Beginning Database-Driven Application Development in Java™ EE

Using GlassFish™

Yuli Vasiliev

Beginning Database-Driven Application Development in Java™ EE: Using GlassFish™

Copyright © 2008 by Yuli Vasiliev

ISBN-13 (paperback): 978-1-4302-0963-8

ISBN-13 (electronic): 978-1-4302-0964-5

Printed and bound in the United States of America 9 8 7 6 5 4 3 2 1

Lead Editor: Steve Anglin
Developmental Editor: Tom Welsh
Technical Reviewer: Gordon Yorke
Editorial Board: Clay Andres, Steve Anglin, Ewan Buckingham, Tony Campbell, Gary Cornell,
    Jonathan Gennick, Matthew Moodie, Joseph Ottinger, Jeffrey Pepper, Frank Pohlmann,
    Ben Renow-Clarke, Dominic Shakeshaft, Matt Wade, Tom Welsh
Project Manager: Tracy Brown Collins
Copy Editor: Kim Wimpsett
Associate Production Director: Kari Brooks-Copony
Production Editor: Ellie Fountain
Compositor: Dina Quan
Proofreader: Linda Seifert
Indexer: Carol Burbo
Artist: Kinetic Publishing Services, LLC
Cover Designer: Kurt Krames
Manufacturing Director: Tom Debolski

Distributed to the book trade worldwide by Springer-Verlag New York, Inc., 233 Spring Street, 6th Floor, New York, NY 10013. Phone 1-800-SPRINGER, fax 201-348-4505, e-mail orders-ny@springer-sbm.com, or visit http://www.springeronline.com.

For information on translations, please contact Apress directly at 2855 Telegraph Avenue, Suite 600, Berkeley, CA 94705. Phone 510-549-5930, fax 510-549-5939, e-mail info@apress.com, or visit http://www.apress.com.

Apress and friends of ED books may be purchased in bulk for academic, corporate, or promotional use. eBook versions and licenses are also available for most titles. For more information, reference our Special Bulk Sales–eBook Licensing web page at http://www.apress.com/info/bulksales.

The source code for this book is available to readers at http://www.apress.com.

To my father.

Contents at a Glance

PART 6 ■■■ Building the Presentation Tier and Testing

PART 7 ■■■ Appendix

Contents

PART 1 ■■■ Introduction

PART 2 ■ ■ ■ Planning the Application

■CHAPTER 5   Planning the Underlying Database 135

PART 3 ■ ■ ■ Building the Database Tier

■CHAPTER 6   Implementing the Database Tier 161

PART 4 ■ ■ ■ Building the Persistence Tier

PART 5 ■ ■ ■ Building the Business Logic Tier

PART 6 ■ ■ ■ Building the Presentation Tier and Testing

PART 7 ■ ■ ■ Appendix

About the Author

YULI VASILIEV is a software developer, freelance author, and consultant currently specializing in open source development, Java technologies, databases, and service-oriented architecture (SOA). He has more than ten years of software development experience as well as several years of technical writing experience. He also wrote a series of technical articles for Oracle Technology Network (OTN) and *Oracle Magazine*.

About the Technical Reviewer

 **GORDON YORKE** is a technical lead on the Oracle TopLink, EclipseLink, and Glassfish TopLink Persistence projects. He is a current member of the JPA 2.0 expert group and the EclipseLink Architecture council. Having worked on Oracle TopLink since its infancy, he has considerable ORM and Java EE application experience; he also has a bachelor's degree in computer science from Acadia University. In addition, he has been known to make speaking appearances at industry conferences.

Introduction

In most cases, developing a data-centric Java EE application doesn't start with building the persistence tier. Instead, you first have to build an underlying database or adjust an existing one to be utilized within your application. Even if you're not charged with building an underlying database for your application, you will look much better if you choose to understand how it works in detail.

Beginning Database-Driven Application Development in Java EE: Using GlassFish is an example-driven, practical book that explains in detail how to develop Java EE applications utilizing relational database technologies with examples using Oracle and MySQL as well as the GlassFish application development framework and deployment platform—all based on Java EE. The book brings together the most useful Java EE technologies such as EJB, JPA, and JSF, providing information that can be immediately put to work.

Over the course of this book, you will be guided through every step of building and deploying a data-centric Java EE application. As you work through the book-length case study, you will learn how to develop each tier of a Java EE application, including the database tier, persistence tier, business logic tier, and presentation tier.

Who Is This Book For?

Beginning Database-Driven Application Development in Java EE: Using GlassFish is aimed at anybody who wants to learn how to build data-centric Java EE applications. Regardless of whether you have already gotten your feet wet with Java EE technologies or just want to start now, there will be something in this book for you. To get the most out of this book, however, you should have some familiarity with the basics of Java EE.

How Is This Book Structured?

The book includes fifteen chapters and an appendix, with the chapters grouped into six logical parts. The first part of the book guides you through the process of installing and configuring the software components required to follow the examples provided in the following chapters. Also, it explains some basics of the Java Persistence API and EJB 3 technologies used to implement the persistence tier and the business logic tier of a Java EE application, respectively. (The basics of relational databases are explained in the appendix.)

In the second part, you will look at the planning stage of the development process. In particular, you will learn how to plan a multitier architecture for your Java EE application and efficiently distribute business logic between the application tiers.

The third part of the book walks you through the process of creating an underlying database to be used with a Java EE application. You will learn how to plan and then develop an underlying database, using Oracle and MySQL—the two most popular databases nowadays.

This part also explains how to set up data sources in your GlassFish server for the underlying database just created.

With the underlying database already in place, the next four chapters grouped into the fourth part cover building the persistence tier, and they explain how to design the JPA entities through which your Java EE application will actually interact with its underlying database. Here, you will also look at the object/relational mapping facility available in Java EE and how to use Java Persistence Query Language (JPQL) as well as native SQL when it comes to querying JPA entities.

The fifth part of the book focuses on building the business logic tier of the Java EE application sample application. In particular, it explains how to create session beans to be utilized within the sample. Also, it covers transactions, explaining how to develop transactional enterprise beans and client applications.

Finally, the sixth part discusses how to build the presentation tier; you'll build JSF beans through which you will access the session beans already in place. Then, you will see how to test the entire application.

What Will You Need to Use This Book?

The examples in the book are designed to be deployed to the GlassFish application server. Also, you will need to implement the underlying database in either MySQL or Oracle. Chapter 1 explains in detail how you can install all these software components. Then, Chapter 2 gives you the information required to get started with GlassFish.

The complete source code for the examples discussed in the book is available in the Source Code/Download section of the Apress website at `http://www.apress.com`.

PART 1

■ ■ ■

Introduction

CHAPTER 1

■■■

Setting Up Your Working Environment

This chapter provides a quick guide to setting up the software components required to follow the samples provided in this book. In particular, it covers how to obtain, install, test, and prepare for using the following pieces of software:

- The GlassFish application server

- The NetBeans IDE

- Oracle Database XE

- MySQL

■**Note** The book assumes you have installed either Oracle Database or MySQL, or both. If you decide on Oracle, you can actually choose any version of Oracle Database. This chapter, though, discusses how to install Oracle Database Express Edition (XE), a lightweight, easy-to-use, free edition of Oracle Database.

It is interesting to note that each of these software components can be downloaded and used for free. The following sections will give you all the information required to quickly set up these components on your system.

Setting Up the GlassFish Application Server

This section explains how to set up the GlassFish application server on your computer. Then, Chapter 2 will give you a good overview of that application server and discuss how you can quickly get started with it. Also, you might want to check out the "GlassFish Quick Start Guide" document available at https://glassfish.dev.java.net/downloads/quickstart/index.html.

Obtaining GlassFish

You can download the latest version of the GlassFish application server from the GlassFish Community web site. As a starting point, you can visit the GlassFish Community home page at https://glassfish.dev.java.net/. At the top-right corner of this page, you should see a set of Download Now buttons, each of which is related to a certain release of GlassFish, as well as the button related to the latest release of TopLink Essentials.

■**Note** In fact, the GlassFish bundle includes the TopLink Essentials implementation of the Java Persistence API by default. So, you don't need to download it separately. This book assumes you will use the TopLink Essentials bundled with GlassFish. For further information, you can refer to the "JPA Implementation at GlassFish" section in Chapter 3. Also, you can visit the TopLink Essentials page at https://glassfish.dev.java.net/javaee5/persistence/index.html.

The https://glassfish.dev.java.net/ page looks like Figure 1-1.

Figure 1-1. *GlassFish Community home page*

On the GlassFish Community home page shown in Figure 1-1, you can click the top Download Now button to move on to the download page of the most up-to-date stable release of GlassFish. The download page offers binary builds for different platforms. Choose what you need, and start downloading.

Installing GlassFish

Once you have downloaded the GlassFish bundle, you can proceed to the installation. Before you can do this, though, you need to have JDK 5 or JDK 6 installed on your computer.

■**Tip** If you still have not installed the JDK on your computer or have an older version of it, you should pick up a recent JDK package at Sun's web site and install it on your system. You can download JDK 5 from `http://java.sun.com/javase/downloads/index_jdk5.jsp` and JDK 6 from `http://java.sun.com/javase/downloads/index.jsp`. Once you have installed the JDK, make sure to set the `JAVA_HOME` environment variable to it.

After you download the GlassFish bundle, follow these steps to unbundle and configure the application server:

1. In the command-line console, change the directory to the one where you have saved the GlassFish bundle file, and run the following command to unbundle it:

```
# java -Xmx256m -jar glassfish-installer-xx-xxxx.jar
```

2. Scroll down the License Agreement window that appears and then click Accept to accept the license agreement terms and proceed with the installation. You should see a lot of text running on the screen and finally the following:

```
Installation complete
```

In fact, the command in step 1 simply creates the `glassfish` directory and unpacks the bundle to it. Although it says the installation is complete, you still have to run an Ant script to complete the installation.

3. Change the directory to the newly created `glassfish` directory:

```
# cd glassfish
```

4. Before you run Ant to complete the installation, make sure that ports 8080 and 8181 are not already in use on your system. If this is the case, edit the following lines in the `setup.xml` file located within the `glassfish` directory:

```
<property name="instance.port" value="8080"/>
<property name="https.port" value="8181"/>
```

so that they refer to other ports, say, as follows:

```
<property name="instance.port" value="2118"/>
<property name="https.port" value="8183"/>
```

5. Run Ant to complete the installation. The following command assumes you are using Ant bundled with GlassFish. On Windows, issue the following command:

```
# lib\ant\bin\ant -f setup.xml
```

On a Unix-like system, issue this:

```
# chmod -R +x lib/ant/bin
# lib/ant/bin/ant -f setup.xml
```

After the Ant build script has completed, you should see the following message at the bottom of the terminal:

```
BUILD SUCCESSFUL
Total time: 48 seconds
```

6. Once the build is completed, read the information in the terminal carefully. Pay close attention to the lines under the `create.domain` section, which tell you what ports will be used with the default GlassFish domain.

Note GlassFish domains are covered in more detail in the section "Understanding GlassFish Domains" in Chapter 2.

After you've completed the previous steps successfully, you have GlassFish installed on your system and can start using it.

Testing the GlassFish Installation

Now that you have GlassFish installed on your system, it is time to verify your installation. To do this, you can follow these steps:

1. Change the directory to the `glassfish\bin` directory:

```
# cd glassfish_install_dir\glassfish\bin
```

2. Run the following command to start GlassFish:

```
# asadmin start-domain domain1
```

3. To make sure your GlassFish application server is up and running, enter the following URL in your browser:

```
http://localhost:8080
```

Note that the port in the previous URL may vary depending on the number specified in the `setup.xml` file during the GlassFish installation.

The previous should output the default GlassFish application server page, which looks like Figure 1-2.

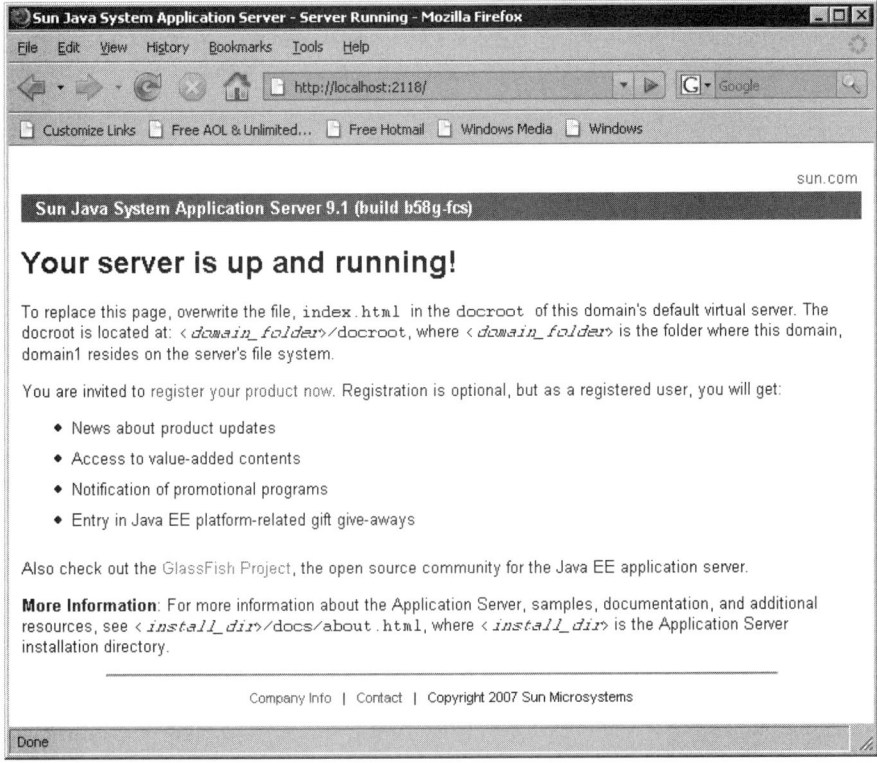

Figure 1-2. *The default GlassFish application server page*

If you see the page shown in Figure 1-2, then your application server is ready for use, meaning you can deploy your applications to it now. That part of deployment is discussed in the "Deploying Applications to the Server" section in Chapter 2.

Testing the GlassFish Admin Console

GlassFish ships with two administrative tools to let you perform administration tasks:

- Admin Console, which is a GUI web interface

- `asadmin`, which is a command-line tool

In the preceding section, you saw how you can use `asadmin` to start an instance of the GlassFish server. Although `asadmin` can be used to perform any administration task on the GlassFish server instances, many developers prefer the web-based Admin Console to it. Before you can test the web-based Admin Console bundled with GlassFish, you need to have GlassFish up and running. If you followed the steps in the preceding section, you should have a running GlassFish server instance now.

To launch Admin Console, enter the following URL in your browser:

```
http://localhost:4848
```

■**Note** In fact, 4848 is the default port for Admin Console. If you changed it in the `setup.xml` file before installing GlassFish to another one, then you must use the specified port number instead.

Once you've loaded Admin Console, you will be prompted to enter a username/password combination, as shown in Figure 1-3.

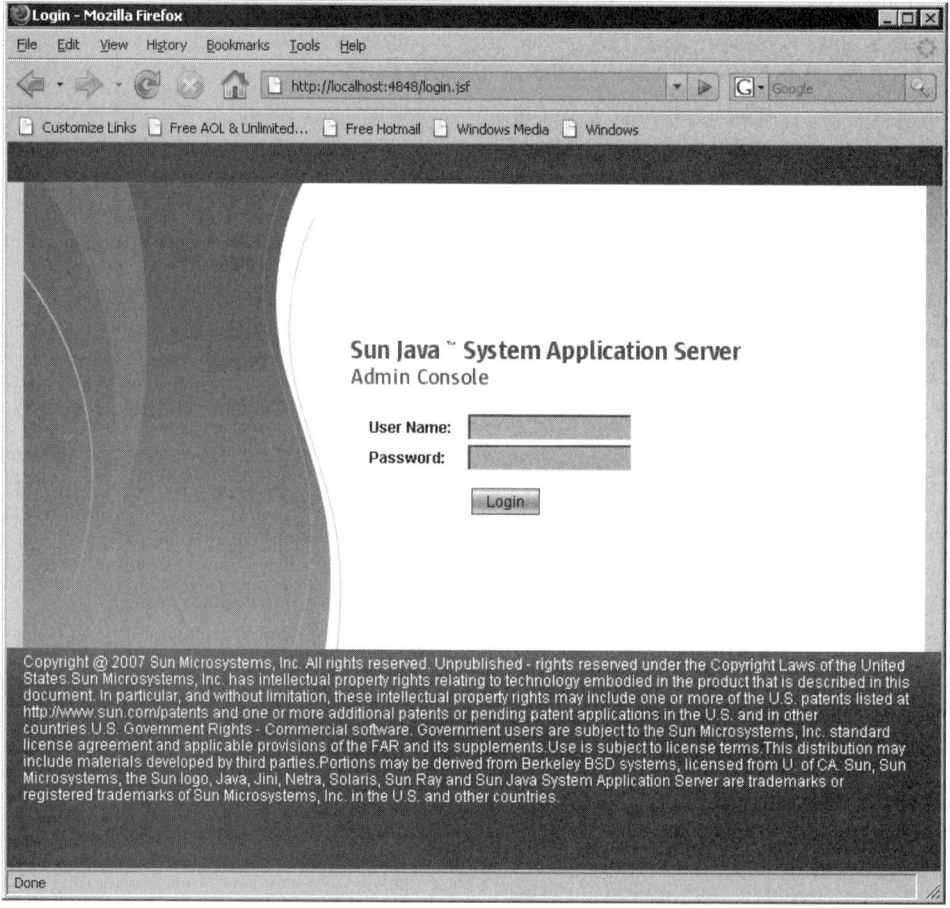

Figure 1-3. *The login page of Admin Console*

To log in to the server, you can use the default username/password pair: admin/adminadmin. It is recommended that you change the default administrator password for security reasons. So, your first administration task to perform might be to change the default password of the admin user. To achieve this, you can follow these steps:

1. Assuming you are already logged in to the server, click the Application Server node under the Common Task column located on the left side of the Admin Console window.

2. Click the Administrator Password tab. As a result, you should see the screen shown in Figure 1-4.

3. On the Administrator Password tab, type in a new password in the New Password text box and then type in the same password in the Confirm New Password text box.

4. Click the Save button on the right side of the display to replace the old password with the new one.

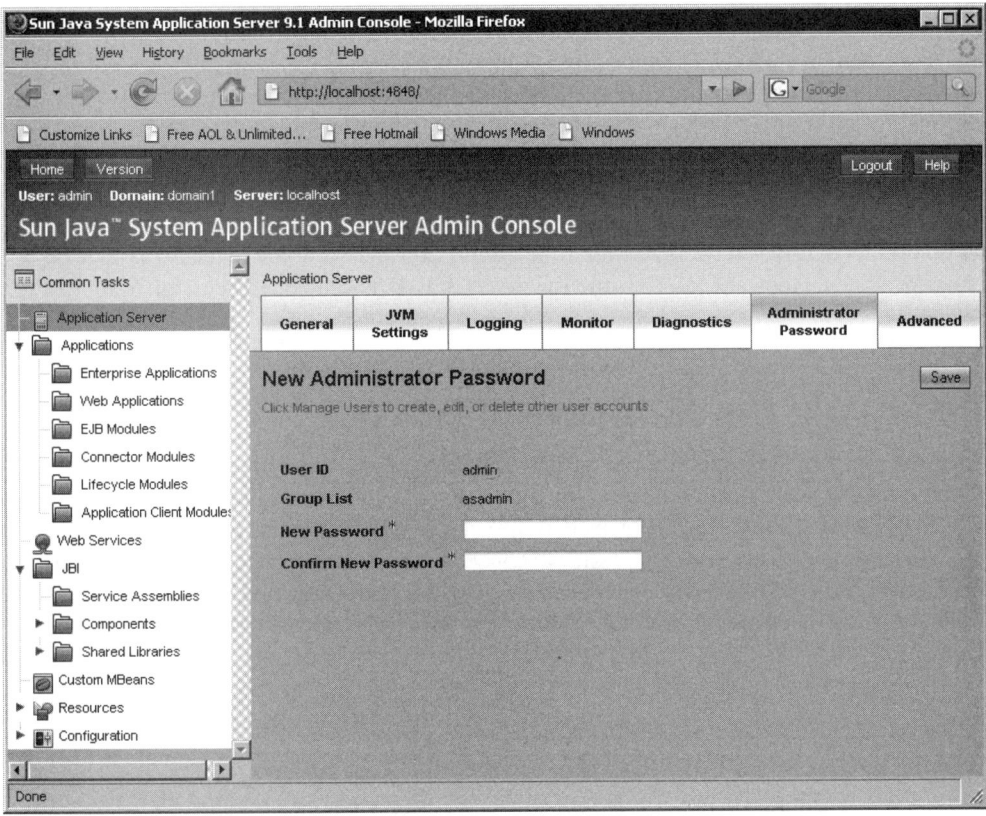

Figure 1-4. *The Administrator Password tab of the Application Server screen in Admin Console*

As you can see in the figure, the Application Server screen in Admin Console includes some other tabs besides Administrator Password discussed here. In the "Configuring the GlassFish Application Server" section in Chapter 2, you will learn how to accomplish major configuration tasks using the menus and buttons located on the Application Server screen's tabs.

■Note Although this section gives you a rough idea of how to use Admin Console, Chapter 2 provides more detailed information on using this browser-based GUI tool, including discussing how you can use it to configure your application server.

Now that you have performed some initial tests of your GlassFish application server, you might want to stop it. To do that, you can execute the following command from a terminal window:

```
# asadmin stop-domain domain1
```

Once you have stopped the server, you cannot manage it with Admin Console anymore—at least, not until you start the server again. In that case, though, you first will be redirected to the login page shown in Figure 1-3 earlier.

As an alternative to stopping the GlassFish application server instance with the asadmin command, you could stop the instance through the Admin Console tool. To do this, you should move to the General tab of the Application Server screen and click the Stop Instance button there.

That concludes this concise guide on installing and testing the GlassFish application server and its GUI-based configuration tool, Admin Console. Now you're ready to move on and take a deeper look at GlassFish and the way it is used. For further discussion, refer to Chapter 2.

Setting Up the NetBeans IDE

The NetBeans IDE is an open source integrated development environment that will be used throughout this book, making it easier for you to develop and deploy the samples discussed.

To learn more about the NetBeans IDE, you can visit its page at http://www.netbeans.org/products/ide/. Also, you might want to check out the NetBeans IDE 5.5.1 Installation Instructions page at http://www.netbeans.org/community/releases/55/1/install.html, which provides the NetBeans IDE 5.5.1 installation instructions for Windows, Solaris OS, Linux, and Macintosh OS X. Another interesting document to check out is the "NetBeans IDE 5.5 Quick Start Guide" that is available at http://www.netbeans.org/kb/55/quickstart.html.

Obtaining the NetBeans IDE

You can download the NetBeans IDE from the NetBeans downloads page at http://www.netbeans.info/downloads/index.php. As of this writing, the most recent stable release of NetBeans IDE is 5.5.1. It is interesting to note that the NetBeans IDE can be downloaded in different bundles. For example, you can download the package containing the NetBeans IDE alone or the NetBeans IDE with the Java EE application server bundle, which contains the NetBeans IDE and a Java EE application server in a single download. For the purpose of this book, though, you should download the package containing nothing but the NetBeans IDE.

■Note When downloading NetBeans bundled with an application server, you in fact have several choices. For example, you can download the NetBeans IDE bundled with a Sun Java system application server or with a JBoss application server. In our situation here, you don't need to download the NetBeans IDE bundled with an application server, since you should have already installed GlassFish on your system.

Once you have obtained the installation package, you can proceed to the installation. Before you can do that, though, make sure you have the JDK installed on your system. To install NetBeans IDE 5.5.1, you must have JDK version 5.0 or later.

Installing the NetBeans IDE on Windows

To install NetBeans IDE 5.5.1 on Windows, follow these steps:

1. Execute the installer file to launch the installation process. As a result, you will see the first installer screen, which looks like Figure 1-5.

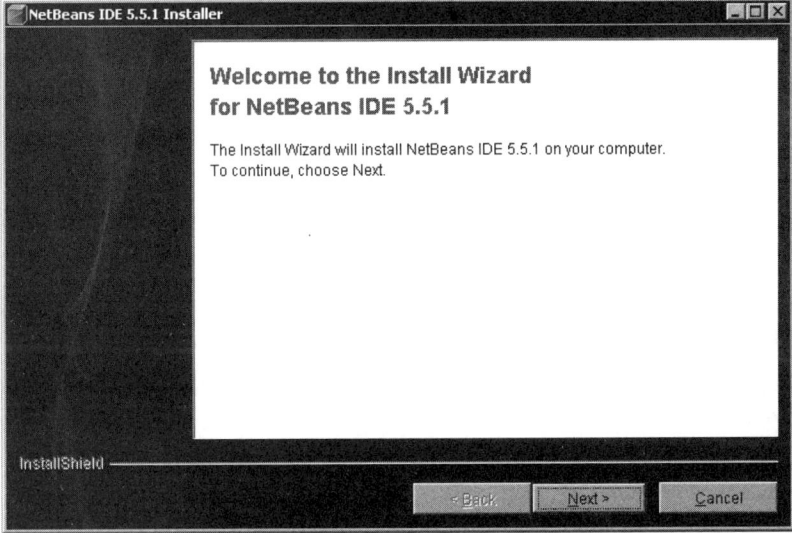

Figure 1-5. *The welcome screen of the NetBeans IDE 5.5.1 Installer*

2. On the welcome screen of the wizard shown in Figure 1-5, click Next.

3. On the License Agreement screen, read the agreement, choose I Accept the Terms in the License Agreement if you agree with it, and then click Next.

4. On the next screen, specify a new or empty directory in which you want to install the NetBeans IDE.

5. On the next screen, choose a JDK from the list of suitable JDKs found on your machine and then click Next.

6. On the next screen, confirm that the specified location is correct and that you have enough space for the installation and then click Next to start the installation.

7. On the last screen of the wizard informing you that the NetBeans IDE has been successfully installed on your computer, click Finish to exit the wizard.

After performing these steps, you should have the NetBeans IDE installed and ready for use.

Installing the NetBeans IDE on Linux

To install NetBeans IDE 5.5.1 on Linux, follow these steps:

1. In the command-line console, change the directory to the directory containing the installer:

```
# cd path_to_install_dir
```

2. Set the execute permission for the installer:

```
# chmod +x netbeans-5_5_1-linux.bin
```

3. Run the installer:

```
# ./netbeans-5_5_1-linux.bin
```

4. On the License Agreement screen, read the agreement, choose I Accept the Terms in the License Agreement if you agree with it, and then click Next.

5. On the next screen, specify a new or empty directory in which you want to install the NetBeans IDE.

6. On the next screen, choose a JDK from the list of suitable JDKs found on your machine and then click Next.

7. On the next screen, confirm that the specified location is correct and that you have enough space for the installation and then click Next to start the installation.

8. On the last screen of the wizard informing you that the NetBeans IDE has been successfully installed on your computer, click Finish to exit the wizard.

After performing the previous steps, you should have the NetBeans IDE installed and ready for use.

Connecting the NetBeans IDE to GlassFish

Now that you have installed the NetBeans IDE, you need to connect it to your GlassFish installation so that applications built with the IDE can be easily deployed to the application server. To do this, follow these steps:

1. Launch the NetBeans IDE from the Start menu of your operating system. When launched, the IDE looks like Figure 1-6.

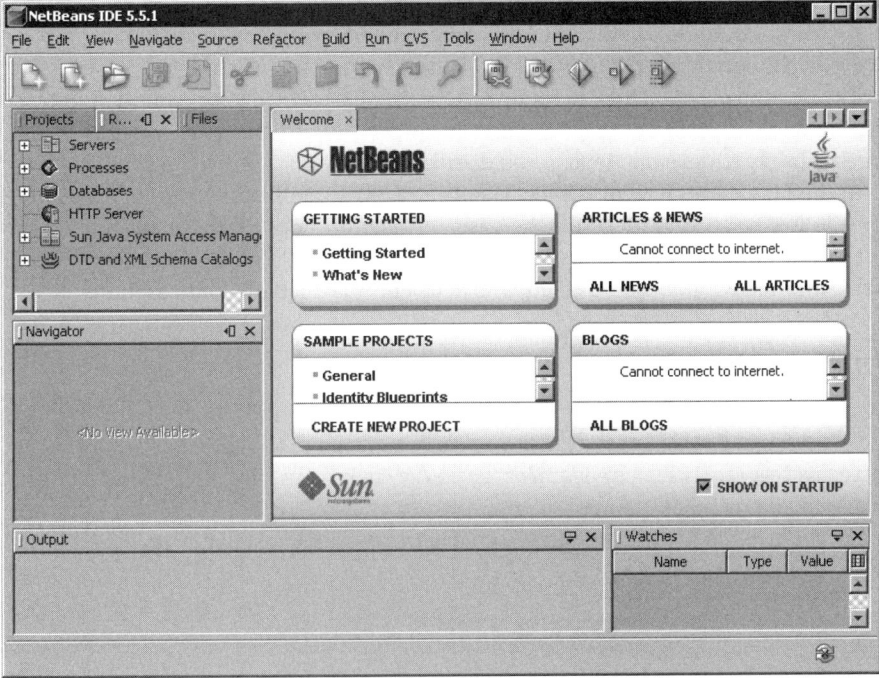

Figure 1-6. *The NetBeans IDE 5.5.1 when you launch it for the first time*

2. In the NetBeans IDE, select Tools ➤ Server Manager.

3. In the Server Manager dialog box, click the Add Server button. As a result, the Add Server Instance dialog box appears.

4. On the Choose Server screen of the Add Server Instance dialog box, choose Sun Java System Application Server in the Server combo box and then type **GlassFish** in the Name box. Then, click Next.

5. On the Platform Folder Location screen of the Add Server Instance dialog box, choose the directory of your GlassFish installation, and click Next.

6. On the Domain Admin Login Info screen of the Add Server Instance dialog box, specify the password for the admin user, and click Finish.

7. In the Server Manager dialog box, click Close.

After you've completed these steps, the NetBeans IDE will deploy your application to the GlassFish application server by default if you select the Deploy Project item from the pop-up menu that appears when right-clicking the application in the Project window. In the "Deploying Applications to the Server" section in Chapter 2, you will see a simple example of how to deploy an application to GlassFish from within the NetBeans IDE.

Setting Up Oracle Database XE

As mentioned earlier, the samples discussed in this book assume you install either an Oracle Database or MySQL on your computer. It is left up to you which one of the previous two to choose. However, there will be nothing wrong with choosing both, because they both can be installed on the same computer and can be used simultaneously.

This section explains how to set up Oracle Database XE on your computer. You can refer to the appendix if you want to learn some advantages of using this lightweight Oracle Database that is free to develop, deploy, and distribute.

At the time of this writing, Oracle Database XE is available only for Windows and Linux. So, the following sections describe the basic installation steps for these two operating systems. Once have completed these steps, you will have an Oracle Database XE server (including a database), Oracle Database XE client, and SQL*Plus installed on your computer.

Obtaining Oracle Database XE

All Oracle Database software is available for download from the Oracle Technology Network (OTN). To obtain Oracle Database XE, you can visit its page on OTN at `http://www.oracle.com/technology/software/products/database/xe/index.html` and then follow a link to the Download page.

On the Download page, obtain the Oracle Database XE installation executable appropriate for your platform.

■Note To follow the Oracle-related examples throughout this book, you are not in fact limited to using Oracle Database XE—any edition of Oracle Database will do. Note, however, that whereas any edition of Oracle Database can be downloaded and then used for developing and prototyping for free, only Oracle Database XE can still be used for free in the production environment.

Installing Oracle Database XE on Windows

To install Oracle Database XE on Windows, follow these steps:

1. Log in to Windows as a user of the Administrators group.

2. Make sure to remove the `ORACLE_HOME` environment variable if it has been set on your system. You can do this in the System Properties dialog box, which can be invoked from the System Control Panel.

3. Launch the Oracle Database XE installation executable downloaded from OTN to run the Oracle Database XE Server installer.

   Figure 1-7 shows what the Oracle Database XE Server installer window looks like after you just ran it.

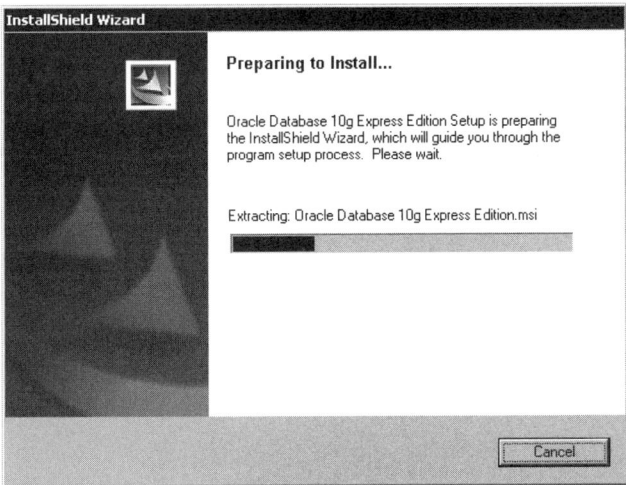

Figure 1-7. *The Preparing to Install screen of the Oracle Database XE Server installer on Windows*

4. On the welcome screen, click Next.

5. On the License Agreement screen, click I Accept and then click Next.

6. On the Choose Destination Location screen, choose the directory in which you want to install Oracle Database XE and then click Next.

7. You will be prompted to enter an available port number or numbers if at least one of the following port numbers is already in use on your system: 1521, 2030, or 8080. Otherwise, these numbers will be used automatically.

8. On the Specify Database Passwords screen, specify the passwords for the SYS and SYSTEM database accounts and click Next.

9. On the Summary screen, click Install to continue with the installation, or click Back to turn back and modify the settings.

10. On the last screen of the wizard that appears after the installation is complete, click Finish.

After you've completed these steps, your database server should be ready for use.

Installing Oracle Database XE on Linux

To install Oracle Database Express Edition on Linux, follow these steps:

1. Log in to your computer as root.

2. Change the directory to the one in which you downloaded the Oracle Database XE oracle-xe-10.2.0.1-1.0.i386.rpm installation executable, and install the RPM:

```
# rpm -ivh oracle-xe-10.2.0.1-1.0.i386.rpm
```

3. When prompted, run the following command to configure the database:

```
# /etc/init.d/oracle-xe configure
```

4. When prompted to enter the configuration information, accept the default port numbers for the Oracle Database XE graphical user interface and Oracle Database listener: 8080 and 1521, respectively. Then, specify the passwords for the SYS and SYSTEM default user accounts.

Assuming that during the installation you answered Yes to the question of whether you want the database to automatically start along with the computer, you should have the database server up and ready for use now. Otherwise, you have to start it manually as follows:

```
# /etc/init.d/oracle-xe start
```

Testing the Database Server with Oracle SQL*Plus

The simplest way to make sure your Oracle Database has been installed successfully and the database server is working properly is to issue a SQL statement against the database.

■**Note** Structured Query Language (SQL) provides a universal way to interact with relational databases. Each database, though, has its own SQL dialect, providing an additional set of commands and functions specific to that particular database. For example, to interact with Oracle Database, you use Oracle SQL.

To issue a SQL statement against an Oracle Database, you can use Oracle SQL*Plus, an interactive and batch query command-line tool that is installed by default with every Oracle Database installation. Assuming you have an Oracle Database server installed and running on your system, you can launch Oracle SQL*Plus from a terminal window by entering sqlplus. Then, you will be prompted to enter a username to connect to the database. You can connect as SYSDBA by entering /as sysdba.

Once you are connected, you should see the SQL> prompt where you can enter a SQL statement to be issued against the database. For example, you might enter the following simple statement to make sure the database server is reachable:

```
SELECT SYSDATE FROM DUAL;
```

The previous statement should produce the output representing the system date, and that might look like this:

```
SYSDATE
---------
07-NOV-07
```

As you no doubt have realized, the previous is a toy example. Here, the only information you receive from the database server is the system date. Practically, you will use SQL*Plus to access database data, as well as perform database administration tasks and manipulate database objects.

Setting Up the hr/hr Demonstration Schema

All Oracle Databases usually come with one or two demonstration schemas installed by default during a typical installation and containing a few related tables populated with data. The most recent Oracle Database releases include the hr/hr demonstration schema, which will be used in some simple Oracle-related samples in this book. So, you first need to make sure this schema is present and unlocked in the database. To find out whether the hr/hr schema exists, you can try to connect to it from within SQL*Plus as follows:

```
CONN hr/hr
```

If the hr/hr account exists but is locked, you should receive the following error message:

```
ERROR:
ORA-28000: the account is locked

Warning: You are no longer connected to ORACLE.
```

In that case, you should reconnect as SYSDBA and then issue the ALTER USER statement to unlock the hr/hr account:

```
CONN /as sysdba
ALTER USER hr ACCOUNT UNLOCK;
```

Now you can connect as hr/hr and perform a query against one of the hr default tables:

```
CONN hr/hr
SELECT count(*) FROM employees;
```

The previous query should count the number of rows in the hr.employees table and produce the following output:

```
COUNT(*)
---------
107
```

Now that you have seen that everything works properly, you may want to quit the SQL*Plus session. To do this, simply enter the following:

```
quit
```

In Chapter 6, which covers how to implement the database tier of a Java EE application, there will be plenty of opportunities to get your hands dirty issuing SQL queries against an Oracle Database from SQL*Plus.

Testing the Database Home Page

Oracle Database XE comes with the Database home page, a browser-based user interface that makes administering the database much easier. You can use this interface as a GUI alternative to the SQL*Plus command-line tool discussed in the preceding section.

After you have installed Oracle Database XE, you can start the Database home page by following these steps:

1. You can launch the Database home page from the Start menu of your operating system—find the Oracle Database Express Edition menu group, and select Go to Database Home Page within it. This launches the Database home page within a browser.

2. On the Database Login page, enter a valid database username and password, and click Login. For example, to log in as an administrator, you can use the SYSTEM account, providing the password specified during the installation.

After performing these steps, you should see the Database home page, which looks similar to the one shown in Figure 1-8.

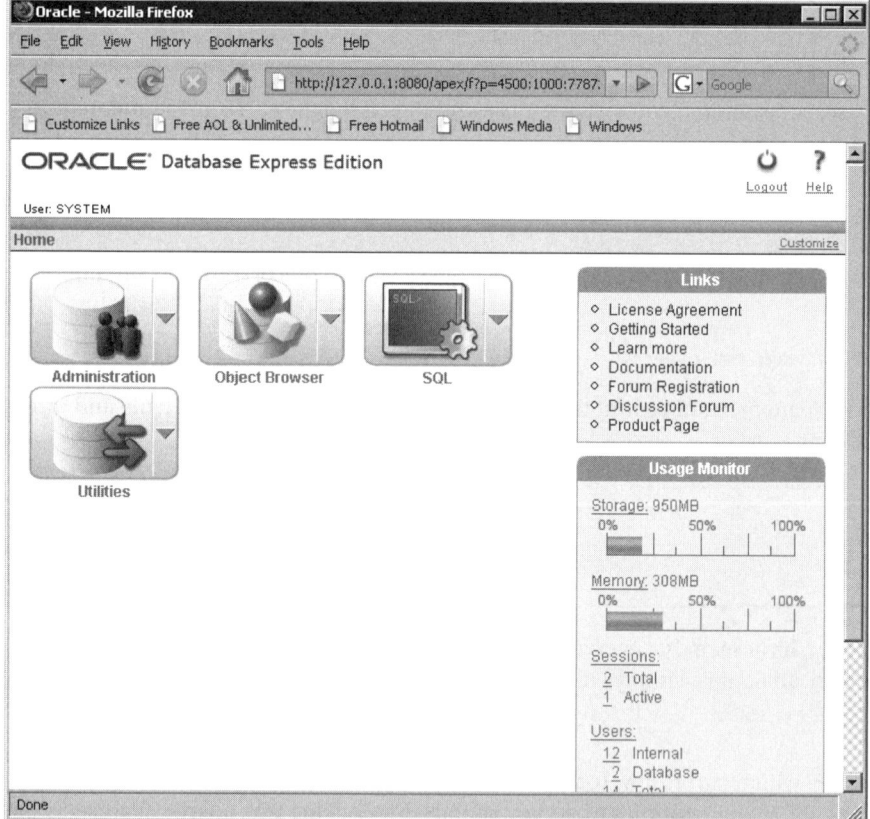

Figure 1-8. *The home page of the Oracle Database XE graphical user interface, a GUI tool installed by default during Oracle Database XE server installation*

Now that you're logged in to the database via the Database home page, you can perform administration tasks, access database data, and manipulate database objects—the same tasks you can do when connected via SQL*Plus discussed in the preceding section. For example, to alter the hr/hr demonstration schema through the Database home page, you can follow these steps:

1. On the Database home page, click the Administration icon.

2. On the Administration page, click the Database Users icon.

3. On the Manage Database Users page, click the HR icon to go to the hr/hr schema page.

4. On the hr/hr schema page, you can change the settings as required and click Alter User to apply the changes made. Otherwise, you can click Cancel.

It is important to note that the Database home page is a highly multifunctional tool. Besides offering an integrated visual environment for performing administration tasks and manipulating database objects and data, this graphical interface also provides integrated tools for monitoring important database parameters, such as current memory allocation and storage space usage. It also allows you to export and import data to and from external data sources, generate reports, and run SQL queries like you would with SQL*Plus.

Concluding this short guide on Oracle Database XE installation and initial testing, it should be noted that if you have managed to execute all the tasks discussed here, this means your Oracle Database installation has been successful and the database server is working properly.

Setting Up MySQL

Although MySQL can be set up on many operating systems, this section provides the installation steps only for Windows and Linux, two most popular platforms nowadays. Then, I'll provide concise instructions for testing your MySQL installation. Also, you might want to check out the MySQL Documentation page at http://dev.mysql.com/doc/. On this page you can find a set of MySQL reference manuals available in a variety of languages and for different MySQL releases.

Obtaining MySQL

When choosing MySQL, you in fact have more than one choice. Generally speaking, you can choose between MySQL Community Server and MySQL Enterprise. The former is a freely downloadable version of MySQL and can be used under the open source GPL license. The latter is used on a commercial basis only. In more detail, the difference between these two editions is discussed in the "Which Should I Use: MySQL Enterprise or MySQL Community Server" document available at http://www.mysql.com/products/which-edition.html.

■**Note** In fact, MySQL Enterprise is available in four levels—Basic, Silver, Gold, and Platinum—thus allowing you to choose the service level most suitable for you. For further information, you can refer to the MySQL Enterprise Features page at `http://www.mysql.com/products/enterprise/features.html`.

The MySQL Downloads page available at `http://dev.mysql.com/downloads/` contains a questionnaire designed to help you choose between MySQL Community Server and MySQL Enterprise. Once you have made your decision, you can move on and start downloading the MySQL distribution. To follow the MySQL-related samples provided in this book, you don't have to purchase MySQL Enterprise—having MySQL Community Server installed will be enough.

You can download the MySQL distribution from the MySQL Downloads page at `http://dev.mysql.com/downloads/mysql`. The MySQL-related book samples assume you will use MySQL Server 5.1 or newer.

If you are a Windows user, pick up the `Windows Essentials` file from the Windows downloads section on the page. This file contains the minimum set of files needed to install MySQL, including the Configuration Wizard. If you want to download the package containing all the MySQL components, consider the Complete Package available on the same page and packed within a zip archive, `mysql-5.1.xx-beta-win32.zip`, assuming that you choose MySQL 5.1. At the time of this writing, though, MySQL 6.0 is available. You can download MySQL 6.0 from `http://dev.mysql.com/downloads/mysql/6.0.html`.

If you're using Linux, then pick up the RPMs for Server and Client from the appropriate section of the MySQL Downloads page. These packages are required for a standard minimal installation.

Installing MySQL on Windows

Installing MySQL on your computer is as easy as choosing the appropriate options and clicking Next buttons in the wizard. To install MySQL on Windows, follow these steps:

1. Execute the downloaded `mysql-essential-5.1.xx-beta-win32.msi` or `Setup.exe` extracted from `mysql-5.1.xx-beta-win32.zip` to start installing MySQL.

2. Click Next on the first screen of MySQL Server's Setup Wizard, which should look like Figure 1-9.

3. On the Setup Type page of the MySQL Setup Wizard, you have to choose Typical, Complete, or Custom. It is OK if you choose the Typical installation type.

4. In the Confirmation screen, click the Install button to begin the installation.

5. On the final screen of the installer, make sure the Configure the MySQL Server Now check box is checked, and click Finish. As a result, the MySQL Configuration Wizard launches.

6. On the Configuration Type screen of the Configuration Wizard, choose the Standard Configuration option to get started with MySQL quickly. The following steps assume that you chose the Standard Configuration option in this step.

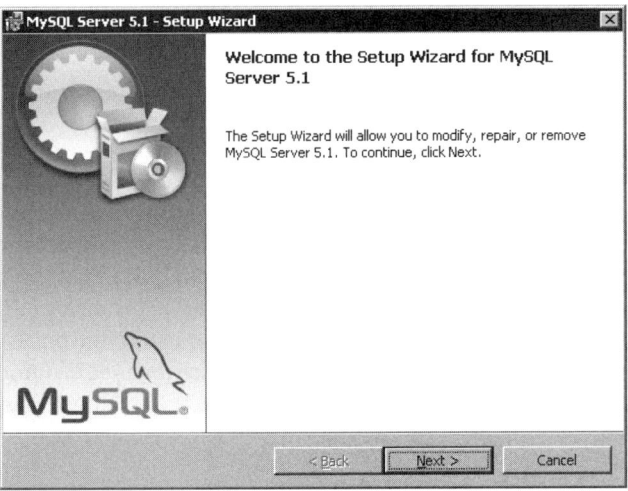

Figure 1-9. *The welcome screen of the Setup Wizard for MySQL Server 5.1*

7. On the next screen, make sure that the Install As Windows Service option is selected, and click Next.

8. On the next screen, set the password for the `root` user.

9. On the final screen of the MySQL Configuration Wizard, click the Execute button to complete the configuration process.

After you have completed these steps, the MySQL server should be up and running on your Windows machine.

Installing MySQL on Linux

Using the RPM packages is the recommended way to install MySQL on Linux. The following steps assume your Linux supports RPMs:

1. Perform the following commands to install the server and client RPMs picked up from the MySQL Downloads page:

   - `# rpm -i MySQL-server-VERSION.i386.rpm`

   - `# rpm -i MySQL-client-VERSION.i386.rpm`

   By default, the server RPM adds the entries to `/etc/init.d/`, which are required to start the `mysqld` server automatically at boot time.

2. After the installation, it is highly recommended you assign the password to the anonymous accounts:

   - `# mysql -u root`

   - `mysql> SET PASSWORD FOR ''@'localhost' = PASSWORD('new_pswd');`

   - `mysql> SET PASSWORD FOR ''@'your_hostname' = PASSWORD('new_pswd');`

After you have completed these steps, the MySQL server should be up and running on your machine.

Setting Up a New User Account with the MySQL Command-Line Client

Now that you have the MySQL database server installed on your computer, it is time to verify that it is up and ready for use. To start with, you might want to set up a new user account on your MySQL database server. This section explains how to do this with the help of the MySQL command-line client, a command prompt tool bundled with the MySQL installation. The user account set up here will be used in the MySQL-related examples throughout the book.

To start a MySQL command-line session from a terminal, you use the mysql command. For example, to connect to the database server as the root user from the localhost, you might enter the following command:

```
mysql -h localhost -u root -p
```

In response, you will be prompted to enter the root password. You should enter the root password specified during installation. If everything is OK, you should see the mysql> prompt through which you can interact with the server.

Now, let's create a new database on the server. To do this, you might enter the following command:

```
CREATE DATABASE mydb;
```

■**Note** It is interesting to note that a MySQL database is implemented as a directory, and the tables belonging to this database are implemented as files within that directory.

The next step is to create a new user account and grant to it the privileges required to operate with the newly created database. You can do this with the following command:

```
GRANT CREATE, DROP, SELECT, INSERT, UPDATE, DELETE
ON mydb.*
TO 'usr'
IDENTIFIED BY 'pswd';
```

The previous command creates the usr user account and grants the privileges to it, which are required to perform a common set of operations on the mydb database. Now you can connect as the usr/pswd user to the server. To do this, you first need to disconnect from the server:

```
EXIT
```

This will take you back to the operating system prompt. Then, you should enter the following command:

```
mysql -h localhost -u usr -p
```

When asked, enter `pswd` as the password. As a result, you will be connected as the `usr` user to the database server. Now you can instruct MySQL to use the `mydb` database by default. To do this, you should issue the following command:

```
USE mydb
```

At the moment, the `mydb` database is empty. You will create tables in it when it comes to performing the first MySQL-related sample in Chapter 4. Also, you can explore examples in the appendix.

Now you might want to quit the MySQL command-line client. To do this, you can issue the following command:

```
QUIT
```

The MySQL command-line client tool will be used throughout this book when it comes to creating and manipulating MySQL database objects utilized within the samples discussed.

Managing the Database Server with MySQL GUI Tools

As an alternative to the MySQL command-line client tool, you might want to use a GUI tool or tools, which allow you to visually perform all the operations you may need to perform on your MySQL database and the data stored in it. To fulfill these needs, MySQL AB has developed the MySQL GUI Tools bundle containing the following tools:

- MySQL Administrator (`http://www.mysql.com/products/tools/administrator/`)

- MySQL Query Browser (`http://www.mysql.com/products/tools/query-browser/`)

- MySQL Migration Toolkit (`http://www.mysql.com/products/tools/migration-toolkit/`)

You can pick up this bundle from the MySQL GUI Tools Downloads page at `http://dev.mysql.com/downloads/gui-tools/`. At the time of this writing, MySQL GUI Tools was available for the MySQL 5.0 release.

The MySQL Administrator tool included in the MySQL GUI Tools bundle allows you to visually perform administrative tasks on your MySQL server. Say, for example, you want to add the `INDEX` privilege to the `usr` user account created in the preceding section so that this account can use the `CREATE INDEX` and `DROP INDEX` statements. To do this using MySQL Administrator, you can follow these steps:

1. Launch MySQL Administrator, and connect as the `root` user.

2. In the left column of MySQL Administrator, click the User Administration node.

3. In the bottom-left corner of the MySQL Administrator window, click usr.

4. In the right frame of the MySQL Administrator window, click the Schema Privileges tab.

5. On the Schema Privileges tab, select the mydb item in the box located on the left side of the tab. As a result, you should see the screen shown in Figure 1-10.

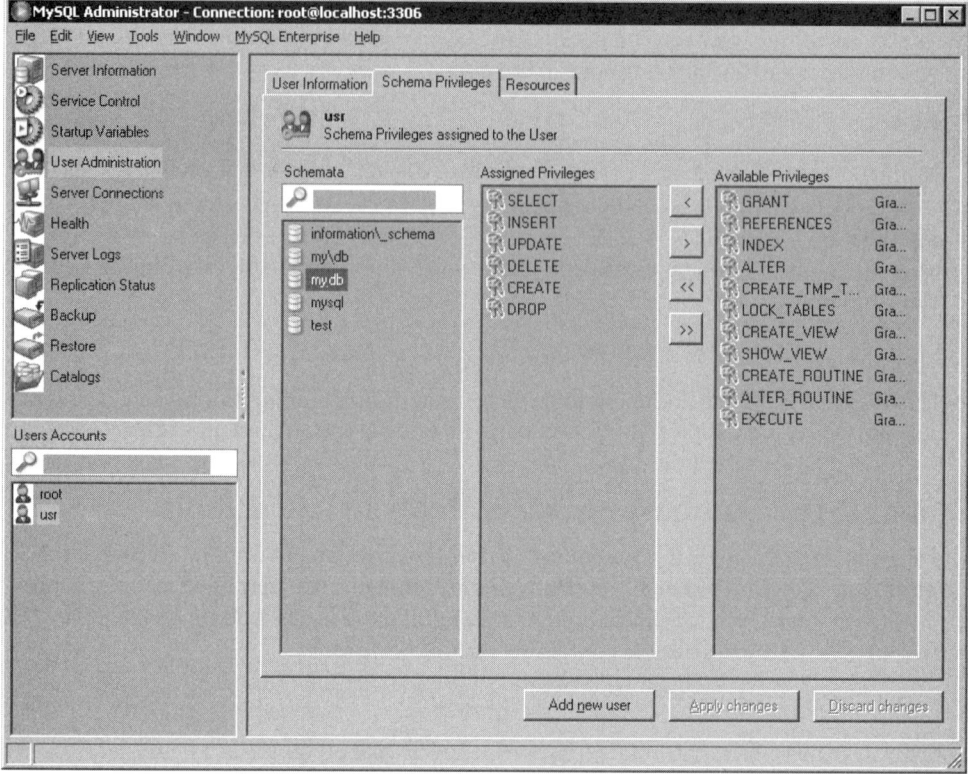

Figure 1-10. *The Schema Privileges tab of the User Administration screen in MySQL Administrator*

6. In the Available Privileges box, select the INDEX item, and click the < button to move the selected item to the Assigned Privileges box.

7. Click the Apply Changes button to apply the changes made.

8. Quit MySQL Administrator by choosing File ➤ Close.

Of course, you could still use the MySQL command-line client tool to accomplish the same goal: granting another privilege to a user account. To achieve that, being connected as root, you might issue the following statement:

```
GRANT INDEX
ON mydb.*
TO 'usr'
```

However, some developers prefer a GUI alternative, since a GUI tool gives a visual representation of the task being performed.

Summary

At this point, you should have set up all the software components required to follow the samples discussed in this book. Moreover, you should have a cursory knowledge of how this software works and how to handle it.

CHAPTER 2

■ ■ ■

Getting Started with GlassFish

Sun's plan to open source its application server was implemented through Project GlassFish, which was announced at JavaOne 2005. Sun and Oracle Corporation became the main source code donors for this project. As a result of this effort, we have a freely available, open source, Java EE 5–compatible application server that is quickly growing in popularity. As of this writing, the final release of GlassFish 2 is available, and the community is working on GlassFish 3.

The purpose of this chapter is to help you get started with GlassFish quickly. After a brief overview, you will learn how to perform a common set of tasks on the application server, including the following:

- Starting an instance of the GlassFish application server

- Configuring the application server with Admin Console

- Deploying applications to the application server

- Creating and managing GlassFish domains

If you already have a basic knowledge of GlassFish and know how to implement the previous tasks, you can skip this introductory chapter and move to Chapter 3.

This chapter assumes you have already installed the GlassFish application server on your system. If not, you should refer to Chapter 1.

Overview of the GlassFish Application Server

This section gives a quick overview of the GlassFish application server. In particular, it explains what GlassFish is, why you might want to choose it over any other Java EE 5–compliant application server, and what the general steps are to start using it quickly.

GlassFish: What Is It?

GlassFish refers to both a community and an application server. The GlassFish community includes developers working on a free, open source, Java EE 5–compatible application server, GlassFish, as well as on a Java Persistence API (JPA) implementation, TopLink Essentials. Henceforth, *GlassFish* will refer to the GlassFish application server in this book.

■**Tip** A good article on GlassFish basics is available on Sun's web site at `http://java.sun.com/`
`developer/technicalArticles/glassfish/GFBasics.html`.

GlassFish is available under the dual-licensing model, which lets you choose one of the
following free software licenses:

- Common Development and Distribution License (CDDL); for information, refer to
  `http://www.sun.com/cddl/`.

- GNU General Public License (GPL); for information, refer to `http://en.wikipedia.org/`
  `wiki/GNU_General_Public_License`.

■**Note** To learn more about open source licenses, you can visit the Open Source Initiative (OSI) web site at
`http://opensource.org/`.

GlassFish can be downloaded from the GlassFish Community page at `https://glassfish.`
`dev.java.net/`. Sun offers GlassFish under the name Sun Java System Application Server. For
example, GlassFish v2 is available from Sun's web site as Sun Java System Application Server 9.1.
You can also download the NetBeans IDE bundled with Sun Java System Application Server;
for further information, refer to `http://www.netbeans.info/downloads/index.php`.

Why GlassFish?

This section gives a quick overview of GlassFish advantages, explaining why you might want to
choose GlassFish over any other Java EE 5–compliant application server.

If you have bought this book, this most likely means you already know what GlassFish is
and which advantages it has over its competitors. If so, you can skip this section. But if you
just picked the book up from the shelf in a bookstore, wondering what GlassFish is all about
and what makes it stand out from the other Java EE application servers available, then you
might find the information provided here interesting.

The following points sum up GlassFish advantages:

- GlassFish is the most widely adopted Java EE reference implementation.

- GlassFish includes the TopLink Essentials implementation of JPA.

- GlassFish is open source and freely available software.

- Sun provides commercial support for GlassFish.

- GlassFish can be used with popular Java IDEs such as NetBeans and Eclipse.

- GlassFish is compatible with many popular frameworks such as Spring and Struts.

- GlassFish ships with Admin Console, a GUI tool to simplify administration tasks.

- GlassFish lets you create different domains with profiles that suit specific needs.

As you no doubt realize, GlassFish is a production-quality Java EE 5 application server available under an open source license, which makes it possible for Java developers to access the source code of this application server and participate in its development.

Although potentially every Java developer concerned can contribute to the development of GlassFish, the great bulk of the source code is developed by teams of professionals, and the main donors for the GlassFish project are Sun and Oracle. For example, JPA, a new Java EE 5 feature providing a standards-based solution for persistence, is implemented in GlassFish using TopLink Essentials, which was contributed by Oracle.

As of this writing, GlassFish offers the most complete Java EE 5 implementation, thus promoting the adoption of the Java EE 5 platform. It enables Java developers to create applications based on the most recent specifications of JSP, JSF, Servlet, EJB, JAX-WS, JAXB, and other Java EE technologies.

■**Note** To find out what application servers used today are Java EE compatible, you can refer to the "Comparison of application servers" wiki document available at http://en.wikipedia.org/wiki/ Comparison_of_application_servers.

GlassFish proves flexible when it comes to creating and configuring administrative domains. When creating a GlassFish administrative domain, you have more than one choice. In particular, you can choose between three different usage profiles, namely, Developer, Cluster, and Enterprise. Each of these profiles is designed to suit specific needs. For example, the Developer profile is chosen when creating a domain to be used in a development environment. After you have created a domain, you can further configure it using tools bundled with GlassFish. Domains are explained in the "Understanding GlassFish Domains" section later in this chapter.

How to Get Started

To get started with GlassFish, follow these general steps:

1. Obtain GlassFish. Download and installation issues are discussed in Chapter 1.

2. Perform any preinstallation steps. Once you have obtained the GlassFish bundle and before you can proceed to installing it, you need to make decisions regarding what type of installation to choose and what port numbers to use for the services being installed to avoid port conflicts.

   If you have to change the default port numbers, you need to make the appropriate changes to the setup.xml configuration file used during installation, as discussed in Chapter 1.

   If you want to choose the clustering-supported installation as an alternative to the installation based on the Developer profile, you will have to use setup-cluster.xml as the parameter of ant when building the application server, rather than using setup.xml.

■**Note** Clustering is beyond the scope of this book. It is assumed that you have performed the installation based on the Developer profile, using `setup.xml` as the parameter of `ant` when building the application server.

---

3. Install GlassFish on your system. This is discussed in detail in Chapter 1.

4. Configure your GlassFish installation by using the tools bundled with GlassFish. After you have installed GlassFish, you might want to further configure the server to simplify development. For example, you might configure the server so that it starts up in debug mode automatically. Postinstallation configuring is discussed in the "Configuring the GlassFish Application Server" section later in this chapter.

5. Deploy a simple web application to GlassFish to verify your installation. This is discussed in detail in the "Deploying Applications to the Server" section later in this chapter.

In addition to these steps, you might take advantage of some GlassFish sample applications demonstrating Java EE technology. For further information, refer to the GlassFish Samples page at `https://glassfish-samples.dev.java.net/`. Also, you can look at the "Glass-Fish Quick Start Guide" document available at `https://glassfish.dev.java.net/downloads/quickstart/index.html`.

GlassFish Documentation

The GlassFish project's Documentation home page is available at `https://glassfish.dev.java.net/javaee5/docs/DocsIndex.html`. On this document index page, you can find a full list of the latest GlassFish documentation.

Also, you might want to visit the following GlassFish resources:

- The GlassFish community's Frequently Asked Questions page at `https://glassfish.dev.java.net/public/faq/index.html`

- The GlassFish discussion forum at `http://forums.java.net/jive/forum.jspa?forumID=56&start=0`

Commercial Support for GlassFish

As discussed earlier, GlassFish is available from the Sun web site as Sun Java System Application Server. Sun also provides commercial support for this product. This support includes services such as e-mail and phone technical support, access to the knowledge database, immediate access to updates and upgrades, and so on.

You can get Sun's support for Sun Java System Application Server by subscribing to any of three tiers: Standard, Premium, and Premium Plus. To learn more about support levels and current prices, you can visit the Java System Application Server Subscriptions page at `http://www.sun.com/service/applicationserversubscriptions/`.

In addition, Sun offers Sun Java System Application Server training courses. For more information on the courses, visit the Sun Java Enterprise System Web and Application Services Course List page at `http://www.sun.com/training/catalog/enterprise/application.xml`.

Starting the Application Server

In Chapter 1, you already saw how to start an instance of the GlassFish application server with the `asadmin` command-line tool. To make this process easier, it is recommended that you add the `[glassfish_dir]/bin` directory to the `PATH` environment variable.

That done, you can launch the server from a terminal window, regardless of the current directory:

```
# asadmin start-domain domain1
```

If the server has launched successfully, you should see the following messages, among some others, of course:

```
Domain domain1 is ready to receive client requests. ➥
Additional services are being started in the background.

...

Domain listens on at least following ports for connections:
[8080 8181 4848 3700 3820 3920 8686]
```

The previous is a set of default port numbers used for the default administrative domain called `domain1` created during the GlassFish installation. These are listed in Table 2-1.

Table 2-1. *The Default* domain1 *Ports for Connections*

Connection	Port Number
HTTP	8080
HTTPS	8181
Administration server	4848
Internet Inter-ORB Protocol (IIOP)	3700
IIOP over SSL	3820
Mutual authentication over SSL	3920
Java Management Extensions (JMX) admin	8686

It is important to understand that the actual port numbers may vary depending on the values specified in the `setup.xml` configuration file utilized during the installation process. Before proceeding to the installation, you can edit `setup.xml` and change the default ports, if required, to avoid port conflicts.

Of particular importance are the first three ports in Table 2-1. User web applications deployed to the server will use the first two ports, 8080 and 8181, which are HTTP and HTTPS ports, respectively. Thus, web applications deployed will be available at the following URLs:

```
http://localhost:8080/appname
https://localhost:8181/appname
```

And the third port in Table 2-1 is 4848, the default administration server port. You can use this port to launch Admin Console:

```
http://localhost:4848
```

Admin Console is discussed in more detail in the next section. Then, in the section "Deploying Applications to the Server," you will learn how to deploy user web applications to the application server so that they are available via HTTP and HTTPS.

Now that you know how to start the server, you might want to learn how to stop it. To do this, you issue the following command:

```
# asadmin stop-domain domain1
```

This will stop the `domain1` instance running on your system.

Performing GlassFish Administration with Admin Console

Now that you have your application server up and running, what is your next step? You might want to learn how you can deploy your web applications to the application server. Also, you might want to learn how to look at the server settings and maybe change something. To fulfill these needs, GlassFish ships with a set of tools, both visual and command line, that let you perform all the previous administration tasks and more. This section discusses Admin Console, a browser-based GUI tool that lets you visually perform administration tasks. In the "GlassFish Administration with asadmin" section later in this chapter, you will learn how you can perform administration tasks with `asadmin`, a command-line tool bundled with GlassFish.

You can use Admin Console to perform the following administration functions:

- Deploying, managing, and undeploying applications

- Creating and manipulating server resources

- Configuring application server settings

- Viewing application server logs

The details of how to perform these administration and configuration tasks are discussed in the later sections of this chapter.

■**Note** As an alternative to Admin Console, GlassFish offers a set of command-line tools for performing administrative tasks. You can find the full list in the Command-Line Tools table within the "GlassFish Quick Start Guide" document at `https://glassfish.dev.java.net/downloads/quickstart/index.html`.

From a user standpoint, the most significant Admin Console features are the following:

- Easy-to-navigate interface

- Online help system

Both are discussed in the following sections.

Using the Admin Console Interface

Admin Console provides an intuitive interface that is easy to navigate and use. You launch it by pointing your browser to `http://localhost:4848`, using the actual host name and port number provided during installation, in case you change the default. As a result, the Admin Console login page appears, where you need to enter an appropriate username/password pair. You can log in as the `admin` user, using the `admin/adminadmin` default pair. Once you are logged in, you can perform configuration tasks, deploy applications, and access application server resources such as connection pools and server logs.

Admin Console has an easy-to-navigate interface implemented as a two-column layout with the menu on the left. Common tasks are grouped into categories displayed in the left column of the console window. To reach a certain page, you should expend appropriate category nodes, moving on to the page of interest. For example, to reach the JDBC Resources page, you need to traverse the following path: Resources/JDBC/JDBC Resources.

Admin Console also includes multitab pages. Figure 2-1 shows the Application Server/ General Information page, which can be reached by clicking the General tab on the Application Server page.

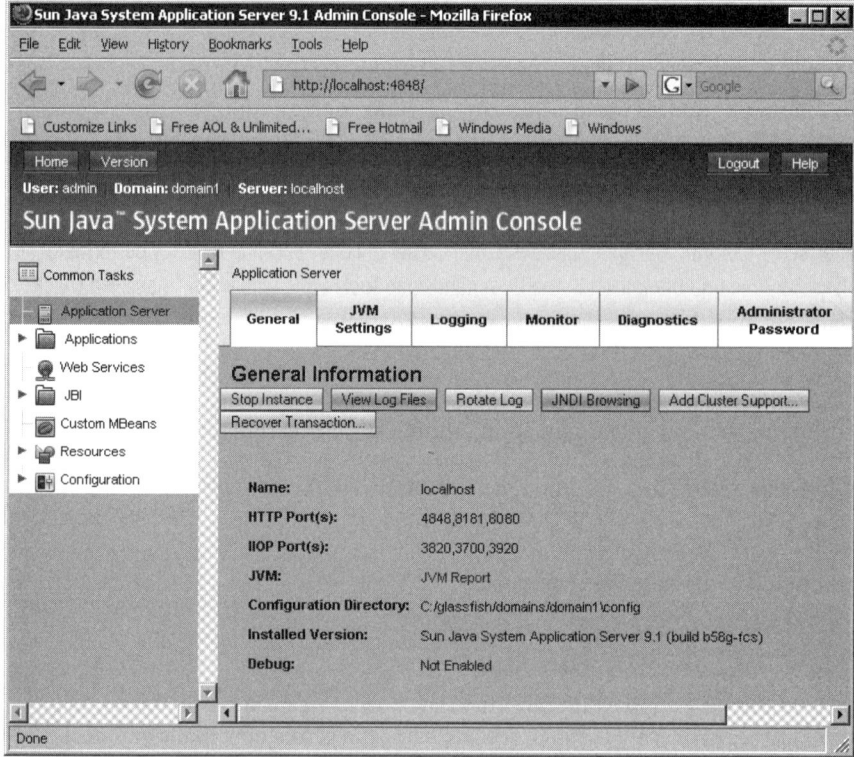

Figure 2-1. *The Admin Console interface*

You can reach some Admin Console pages via buttons on their parent pages. For example, to view the server logs, you can click the View Log Files button on the Application Server/ General Information page shown in Figure 2-1. As a result, the Log Viewer page will be loaded in a separate browser window.

Using the Admin Console Help System

Admin Console comes with an online help system allowing you to get context-sensitive help. To get help on the topic related to a particular Admin Console page, you need to have this page open and then click the Help button located at the top-right corner of the Admin Console window. As a result, the Help window appears in a separate window, with the topic of interest displayed.

For example, if you click the Help button when the Application Server/JVM Settings page is open, you should see the "To configure the JVM settings" information in the Help window, as shown in Figure 2-2.

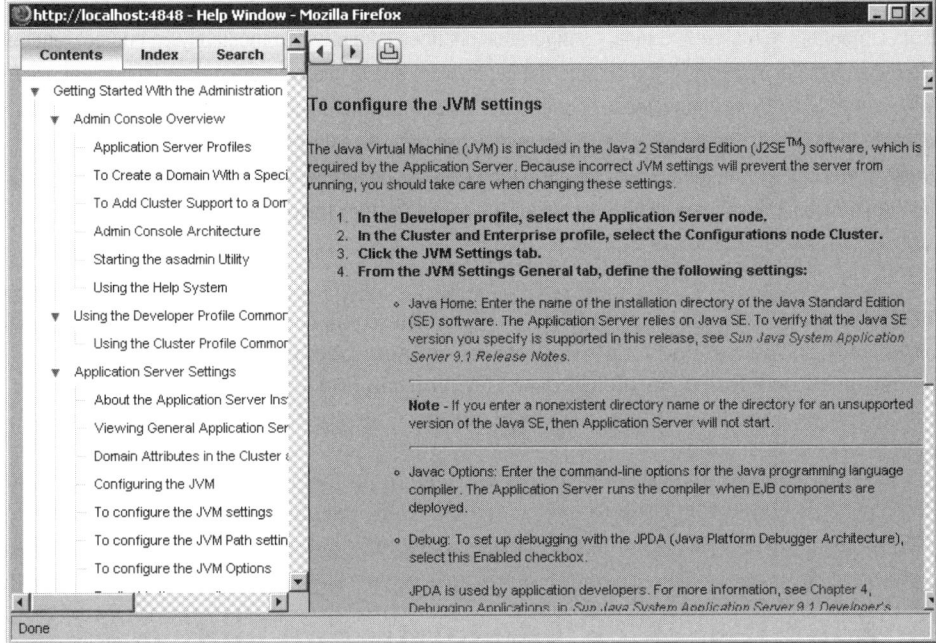

Figure 2-2. *The Help window of the online help system bundled with Admin Console*

As you can see, the Help window provides index and search functionality and also allows you to send the page currently being displayed to the printer.

Configuring the GlassFish Application Server

As mentioned earlier, Admin Console lets you perform a full set of administration and configuration tasks on your application server, including accessing and manipulating settings of the server.

You can start by viewing the server setting on the Application Server page that can be loaded by clicking the Application Server item in the left column. The Application Server page is a multitab screen allowing you to access the server settings. Some tabs of this screen are multitab screens themselves. For example, the Monitor screen contains six tabs.

It is interesting to note that not only can you view the server settings, but you also can change them. In particular, you can change the admin password, JVM settings, logging, monitor, and other server settings. To do this, you should navigate to the page of interest, change the settings as needed, and then click the Save button located at the top-right side of the page.

■Note It is important to realize that most configuration changes take effect immediately and do not require restarting the server. For example, if you change the log level for one or more server modules on the Application Server/Logging/Log Levels page, these changes will take effect immediately, impacting the information being saved in the log files. On the other hand, some changes require restarting the server to take effect. For example, if you change the Admin Console port when editing Configuration/HTTP Service/HTTP Listeners/admin-listener, then you will have to restart the server for the change to take effect.

The Application Server page is not the only place where you can find and edit the application server settings. You can find many more server settings under the Configuration node in the left column of the Admin Console window. Here you can find and manipulate the web container and EJB container settings, HTTP and admin service settings, security, monitoring, and some other server settings.

Another important configuration task you will need to perform is setting up a data source that will be used by your application to interact with a relational database. Chapter 7 explains in detail how to set up a reusable connection for a particular database.

Performing GlassFish Administration with asadmin

It is interesting to note that everything you can do using Admin Console can also be done with one of the command-line tools bundled with GlassFish. The most powerful of these is asadmin.

You can issue an asadmin command either at the asadmin prompt or at the operating system command prompt. To switch to the asadmin prompt from the system command prompt, just type the following:

```
# asadmin
```

As a result, you should see the following prompt:

```
asadmin>
```

To look through the list of all the asadmin commands, you can use the asadmin help command:

```
asadmin>help
```

To obtain the usage information for a particular asadmin command, you can use the following syntax:

```
asadmin>help asadmin's_command_of_interest
```

For example, to obtain the usage information for asadmin's create-domain command, you might issue the following command:

```
asadmin>help create-domain
```

The information provided contains not only the synopsis and detailed description of the command specified but also a detailed description of each command parameter and several examples. Often, the information to be displayed cannot fit entirely in the terminal window. In that case, asadmin divides the information into several pages. You pass on to the next page by pressing Enter, or you quit by typing q.

Sometimes you might want to obtain just a synopsis briefly describing how to use the command. If so, you can simply enter the command of interest at the asadmin prompt like this:

```
asadmin>create-domain
```

As a result, you should see the following synopsis:

```
Usage: create-domain  [--user user] [--passwordfile passwordfile]
[(--adminport port_number | --portbase portbase)]
[(--profile developer | cluster | enterprise ] --template domain_template)]
[--domaindir domain_directory/domains]
[--instanceport port_number] [--savemasterpassword=false]
[--domainproperties (name=value)[:name=value]*]
[--savelogin=false] [--terse=false]
[--echo=false] [--interactive=true]
domain_name
```

With that in hand, you can easily compose the right command to issue, using the command parameters properly. You can find an example of the create-domain command in the section "Creating a Domain" later in this chapter.

To exit the asadmin prompt and return to the system command prompt, use the exit command:

```
asadmin>exit
```

Deploying Applications to the Server

Now that you have an idea of how to configure GlassFish, how might you deploy an application to it? After all, the reason for using an application server is that you will deploy your applications to it, thus making them available to users.

The following sections discuss several different ways in which you can deploy an application to GlassFish. First, you will learn how to manually develop and then deploy a simple web application. Later, in the section "Creating and Deploying a Web Application with the NetBeans IDE," you will see how to perform the same task with the NetBeans IDE, a GUI tool.

Creating a Simple Web Application

Before you can deploy an application to your application server, you should have that application created and packed properly. This section discusses how you can manually create a "Hello World!" web application to be packed and deployed to GlassFish.

For simplicity, the application will contain a single JSP page displaying the message "Hello World!"

First, let's develop the directory structure for the application. In fact, a web application is deployed as a WAR archive having a predetermined structure. Figure 2-3 gives a graphical depiction of that structure.

Figure 2-3. *The structure of a web application*

As you can see in the figure, the application's root directory contains JSP files. In a real-world example, there may be many more JSP, HTML, and CSS files here. Aside from these files, the root directory contains the META-INF and WEB-INF directories.

You don't need to worry about creating the META-INF directory and the MANIFEST.MF file within it. The jar utility that you will use to build the WAR archive takes care of that nuance for you.

The WEB-INF directory has a somewhat more complicated structure. In particular, it contains the configuration files required for deployment, as well as the classes and lib directories containing the compiled Java classes and library dependencies, respectively. When developing the "Hello World!" application discussed here, though, you don't need to create the classes and lib directories within WEB-INF. This is because this simple application does not utilize any Java classes at all. What you must create, however, is the sun-web.xml runtime deployment descriptor containing information required when deploying the application to GlassFish. Also, you might include the web.xml deployment descriptor.

■Note In this particular example, including web.xml is optional. You don't have to include this application deployment descriptor if your application contains only JSP pages and static files and does not contain any servlets, filters, or listeners. In that case, though, you may still want to use web.xml, for example, to set a particular JSP file to be a welcome page.

Finally, for your "Hello World!" application, you might create the directory structure shown in Figure 2-4.

Figure 2-4. *The structure of a "Hello World!" application*

You can create the structure shown in the figure in any folder in your system. Once you have created the directories, you can move on and create the files. The index.jsp file responsible for displaying the "Hello World!" message might look like the one shown in Listing 2-1.

Listing 2-1. *The* index.jsp *File of the "Hello World!" Application*

```
<%@page contentType="text/html"%>
<%@page pageEncoding="UTF-8"%>
<html>
  <head>
    <title>Hello World! Page</title>
  </head>
  <body>
    <h1>Hello World!</h1>
  </body>
</html>
```

As you can see, the index.jsp page does not contain any dynamic content—it does not access any Java object. It simply uses static HTML to display the message.

Creating Deployment Descriptors

The next step in building the "Hello World!" application is to create the web.xml and sun-web.xml configuration files containing information to be utilized during the deployment process.

web.xml is a deployment descriptor whose elements are used to configure your web application. As mentioned in the preceding section, using web.xml in this particular example is optional, as long as the application does not contain any servlets, filters, or listeners. However, you are using it here to explicitly set the index.jsp page to a welcome page.

Listing 2-2 shows a simple deployment descriptor that might be used in the "Hello World!" application.

Listing 2-2. *A (Simple)* web.xml *Deployment Descriptor*

```
<?xml version="1.0" encoding="UTF-8"?>
<web-app xmlns="http://java.sun.com/xml/ns/javaee"
    xmlns:xsi="http://www.w3.org/2001/XMLSchema-instance"
    xsi:schemaLocation="http://java.sun.com/xml/ns/javaee
                http://java.sun.com/xml/ns/javaee/web-app_2_5.xsd"
                version="2.5">
    <welcome-file-list>
        <welcome-file>
            index.jsp
        </welcome-file>
    </welcome-file-list>
</web-app>
```

Remember to save this file in the WEB-INF directory within the root directory of your application.

The next step is to create the sun-web.xml runtime deployment descriptor, providing the information required for deploying the application to GlassFish. In this particular example, you need to specify only the information about the context root of the application.

The sun-web.xml runtime deployment descriptor of the "Hello World!" application might look like Listing 2-3.

Listing 2-3. *A (Simple)* sun-web.xml *Runtime Deployment Descriptor*

```
<?xml version="1.0" encoding="UTF-8"?>
<!DOCTYPE sun-web-app PUBLIC "-//Sun Microsystems,
Inc.//DTD Application Server 9.0 Servlet 2.5//EN"
"http://www.sun.com/software/appserver/dtds/sun-web-app_2_5-0.dtd">
<sun-web-app>
    <context-root>/HelloWorld</context-root>
</sun-web-app>
```

You must save this file in the WEB-INF directory within the root directory of your application.

Packaging the Application

Now that you have created the application sources, you can move on and build the WAR file. To do this, you should change the directory to the root directory of your application and then use the jar program as shown here. And don't forget to put the period at the end of this command:

```
#jar cvf helloworld.war .
```

As a result, the helloworld.war file should appear in the HelloWorld directory. Now you can use this archive to deploy the application to the application server.

Deploying the Application Using Autodeploy

Deployment can be accomplished in different ways. The simplest way to deploy an application is to copy its WAR deployment archive to the autodeploy directory under [glassfish_dir]/domains]/your_domain. If you are using the default domain, this should be the following directory: [glassfish_dir]/domains/domain1/autodeploy.

Once you have copied the WAR file to the previous directory, the application will be automatically deployed to the server. To make sure it has been done, you can check out the server.log file located in the [glassfish_dir]/domains/domain1/logs/ directory. The last two lines in this file should look similar to the following ones:

```
[#|2007-11-18T20:30:00.781-0800|INFO|sun-appserver9.1 ➥|
javax.enterprise.system.tools.deployment|_ThreadID=13;_ThreadName=Timer-5;| ➥
deployed with moduleid = helloworld|#]

[#|2007-11-18T20:30:00.906-0800|INFO|sun-appserver9.1| ➥
javax.enterprise.system.tools.deployment|_ThreadID=13;_ThreadName=Timer-5;| ➥
[AutoDeploy] Successfully autodeployed : ➥
C:\glassfish\domains\domain1\autodeploy\helloworld.war.|#]
```

Tip You will have more readable results if you look at the logs in Admin Console. This is discussed in the "Deploying the Application with Admin Console" section later in this chapter.

You can undeploy the application by removing the `helloworld.war` file from the `[glassfish_dir]/domains/domain1/autodeploy` directory.

Deploying the Application with asadmin

Copying the WAR file from one directory to another may take a long time if you have to type the full path to `[glassfish_dir]/domains/domain1/autodeploy` by hand. So, you may find it easier to accomplish the deployment using the `asadmin` tool. To do this, change the directory to the `HelloWorld` directory and then issue the following command:

```
#asadmin deploy helloworld.war
```

If everything is OK, you should see the following output:

```
Command deploy executed successfully.
```

To make sure this has been done, you can issue the following command:

```
#asadmin list-components
```

The previous should produce the following output:

```
helloworld <web-module>
Command list-components executed successfully.
```

You can undeploy the application by issuing the following command:

```
#asadmin undeploy helloworld
```

It is interesting to note that you can use the `asadmin undeploy` command to undeploy the application deployed by copying the WAR application deployment file to the `autodeploy` directory, as discussed in the preceding section.

Another important thing to note is that deploying and undeploying applications takes effect immediately and does not require restarting the server.

Deploying the Application with Admin Console

If you prefer a GUI tool to a command-line one, you might deploy your applications using Admin Console. To do this, follow these steps:

1. Launch Admin Console.

2. Log in to Admin Console.

3. Navigate to the Applications/Web Applications page.

4. On the Web Applications page, click the Deploy button. As a result, the Deploy Enterprise Applications/Modules page appears.

5. On the Deploy Enterprise Applications/Modules page, make sure that Web Application (.war) is chosen in the Type combo box.

6. Move down to the Location group, and make sure that the Packaged File to Be Uploaded to the Server button is selected.

7. Click the Browse button located on the right of the Packaged File to Be Uploaded to the Server button, and navigate to the `helloworld.war` file discussed in the preceding sections.

8. After you have specified the location of the `helloworld.war` file, the Application Name and Context Root boxes will be filled in with helloworld.

9. In the Context Root box, replace helloworld with **/HelloWorld**.

10. Leave the other fields at their defaults, and click OK at the top-right side of the page.

After performing these steps, you will be taken back to the Applications/Web Applications page. This time, the Deployed Web Applications dialog box within the Applications/Web Applications page should show one deployed application, namely, `helloworld`.

Figure 2-5 shows the Deployed Web Applications area within the Applications/Web Applications page after you have deployed the "Hello World!" application.

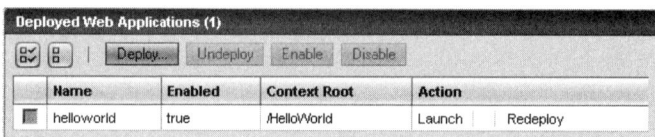

Figure 2-5. *Mock-up of the Deployed Web Applications area located within the Applications/Web Applications page of Admin Console*

It is interesting to note that the Deployed Web Applications area shown in Figure 2-5 shows all the applications deployed on this domain, regardless of the way you deployed them. So, if you now undeploy the "Hello World!" application and then deploy it again using one of the methods discussed in the preceding sections, you will see the same results as shown in Figure 2-5.

Once the "Hello World!" application is deployed, an appropriate entry appears in the log file. To make sure that is the case, follow these steps:

1. In Admin Console, navigate to the Application Server/General page.

2. On the Application Server/General page, click the View Log Files button. This opens the Log Viewer window.

3. In the Log Viewer window, move on to the Log Viewer Results table, and find the upper row containing the following message: `deployed with moduleid = helloworld(details)`.

4. In the message `deployed with moduleid = helloworld(details)`, click `details`. This should open the Log Entry Detail dialog box shown in Figure 2-6.

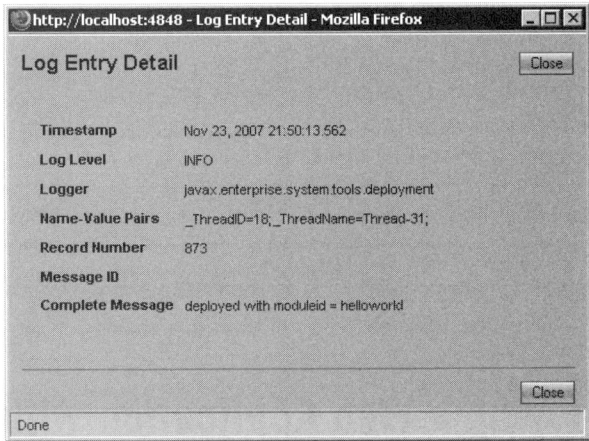

Figure 2-6. *Log Entry Detail dialog box*

As you can see in the figure, the server has created a log entry upon deploying the application.

Testing the Application

Checking out the logs to make sure the application has been successfully deployed is definitely not the fastest way to go in this case. You can quickly check your application if you simply point a browser to the URL of the application.

To run the "Hello World!" application discussed here, point your browser to `http://localhost:8080/HelloWorld/`. As a result, the browser should output the page shown in Figure 2-7.

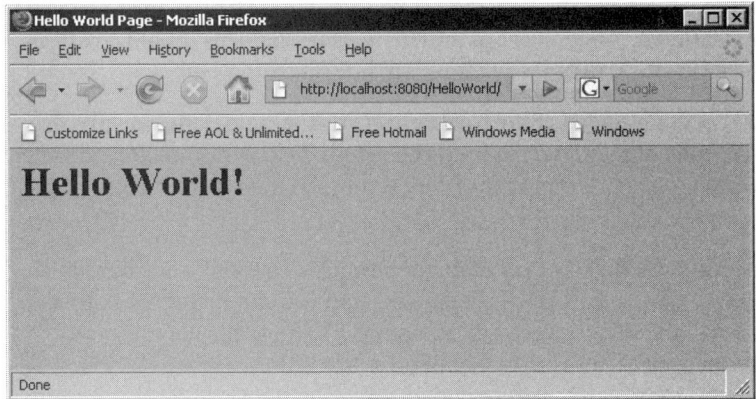

Figure 2-7. *The "Hello World!" page*

If you undeploy the application and then point your browser to `http://localhost:8080/HelloWorld/` again, you will see the following messages:

```
HTTP Status 404 -
--------------------------------------------------------------------------------
type Status report
message
description The requested resource () is not available.
--------------------------------------------------------------------------------
Sun Java System Application Server 9.1
```

This indicates that the application is not deployed on the server and, therefore, is not available.

Creating and Deploying a Web Application with the NetBeans IDE

The preceding example illustrates how to create a simple web application and then deploy it to the application server in several ways. In the following sections, I will illustrate how to perform this same task using the NetBeans IDE, an open source integrated development environment that can be used as a single, easy-to-use interface when it comes to building and deploying Java EE applications.

Creating a "Hello World!" Application

Follow these steps to build a "Hello World!" application using the NetBeans IDE:

1. Launch the NetBeans IDE.

2. In the NetBeans IDE, select File ➤ New Project.

3. On the Choose Project screen of the New Project Wizard, choose Web in the Categories box and Web Application in the Project box and then click Next. This should create an empty web application as a standard NetBeans IDE project.

4. On the Name and Location screen of the New Project Wizard, type **HelloWorldWithIDE** in the Project Name box, and set the Project Location box to the directory in which you want to save the project files. Leave the other settings at their defaults, and click Next.

5. On the Frameworks screen, make sure that no framework is checked, and click Finish. As a result, the HelloWorld project will be generated, and you should see the contents of the `index.jsp` file in the IDE's Source Editor. Listing 2-4 shows the file (the comments have been removed to improve readability).

Listing 2-4. *The* `index.jsp` *Page Automatically Generated with the NetBeans IDE When Creating a Web Application Project*

```
<%@page contentType="text/html"%>
<%@page pageEncoding="UTF-8"%>
<!DOCTYPE HTML PUBLIC "-//W3C//DTD HTML 4.01 Transitional//EN"
    "http://www.w3.org/TR/html4/loose.dtd">
<html>
    <head>
        <meta http-equiv="Content-Type" content="text/html; charset=UTF-8">
        <title>JSP Page</title>
    </head>
    <body>
     <h1>JSP Page</h1>
    </body>
</html>
```

6. In the Source Editor, change the body of the `index.jsp` page as follows:

```
<body>
 <h1>Hello World!!!</h1>
</body>
```

Note that you put three exclamation marks at the end of the "Hello World" message to distinguish it from the "Hello World!" application discussed earlier in this chapter.

7. In the NetBeans IDE, select File ➤ Save to save the changes made in the `index.jsp` page.

8. On the Projects tab of the IDE, right-click the `HelloWorldWithIDE` project, and select Build Project.

If everything is OK, you should see the `BUILD SUCCESSFUL` message in the Output window of the IDE.

After performing these steps, you should have the "Hello World!" application project created and ready for deployment.

Deploying an Application with NetBeans

Deployment with NetBeans is straightforward. Once you have finished creating your application, you can deploy it as follows:

1. On the Projects tab of the IDE, right-click the `HelloWorldWithIDE` project.

2. In the pop-up menu, select Deploy Project.

After performing these steps, you should have your "Hello World!" application deployed to the application server. To make sure it has done so, you can point your browser to `http://localhost:8080/HelloWorldWithIDE/`. As a result, you should see the page displaying the `Hello World!!!` message.

Understanding GlassFish Domains

GlassFish uses the concept of *domains* to organize application server instances into groups, each of which shares the same configuration settings, log files, and user applications deployed.

You might create more than one domain in your application server if you need to use the deployed applications in different environments.

■Note This discussion assumes that you run your GlassFish server in the Single Instance mode. In this mode, although you can create more than one domain and then run them simultaneously, each domain can access and manipulate only its own configuration, resources, and deployed applications. Alternatively, you might take advantage of the Cluster mode available in GlassFish 2. The Cluster mode assumes you're using a group of server instances sharing the same resources. For more information on clustering with GlassFish, you can refer to the "Cluster Support in GlassFish V2" document at http://wiki.glassfish.java.net/Wiki.jsp?page=GlassFishV2Architecture.

Creating a Domain

You can create a new domain with the asadmin's create-domain command. In the following example, you bring up the asadmin prompt in a terminal window:

```
# asadmin
```

Then, you issue the following command:

```
asadmin>create-domain --user admin --profile developer --portbase 9000 domain2
```

Let's take a closer look at the create-domain command. You issue this command here with three parameters. In particular, you use the --user parameter to specify the username of the administrator of the domain being created. Then, you explicitly define the profile of the domain. Finally, you set the port base, defining the number with which the ports of the domain being created should start.

When you enter the create-domain command, you are prompted to enter the admin password:

```
Please enter the admin password>
```

After you have entered the admin password and confirmed it, you will be asked to enter the master password or hit Enter to accept the default:

```
Please enter the master password [Enter to accept the default]>
```

You can hit Enter here. After the confirmation, the creation of the domain begins. You should see the following output:

```
Using port 9048 for Admin.
Using port 9080 for HTTP Instance.
Using port 9076 for JMS.
Using port 9037 for IIOP.
Using port 9081 for HTTP_SSL.
Using port 9038 for IIOP_SSL.
Using port 9039 for IIOP_MATUALAUTH.
Using port 9086 for JMX_ADMIN
Domain being created with profile: developer, as specified on command line or ➡
environment.
Security Store uses: JKS
Domain domain2 created.
```

Running Several Domains Simultaneously

If required, you can run several domains simultaneously. For example, you might issue these commands one after another:

```
asadmin>start-domain domain1
asadmin>start-domain domain2
```

Once both the domains are up and running, you can run the applications deployed under those domains. For example, if you deployed the "Hello World!" application under both domains, you can launch two browser windows and point one of them to `http://localhost:8080/HelloWorld` and the other one to `http://localhost:9080/HelloWorld`.

Deleting a Domain

When deleting a domain, you should understand that you in fact delete all the configuration associated with that domain, including deployed applications.

To delete a domain, you first have to leave the `asadmin` prompt:

```
asadmin>exit
```

Then, you can delete the domain as follows:

```
# asadmin delete-domain domain2
```

If everything is OK, you should see the following message:

```
Domain domain2 deleted
```

Summary

In this chapter, you learned what GlassFish is and why you might want to choose it over any other Java EE 5–compliant application server. Then, you looked at the GlassFish tools for administration, both visual and command line. You learned how to configure your GlassFish application server, as well as how to deploy and undeploy applications using different techniques.

The knowledge and techniques you learned in this chapter are required to follow the samples discussed in the later chapters of this book. This is because all the book sample applications assume that you deploy them to GlassFish.

CHAPTER 3

■ ■ ■

Introducing EJB 3 and the Java Persistence API

In the preceding chapter, you learned about GlassFish, one of the most powerful Java EE 5–compatible application servers. By Java EE 5 compatible, I mean you can deploy Java applications, which are built in compliance with the Java EE 5 specification, to this application server.

In fact, the Java EE 5 platform involves several Java APIs, such as JSP 2.1, JSF 1.2, EJB 3.0, and JAX-WS 2.0, to name a few. JSP and JSF are web tier technologies utilized in developing the presentation layer of a Java EE 5 application. You saw an example of using a JSP page in the preceding chapter when developing a "Hello World!" application. In Chapter 14, you will learn how to use the JSF technology when building the presentation tier of an enterprise application.

This chapter discusses the basics of Enterprise JavaBeans 3.0 (EJB 3), which is one of the key Java EE 5 specifications, providing a standard way to implement server-side components that encapsulate the business logic of enterprise applications. The chapter also introduces the EJB 3 Java Persistence API (JPA), a new Java EE 5 technology used for accessing relational databases from Java EE applications.

Here are the main topics covered in the chapter:

- Overview of EJB 3

- Building and deploying a "Hello World!" session enterprise bean

- Creating a client application to test the "Hello World!" bean

- Overview of JPA

- Building, deploying, and testing a simple application using EJB and JPA technologies together

You can skip this chapter if you already have some basic knowledge of the EJB 3 and JPA technologies.

To follow the examples discussed in this chapter, you need to have GlassFish installed in your system. If you still have not installed it, you can refer to Chapter 1.

Overview of EJB 3

This section provides a brief overview of the EJB 3 technology. It discusses what EJB 3 is and what the advantages of using EJB 3 as a technology are.

This section is followed by the "Your First EJB 3 Application" section, providing a simple example of using the EJB 3 technology.

What Is EJB 3?

Depending on how you look at it, EJB may be one of the following:

- *A technology*: As a technology, EJB 3 is based on the EJB 3.0 specification (JSR-220) available at `http://jcp.org/en/jsr/detail?id=220`, and it provides a platform for developing reusable, scalable, and mission-critical enterprise applications.

- *A component*: EJB components, also known as *enterprise beans*, implement the EJB technology. An EJB component is a reusable, server-side piece of code implementing a business method or methods to be utilized within enterprise applications. For further details on EJB components, refer to the "EJB 3 Components" section later in this overview.

- *A container*: An EJB container is a runtime environment implemented within the application server, which enables deployment of enterprise beans and provides runtime support for beans' instances in the form of services, such as persistence and transaction management, concurrency control, and security authorization. For further details on EJB containers, refer to the "EJB Container" section later.

As you can see, EJB may mean different things in different situations. Throughout this book, though, *EJB* will typically refer to an EJB component, while *EJB 3* will refer to the EJB 3 technology, unless noted otherwise.

Advantages of EJB 3

Now that you have learned what EJB 3 is, it's time to look at the advantages of using this technology and why you might want to choose it.

The following are some advantages of the EJB 3 technology:

- The EJB platform provides a standard way for developing and deploying reliable component-based Java enterprise applications that scale.

- The fact that EJB 3 is a standard Java EE 5 technology enables you to deploy your EJB components on any Java EE 5–compliant application server.

- On the EJB 3 platform, the back-end code, encapsulating most of the repetitive tasks, was moved into the framework, making the development process easier and making the technology much friendlier, especially for beginners.

- When using the EJB technology, the developer can concentrate on implementing business logic to be utilized within particular enterprise applications, rather than on reimplementing logic related to the problems commonly found in enterprise applications.

- When it comes to performing configuration tasks, EJB 3 developers have choices. Annotations can be used in favor of XML descriptors or together with them.

- Typically used to implement the business logic and persistence tiers of an enterprise application, EJB 3 can be seamlessly used with other Java EE APIs, such as JSP and JSF that are employed for building the application presentation tier.

Looking through this list, you may conclude that EJB 3 as a technology provides a powerful yet easy-to-use way of developing enterprise applications in the Java programming language. The most important thing about EJB 3 is that it doesn't require you to perform a set of repetitive tasks typically found in enterprise applications. Such tasks are implemented as services provided by the EJB container and include transaction management, concurrency control, persistence, security, and some others described in the EJB 3 specification. This approach based on moving the back-end code into the framework allows you to focus your efforts entirely on solving particular problems related to your application rather than on making desperate efforts to develop back-end code yourself.

EJB Container

The EJB container represents a runtime environment in the application server, providing core functionality common to many EJB components.

The EJB components deployed to the application server are executed within the EJB container that provides system-level services such as transaction management and security authorization to those components. As mentioned, this architecture allows developers to concentrate on the particular business problems, rather than on reimplementing solutions to the common problems usually found in enterprise applications.

It is interesting to note that the EJB container is not the only container running within an instance of a Java EE 5–compliant application server. Another important container of an application server is a web container that is responsible for managing the execution of JSP and JSF pages, as well as servlet components.

EJB 3 Components

As mentioned, an EJB is a server-side, reusable component that encapsulates specific business logic and is activated and executed by the EJB container within an application server.

An EJB component may be one of the following two:

- Session bean

- Message-driven bean

■**Note** Also, there are Java Persistence API entities (formerly, entity beans). You will see a JPA entity in action in the "Your First EJB JPA Application" section later in this chapter.

It is interesting to note that all EJB components are plain old Java objects (POJOs) with Java EE annotations incorporated.

Session Beans

Session beans are used to encapsulate the business logic of enterprise applications, executing business tasks inside the EJB container on the application server. A session bean can be either stateless or stateful. The following two sections explain these two types of session beans.

Stateful Session Beans

When a client application invokes a stateful session bean, the EJB container provides the same instance for each subsequent method invocation performed by the client during the session. You might want to use a stateful session bean when you need, for example, to implement a business process involving several steps, each of which may rely on the state maintained in a previous step.

A typical example is creating a user account on a web site. The process of collecting user information is usually divided into several steps. For example, when creating a new e-mail account, you first may be asked to provide the information of vital importance, such as an account name and password. If the information provided in this stage is OK, you will be taken to the next page of the wizard, which may ask you to enter your personal information, such as your name and birthday. Finally, on the last page, you will be asked to confirm the information you have provided so far.

As you have no doubt realized, the previous business process requires maintaining state information all the way through. It's fairly obvious that when you click the Create Account button in the last step, you expect that all the information provided so far will be properly saved to the database on the server. Using a session bean in the previous situation is a standard way to go. Instead of implementing a custom, likely to be error-prone, solution, you gain the advantages provided by the container. In particular, the container automatically takes care of maintaining session state, also known as *conversational state*, during the entire process of collecting user information.

The downside of using stateful beans is that each stateful bean instance is one-to-one related to a certain client and cannot be reused with another client. Diagrammatically, it might look like Figure 3-1.

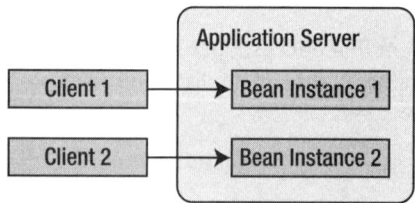

Figure 3-1. *One-to-one mapping of client applications and stateful session bean instances*

A stateful bean instance terminates when either the client removes it or the session ends. This can add considerable memory overhead if the stateful bean has a great number of concurrent clients.

You will see an example of using a stateful session bean in Chapter 12 of this book.

Stateless Session Beans

As you learned in the previous discussion, stateful session beans come in handy when you need to retain the state. In practice, though, stateless session beans are used more often than stateful ones. Stateless beans provide business methods to their clients, while not maintaining a conversational state with them. The latter makes it possible for the container to pool and reuse instances of stateless beans, sharing them between clients. This is graphically depicted in Figure 3-2.

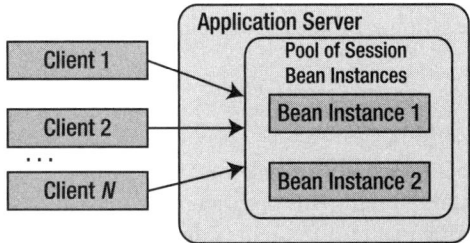

Figure 3-2. *Using a pool of stateless session bean instances*

Using a stateless bean is ideal when you need to implement the task that can be concluded with a single method call performed by a client. Listing 3-1 shows a simplified example of a stateless session bean class.

Listing 3-1. *A Simple Example of a Stateless Session Bean Class*

```
package example.ejb;
import javax.ejb.Stateless;
@Stateless
public class HelloSessionBean implements example.ejb.HelloSession {
  private String helloMessage;
  public String outputHelloMessage(String usrname) {
    helloMessage = "Hi, "+ usrname;
    return helloMessage;
  }
}
```

As you can see, the previous session bean provides the only business method, namely, outputHelloMessage. This method takes the parameter name and compiles a "hello" message based on the value passed in with that parameter, returning the compiled message to the client.

Note that in the outputHelloMessage business method, you modify the helloMessage bean variable. You can safely perform this operation, since each new invocation of the outputHelloMessage business method will rewrite the value of the helloMessage instance variable with new data. However, since HelloSessionBean used here is defined as stateless, a more elegant way of using the helloMessage bean variable would be as follows:

```
@Stateless
public class HelloSessionBean implements example.ejb.HelloSession {
  private String helloMessage = "Hi, ";
  public String outputHelloMessage(String usrname) {
    return helloMessage + usrname;
  }
}
```

You will see a simple working example of a stateless session bean in the "Your First EJB 3 Application" section later in this chapter. More interesting examples of session beans are discussed in Chapter 12.

Interfaces Defining Access to Session Beans

Continuing with the discussion on session beans, it is interesting to note that they can be accessed only through the business interfaces they implement. This programming model makes it easier for you to change beans without having to alter the client code. You can change the bean class while leaving its business interface untouched.

A session bean can implement a local or remote business interface, or both. You can use a local business interface only if the bean and the client application consuming that bean are running in the same JVM. Otherwise, you have to use a remote interface.

■Note It is recommended that you use a local interface for the enterprise beans that are utilized by applications deployed on the same server. This will allow you to avoid the performance overhead associated with supporting a distributed computing environment. However, if you develop an enterprise bean that will be then utilized by applications distributed across a network, you have to use a remote interface with that bean.

Listing 3-2 shows a local interface that might be implemented by the HelloSession bean shown in Listing 3-1 earlier.

Listing 3-2. *The Business Interface for the* HelloSession *Bean*

```
package example.ejb;
import javax.ejb.Local;
@Local
public interface HelloSession {
  public String outputHelloMessage(String usrname);
}
```

Note the use of the @Local annotation in the previous example. With that, you declare the HelloSession business interface as local.

Alternatively, you might specify the interface in the bean's class. In that case, you would have to include the @Local annotation in the HelloSession bean class shown in Listing 3-1 as follows:

```
package example.ejb;
import javax.ejb.Local;
import javax.ejb.Stateless;
@Stateless
@Local(HelloSession.class)
public class HelloSessionBean implements example.ejb.HelloSession {
...
}
```

Now the HelloSession interface shown in Listing 3-2 might look like this:

```
package example.ejb;
public interface HelloSession {
  public String outputHelloMessage(String usrname);
}
```

With this approach, you are free to use the HelloSession interface as local or remote as appropriate.

Client Code Utilizing Session Beans

Now that you have seen an example of a session bean, you might want to look at the client code utilizing that bean. Listing 3-3 shows a simple example of such a client.

Listing 3-3. *The Client Code Utilizing the* outputHelloMessage *Business Method of the* HelloSession *Bean*

```
package example.client;
import javax.ejb.EJB;
import example.ejb.HelloSession;
public class HelloSessionClient {
    @EJB
    private static HelloSession helloSession;
    public static void main (String[] args)
      {
          System.out.println(helloSession.outputHelloMessage("John"));
      }
}
```

The most interesting thing to notice in this code is the use of the @EJB annotation. In this example, you use @EJB to annotate the static field helloSession that represents the HelloSession bean business interface.

■**Note** This is an example of how a client can obtain a session bean's business interface using dependency injection. In a nutshell, dependency injection lets the container automatically insert (*inject*) references to other components and resources with the help of annotations. In this particular example, you acquire a reference to the HelloSession interface by annotating the private, static HelloSession helloSession with @EJB.

A little later, in the "Your First EJB 3 Application" section, you will learn how to build a simple stateless session bean, deploy it to the GlassFish application server, and then test it with a client application. Then, in Chapter 12, you will see more realistic examples of using session beans. For the time being, though, that concludes this concise discussion of session beans.

Message-Driven Beans

It is important to realize that all communications between session bean instances and their clients are synchronous. What this means in practice is that the client cannot continue execution until the bean instance completes the request. In some situations, though, you may need to develop an asynchronous solution built upon loosely coupled components. This is where message-driven beans come in handy.

Unlike session beans, message-driven beans enable asynchronous communications between the server and client, thus avoiding tying up server resources. Instead of directly invoking bean's methods, a client sends a message to a JMS queue or a JMS topic. Listing 3-4 illustrates the source code for a simple message-driven bean.

Listing 3-4. *An Example of a Message-Driven Bean*

```
package example.ejb;
import javax.ejb.MessageDriven;
import javax.ejb.MessageDrivenContext;
import javax.jms.MessageListener;
import javax.jms.Message;
import javax.jms.TextMessage;
import javax.jms.JMSException;

@MessageDriven(mappedName = "jms/Queue")
public class SimpleMessageDrivenBean implements MessageListener {

public void onMessage(Message msg) {
  TextMessage txtMsg = null;
  try
  {
    txtMsg = (TextMessage) msg;
    System.out.println("The following message received: " +txtMsg.getText());
```

```
  } catch (JMSException e) {
    e.printStackTrace();
  }
 }
}
```

As you can see, a message-driven bean is decorated with the @MessageDriven annotation. You use the mappedName attribute with this annotation in order to specify the name of the JMS queue or topic from which the bean will consume messages.

The SimpleMessageDrivenBean message-driven bean shown in the listing implements the javax.jms.MessageListener interface providing the onMessage method. This method is automatically invoked by the EJB container when the queue specified with the mappedName attribute of the @MessageDriven annotation receives a message.

In this particular example, the bean simply prints the message, sending it to the application server log.

Your First EJB 3 Application

Now that you have a rough idea of EJB 3, let's take a look at a simple application based on this technology. This application will surprise you with its simplicity, but it will also give you a high-level view of how to build and deploy applications utilizing EJB 3 components.

The following sections explain how to build, deploy, and test a "Hello World!" enterprise bean. You will learn how to do it using only command-line tools, which will allow you to better understand the structure of an EJB application.

■**Note** The fact is that visual tools like NetBeans IDE do a lot of work behind the scenes, hiding some details from the developer. This is generally good, since it makes the development process easier. However, if you are a beginner, you might want to go into more detail. The NetBeans IDE will be used in later chapters.

Creating a Simple Enterprise Bean

In this section, you'll create a "Hello World!" session enterprise bean, compiling it with the javac command-line tool. In the next section, you'll package this bean and then deploy it to the GlassFish application server.

What you really need to develop here is a session enterprise bean, which you will then deploy to the application server, thus making it available for a client application. To achieve this goal, you have to create the enterprise bean class and business interface defining the methods implemented by that class. In this particular example, the enterprise bean class named HelloWorldBean will contain only one method, outputHelloWorld. The business interface, HelloWorld, will be remote. Thus, all you need to do to develop a simple EJB is build two Java files.

■Note In EJB 3, unlike its predecessor EJB 2.*x*, you don't have to define a deployment descriptor that provides the information required for deployment. Instead, you can use metadata annotations; this simplifies the development work.

Before you move on and develop the previous files, though, take some time to build the directory structure for the project. To do this, follow these steps:

1. Under any directory in your system, create the root project directory, say, HelloWorldProject. In fact, you will have two projects under this directory, each of which is in a separate subdirectory, of course. The first one will be used to build the HelloWorld enterprise bean, and the second will be used to build a client application to test that bean.

2. Within the HelloWorldProject directory, create the directory HelloWorldEJB that will contain files and folders required for building the HelloWorld enterprise bean discussed here.

3. Within the HelloWorldEJB directory, create three directories, namely, dist, src, and target.

4. In the src directory, create a helloworld/ejb directory. In this directory, you will then create the enterprise bean class, HelloWorldBean.java, and its business interface, HelloWorld.java.

Finally, the directory structure for the project will look like the one shown in Figure 3-3.

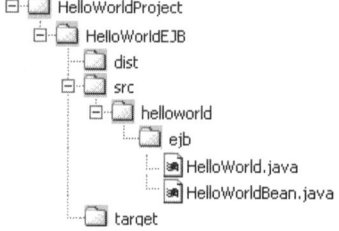

Figure 3-3. *The directory structure of the "Hello World!" EJB project*

After you have created the directory structure for the HelloWorld EJB project, you can switch your focus to developing the project sources.

You might start by creating the HelloWorld.java file implementing the remote interface for the HelloWorldBean enterprise bean class. This interface will be used by the clients of the bean. The source code for the HelloWorld.java file might look like Listing 3-5.

Listing 3-5. *The Remote Business Interface for the* HelloWorldBean *Enterprise Bean Class*

```
package helloworld.ejb;
import javax.ejb.Remote;
@Remote
public interface HelloWorld {
  public String outputHelloWorld();
}
```

Now that you have the business interface created for your enterprise bean, it is time to create the enterprise bean class. Listing 3-6 shows the source code for the HelloWorldBean. java file.

Listing 3-6. *The Source Code for the* HelloWorldBean *Enterprise Bean Class*

```
package helloworld.ejb;
import javax.ejb.Stateless;
@Stateless
public class HelloWorldBean implements helloworld.ejb.HelloWorld {
  public String outputHelloWorld() {
    return "Hello World!";
  }
}
```

As you can see, this is a very simple session bean. All it does is return the string Hello World!

Now that you have both the session bean class and the business interface for that bean, you can compile them. Since this is a very simple example, you can compile the sources using the javac compiler. First, change the directory to the root directory of your project, HelloWorldEJB, and then use the javac program as shown here:

```
# javac -cp /glassfish_dir/lib/javaee.jar -d target src/helloworld/ejb/*.java
```

In this command, you explicitly specify the path to the Java EE library, javaee.jar, located in the GlassFish's lib directory. You might exclude this parameter from the command if you include the path to this library to the CLASSPATH environment variable. In that case, the previous command might be shortened to the following one:

```
 # javac -d target src/helloworld/ejb/*.java
```

After executing the previous, the target\helloworld\ejb directory should appear within the HelloWorldEJB directory. In this directory, you should find the HelloWorld.class and HelloWorldEJB.class files.

Now the target directory should have the structure shown in Figure 3-4.

Figure 3-4. *The directory structure of the target directory located within the root directory of the* HelloWorld *EJB project*

Packaging the Enterprise Bean

Now that you have compiled class files, you are ready to package them into an EJB JAR archive to be then deployed to the application server. For the purpose of this example, you package the HelloWorld session bean code into a .jar file named helloworldejb.jar.

To do this, change the directory to the target directory located within the HelloWorldEJB root directory of the project:

```
# cd target
```

Then issue the following command:

```
# jar cvf ..\dist\helloworldejb.jar .
```

This command should create the helloworldejb.jar file in the HelloWorldEJB\dist directory. If you list this archive, you should see that it has the structure shown in Figure 3-5.

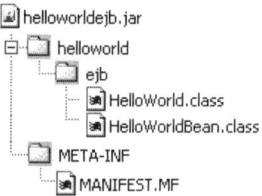

Figure 3-5. *The directory structure of the JAR archive containing the* HelloWorld *session bean*

As you can see, the jar utility automatically created the MANIFEST.MF file in the META-INF directory. All the other files and the directory structure are equal to the ones found under the target directory.

Deploying the Enterprise Bean to GlassFish

Now that you have packaged the HelloWorld session bean into the JAR archive, you can move on and deploy it to the GlassFish application server.

If you recall from Chapter 2, you can deploy your deployment archive to the GlassFish application server in several ways. One of the simplest ways to perform deployment is to copy the deployment archive to the autodeploy subdirectory under the [glassfish_dir]/domains/ your_domain directory. If you are using the default domain, domain1, this should be the following directory: [glassfish_dir]/domains/domain1/autodeploy.The obvious disadvantage of this autodeploying approach is that it doesn't immediately show you whether the deployment operation has been successful. You need to check with the logs to find it out.

So, you might want to use the asadmin's deploy command to deploy the HelloWorld session bean. After executing, this command gives a message informing you about the result of the deployment operation.

Before you can deploy the archive, make sure to start the application server. If you recall from Chapter 2, this can be done with asadmin as follows:

```
# asadmin start-domain domain1
```

With that done, you can change the directory to dist. Assuming that you are currently in the target directory, you need to perform the following commands:

```
# cd ..
# cd dist
```

And then issue the following command:

```
# asadmin deploy helloworldejb.jar
```

If the deployment operation is successful, you should see the following message in the terminal:

```
Command deploy executed successfully
```

To make sure this has been done, you can check the Applications/EJB Modules page of Admin Console. On this page, you should see the helloworldejb module in the list of deployed EJB modules.

Creating the Client Application

Now that you have created and deployed the HelloWorld enterprise bean, you might want to test it. For this, you need to create a client application that will make the EJB container create an instance of that bean and invoke its outputHelloWorld method.

The first thing to take care of is building the directory structure for the client application project. To do this, follow these steps:

1. Within the HelloWorldProject directory, create the directory HelloWorldClient that will contain files and folders required for building the client application discussed here.

2. Within the HelloWorldClient directory, create three directories, namely, dist, src, and target.

3. In the src directory, create directory helloworld/client. In this directory, you will then create the client class in the file HelloWorldClient.java.

4. In the target directory, create the directory META-INF. In this directory, you will then create the MANIFEST.MF file.

Finally, the directory structure for the client project should look like the one shown in Figure 3-6.

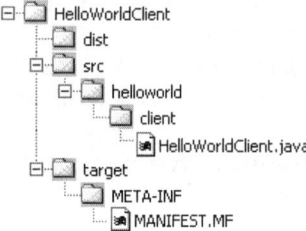

Figure 3-6. *The directory structure of the client application project*

Now that you have created the directory structure for the project, it is time to create the HelloWorldClient class. Listing 3-7 shows the source code for the HelloWorldBean.java file.

Listing 3-7. *The Source Code for the* HelloWorldClient *Client Application*

```
package helloworld.client;
import javax.ejb.EJB;
import helloworld.ejb.HelloWorld;
public class HelloWorldClient {
    @EJB
    private static HelloWorld helloWorld;
    public static void main (String[] args)
    {
        System.out.println(helloWorld.outputHelloWorld());
     }
}
```

As you can see, the client code simply invokes the outputHelloWorld method of a HelloWorld bean instance, printing the method's output in the terminal.

After you have saved the HelloWorldClient.java file in the HelloWorldClient/src/ helloworld/client directory, you can compile it. For this, first make sure to change to the HelloWorldClient directory:

```
# cd HelloWorldClient
```

And then issue the following command:

```
# javac -cp /glassfish_dir/lib/javaee.jar; ➥
../HelloWorldEJB/dist/helloworldejb.jar -d target src/helloworld/client/*.java
```

Although the previous command is broken in two lines here, you must type it on a single line. When you hit the Enter, javac starts execution. If everything is OK, you should see no error message.

Packaging the Client Application

The next step in building the client application discussed here is packaging it into a JAR archive. Before you can do that, though, you need to create the MANIFEST.MF file in the target/META-INF directory. Listing 3-8 shows the source code for the MANIFEST.MF file.

Listing 3-8. *The Source Code for the* `MANIFEST.MF` *File*

```
Manifest-Version: 1.0
Main-Class: helloworld.client.HelloWorldClient
```

The next step is to build the `helloworldclient.jar` archive. To do this, first change the directory to the `HelloWorldClient/target` directory:

```
# cd target
```

And then issue the following command:

```
# jar cvfM ../dist/helloworldclient.jar .
```

Note the use of the `M` option along with the other options usually used when building a `.jar` archive. You specify the `M` option here to force the `jar` utility not to generate a new manifest file. This guarantees that the `MANIFEST.MF` file you created earlier will be used in the archive.

Creating the Application Archive

By now you should have the `helloworldclient.jar` file in the `HelloWorldClient/dist` directory and the `helloworldejb.jar` file in the `HelloWorldEJB/dist` directory. In the next step, you should place these files in a single `.jar` archive, say, `helloworldapp.jar`, that will be then executed with the `appclient` utility that comes with GlassFish and can be found in its `bin` directory.

To begin with, you need to create the directory structure for the `helloworldapp.jar` archive. To do this, follow these steps:

1. Within the `HelloWorldProject` directory, create the `dist` directory to which you will save the `helloworldapp.jar` file.

2. Within the `HelloWorldProject` directory, create the `target` directory.

3. To the `HelloWorldProject/target` directory created in the preceding step, copy the `helloworldejb.jar` and `helloworldclient.jar` archives created as described earlier.

4. In the `HelloWorldProject/target` directory, create the directory `META-INF`. In this directory, you will then create the Java EE deployment descriptor, `application.xml`.

Finally, you should have the directory structure shown in Figure 3-7.

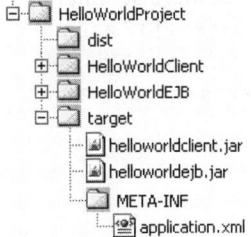

Figure 3-7. *The directory structure of the* `HelloWorld` *project*

For the application discussed here, you can define the Java EE deployment descriptor, application.xml, as shown in Listing 3-9.

Listing 3-9. *The Source Code for the* application.xml *Deployment Descriptor*

```
<?xml version="1.0" encoding="UTF-8"?>
<application version="5" xmlns="http://java.sun.com/xml/ns/javaee"
   xmlns:xsi="http://www.w3.org/2001/XMLSchema-instance"
   xsi:schemaLocation="http://java.sun.com/xml/ns/javaee
   http://java.sun.com/xml/ns/javaee/application_5.xsd">
   <display-name>helloworldejb</display-name>
   <module>
     <ejb>helloworldejb.jar</ejb>
   </module>
   <module>
     <java>helloworldclient.jar</java>
   </module>
</application>
```

After you have created the application.xml deployment descriptor shown in the listing, you can move on and build the helloworldapp.jar archive:

```
# jar cvf ..\dist\helloworldapp.jar .
```

As a result, the helloworldapp.jar file should appear in the HelloWorldEJB/dist directory.

Testing the Application

Finally, you can test your first EJB 3 application built as described in the preceding sections. To do this, change the directory to HelloWorldEJB/dist, and issue the following command:

```
# appclient -client helloworldapp.jar
```

This command assumes that the glassfish_dir/bin directory is included in the PATH environment variable. This should produce the following output:

```
# Hello World!
```

Believe it or not, you just successfully created and tested your first EJB 3 application. Although it simply says Hello World! in a terminal window, it illustrates the ideas behind EJB 3 development well enough. In particular, this example showed you how to use EJB 3 annotations when developing EJB components. Also, it illustrated that clients can access EJBs only via interfaces and that a deployment archive containing an EJB must have a certain structure to be successfully deployed to the application server.

JPA at a Glance

The following two sections briefly describe JPA, giving you the basics required to start building solutions utilizing this exciting technology.

What Is JPA?

In a nutshell, JPA, a new Java EE 5 technology, was created as an answer to the problem of data persistence. It brings the object-oriented and relational models together, making Java EE developers more productive.

As you have no doubt guessed, the Java Persistence API represents a standard way of accessing relational databases from Java EE applications. You can use this API to access and manipulate relational data in EJB and web components, as well as application clients.

■**Note** It is important to note that JPA can also be used in J2EE 1.4 and Java SE applications.

Java Persistence provides the following features:

- Object/relational mapping (ORM)

- The EntityManager API

- The Java Persistence Query Language (JPQL)

Each of these features is discussed in great detail later in this book. For the time being, though, it is important to understand that the ORM mechanism allows you to map POJOs to relational data stored in a database, with the help of ORM annotations or XML. Such POJOs are called JPA *entities* and must be annotated with the `javax.persistence.Entity` annotation or described in an object/relational mapping XML configuration file. When developing a JPA entity, there is no need to include any methods performing database-related operations, such as save or update. Instead, you can use the EntityManager API to manipulate JPA entity instances. This prevents you from using the JDBC API directly, which means you don't need to write your own SQL code to manipulate database data.

JPA Implementation at GlassFish

In GlassFish, the Java Persistence API is implemented with the TopLink Essentials product donated by Oracle Corporation. TopLink Essentials is an open source edition of Oracle's TopLink product. It comes with the GlassFish application server and also can be downloaded as a stand-alone product.

For further information, you can visit the TopLink Essential page on the GlassFish Community web site at `https://glassfish.dev.java.net/javaee5/persistence/`. You can also visit the TopLink Essential microsite on the Oracle Technology Network (OTN) at `http://www.oracle.com/technology/products/ias/toplink/jpa/index.html`.

JPA Entities and ORM Mapping

As mentioned earlier, JPA entities are POJOs. So, you can safely say that the JPA technology brings POJO programming to persistence. You incorporate ORM annotations into an entity, applying them to either the entity's instance variables or the properties. With ORM annotations, you describe how objects are mapped to relational tables. For example, you use the

@Table annotation to specify the name of the underlying database table, and you use @Column to specify the column name in that table.

Although an example of an entity is provided a little later, Figure 3-8 provides a conceptual depiction of the mechanism called *object/relational mapping*.

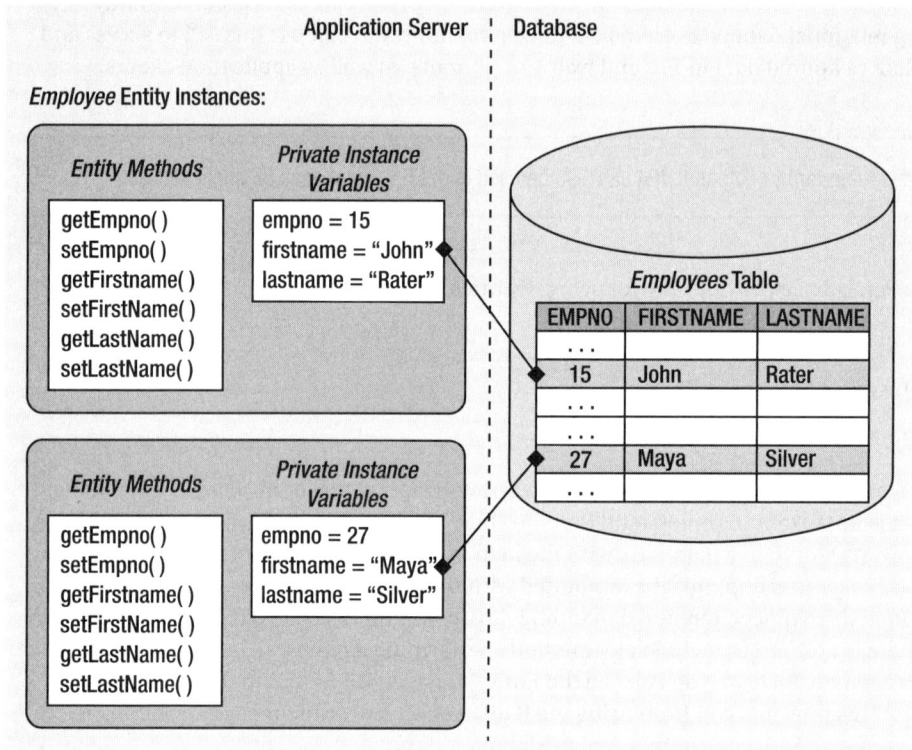

Figure 3-8. *A conceptual depiction of object/relational mapping*

You will see a simple example of an entity in action when building your first EJB JPA application, as described in the next section. In later chapters, you will see more realistic examples showing you how to use JPA entities and define relationships between them, much like you do with relational objects when setting up a database schema.

Your First EJB JPA Application

Now that you have a grasp of the ideas behind the JPA technology, it's time to see how you can put it into action. In the following sections, you will build a simple application using the EJB and JPA technologies. Along the way, you will set up and configure the following components utilized within the application:

- The myderbydb database schema within the default Java DB database

- The employees table within the myderbydb database

- The `jdbc/myderbypool` data source

- The `employee` JPA entity

- The `EmployeeSessionBean` stateless session bean

- The `EmployeeSessionClient` stand-alone client application

Figure 3-9 illustrates how these components fit together, giving you a high-level view of their interactions at runtime.

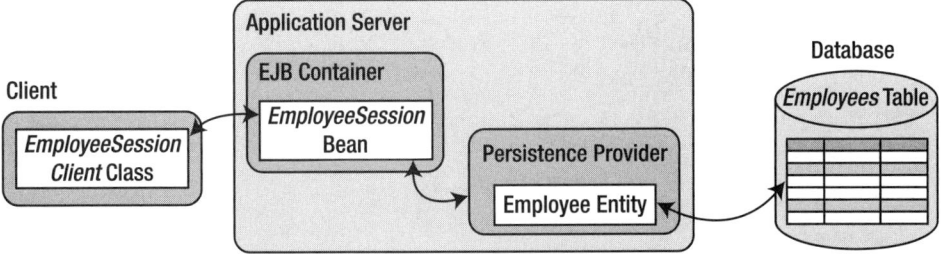

Figure 3-9. *A high-level view of component interactions in the EJB JPA application discussed here*

The following sections walk you through the process of developing the application depicted in the figure.

The Project Structure

As mentioned, before you can deploy a bean to the application server, you need to create a certain structure for a JAR archive packaging the bean's components. Similarly, the first step in developing the application discussed here is to develop the directory structure for the project.

Similarly to the preceding application, the entire application project will include two smaller projects, the enterprise bean project and the application client project, which are called in this particular example `EJBJPA` and `AppClient`, respectively. Returning to creating the directory structure, this means you need to create the `EJBJPA` and `AppClient` directories within the root project directory that you can create in any directory in your system and name, say, `EJBJPAProject`. Under this directory, you also need to create the `target` and `dist` directories.

Since the directory structure to be created is similar to the one discussed in the preceding example, this section will not give you step-by-step instructions on how to complete this task. Instead, you might do it yourself by referring to the directory structure shown in Figure 3-10.

■Note Right now, you don't need to worry about creating the files within the directories. All you need to do right away is to create the directories. You will create the files later as discussed in the next sections.

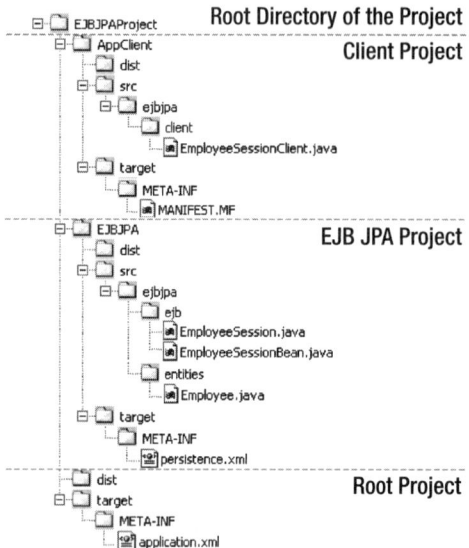

Figure 3-10. *The directory structure for the application project*

Using the Java DB Database

For simplicity, the EJB JPA application discussed here will interact with the Java DB database included with the GlassFish application server by default. To learn more about this database, you can visit the Apache Derby Project web site at http://db.apache.org/derby/.

You can start the database using the following command:

```
# asadmin start-database
```

If everything is OK, you should see the following messages on your terminal:

```
Starting database in the background.
Log redirected to C:\\derby.log.
Command start-database executed successfully.
```

Now that you have started the database, you need a way to connect to it and then issue a few SQL commands against it in order to create a new database and a table within the newly created schema.

In fact, the Derby database provides several tools that you might use to interact with the database. The simplest one is probably ij, which allows you to enter SQL commands at a command prompt. To move on to the ij prompt, you need to start the ij script from a terminal window:

```
# cd glassfish_dir/javadb/bin
# ij
```

As a result, the ij prompt should appear. The next step is to create a new database. The Derby SQL does not provide a create database command. Instead, you should use the create attribute set to `true` when connecting to the database. So, you can create a new database and connect to it with a single command, as shown here:

```
connect 'jdbc:derby://localhost:1527/myderbydb;create=true';
```

If no error messages appeared, then you successfully connected to the newly created `myderbydb` database.

The next time you will connect to the `myderbydb` database, you can use the following command:

```
connect 'jdbc:derby://localhost:1527/myderbydb';
```

Now you can create the `employees` table by issuing the following command from the `ij` prompt:

```
CREATE TABLE employees(
 empno INT PRIMARY KEY,
 firstname VARCHAR(24),
 lastname VARCHAR(24)
);
```

Although you are not performing an operation on a row, the previous command should produce the following output:

```
0 rows inserted/updated/deleted
```

The next step is to insert a row into the newly created `employees` table. You can do this with the following command issued from the `ij` prompt:

```
INSERT INTO employees VALUES(10, 'John', 'Rater');
```

This time the following message should appear:

```
1 rows inserted/updated/deleted
```

Setting Up the Data Source

The `ij` tool used in the preceding section is well and good if you need to interact with the database directly, from within a terminal window. Now, you need to find a way to interact with the database from within the application discussed here.

To do this, you first have to define a data source within the application server. This can be easily done with the help of Admin Console, as follows:

■Note This task is discussed in more detail in Chapter 7. In particular, Chapter 7 explains in extensive detail how to set up data sources in GlassFish for Oracle and MySQL databases.

1. Start Admin Console by pointing your browser to `http://localhost:4848`.

2. Log in to Admin Console as `admin`.

3. In Admin Console, go to the Resources/JDBC/Connection Pools page.

4. On the Resources/JDBC/Connection Pools page, click the New button.

5. In the first step of the wizard, before you click Next, enter the general settings as follows:

   - Name: `myderbypool`

   - Resource Type: `javax.sql.DataSource`

   - Database Vendor: `JavaDB`

6. In the next step of the wizard, scroll down to the Additional Properties table and make sure to set up the following five settings before you click Finish:

   - Database Name: `myderbydb`

   - User: `APP`

   - Password: `APP`

   - Server Name: `localhost`

   - Port Number: `1527`

7. In Admin Console, move on to the Resources/JDBC/JDBC Resources page and then click the New button.

8. In the New JNDI Resource page, set the properties as shown here and then click Finish:

   - JNDI Name: `jdbc/myderbypool`

   - Pool Name: `myderbypool`

   - Status: `Enabled`

After performing these steps, you should have the `jdbc/myderbypool` data source through which the application will interact with the database.

Creating the Entity

Now that you have set up the database and created the data source required to programmatically interact with that database, it's time to develop the JPA entity that will be mapped to the database table `employees` that is created and populated with data as described in the "Using the Java DB Database" section earlier.

Listing 3-10 shows the source code for the `Employee` entity that you have to save as `Employee.java` to the `EJBJPAProject/EJBJPA/src/ejbjpa/entities` directory, according to the project structure shown in Figure 3-10 earlier.

Listing 3-10. *The Source Code for the* Employee.java *File*

```
package ejbjpa.entities;
import java.io.Serializable;
import javax.persistence.Column;
import javax.persistence.Entity;
import javax.persistence.Id;
import javax.persistence.Table;
@Entity
@Table(name = "employees")
public class Employee implements Serializable {
    @Id
    @Column(name = "empno")
    private Integer empno;
    @Column(name = "firstname" )
    private String firstname;
    @Column(name = "lastname")
    private String lastname;
    public Employee() {
    }
    public Integer getEmpno() {
        return this.empno;
    }
    public void setEmpno(Integer empno) {
        this.empno = empno;
    }
    public String getFirstname() {
        return this.firstname;
    }
    public void setFirstname(String firstname) {
        this.firstname = firstname;
    }
    public String getLastname() {
        return this.lastname;
    }
    public void setLastname(String lastname) {
        this.lastname = lastname;
    }
}
```

As you can see, the Employee entity shown in the listing doesn't include any methods used to perform database-related operations, such as save or update. You may be asking yourself, how can I store that entity to the database, or how can I update the database table row representing this entity? The answer is to use the EntityManager, a JPA interface providing all the methods for manipulating JPA entities mapped to relational tables. In the next section, you will see the EntityManager in action. You can find more thorough information on this tool in Chapter 10.

Creating the Session Bean

The next step is to create the `EmployeeSessionBean` session bean that will utilize the `Employee` entity discussed in the preceding section. You start by creating the bean's business interface.

Listing 3-11 shows the source code for the remote business interface to be used in this example. You have to save it as `Employee.java` to the `EJBJPAProject/EJBJPA/src/ejbjpa/ejb` directory.

Listing 3-11. *The Source Code for the* `EmployeeSession.java` *File*

```
package ejbjpa.ejb;
import javax.ejb.Remote;
@Remote
public interface EmployeeSession  {
    public String getEmplastname(Integer empno);
}
```

Next, you can create the bean implementing this interface. Listing 3-12 shows the source code for the `EmployeeSessionBean` stateless session bean.

Listing 3-12. *The Source Code for the* `EmployeeSessionBean.java` *File*

```
package ejbjpa.ejb;
import java.io.Serializable;
import javax.ejb.EJBException;
import javax.ejb.Stateless;
import javax.persistence.EntityManager;
import javax.persistence.EntityManagerFactory;
import javax.persistence.PersistenceUnit;
import ejbjpa.entities.*;

@Stateless
public class EmployeeSessionBean implements EmployeeSession {
    @PersistenceUnit(unitName = "ejbjpa-pu")
    private EntityManagerFactory emf;
    public String getEmplastname(Integer empno) {
        String fullname;
        try {
            EntityManager em = emf.createEntityManager();
            Employee emp = em.find(Employee.class, empno);
            fullname = emp.getFirstname()+" "+emp.getLastname();
        } catch (Exception e) {
            throw new EJBException(e.getMessage());
        }
        return fullname;
    }
}
```

In this example, you create an instance of the EntityManager by invoking the createEntityManager method of `javax.persistence.EntityManagerFactory`. Then, you obtain an instance of the Employee entity with the `find` method of the EntityManager, specifying the primary key of the record to be obtained. Once you have obtained the record, you invoke the getFirstname and getLastname methods of the Employee instance to set the `fullname` variable being returned by the bean's business method.

It is interesting to notice the use of the `@PersistenceUnit` annotation in the previous code, with which you inject the EntityManagerFactory instance into your code. With the `unitName` parameter of `@PersistenceUnit`, you specify the persistence unit, namely, ejbjpa-pu, defined in the `persistence.xml` configuration file. In this particular example, however, you might not use the `unitName` parameter to explicitly specify the persistence unit. This is because you're using a single persistence unit here, and therefore, the container will use it by default.

Creating the persistence.xml Configuration File

In the `persistence.xml` configuration file, you define the persistence unit to be utilized with the application.

Listing 3-13 shows the source code for the `persistence.xml` configuration file to be used in this example. You have to save this file to the `EJBJPAProject/EJBJPA/target/META-INF` directory.

Listing 3-13. *The Source Code for the* persistence.xml *Configuration File*

```
<?xml version="1.0" encoding="UTF-8"?>
<persistence xmlns="http://java.sun.com/xml/ns/persistence"
xmlns:xsi="http://www.w3.org/2001/XMLSchema-instance"
xsi:schemaLocation="http://java.sun.com/xml/ns/persistence
   http://java.sun.com/xml/ns/persistence/persistence_1_0.xsd" version="1.0">
    <persistence-unit name="ejbjpa-pu" transaction-type="JTA">
        <jta-data-source>jdbc/myderbypool</jta-data-source>

        <class>ejbjpa.entities.Employee</class>

    </persistence-unit>
</persistence>
```

In this example, the `persistence.xml` file contains configuration information describing the persistence unit named ejbjpa-pu.

Packaging and Deploying the Session Bean

Now that you have created the sources, you can compile them. First you need to change the directory to `EJBJPAProject/EJBJPA`. Once you are there, you can use the `javac` compiler:

```
# javac -d target src\ejbjpa\entities\*.java src\ejbjpa\ejb\*.java
```

This command will compile both the Employee entity and the EmployeeSession bean files.

In the next step, you change directory to the target directory and build the ejbjpa.jar archive:

```
# cd target
# jar cvf ../dist/ejbjpa.jar .
```

Finally, you need to deploy the session bean archive to the application server. To achieve this, issue the following commands:

```
# cd ..
# cd dist
# asadmin deploy ejbjpa.jar
```

As a result, you should see the following message:

```
Command deploy executed successfully
```

If you see this result, you just successfully completed creating and deploying the EmployeeSession stateless session bean utilizing the Employee JPA entity.

Creating the Client

Now that you have created and deployed the bean, it's time to develop a client application to test it.

Listing 3-14 shows the source for the MANIFEST.MF file you need to create in the EJBJPAProject/AppClient/target/META-INF directory.

Listing 3-14. *The Source Code for the* MANIFEST.MF *File*

```
Manifest-Version: 1.0
Main-Class: ejbjpa.client.EmployeeSessionClient
```

Listing 3-15 shows the source for the EmployeeSessionClient.java file you have to create in the EJBJPAProject/AppClient/src/ejbjpa/client directory.

Listing 3-15. *The Source Code for the* EmployeeSessionClient.java *File*

```
package ejbjpa.client;
import javax.ejb.EJB;
import ejbjpa.ejb.EmployeeSession;
public class EmployeeSessionClient {
    @EJB
    private static EmployeeSession employeeSession;
    public static void main (String[] args)
      {
          System.out.println(employeeSession.getEmplastname(10));
      }
}
```

As you can see, the client code is very straightforward. You simply inject an instance of the EmployeeSession bean and then invoke its method getEmplastname, passing 10 as the parameter. The result returned is printed with System.out.println.

Compiling and Packaging the Client

Although the previous section provides the source code for the client, the appclient program that comes with GlassFish requires you to provide the compiled code.

To compile the EmployeeSessionClient.java file shown in Listing 3-15, you need to change the directory to EJBJPAProject/AppClient and then issue the following command:

```
# javac -cp /glassfish_dir/lib/javaee.jar; ../EJBJPA/dist/ejbjpa.jar ➥
-d target src/ejbjpa/client/*.java
```

Then, you can change directory to the target directory and build the appclient.jar archive as follows:

```
# cd target
# jar cvfM ../dist/appclient.jar .
```

As a result, the appclient.jar file should appear in the EJBJPAProject/AppClient/dist directory.

Now you are ready to build the application archive that you will run with the appclient program. First, copy the ejbjpa.jar and appclient.jar archives created earlier to the EJBJPAProject/target directory. Then, create the application.xml deployment descriptor in the EJBJPAProject/target/META-INF directory. Listing 3-16 shows the source code for this file.

Listing 3-16. *The Source Code for the* application.xml *Deployment Descriptor*

```
<?xml version="1.0" encoding="UTF-8"?>
<application version="5" xmlns="http://java.sun.com/xml/ns/javaee"
 xmlns:xsi="http://www.w3.org/2001/XMLSchema-instance"
xsi:schemaLocation="http://java.sun.com/xml/ns/javaee
   http://java.sun.com/xml/ns/javaee/application_5.xsd">
  <display-name>ejbjpa</display-name>
  <module>
    <ejb>ejbjpa.jar</ejb>
  </module>
  <module>
    <java>appclient.jar</java>
  </module>
</application>
```

After you have created the application.xml deployment descriptor shown in the listing, you can move on and build the ejbjpaapp.jar archive. To do this, you need to change the directory to EJBJPAProject/target and then issue the following command:

```
# jar cvf ..\dist\ejbjpaapp.jar .
```

As a result, the ejbjpaapp.jar file should appear in the EJBJPAProject/dist directory.

Testing the Application

Before you can run the application, you must have the Java DB database running. You can start it as described in the "Using the Java DB Database" section earlier. Also, make sure you have started your default application server domain. After that, you can test the application created in the preceding sections. To do this, change the directory to `EJBJPAProject/dist`, and issue the following command:

```
# appclient -client ejbjpaapp.jar
```

This should produce the following output:

```
John Rater
```

As you have no doubt realized, the previous is a simple example, but it should have given you a taste of how JPA can be used and what it can do for you.

Summary

This chapter started by explaining some basic concepts of EJB 3. Then, you looked at a simple stand-alone application based on this technology. To build it, you used only command-line tools. This approach of manually building and deploying was chosen to help you better understand the structure of EJB components and how they work.

Then, the chapter covered the basics of the JPA technology. You also looked at a simple example of the application demonstrating the JPA technology in action.

PART 2

■ ■ ■

Planning the Application

CHAPTER 4

■■■

Planning a Java EE Application

At the planning stage, you first analyze the needs of potential users of your application, determining how it will be used and what it must do. After you have realized what kind of application you want to develop and what results it must produce, you then need to decide what technologies will be used and plan the application structure. Finally, you need to determine what application modules you have to develop and how these modules will interact with each other, planning the steps for building and deploying each application component.

As its title implies, this chapter discusses the planning stage of a Java EE application project. In particular, you will look at the following:

- Planning a multitier architecture for your Java EE application

- Distributing business logic between the application tiers

- Planning Java EE application components

- Using XML deployment descriptors vs. annotations

After reading this chapter, you will have a good understanding of the issues related to the planning stage of the development process. Along the way, you will look at the architecture of a typical Java EE application and learn how that architecture might be implemented in your particular application.

Understanding the Structure of a Java EE Application

Before you start developing your application, it is important to take the time to look at the application architecture and to understand what components you need to build and how they will fit into the big picture.

Understanding the Multitier Architecture

A Java EE application typically employs a multitier architecture. One of the greatest strengths of the multitier architecture is scalability. You build your application from a set of reusable components executed within the containers of a Java EE server. This means you can change one or more components without impacting client applications. For example, you can modify an EJB component implementing a piece of business logic so that it has no impact on the other EJB components utilized within the application and, of course, has no impact on the components implementing the other tiers of the application.

Figure 4-1 gives a graphical depiction of the four-tier architecture that is often employed by enterprise applications.

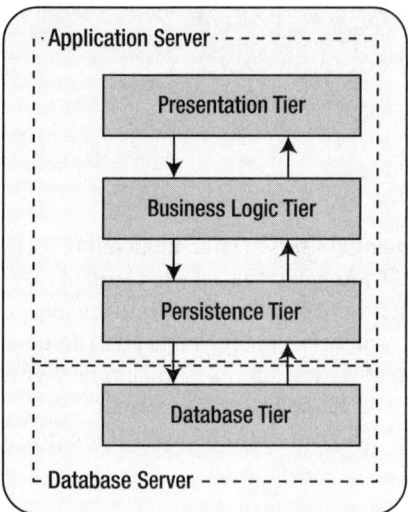

Figure 4-1. *Graphical depiction of the four-tier architecture*

As you can see in the figure, the presentation, business logic, and persistence tiers are implemented within the application server, whereas the database tier resides within the database server. As you will learn in the next section, the Java EE application server provides the underlying services to the components implementing the presentation logic, business logic, and persistence logic of your application.

While Figure 4-1 gives a graphical depiction of the four-tier architecture, Table 4-1 summarizes each tier.

Table 4-1. *Layers of the Four-Tier Architecture*

Layer	Description
Presentation tier	Includes the user interface elements of your application, making it possible for users to interact with the application.
Business logic tier	Implements the business logic of your application. Processes the user requests coming from the presentation tier.
Persistence tier	Implements the persistence logic of your application. The business logic tier interacts with the underlying database via the persistence tier, rather than directly interacting with the database.
Database tier	Includes a relational database that is used to persist the objects, which are part of the persistence tier.

As you can see, each tier plays a certain role in the entire architecture and can interact only with neighboring tiers. For example, you can create an instance of an enterprise bean and then invoke its business methods from within a JSP page belonging to the presentation tier. However, a JSP page cannot be used to directly interact with the database tier.

Understanding the Architecture of the Java EE Container

As stated earlier, the Java EE application server provides underlying services to the deployed components so that you can concentrate on implementing business logic related to your particular application, rather than reimplementing logic related to the problems often found in enterprise applications.

These underlying services are logically grouped into *containers*. For example, the web container provides the services that enable you to build web components based on the JSP and JSF technologies typically used when developing the presentation layer of a Java EE application. You saw a simple example of using JSP pages in Chapter 2 when developing a "Hello World!" application. In Chapter 14, you will learn how to use the JSF technology when building the presentation tier of an enterprise application.

The EJB container provides the services required to deploy and execute enterprise beans. Typically used to implement the business logic of an enterprise application, EJB 3 can be seamlessly used with other Java EE APIs, such as JSP and JSF that are employed for building the application presentation tier.

Figure 4-2 gives a simple representation of how the tiers of a Java EE application are implemented within the Java EE server.

Application Server

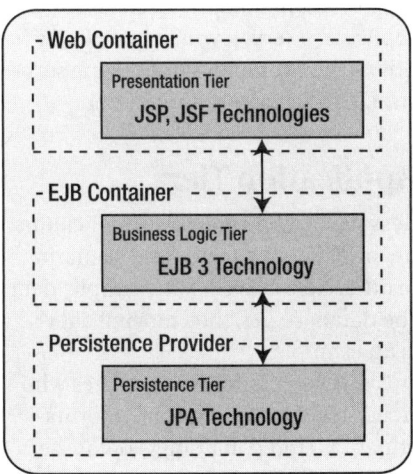

Figure 4-2. *Most tiers of a Java EE application are implemented using the technologies that let you build components executed within the application server containers.*

As you can see in the figure, each application tier is implemented in a single Java EE container, using different technologies.

■Note It's important to note here that the technologies used in the neighboring tiers can seamlessly inter-act with each other. For example, you don't need to worry a lot about how to invoke an EJB bean method from within a JSP page or how to manipulate JPA entities from the code of a session bean. Both of these tasks can be easily accomplished because EJB 3 is seamlessly integrated with the other Java EE technolo-gies, such as Java Server Pages (JSP) and Java Persistence API (JPA).

Table 4-2 summarizes the Java EE server containers depicted in Figure 4-2.

Table 4-2. *Java EE Server Containers Providing Configurable Services to the Components of a Java EE Application*

Java EE Server Container	Description
Web container	Provides underlying services for and manages the execution of the web pages comprising the presentation tier of your Java EE application, which can be built using JSP and JSF technologies
EJB container	Provides underlying services for and manages the execution of the enterprise beans comprising the business logic tier of your Java EE application
JPA provider	Provides persistence services, allowing you to map JPA entities to the underlying datastore

When deploying an application component to the application server, you actually deploy it to the corresponding server container to provide the low-level functionality needed by that component. Thus, when deploying an EJB bean to the application server, you in fact deploy it into the EJB container, therefore enabling that bean to utilize the container's underlying serv-ices such as transaction management, concurrency control, and security authorization.

Distributing Business Logic Between Application Tiers

According to the diagram shown in Figure 4-2, the business logic of an enterprise application is implemented at the business logic tier with the EJB 3 technology. In a real-world scenario, though, some business logic may be implemented in the other tiers as well. For example, data processing logic may be and often should be moved to the database tier, thus moving data processing to the data. This can be best understood with an example.

Suppose your company wants to pay an annual bonus of 5 percent to its employees who work in the accounting department and a bonus of 4 percent to all the others. The informa-tion about what bonuses are awarded to a certain department is stored in a single database table, say, bonuses. Now, based on this information, you need to calculate the amount of the bonus to be paid to an employee and then also store this information in the database, this time, in the table payments. Another interesting thing to note here is that the information about employees' salaries that is needed to calculate bonuses is also stored in the database, in the employees table.

As you can see, in this example the starting data and resultant data are stored in the data-base. Therefore, it's a good idea to perform all the required processing inside the database, rather than first moving the starting data from the database and then, after processing that data, moving the results back to the database. To accomplish this, you might develop one or more stored procedures to perform all the required processing inside the database. You will see stored procedures in action in Chapter 6.

Sometimes, though, it is a good idea to implement some data processing logic with the components executed within the application server rather than inside the database. Again, this can be best understood with an example.

Suppose you need to implement functionality enabling an employee to place an order by filling out the order form and then submitting it. Upon setting the order details, the order total sum should be automatically recalculated, showing the updated figure after each item is inserted or updated. As someone who already has experience with Java EE technologies, you might guess that each time an employee adds a new item line to the order, the information about this item is retrieved from the database and then shown in the form. This means the information about the items chosen and their quantity is accumulated on the application server side rather than on the database server side. So, in this particular example, it would be much more efficient to perform the required processing on the application server side.

As you can see from these examples, the decision of whether to move business logic into the database should be made in the context of the task you are dealing with. Figure 4-3 diagrammatically shows that the data-processing logic of an enterprise application may be implemented within either the application server or the database server (in reality, though, it is usually implemented partly within the application server and partly within the database server).

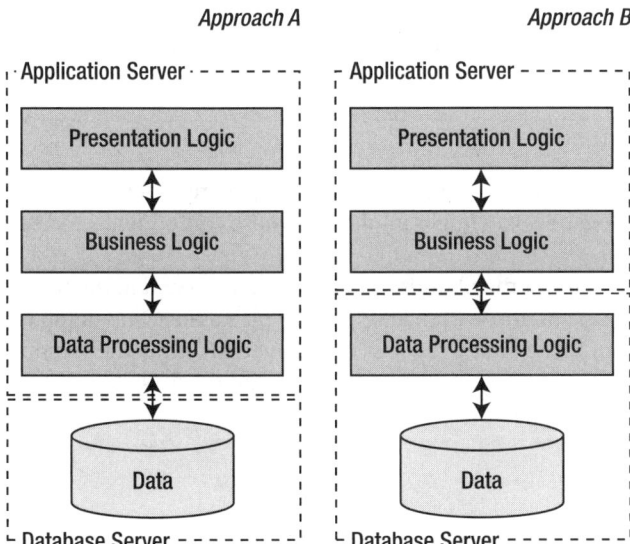

Figure 4-3. *Most data-processing logic within an application can and should be implemented inside the database, if it doesn't hurt application flexibility, of course.*

You will see more detailed examples on moving data processing to the underlying database in Chapter 5 and in Chapter 6.

Planning Application Components and Their Interactions

Now that you have a good initial understanding of the structure of a typical Java EE application, you might want to perform some sort of analysis, trying to figure out how the four-tier architecture might be implemented in the application you are going to build.

Assuming you have a clear understanding of what your application is supposed to do, your first task in the application planning is to determine what application components you need to build and how they will interact with each other. Let's look at a very simple example.

Suppose you need to develop an application that accesses and manipulates the information about the customers your company deals with. One of the tasks to be implemented within the application is retrieving the information about a certain customer whose ID is equal to the specified one. For the sake of simplicity, let's assume the information about the customers can be stored in just two database tables: `customers` and `billing_addresses`. If so, you might need to create the following components distributed between the application tiers:

- *Business logic tier*: `CustomerSessionBean` session bean

- *Persistence tier*: `Customer` and `Address` entities

- *Database tier*: `customers` and `billing_addresses` tables

■Note Although a typical Java EE application is a four-tier architecture, this example focuses only on the business, persistence, and database tiers.

Now that you know what components should be created in the application tiers, you'll want to look into the details concerning how you might implement these components and set up relationships between them.

The following few sections will discuss some planning considerations related to the previous components, placing most emphasis on those that belong to the persistence and database tiers. After all, this is a book about TopLink, which is the Java Persistence API implementation at GlassFish. As you will see in the following sections, the persistence and database tiers are very closely related, so it's always a good idea to plan them together.

Planning JPA Entities

As you might recall from the "JPA Entities and ORM Mapping" section in Chapter 3, a JPA entity is a POJO with object/relational mapping (ORM) annotations incorporated, which you use to specify how the entity is mapped to the database.

■Note This section gives you some insight into the things to consider when planning JPA entities to be then utilized within your application, providing examples along the way to help you. JPA entities are discussed in further detail in Chapter 8 and Chapter 9.

At first glance, it may be fairly obvious how entities can be used in your application. You define entities so that each entity represents a database table in the underlying database, creating entities upon only those tables that store the data needed by your application. If you create two entities corresponding to the tables related through a parent key/foreign key association, you define a relationship between these entities using an appropriate relationship annotation such as @OneToOne and @OneToMany.

Although this is the most common approach to the problem, in practice, though, you have a few other options. This is best understood with an example.

Continuing the example of retrieving the information about a certain customer, let's first look at how the customers and billing_addresses tables might be organized. Suppose you have created these tables as shown in Listing 4-1.

Listing 4-1. *Creating the* customers *and* billing_addresses *Tables*

```
CREATE TABLE customers (
  cust_id INTEGER PRIMARY KEY,
  company_name VARCHAR(100),
  phone VARCHAR(20)
);

CREATE TABLE billing_addresses (
  cust_address_id INTEGER PRIMARY KEY REFERENCES customers(cust_id),
  street VARCHAR(100),
  city VARCHAR(100),
  state VARCHAR(2),
  zipcode VARCHAR(20)
);
```

As you might guess, in this example you use a one-to-one relationship between the customers and billing_addresses tables, assuming each customer has only one billing address. Listing 4-2 illustrates how you might populate these tables with data. First you insert a row into the customers table, and then you can insert a row with the same ID into the billing_addresses table.

Listing 4-2. *Populating the* customers *and* billing_addresses *Tables with Data*

```
INSERT INTO customers VALUES(1, 'Fast Express', '(650)777-5665');
INSERT INTO billing_addresses VALUES(1, '10000 Broadway Street', 'San Mateo', ➥
'CA', '94400');
```

Now, once you have the underlying tables in place, you can move on and create the persistence tier, building JPA entities mapped to these tables. Here are some ways in which you can do that:

- Create the Customer and Address entities in the customers and billing_addresses underlying database tables, and define a relationship between these entities. You can define either a unidirectional relationship or a bidirectional relationship. You'll be looking at the details of this a little later.

- Create the Customer entity in the customers and billing_addresses underlying tables so that the Customer entity includes fields from both tables. In the "Mapping an Entity to More Than One Table" section, you will see how you can do this using the @SecondaryTable annotation.

- Create the Customer entity upon a database view built on the customers and billing_addresses underlying tables, using this view as if it were a single table. This approach is discussed in detail in the later section "Mapping an Entity to a Database View."

Figure 4-4 gives a graphical depiction of each approach outlined in the previous list. Note that although the diagram for approach A shows a unidirectional relationship between the Customer and Address entities (in this example, the Customer entity refers to the Address entity), it might be a bidirectional relationship here. You will look at how to establish a bidirectional relationship between these two entities in the "Using Bidirectional Relationships Between Entities" section a little later.

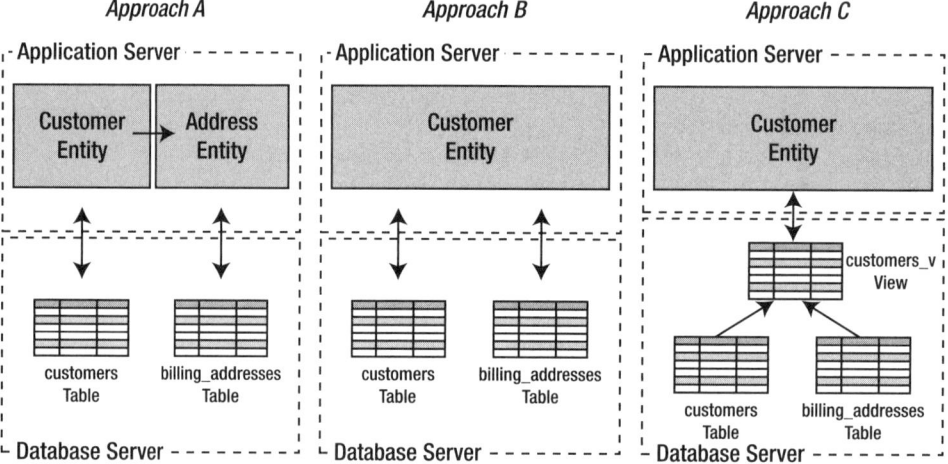

Figure 4-4. *You can design the database and persistence tiers of your application in a few different ways.*

Note As you no doubt have guessed, approaches B and C make sense only if the underlying tables use a one-to-one relationship, as in the example discussed here. If your underlying tables use a one-to-many relationship, then approach A is the only one you should seriously consider.

There are some nuances to consider when choosing between these options. Although it is generally OK to choose approach A, with which you create an entity upon each underlying table and define relationships between the entities as needed, you should consider whether you really need to have two entities related with a relationship rather than a single entity containing the fields from both underlying tables. To determine this, you might ask yourself a simple question: "Is there any situation where I might want to use only one entity without using the other one?" If the answer is no and you will always use the corresponding instances of these two entities together, you might consider using approach B, as shown in Figure 4-4. Also, you might consider approach C, which assumes you use a view derived from your two underlying tables so that this view appears as a single table to the application. Returning to approach A, you might consider using lazy loading, which assumes that, upon retrieving a Customer instance, its related Address entity instance is not automatically loaded—it may happen later when you first access that Address instance through the corresponding method of the Customer instance.

The following sections discuss how to implement each of the approaches outlined here.

Using Unidirectional Relationships Between Entities

When planning entities to be then utilized within your application, you also have to plan the relationships between those entities. Just like relational tables, entities can be related with a one-to-one, one-to-many, or many-to-many relationship. The relationship you establish between entities can be either unidirectional or bidirectional.

The example discussed in this section illustrates a unidirectional relationship between entities. This means only one entity (it's Customer in this particular example) contains a relationship property that refers to the other (it's Address here).

Listing 4-3 shows what the source code for the Address entity might look like (the getter and setter methods of the entity have been removed to save space).

Listing 4-3. *Source Code for the* Address *Entity Mapped to the* billing_addresses *Database Table*

```
package ejbjpa.entities;
import java.io.Serializable;
import javax.persistence.Column;
import javax.persistence.Entity;
import javax.persistence.Id;
import javax.persistence.Table;
@Entity
@Table(name = "BILLING_ADDRESSES")
public class Address implements Serializable {
    @Id
    @Column(name = "CUST_ADDRESS_ID")
    private Integer cust_address_id;
    @Column(name = "STREET", nullable = false)
    private String street;
    @Column(name = "CITY", nullable = false)
    private String city;
    @Column(name = "STATE", nullable = false)
    private String state;
    @Column(name = "ZIPCODE", nullable = false)
    private String zipcode;
    public Address() {
    }
```

```
//The Address entity setter and getter methods
...
}
```

As you can see, the `Address` entity doesn't refer to the `Customer` entity. Put simply, the `Address` entity knows nothing about the `Customer` entity.

Now let's look at Listing 4-4, which shows what the source code for the `Customer` entity might look like (again, the getter and setter methods of the entity have been removed to save space).

Listing 4-4. *Source Code for the* Customer *Entity Mapped to the* customers *Database Table*

```
package ejbjpa.entities;
import java.io.Serializable;
import javax.persistence.Column;
import javax.persistence.Entity;
import javax.persistence.Id;
import javax.persistence.Table;
import javax.persistence.OneToOne;
import javax.persistence.PrimaryKeyJoinColumn;
@Entity
@Table(name = "CUSTOMERS")
public class Customer implements Serializable {
    @Id
    @Column(name = "CUST_ID")
    private Integer cust_id;
    @Column(name = "COMPANY_NAME", nullable = false)
    private String company_name;
    @Column(name = "PHONE", nullable = false)
    private String phone;
    @OneToOne
    @PrimaryKeyJoinColumn(
      name="CUST_ID",
      referencedColumnName="CUST_ADDRESS_ID")
    private Address address;
    public Customer() {
    }
    public Address getAddress() {
        return this.address;
    }
    public void setAddress(Address address) {
        this.address = address;
    }
//The other Customer entity setter and getter methods
...
}
```

In Listing 4-4, the lines in bold are what you added to the `Customer` entity code to establish a one-to-one relationship to the `Address` entity shown in Listing 4-3 earlier. With that in place, you can obtain an `Address` instance corresponding to the `Customer` instance being used, using the `getAddress` method of the latter. On the other hand, you should remember that the `Address` entity doesn't contain any code allowing that entity to reach the `Customer` entity. That is, you have no way to obtain a `Customer` instance corresponding to the `Address` instance by using one of the methods of the latter. This is what is called a *unidirectional relationship*.

Now that you know how to establish a unidirectional relationship between entities, it's time to see how you can put these entities into action. Listing 4-5 shows how, by using the `getAddress` method of the `Customer` instance, you might create a `Customer` instance within the code of a session bean and then obtain the corresponding `Address` instance (the import declarations have been removed to save space).

Listing 4-5. *Source Code for the* `CustomerSessionBean` *Bean That Consumes the* `Customer` *Entity*

```
//import declarations
...
@Stateless
public class CustomerSessionBean implements CustomerSession {
    @PersistenceUnit(unitName = "jpaplanning-pu")
    private EntityManagerFactory emf;
    public String getCustomerAddress(Integer cust_id) {
        String cust_address;
        try {
            EntityManager em = emf.createEntityManager();
            Customer cust = em.find(Customer.class, cust_id);
            cust_address = cust.getAddress().getStreet()+", "+
                           cust.getAddress().getCity()+", "+
                           cust.getAddress().getState()+", "+
                           cust.getAddress().getZipcode();
        } catch (Exception e) {
            throw new EJBException(e.getMessage());
        }
        return cust_address;
    }
}
```

As this snippet shows, you obtain the values of the `Address` instance properties through the instance of the `Customer` entity by using the `getAddress` method of `Customer`. Note that you don't pass any parameters to the `getAddress` method. This is because the JPA provider knows what row to select from the `billing_addresses` underlying table when setting the `Address` entity instance, without you specifying any additional information. In particular, the JPA provider will select the `billing_addresses`'s record that refers to the `customers`'s record used when setting the `Customer` entity. This can be easily done, since the `billing_addresses` and `customers` underlying tables connected through the primary/foreign keys assume, in this particular case, a one-to-one relationship.

Finally, you might want to look at the client code that can be used to create an instance of the CustomerSessionBean bean discussed here and then invoke its getCustomerAddress business method, as shown in Listing 4-6.

Listing 4-6. *Source Code for the Client Consuming the* CustomerSessionBean *Bean*

```
package ejbjpa.client;
import javax.ejb.EJB;
import ejbjpa.ejb.CustomerSession;
public class CustomerSessionClient {
    @EJB
    private static CustomerSession customerSession;
    public static void main (String[] args)
    {
        System.out.println("Billing address of the customer whose id=1 is: "➥
                            + customerSession.getCustomerAddress(1));
    }
}
```

Provided that you populated the customers and billing_addresses tables with data as shown in Listing 4-2 earlier, the client just shown, when executed, should output the following message:

```
Billing address of the customer whose id=1 is: 10000 Broadway Street, ➥
San Mateo, CA, 94400
```

As you might expect, the resultant string contains information taken from both underlying tables.

Using Bidirectional Relationships Between Entities

In the preceding example, you use a unidirectional relationship between the Customer and Address entities. In particular, you define the Address property within the Customer entity, which refers to the Address entity.

In practice, you may need to establish a bidirectional relationship between these entities. In that case, you will be able not only to obtain the Address entity instance corresponding to the Customer entity instance you are dealing with but also to perform a reverse operation—obtaining the Customer instance from within the corresponding Address instance. Listing 4-7 shows the updated version of the Address entity originally shown in Listing 4-3.

Listing 4-7. *Source Code for the* Address *Entity That Allows You to Obtain the Corresponding Instance of the* Customer *Entity*

```
package ejbjpa.entities;
import java.io.Serializable;
import javax.persistence.Column;
import javax.persistence.Entity;
import javax.persistence.Id;
import javax.persistence.Table;
```

```
import javax.persistence.OneToOne;
@Entity
@Table(name = "BILLING_ADDRESSES")
public class Address implements Serializable {
    @Id
    @Column(name = "CUST_ADDRESS_ID")
    private Integer cust_address_id;
    @Column(name = "STREET", nullable = false)
    private String street;
    @Column(name = "CITY", nullable = false)
    private String city;
    @Column(name = "STATE", nullable = false)
    private String state;
    @Column(name = "ZIPCODE", nullable = false)
    private String zipcode;
    @OneToOne(mappedBy="address")
    private Customer customer;
    public Address() {
    }
    public Customer getCustomer () {
        return this.customer;
    }
    public void setCustomer(Customer customer) {
        this.customer= customer;
    }
//The other Address entity setter and getter methods
...
}
```

Note that with the Address entity shown in the listing you might use the same Customer entity you saw in Listing 4-4 in the preceding section. In this example, the Address entity represents the inverse side of the bidirectional relationship, referring to the owning side with the mappedBy element of the @OneToOne annotation. You also added the customer property with its setter and getter methods, thus explicitly specifying the owning side of the relationship.

To see the bidirectional relationship discussed here in action, you could modify the CustomerSessionBean bean as shown in Listing 4-8.

Listing 4-8. *Source Code for the* CustomerSessionBean *Bean That Shows How You Might Use the Bidirectional One-to-One Relationship Between Entities*

```
//import declarations
...
@Stateless
public class CustomerSessionBean implements CustomerSession {
    @PersistenceUnit(unitName = "jpaplanning-pu")
    private EntityManagerFactory emf;
    public String getCustomerDetails(Integer cust_address_id) {
        String cust_details;
```

```
    try {
        EntityManager em = emf.createEntityManager();
        Address addr = em.find(Address.class, cust_address_id);
        cust_details = addr.getCustomer().getCompany_name()+", "+
                       addr.getCustomer().getPhone()+", "+
                       "address id is "+" "+
                       addr.getCustomer().getAddress().getCust_address_id();
    } catch (Exception e) {
        throw new EJBException(e.getMessage());
    }
    return cust_details;
    }
}
```

In Listing 4-8, pay close attention to the code highlighted in bold. Note that unlike the example shown in Listing 4-5 in the preceding section, you first obtain the instance of the Address entity and then get the corresponding instance of Customer through the getCustomer method of the Address instance.

It is interesting to note that the Customer instance obtained through the getCustomer method of the Address instance in turn will refer to this same Address instance. So, as the last line highlighted in bold shows, you can refer to the Address instance properties via the Customer instance obtained in turn via the Address's getCustomer method. This is how a bidirectional relationship works.

Listing 4-9 illustrates how you might put the previously shown CustomerSessionBean bean into action.

Listing 4-9. *Source Code for the Client Consuming the* CustomerSessionBean *Bean Shown in Listing 4-8*

```
package ejbjpa.client;
import javax.ejb.EJB;
import ejbjpa.ejb.CustomerSession;
public class CustomerSessionClient {
    @EJB
    private static CustomerSession customerSession;
    public static void main (String[] args)
    {
        System.out.println("Customer details: "➥
                                +customerSession.getCustomerDetails(1));
    }
}
```

When executed, the client shown in the listing should output the following message:

```
Customer details: Fast Express, (650)777-5665, address id is 1
```

As you can see, like in the preceding example, the resultant string contains information taken from both underlying tables.

Mapping an Entity to More Than One Table

Taking a closer look at the preceding example, you might find it redundant to have information related to a single customer presented in the form of two entities. If you are planning to use these two entities together in any scenario, you might safely consider combining them into one.

Consider the updated Customer entity shown in Listing 4-10.

Listing 4-10. *Source Code for the* Customer *Entity Mapped to Two Underlying Tables*

```
package ejbjpa.entities;
import java.io.Serializable;
import javax.persistence.Column;
import javax.persistence.Entity;
import javax.persistence.Id;
import javax.persistence.Table;
import javax.persistence.SecondaryTable;
import javax.persistence.PrimaryKeyJoinColumn;
@Entity
@Table(name = "CUSTOMERS")
@SecondaryTable(name="BILLING_ADDRESSES",
  pkJoinColumns=@PrimaryKeyJoinColumn(
      name="CUST_ADDRESS_ID",
      referencedColumnName="CUST_ID"))
public class Customer implements Serializable {
    @Id
    @Column(name = "CUST_ID")
    private Integer cust_id;
    @Column(name = "COMPANY_NAME", nullable = false)
    private String company_name;
    @Column(name = "PHONE", nullable = false)
    private String phone;
    @Column(name = "STREET", table="BILLING_ADDRESSES", nullable = false)
    private String street;
    @Column(name = "CITY", table="BILLING_ADDRESSES", nullable = false)
    private String city;
    @Column(name = "STATE", table="BILLING_ADDRESSES", nullable = false)
    private String state;
    @Column(name = "ZIPCODE", table="BILLING_ADDRESSES", nullable = false)
    private String zipcode;
    public Customer() {
    }
//The Customer entity setter and getter methods
...
}
```

Note the use of the @SecondaryTable annotation, with which you specify the billing_addresses table to be used as the secondary underlying table for the Customer entity. Next, when defining the entity fields derived from the `billing_addresses` table, you set the `table` element of the `@Column` annotation to `BILLING_ADDRESSES`, thus explicitly specifying the table name.

You might wonder what SQL query will be generated by the JPA provider when setting up an instance of the `Customer` entity discussed here. Listing 4-11 shows how this query might look.

Listing 4-11. *SQL Query Generated by the JPA Provider to Fill in the Fields of an Instance of the* `Customer` *Entity*

```
SELECT t0.CUST_ID, t1.CUST_ADDRESS_ID, t1.STREET, t1.CITY, t0.PHONE, t1.STATE, ➥
 t0.COMPANY_NAME, t1.ZIPCODE FROM CUSTOMERS t0, BILLING_ADDRESSES t1 ➥
WHERE ((t0.CUST_ID = ?) AND (t1. CUST_ADDRESS_ID = t0.CUST_ID))
bind => [1]
```

As you can see, the previous is a join query over two base tables, namely, `customers` and `billing_addresses`.

In this example, the `CustomerSessionBean` bean utilizing the `Customer` entity might look like the one shown in Listing 4-12.

Listing 4-12. *Source Code for the* `CustomerSessionBean` *Bean That Shows How You Might Use the* `Customer` *Entity Built Upon Two Underlying Tables*

```
//import declarations
...
@Stateless
public class CustomerSessionBean implements CustomerSession {
    @PersistenceUnit(unitName = "jpaplanning-twotables-pu")
    private EntityManagerFactory emf;
    public String getCustomerDetails(Integer cust_id) {
        String cust_details;
        try {
            EntityManager em = emf.createEntityManager();
            Customer cust = em.find(Customer.class, cust_id);
            cust_details = cust.getCompany_name()+", "+
                            cust.getPhone()+", "+
                            "address is: "+" "+
                            cust.getStreet()+", "+
                            cust.getCity()+", "+
                            cust.getState()+", "+
                            cust.getZipcode();
        } catch (Exception e) {
            throw new EJBException(e.getMessage());
        }
        return cust_details;
    }
}
```

In this example, you deal only with an instance of the Customer entity, which includes all the fields of both the customers and billing_addresses tables.

The client invoking the getCustomerDetails method of the CustomerSessionBean bean discussed here might look like the one shown in Listing 4-9 in the preceding section. This time, it should output the following message:

```
Customer details: Fast Express, (650)777-5665, address is: 10000 Broadway ➡
Street, San Mateo, CA, 94400
```

As you can see, the previous string is composed of the data derived from the fields of the two related records stored in the customers and billing_addresses tables, respectively.

Mapping an Entity to a Database View

Looking at the query shown in Listing 4-11, you might wonder what would happen if this query were used as the query for the view upon which the Customer entity would be then built. Although the example in the preceding section showed how you might map a single entity to two underlying database tables, the example discussed in this section takes it one step further, showing how you can map an entity to a database view derived from two or more underlying tables.

The advantage of this technique is that it allows you to use a view as if it were a single table. It is interesting to note that you might use the same technique when the base tables from which the view is derived use a one-to-many relationship. In that case, though, the view records representing the line items of an order would provide repetitive data, including the same information related to the order in each record.

Returning to the customers and billing_addresses tables, you start by creating the view derived from these tables. You can do this as shown in Listing 4-13.

Listing 4-13. *Creating the* customers_v *View Built Upon the* customers *and* billing_addresses *Tables*

```
CREATE VIEW customers_v AS
SELECT c.cust_id, c.company_name, c.phone, a.street, a.city, a.state, a.zipcode
FROM customers c, billing_addresses a
WHERE c.cust_id = a.cust_address_id
```

After you've created the customers_v view, you can build a Customer entity mapped to this view. Listing 4-14 shows how this entity looks like.

Listing 4-14. *Source Code for the* Customer *Entity Mapped to the* customers_v *View Built Upon the* customers *and* billing_addresses *Tables*

```
package ejbjpa.entities;
import java.io.Serializable;
import javax.persistence.Column;
import javax.persistence.Entity;
import javax.persistence.Id;
import javax.persistence.Table;
@Entity
```

```
@Table(name = "CUSTOMERS_V")
public class Customer implements Serializable {
    @Id
    @Column(name = "CUST_ID")
    private Integer cust_id;
    @Column(name = "COMPANY_NAME", nullable = false)
    private String company_name;
    @Column(name = "PHONE", nullable = false)
    private String phone;
    @Column(name = "STREET", nullable = false)
    private String street;
    @Column(name = "CITY", nullable = false)
    private String city;
    @Column(name = "STATE", nullable = false)
    private String state;
    @Column(name = "ZIPCODE", nullable = false)
    private String zipcode;

    public Customer() {
    }
//The Customer entity setter and getter methods
...
}
```

The code line highlighted in bold illustrates the use of the @Table annotation to identify the name of the database view rather than database table.

Listing 4-15 shows what the CustomerSessionBean bean utilizing the Customer entity might look like.

Listing 4-15. *Source Code for the* CustomerSessionBean *Bean Utilizing the* Customer *Entity Built Upon the* customers_v *View*

```
//import declarations
...
@Stateless
public class CustomerSessionBean implements CustomerSession {
    @PersistenceUnit(unitName = "jpaplanning-view-pu")
    private EntityManagerFactory emf;
    public String getCustomerDetails(Integer cust_id) {
        String cust_details;
        try {
            EntityManager em = emf.createEntityManager();
            Customer cust = em.find(Customer.class, cust_id);
            cust_details = cust.getCompany_name()+", "+
                           cust.getPhone()+", "+
                           "address is: "+" "+
                           cust.getStreet()+", "+
                           cust.getCity()+", "+
```

```
                           cust.getState()+", "+
                           cust.getZipcode();
        } catch (Exception e) {
            throw new EJBException(e.getMessage());
        }
        return cust_details;
    }
}
```

Again, as in the example from the preceding section, here you deal only with an instance of the `Customer` entity that includes all the fields of both the `customers` and `billing_addresses` tables.

To test the `CustomerSessionBean` bean discussed here, you might use the client code shown in Listing 4-9 earlier.

Finally, I must issue a word of caution. Although this view-based approach helps simplify dealing with JPA entities being used to access data derived from multiple database tables, you need to use it with caution when you are planning to use those entities for updating the data. The fact is that neither MySQL nor Oracle allows you to update fields from different base tables within a single `UPDATE` statement issued against a view. For example, if you issue the statement shown in Listing 4-16 against the `customer_v` view discussed here, you will receive the following error message:

```
Can not modify more than one base table through a join view
```

Listing 4-16. *An Attempt to Update the Join View Fields Derived from Different Base Tables Inevitably Leads to Failure When Trying to Do This with a Single* UPDATE *Statement*

```
UPDATE customer_v
SET phone = '(650)777-5667',
zipcode = '94401';
```

What this means for the bean code utilizing the entity deriving data from a multitable view is that you cannot update the entity properties mapped to different base tables within a single statement.

■**Note** The default transaction mode used in EJB assumes that a transaction starts when an EJB business method is invoked and ends when the method execution completes. Utilizing this model, the container doesn't perform entity updates immediately, synchronizing the changes made to the database. Rather, it batches up all the entity updates and executes a single UPDATE statement for each entity at the end of the transaction. Transactions are touched upon briefly in the "Transaction Considerations" section later in this chapter and are discussed in more detail in Chapter 13.

For example, if you try to invoke the `getCustomerDetails` method of the `CustomerSessionBean` bean updated as shown in Listing 4-17, you will end up with the error caused by not being able to modify more than one base table through a join view.

Listing 4-17. *The* `CustomerSessionBean` *Bean Trying to Update the* `Customer` *Entity Built Upon the* `customers_v` *View*

```
//import declarations
...
@Stateless
public class CustomerSessionBean implements CustomerSession {
    @PersistenceUnit(unitName = "jpaplanning-view-pu")
    private EntityManagerFactory emf;
    public String getCustomerDetails(Integer cust_id) {
        String cust_details;
        try {
            EntityManager em = emf.createEntityManager();
            Customer cust = em.find(Customer.class, cust_id);
            cust.setPhone("(650)777-5667");
            cust.setZipcode("94401");
            cust_details = cust.getCompany_name()+", "+
                            cust.getPhone()+", "+
                            "address is: "+" "+
                            cust.getStreet()+", "+
                            cust.getCity()+", "+
                            cust.getState()+", "+
                            cust.getZipcode();
        } catch (Exception e) {
            throw new EJBException(e.getMessage());
        }
        return cust_details;
    }
}
```

As stated earlier, if you try to invoke the `getCustomerDetails` method shown in the listing, you will end up with an error. The fact is that the JPA provider when dealing with the previous code implicitly generates the `UPDATE` statement shown in Listing 4-16.

However, if you try to perform this update operation with two separate `UPDATE` statements, this should work. Listing 4-18 shows how to do this.

Listing 4-18. *Updating the Join View Fields Derived from Different Base Tables with Several* `UPDATE` *Statements*

```
UPDATE customer_v
SET phone = '(650)777-5667';

UPDATE customer_v
SET zipcode = '94401';
```

Listing 4-19 shows how you might make the JPA provider perform two `UPDATE` statements shown in Listing 4-18 rather than performing the one shown in Listing 4-16.

Listing 4-19. *The* `CustomerSessionBean` *Bean Trying to Update the* `Customer` *Entity Built Upon the* `customers_v` *View*

```
//import declarations
...
@Stateless
public class CustomerSessionBean implements CustomerSession {
    @PersistenceUnit(unitName = "jpaplanning-view-update-pu")
    private EntityManagerFactory emf;
    public String getCustomerDetails(Integer cust_id) {
        String cust_details;
        try {
            EntityManager em = emf.createEntityManager();
            Customer cust = em.find(Customer.class, cust_id);
            cust.setPhone("(650)777-5669");
            em.flush();
            cust.setZipcode("94401");
            em.flush();
            cust_details = cust.getCompany_name()+", "+
                           cust.getPhone()+", "+
                           "address is: "+" "+
                           cust.getStreet()+", "+
                           cust.getCity()+", "+
                           cust.getState()+", "+
                           cust.getZipcode();
        } catch (Exception e) {
            throw new EJBException(e.getMessage());
        }
        return cust_details;
    }
}
```

In this example, after each update of the `Customer` entity instance, you explicitly tell the JPA provider to synchronize all the changes made with the database.

Transaction Considerations

Transactions are another important thing to look at when planning your application. What makes using transactions extremely important in application development is that they make it possible for multiple applications to concurrently access the same data without compromising data integrity and consistency. Transactions are discussed in more detail in Chapter 13, but this section looks at some transaction-related issues to consider when planning your application.

At the planning stage, you should determine the transactional behavior of the entire application and each of its components. Even if you're going to rely on the default transactional behavior of the application components, you should clearly understand the sequence of the implicit transactions that will take place.

The first question you might ask in planning application transactional behavior is, what application components will be involved in transaction-related interactions? It is fairly obvious that transactions can be implemented at the application tiers where business logic resides. Therefore, as for a Java EE application, transactional code can be implemented at the business tier and the database tier. Diagrammatically, this might look like Figure 4-5.

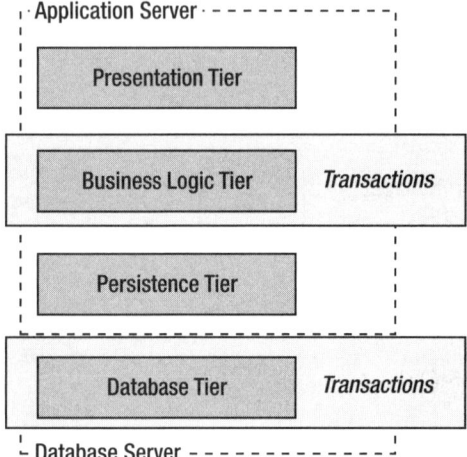

Figure 4-5. *In a Java EE application, transactional code is implemented at the business logic tier and database tier.*

Using transactions in a Java EE application is best understood by example. Suppose you run an online bookstore, where customers may order one or more books from those that are in stock. In a reality, bookstores also let their customers order books that are temporarily out of stock. In that case, however, the orders placed are shipped in a few weeks, since the bookstore first needs to obtain a copy or copies of the ordered book and then perform the order. This particular example, though, assumes that customers can place orders only for those books that are available right now. If a customer tries to place an order for a copy of the book that is out of stock, then an error is generated, and the transaction is rolled back.

To keep things simple, suppose you store all the information about the books you are selling in a single table, say, books. Also, you store information about users' orders in the table orders.

The next problem is, how do you enforce the integrity rule requiring the values of the quantity field in the books table to be not less than 0? The solution to this problem has two approaches.

When creating the books table, you might define a CHECK constraint on the quantity column. This will restrict insert and update operations issued against the books table to only those that do not attempt to set the quantity field to something less than 0. Although this approach is a good example of using database features when implementing the business logic of your application, you won't be able to enjoy it in MySQL (at least not in MySQL 5.1). The MySQL documentation says unambiguously that although the CHECK clause in the CREATE TABLE statement is parsed, all storage engines ignore it.

The second approach is based on using a BEFORE UPDATE trigger defined on the books table to prevent the updates that modify the quantity field to become a negative integer. Unlike the preceding approach, this one can be used in both MySQL and Oracle. However, the implementation of the trigger will differ radically, depending on the database platform.

■**Note** In addition, you might implement validation in the presentation tier, utilizing client-side validation. The advantage of this approach is that it allows your application to immediately block bad input, without having to check it with the underlying database.

Figure 4-6 gives a graphical depiction of the second approach, the one based on using a BEFORE UPDATE trigger defined on the books table.

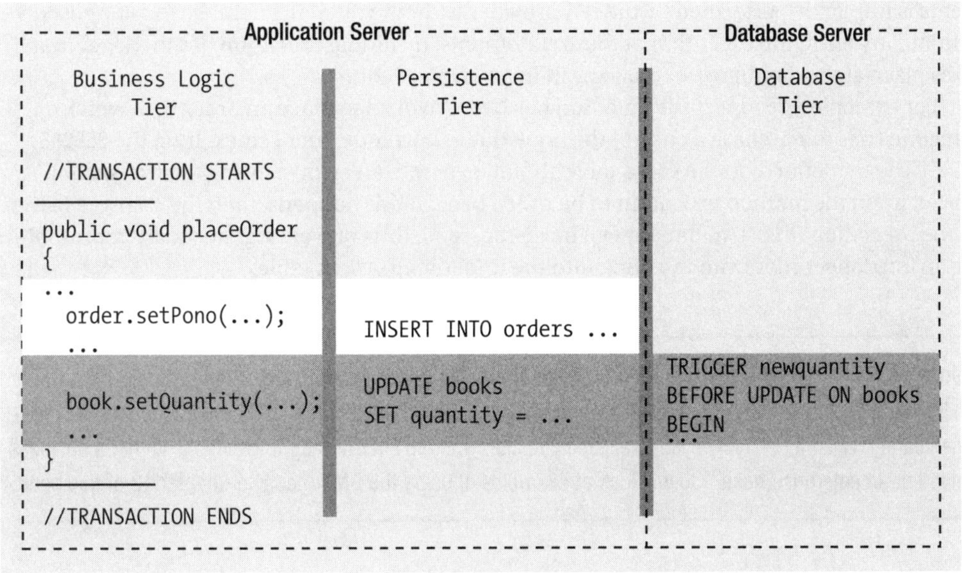

Figure 4-6. *By default, a transaction starts when an enterprise bean business method is invoked and ends on a return from this method.*

In this example, you implement the functionality related to placing an order in the placeOrder method of an enterprise bean. In this method, you first create an instance of the order entity, setting its fields to the data derived from the order being placed. Then, you obtain an instance of the book entity, deriving the data from the books table's record whose quantity field must be modified to correspond to the changes in the number of available book copies. You change the quantity field of the book entity instance, reducing the number of available copies for the book by the number of book copies specified in the order.

So, to make a long story short, you have to complete two operations in this example. In particular, you have to create an order and modify the number of available in-stock copies, completing both of these operations in a single transaction. This means either both of these operations or none should take place.

As you will learn in Chapter 13, when developing an enterprise bean, you can choose between the container-managed transaction (CMT) and bean-managed transaction (BMT) transaction models. The CMT model is used by default and assumes that a transaction starts when an enterprise bean business method is invoked and ends on return from this method. In the example discussed here, you employ a CMT model, assuming that the container automatically starts a transaction when the placeOrder business method is invoked. If no error occurs during execution of the method, the transaction is committed. Otherwise, it is rolled back.

Figure 4-6 shown earlier illustrates that the code of the placeOrder business method considered among the business logic tier implicitly uses the SQL statements generated by the JPA provider at the persistence tier. And one of these statements, namely, UPDATE, invokes a trigger implemented in the database tier. While the process of generating the underlying SQL statements is implicitly performed by the JPA provider without you doing a thing, and supposedly without any error, the execution of these statements, including execution of the trigger that takes place at the database tier, may result in an error, of course.

For example, the placeOrder method has been invoked to place an order with which someone tries to purchase a copy of the book that is currently out of stock. If so, the BEFORE UPDATE trigger defined on the books table should generate an error, causing the transaction started upon the method execution to be rolled back. If this happens, then the changes made by the preceding INSERT statement will be disregarded, thus preventing the record representing an improper order from inserting into the underlying orders table.

■**Note** So, if an error occurs at the database tier, the entire transaction started at the business logic tier will be rolled back by default. You have more choices, though, when using the BMT transaction model mentioned earlier. This model allows you to explicitly decide when to start or stop transactions within a business method of an enterprise bean. You will look at examples of using the BMT model in Chapter 13 of this book.

Now let's look at how you might implement the previous example. You start by creating the books and orders tables, as shown in Listing 4-20.

Listing 4-20. *Creating the* books *and* orders *Tables*

```
CREATE TABLE books(
  isbn VARCHAR(20) PRIMARY KEY,
  title VARCHAR(150),
  author VARCHAR(150),
  quantity INTEGER,
  price NUMERIC(8,2)
);
```

```
CREATE TABLE orders(
  pono INTEGER PRIMARY KEY,
  cust_id INTEGER,
  book_id VARCHAR(20),
  units INTEGER,
  FOREIGN KEY(cust_id) REFERENCES customers(cust_id),
  FOREIGN KEY(book_id) REFERENCES books(isbn)
);
```

The INSERT statement in Listing 4-21 illustrates how you might populate the books table with data.

Listing 4-21. *Populating the* books *Table with Data*

```
INSERT INTO books VALUES('1430209631', 'Beginning GlassFish TopLink: ➥
From Novice to Professional', 'Yuli Vasiliev', 1, 44.99);
```

In this example, you set the number of available copies for the book you're reading now to 1. You don't need to worry about populating the orders table with data at this stage, because it should be done later with the placeOrder business method of the orderSessionBean enterprise bean.

The next step in building the sample is to define the BEFORE UPDATE trigger on the books table. As stated earlier, there are some differences between trigger implementations in MySQL and Oracle. First, let's look at how things work in MySQL.

Before you can create a trigger, you need to grant the TRIGGER privilege for the table on which you want to create the trigger. Or you can grant that privilege for the entire database to the user. To do this, you need to connect as root and then issue the statement shown here:

```
GRANT TRIGGER ON mydb.* TO 'usr'@'localhost'
```

With that done, you can reconnect as usr and create the BEFORE UPDATE trigger on the books table, as shown in Listing 4-22.

Listing 4-22. *Creating the* BEFORE UPDATE *Trigger on the* books *Table, Which Won't Change the Quantity Field If Its New Value Less Than 0*

```
use mydb
delimiter //
CREATE TRIGGER newquantity BEFORE UPDATE ON books
FOR EACH ROW
BEGIN
 DECLARE x INT;
 DECLARE EXIT HANDLER FOR NOT FOUND SET NEW.quantity = OLD.quantity;
 IF NEW.quantity<0 THEN
  SELECT 1 INTO x FROM dual WHERE 1=0;
 END IF;
END;
//
delimiter ;
```

The idea behind this implementation is very straightforward. If the new value for the quantity field of the record being updated is less than 0, you perform a SELECT statement that definitely returns no rows, thus causing the NOT FOUND SQL condition. To handle that condition, you define the handler that sets the quantity field to its original value and terminates the trigger execution.

The problem with the BEFORE UPDATE trigger shown in Listing 4-22 is that it doesn't actually cause an error when you try to set the quantity field to a negative integer. Rather, it prevents such an update from taking place. The following example illustrates this in action. Provided that you've populated the books table with data as shown in Listing 4-21 earlier in this section, you might now issue the following UPDATE statement:

```
UPDATE books
SET quantity=quantity -2
WHERE isbn ='1430209631';
```

Looking at the message generated by the server, you may notice that the previous statement affected no row despite that one row matched the selection criteria.

```
Query OK, 0 rows affected (0.00 sec)
Rows matched: 1 Changed: 0 Warnings 0
```

But what is really worth your attention here is that the previous UPDATE statement doesn't result in an error. As you may notice, even a warning was not issued.

Things like that should be always noted at the planning stage. At first glance, it looks like the BEFORE UPDATE trigger shown in Listing 4-22 serves the purpose very well—it prevents improper update operations from taking place. From the point of view of transactional behavior, though, it turns out that this trigger will not cause an error forcing the transaction within which it is executed to be rolled back.

Put simply, the BEFORE UPDATE trigger shown in Listing 4-22 is not the best way to go in the example discussed here. What you really need here is the BEFORE UPDATE trigger that ends up with an error each time you try to update a row in the books table, when setting the quantity field of that row to a negative integer. So, you can drop the trigger you have as follows:

```
DROP TRIGGER newquantity;
```

Then, you can create the updated trigger as shown in Listing 4-23.

Listing 4-23. *Creating the* BEFORE UPDATE *Trigger on the* books *Table, Which Causes an Error If the New Value of the* quantity *Field Is Less Than 0*

```
delimiter //
CREATE TRIGGER newquantity BEFORE UPDATE ON books
FOR EACH ROW
BEGIN
 IF NEW.quantity<0 THEN
  INSERT INTO books VALUES();
 END IF;
END;
//
delimiter ;
```

This time, when attempting to set the `quantity` field to a negative integer, you simply issue a statement that always results in an error, inevitably forcing the transaction within which the `UPDATE` statement has been issued to be rolled back. For example, you might issue the following statement:

```
UPDATE books
SET quantity=quantity -2
WHERE isbn ='1430209631';
```

This should result in the following error:

```
ERROR 1364 (HY000): Field 'isbn' doesn't have a default value
```

As you might guess, this error occurred because you tried to insert a row into the books table in the trigger, specifying actually no data to be inserted. In fact, it doesn't matter what error will occur and how you achieve this. What really matters is that the trigger execution is terminated with an error.

When examining Listing 4-22 and Listing 4-23, which contain the code for the `BEFORE UPDATE` trigger, you might notice that building triggers in MySQL is a bit tricky. Triggers as well as stored procedures are new MySQL features that first appeared in MySQL 5.0 and, of course, are not perfect yet.

Now let's look at how you might create the `BEFORE UPDATE` trigger for the books table in Oracle, similar to the one in Listing 4-23. Before you can do that, you must grant the `CREATE TRIGGER` privilege to the `usr` schema. Just connect `/as sysdba` to Oracle and then issue the following statement:

```
GRANT CREATE TRIGGER TO usr
```

With that done, you can reconnect as the `usr` user and create the `BEFORE UPDATE` trigger on the books table, as shown in Listing 4-24.

Listing 4-24. *Creating the* `BEFORE UPDATE` *Trigger on the* books *Table in Oracle, Which Generates an Error If the New Value of the* quantity *Field Is Less Than 0*

```
CREATE OR REPLACE TRIGGER newquantity
BEFORE INSERT OR UPDATE ON books
FOR EACH ROW
WHEN (new.quantity < 0)
BEGIN
 RAISE_APPLICATION_ERROR(-20001, 'Improper quantity');
END;
/
```

As you can see, unlike MySQL, Oracle allows you to explicitly raise a user-defined exception, which, nevertheless, brings the trigger to the point of failure. Note the use of the `WHEN` clause, which instructs the database to fire the trigger only if the specified condition is satisfied. In this particular example, the condition specified in the `WHEN` clause is used to ensure that the trigger will fire only when attempting to insert or update the record whose new quantity value is less than 0. To make sure everything works as expected, you can issue the following `UPDATE` statement:

```
UPDATE books
SET quantity=quantity -2
WHERE isbn ='1430209631';
```

This should result in the following error:

```
ERROR at line 2:
ORA-20001: Improper quantity
ORA-06512: at "USR.NEWQUANTITY", line 2
ORA-04088: error during execution of trigger 'USR.NEWQUANTITY'
```

Now that you have seen how to implement the newquantity BEFORE UPDATE trigger defined on the books table, it's time to look at the components implemented in the persistence and business logic tiers. To start with, let's look at the Order and Book entities defined upon the orders and books tables, respectively. Listing 4-25 shows what the Order entity might look like.

Listing 4-25. *Source Code for the* Order *Entity*

```java
package ejbjpa.entities;
import java.io.Serializable;
import javax.persistence.Column;
import javax.persistence.Entity;
import javax.persistence.Id;
import javax.persistence.Table;
import javax.persistence.ManyToOne;
import javax.persistence.JoinColumn;
@Entity
@Table(name = "ORDERS")
public class Order implements Serializable {
    @Id
    @Column(name = "PONO")
    private Integer pono;
    @Column(name = "CUST_ID", nullable = false)
    private Integer cust_id;
    @Column(name = "UNITS", nullable = false)
    private Integer units;
    @ManyToOne
    @JoinColumn(
      name="BOOK_ID",
      referencedColumnName="ISBN")
    private Book book;
    public Order() {
    }
    public Book getBook() {
        return this.book;
    }
    public void setBook(Book book) {
        this.book = book;
    }
```

```
//The other setter and getter methods of the Order entity
...
}
```

Looking at the code in the listing, you may notice that the Order entity contains no specification for the book_id column presented in the underlying orders table nevertheless. You don't need that specification here because book_id is the foreign key column through which you establish a many-to-one relationship with the Book entity. To achieve this, you use the @ManyToOne and @JoinColumn annotations highlighted in bold.

Following this pattern, you might also remove the specification for the cust_id column that is the foreign key referencing the primary key column in the customers table, thus establishing a many-to-one relationship between the Order and Customer entities with the @ManyToOne and @JoinColumn annotations, like you do with the Order and Book entities.

■Note In practice, you may deal with tables that have a few foreign key columns referencing a number of different tables. When creating JPA entities upon such tables, you have to include a lot of annotations such as @ManyToOne, @OneToMany, and @JoinColumn, which are required for establishing relationships between entities. As a result, the source code for those entities may grow quite large. One possible way to solve this problem is to reduce the number of entities being used by your application, moving some business logic into the database. You will see an example on how this can be implemented in the next chapter in the "Implementing Some Business Logic of an Application Inside the Database" section.

Listing 4-26 shows the Book entity to which you establish a many-to-one relationship in the Order entity.

Listing 4-26. *Source Code for the* Book *Entity*

```
package ejbjpa.entities;
import java.util.List;
import javax.persistence.CascadeType;
import java.io.Serializable;
import javax.persistence.Column;
import javax.persistence.Entity;
import javax.persistence.Id;
import javax.persistence.Table;
import javax.persistence.OneToMany;
@Entity
@Table(name = "BOOKS")
public class Book implements Serializable {
    @Id
    @Column(name = "ISBN")
    private String isbn;
    @Column(name = "TITLE", nullable = false)
    private String title;
    @Column(name = "AUTHOR", nullable = false)
```

```
    private String author;
    @Column(name = "PRICE", nullable = false)
    private Double price;
    @Column(name = "QUANTITY", nullable = false)
    private Integer quantity;
    @OneToMany(mappedBy="book", cascade = CascadeType.ALL)
    private List<Order> orders;
    public List<Order> getOrders(){
        return orders;
    }
    public void setOrders(List<Order> orders) {
        this.orders = orders;
    }
    public Book() {
    }
//The Book entity setter and getter methods
...
}
```

As far as a bidirectional relationship is concerned, you use the @OneToMany annotation in the Book entity shown in the listing to establish a relation with the Order entity shown in Listing 4-25 earlier.

Now that you have seen the components being used in the persistence tier, let's look at the business logic tier. Listing 4-27 shows what the OrderSessionBean enterprise bean might look like. In the listing, take a close look at the placeOrder business method of the enterprise bean, whose invocation starts the transaction within which the newquantity trigger discussed earlier in this section may fire.

Listing 4-27. *Source Code for the* OrderSessionBean *Enterprise Bean*

```
//import declarations
...
@Stateless
public class OrderSessionBean implements OrderSession {
    @PersistenceUnit(unitName = "order-pu")
    private EntityManagerFactory emf;
    public void placeOrder(Integer pono,
                           Integer cust_id,
                           Integer units,
                           String book_id) {
        try {
            EntityManager em = emf.createEntityManager();
            Book book = (Book) em.find(Book.class, book_id);
            Order order = new Order();
            order.setPono(pono);
            order.setCust_id(cust_id);
            order.setUnits(units);
            book.setQuantity(book.getQuantity()-units);
```

```
        order.setBook(book);
        em.persist(order);
    } catch (Exception e) {
        throw new EJBException(e.getMessage());
    }
}
}
}
```

The most interesting code in this listing is highlighted in bold. First, you find the book record of interest using the find method of the EntityManager instance created in this method earlier. Next, you create an instance of the Order entity and set its cust_id and units fields to the values of the respective arguments passed to the placeOrder method discussed here. You also calculate the new value for the quantity field of the Book entity instance, subtracting the number of units to which you set the units field of the Order entity instance from the current value of the quantity field. Then, you use the setBook method to set the book field of order. Finally, you persist the order instance using the persist method of the EntityManager instance.

It is interesting to note here that although you explicitly persist only the order instance, the changes made to the book instance will be stored to the database as well. If you recall from Listing 4-26, when defining the Book entity, you set cascade = CascadeType.ALL in the @OneToMany annotation that is used to establish a relationship to the Order entity. This means every time an instance of the Order entity is persisted to the database, the related instance of the Book entity is also persisted. Behind the scenes, as you might recall from Figure 4-6, the JPA provider issues the two SQL statements, namely, INSERT that is issued against the orders table and UPDATE issued against the books table. You don't need to worry about the order in which these statements will be issued, since they are both performed in a single transaction. If one of these statements fails, the changes made by the other will be automatically disregarded.

Now let's look at the client that might be used to invoke the placeOrder method. For the sake of simplicity, like in all the preceding examples, the client shown in Listing 4-28 is a terminal client that you will launch from your operating system prompt.

Listing 4-28. *Source Code for the Client That Might Be Used to Test the* OrderSessionBean *Enterprise Bean Shown in Listing 4-27*

```
package ejbjpa.client;
import javax.ejb.EJB;
import ejbjpa.ejb.OrderSession;
public class OrderSessionClient {
    @EJB
    private static OrderSession orderSession;
    public static void main (String[] args)
    {
        Integer pono = Integer.parseInt(args[0]);
        Integer cust_id = Integer.parseInt(args[1]);
        Integer units = Integer.parseInt(args[2]);
        String book_id = args[3];
        orderSession.placeOrder(pono, cust_id, units, book_id);
    }
}
```

Examining the code in this listing, you may notice that this client assumes you will specify the parameters of the order being processed as the input arguments of the client's main method. As you might guess from the code, the order in which the arguments should be specified when invoking the client matters. Here is the proper order: pono, cust_id, units, book_id.

Now, assuming you packed the application in the transactions-planning.jar archive, you might issue the appclient command from a terminal window, specifying the main method parameters as follows:

```
appclient -client transactions-planning.jar 1 1 1 1430209631
```

■**Note** This example illustrates an interesting use of the GlassFish's appclient command. You provide the input arguments for the client's main method, adding them to the end of the command line with which you invoke the client.

The previous command runs the client that invokes the placeOrder business method, passing the parameters specified in the prompt. This particular invocation should result in persisting the order whose pono is 1, cust_id is 1, units is 1, and book_id is 1430209631. Also, the books table will be modified, reducing the quantity of available copies for the book included in the order by the number of units specified (by 1, in this example). To make sure this has been done correctly, you can issue the following two queries, shown with the output:

```
SELECT * FROM orders;
```

```
pono   cust_id  book_id            units
1      1          1430209631 1
```

```
SELECT * FROM books;
```

```
isbn         title          author         quantity  price
1430209631  Beginning GlassFish  Yuli Vasiliev  0         44.99
```

The result generated by the first query shows that a new record appeared in the orders table. The second query shows you that the value of the quantity field in the record from the books table has changed and is set to 0. This means that both operations, namely, the insert into the orders table and update of the books table, have been successfully completed.

Now, you might try to insert another record into the orders table by issuing the following command:

```
appclient -client transactions-planning.jar 2 1 1 1430209631
```

Although in the previous command you change the value for the pono field in order to avoid the primary key constraint violation, this will end up with an error anyway. The reason for this is that the value of the quantity field in the record representing the book specified in the order is 0, meaning the item is out of stock at the moment. In this case, the UPDATE operation implicitly issued by the JPA provider against the books table is attempting to change the preceding `quantity` field to a negative integer, which leads to an error generated by the `BEFORE UPDATE` trigger defined on the `books` table, as discussed earlier. As a result, both operations, the insert into the `orders` table and the update of the `books` table, are rolled back.

The sample you looked at in this section should give you a clear idea of what you're facing when planning the transactional behavior of your Java EE application. In particular, you learned that although a transaction typically starts and ends with the code implemented at the business logic tier, the underlying SQL statements and triggers executed at the database tier affect profoundly whether the transaction is committed or rolled back.

Planning for Security

Applications that manipulate sensitive information need to be protected. It is important to plan a strategy for security from the beginning, at the planning stage. In particular, you should choose the security model that suits you best. As you will learn in Chapter 12, when developing a Java EE application, you can employ declarative or programmatic security in the business logic tier.

In reality, though, it is often a good idea to implement security not only in the business logic tier but also in the other tiers of your application. For example, when planning an application that will heavily access and/or manipulate database data, it is wise to think about implementing security in the database tier in addition to implementing security measures in the business logic tier.

Before you start planning security at the database level, you need to understand that database security is based on the permissions you grant to user accounts. Therefore, it is always a good idea to give users only those permissions that they need to accomplish their tasks—not less, not more. Again, this is best understood by example.

Taking a closer look at the example discussed in the preceding section, you might notice that using the `Book` entity was not actually a necessity and in fact poses a security risk because it makes it possible to modify the data stored in the `books` table from within the business logic tier.

The simplest solution to this problem is to move some business logic implemented in the `placeOrder` business method of the `OrderSessionBean` enterprise bean shown in Listing 4-27 earlier into the database so that reducing the number of available book copies by modifying the `books` table takes place inside the database, thus making the `Book` entity unnecessary. You will see how to do this in the next chapter in the "Implementing Some Business Logic of an Application Inside the Database" section.

From a security standpoint, though, removing the `Book` entity from the project doesn't make things much better. The problem is that the `books` table still can be modified from within the business logic tier with the help of a SQL statement issued against that table directly.

■**Note** As you will learn in Chapter 11, using entities is recommended but not the only way in which you can access and manipulate database data from within enterprise beans. Alternatively, you can always issue a native SQL query.

A good solution to this problem is to create another user account in the database through which your application will interact with the database.

Returning to the example from the preceding section, you might create the sec_usr account and grant it the privileges only to the orders table. Although the newly created sec_usr account will be used by the application to connect to the database, the database administrator (DBA) will still use the usr account to manipulate database data and metadata as required.

Provided that the books table will be automatically updated from within the BEFORE INSERT trigger defined on the orders table every time you insert a new record into that table, you don't have to grant any privilege to the books table to the sec_usr account. The details of how to implement this BEFORE INSERT trigger will be discussed in the next chapter in the "Implementing Some Business Logic of an Application Inside the Database" section. In this section, however, let's look at a more comprehensive and general example that shows how you might implement security at the database level.

Suppose your application needs only to access some columns in the orders and books tables. Following the least privilege pattern, you should give the sec_usr account (the one the application server will use to connect to the database) only those permissions that enable your application to access the needed columns in the previous tables and nothing more. So, what you need to do here is to implement a mechanism that provides column-level access control over the orders and books tables.

This is where a view built upon these tables comes in handy. The trick is to include in the view's query only the needed columns from the underlying tables and then grant the sec_usr account only the SELECT privilege on this view, while not granting this account any access privilege to the orders or books table. Diagrammatically, this might look like Figure 4-7.

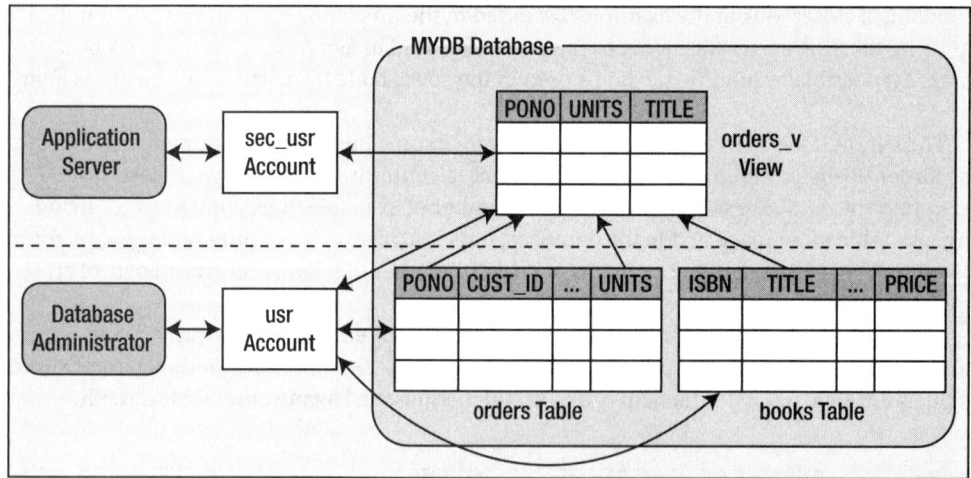

Figure 4-7. *The application server interacts with the database via the* sec_usr *account that can see only the* orders_v *view. The DBA can still use the* usr *account to manipulate database data and metadata as required.*

Now, let's look at how you might implement this in MySQL. The following commands assume you're using the MySQL command-line tool. To start with, you connect to the MySQL server as usr from your operating system prompt:

```
mysql -u usr -p
Enter password: ****
```

Next, you create the orders_v view in the mydb database:

```
use mydb
CREATE VIEW orders_v AS
SELECT o.pono, b.title, o.units FROM orders o, books b WHERE o.book_id=b.isbn;
```

To make sure everything works as expected, you can issue a SELECT statement against the newly created view:

```
SELECT * FROM orders_v;
```

This should generate the following output:

```
pono  title               units
1     Beginning GlassFish ... 1
```

Now you should exit the MySQL command-line tool and then reconnect as root:

```
mysql -u root -p
Enter password: ****
```

After this, you can create the sec_usr account and grant it the SELECT privilege on the orders_v view with the help of the following statement:

```
GRANT SELECT
ON mydb.orders_v
TO 'sec_usr'@'localhost'
IDENTIFIED BY 'pswd';
```

Then, you exit the MySQL command-line tool and reconnect as sec_usr:

```
mysql -u sec_usr -p
Enter password: ****
```

Now, if you issue a SELECT statement against the orders_v view as follows:

```
use mydb
SELECT * FROM orders_v;
```

you should receive the following output:

```
pono  title               units
1     Beginning GlassFish ... 1
```

However, if you try to issue a SELECT statement against the orders or books table directly, say, like this:

```
SELECT * FROM orders;
```

you will see the following error message:

```
ERROR 1142 (42000): SELECT command denied to user 'sec__usr'@'localhost' ➥
for table 'orders'
```

The most interesting thing about this approach is that it allows the user to selectively access fields of the underlying tables, keeping that user from being able to access the other fields of those tables. In this particular example, you create the view through which an application will be able to access only three fields from the underlying orders or books table.

Now, let's look at how the previous sample might be implemented in Oracle. Oracle, unlike MySQL, automatically assigns a working area for a new user account. So, if you connect as usr, then everything you create in the database will, by default, belong to this schema.

To execute the statements discussed next, you will need a SQL command-line tool interacting with Oracle, such as Oracle SQL*Plus. You can start by connecting as usr and then creating the orders_v view upon the orders or books table in the same way you would in MySQL:

```
CONN usr/pswd

CREATE VIEW orders_v AS
SELECT o.pono, b.title, o.units FROM orders o, books b WHERE o.book_id=b.isbn;
```

Then, you need to reconnect as sysdba and create the sec_usr account, to which you grant the SELECT privilege on the usr.orders_v view just created in the usr schema:

```
CONN /as sysdba

CREATE USER sec_usr
IDENTIFIED BY pswd;
GRANT connect, resource TO sec_usr;

GRANT SELECT ON usr.orders_v
TO sec_usr;
```

Now you can connect as sec_usr and then issue a SELECT query against the orders_v view:

```
CONN sec_usr/pswd

SELECT * FROM usr.orders_v;
```

As a result, you should see the same output you saw in the MySQL example discussed a bit earlier:

```
pono title                 units
1    Beginning GlassFish ... 1
```

As in MySQL, if you try to query an underlying table, connected as sec_usr, you will receive an error message. In Oracle, this error message might look like the following:

```
ERROR at line 1:
ORA-00942: table or view does not exist
```

The example provided in this section should have given you a taste of what database-level security is and how this can be implemented. Of course, it is impossible for a single section to cover all the security features your database may offer you. The main purpose of this section, though, is to show you that it is always a good idea to implement some security measures at the database level, where the data resides. Another important conclusion you can draw is that it is a necessity to spend some time thinking about security during the planning stage, rather than trying to incorporate security measures afterward.

XML Deployment Descriptors vs. Annotations

Prior to Java EE 5, you had to use XML deployment descriptors describing the metadata for an application, a component, or a module. One of the significant improvements the Java EE 5 platform offers is that XML deployment descriptors are now optional. Instead, you can use annotations that are inserted directly into your Java code, associating metadata with program components.

This section briefly explains when you might prefer using deployment descriptors to annotations and gives an example of how you might replace annotations with deployment descriptors.

■**Note** It is important to understand that you can use both annotations and deployment descriptors within the same project simultaneously. Almost all the samples discussed so far used both of these approaches. For example, in each sample interacting with a database, you used the `persistence.xml` descriptor file defining a persistence unit being utilized in the application. Also, you used the `application.xml` deployment descriptor in which you included information about modules utilized within the application. To describe the other metadata, you used annotations, such as `@Entity`, `@Table`, `@EJB`, and many others.

Now that you have two choices when it comes to defining metadata in your Java EE application, you should consider the pros and cons for both approaches, taking into account the specifics of a particular project.

Annotations are built on the idea that metadata can be more intuitive and vivid. You embed annotations in your Java code, providing the application server with the required configuration information and leaving the actual work of creating deployment descriptors to the application server.

However, many developers think that keeping configuration data apart from the code is a good design practice. Figure 4-8 depicts these two approaches to providing configuration information when developing a Java EE component.

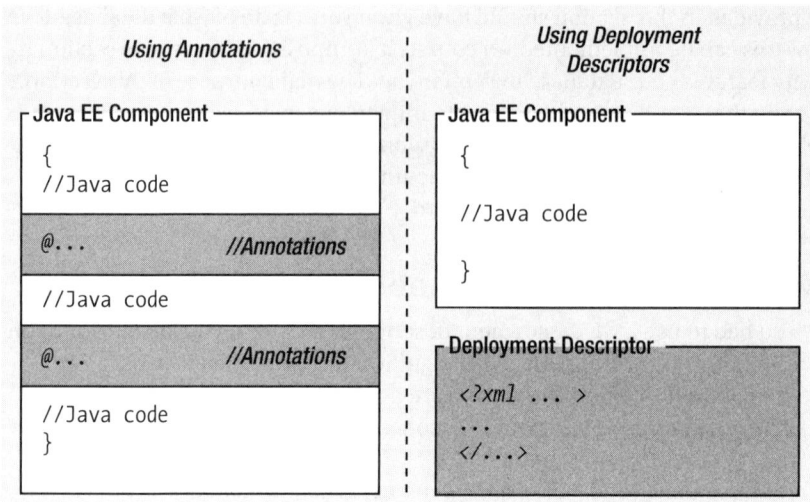

Figure 4-8. *When developing a Java EE component, you provide configuration information using annotations or deployment descriptors.*

At first glance, it seems that using annotations can improve productivity and reduce development time, since annotations are intuitive to use and allow the developer to keep the code and configuration data in one place, thus reducing the number of project files. You might be surprised to learn, however, that annotations are best used only in small to middle-sized projects. Large projects require more granularity. In such projects, manageability is the challenge; therefore, keeping the metadata apart from the code is typically a requirement. Not following this rule can lead to a poorly designed solutions, reducing scalability, maintainability, and component reusability.

So, it is always a good idea to decide at the planning stage whether to use annotations, deployment descriptors, or a mix in your project.

■**Note** It is interesting to note that annotations can be overridden with deployment descriptors. This approach is not recommended, though, since duplicating configuration information is wasteful and pretty error-prone.

By now, you have seen a lot of examples of how to define a session bean using annotations. In particular, you saw how to define stateless session beans implementing a remote interface with the help of the @Stateless and @Remote annotations used in the class and business interface of a bean, respectively. In the OrderSessionBean bean shown in Listing 4-27 (in the "Transaction Considerations" section earlier), you also saw the @PersistenceUnit annotation in action.

Returning to the example discussed in the "Transaction Considerations" section, let's look at how the OrderSessionBean bean might be implemented with no annotations. Listing 4-29 shows how you can implement the business interface for the OrderSessionBean bean without using annotations (annotations are still included but have been commented out and high-lighted in bold for clarity).

Listing 4-29. *The Business Interface for the* OrderSessionBean *Bean Without Using Annotations*

```
package ejbjpa.ejb;
//import javax.ejb.Remote;
//@Remote
public interface OrderSession  {
   public void placeOrder(Integer pono,
                          Integer cust_id,
                          Integer units,
                          String book_id);
}
```

In the same way, you can remove the annotations from the OrderSessionBean bean class. Listing 4-30 shows the updated bean's code, with annotations commented out.

Listing 4-30. *A Snippet of the* OrderSessionBean *Enterprise Bean Originally Shown in Listing 4-27, with No Annotations This Time*

```
package ejbjpa.ejb;
import java.io.Serializable;
import javax.ejb.EJBException;
//import javax.ejb.Stateless;
import javax.persistence.EntityManager;
import javax.persistence.EntityManagerFactory;
//import javax.persistence.PersistenceUnit;
import ejbjpa.entities.*;
//@Stateless
public class OrderSessionBean implements OrderSession {
//    @PersistenceUnit(unitName = "order-pu")
    private EntityManagerFactory emf;
    public void placeOrder(Integer pono,
                           Integer cust_id,
                           Integer units,
                           String book_id)
    {
     //the placeOrder method code
  ...
    }
}
```

Examining the code in the previous two listings, you may notice that removing annotations made the OrderSessionBean bean more flexible. Now you won't need to change the source code if you want to use the bean with a local interface, employ it as a stateful bean, or utilize another persistence unit. However, since the configuration data has been removed from the code, the following question arises: where can all this specification information can be found now? The answer is, in the deployment descriptor describing the OrderSessionBean

bean. Listing 4-31 shows what the `ejb-jar.xml` deployment descriptor describing `OrderSessionBean` might look like.

Listing 4-31. *Source Code for the* `ejb-jar.xml` *Deployment Descriptor Describing the* `OrderSessionBean` *Enterprise Bean Shown in Listing 4-30*

```xml
<?xml version="1.0" encoding="UTF-8" standalone="no"?>
<ejb-jar xmlns="http://java.sun.com/xml/ns/javaee"
xmlns:xsi="http://www.w3.org/2001/XMLSchema-instance"
metadata-complete="true" version="3.0"
xsi:schemaLocation="http://java.sun.com/xml/ns/javaee
                          http://java.sun.com/xml/ns/javaee/ejb-jar_3_0.xsd">
  <enterprise-beans>
    <session>
      <display-name>OrderSessionBean</display-name>
      <ejb-name>OrderSessionBean</ejb-name>
      <business-remote>ejbjpa.ejb.OrderSession</business-remote>
      <ejb-class>ejbjpa.ejb.OrderSessionBean</ejb-class>
      <session-type>Stateless</session-type>
      <transaction-type>Container</transaction-type>
      <persistence-unit-ref>
        <persistence-unit-ref-name>ejbjpa.ejb.OrderSessionBean/emf➥
</persistence-unit-ref-name>
        <persistence-unit-name>order-pu</persistence-unit-name>
        <injection-target>
          <injection-target-class>ejbjpa.ejb.OrderSessionBean➥
</injection-target-class>
          <injection-target-name>emf</injection-target-name>
        </injection-target>
      </persistence-unit-ref>
      <security-identity>
        <use-caller-identity/>
      </security-identity>
    </session>
  </enterprise-beans>
</ejb-jar>
```

Looking at this listing, you may not like the idea of replacing annotations with deployment descriptors. As you might guess, writing deployment descriptors takes more time and energy than dealing with annotations. As the previous listing shows, writing descriptors by hand may be extremely tedious and very error-prone.

The best way to start learning deployment descriptors is to look at the ones generated by your application server. The application server automatically generates the deployment descriptors that will actually be used at runtime, when you're deploying your Java EE component to that server, assuming that all the configuration information has been specified with annotations. In particular, you should examine the `glassfish_dir/domains/domain1/generated/xml/j2ee-modules/your_ejb_name/ META-INF` directory to find the deployment descriptors generated by the container when you deployed your bean.

In other words, this approach assumes you first utilize annotations in the Java code of your component. Then, you deploy the component to the application server, making the latter generate the deployment descriptors based on the data specified with annotations. Finally, you can return to your component and remove the annotations from the source code, including the generated deployment descriptors to the deployment archive instead.

This approach generally takes away the need for you to write deployment descriptors by hand and may be especially helpful if you're new to XML in general and deployment descriptors in particular. The downside is that you need to compile and deploy your component twice—first with annotations and then with deployment descriptors.

Returning to the `ejb-jar.xml` deployment descriptor shown in Listing 4-31, you will probably not be surprised to learn that this one was generated by the application server when deploying the `OrderSessionBean` bean shown in Listing 4-27 in the "Transaction Considerations" section earlier in this chapter. Including this `ejb-jar.xml` file into the `META-INF` directory of the bean's deployment archive makes it possible for you to completely remove annotations from the `OrderSessionBean` bean's source, as you did in Listing 4-29 and Listing 4-30 earlier in this section.

A good example of when you might prefer using deployment descriptors to annotations is when developing JPA entities. If you recall from the "Planning JPA Entities" section, the source code for an entity may grow quite large if you include annotations required for establishing relationships with related entities. This is where moving the configuration information from annotations to deployment descriptors may come in very handy. You will see an example of how this can be accomplished in Chapter 9 later in this book.

However, for the time being, that concludes this brief discussion on the pros and cons of using annotations and XML deployment descriptors. After reading this section, you should realize that although using annotations, a new Java EE 5 feature, makes the process of developing Java EE components easier, this approach may even increase the complexity when it comes to large projects. This is because mixing source code with configuration data reduces the flexibility, scalability, and reusability of application components—things that cannot be ignored in large projects. In contrast, the approach based on deployment descriptors, while not obvious and may require more expertise, lets you reconfigure your Java EE component without touching the original source, which is particularly welcome in real-world projects.

Application Organization and Reuse

Now that you have some understanding of the structure of a typical Java EE application and have looked at some common issues to consider at the application planning stage, it's time to move on and look at how you can organize your Java EE solution.

Collecting Information

Admittedly, planning any application begins with collecting information. Although in reality the planning stage actually starts with a discussion between the developer responsible for the application planning and the business decision maker and/or some other people who are interested in the application, our discussion here assumes that you, as the developer responsible for planning, already know what potential users expect from the application.

Before you move on to drawing up a plan of what exactly has to be done at the development phase, you need to collect some information on what you already have, what is missing, and what has to be done to complete the project. In particular, you need to consider the answers to the following questions:

- Is the underlying database already in place, or are you going to generate a new one from scratch?

- What Java EE components are already in use, and which of those might be reused in your application?

- What Java EE components are missing and need to be built from scratch?

The answers to these questions help you determine what you can reconfigure and then reuse in your application and what has to be built from scratch.

For example, you may already have the underlying database upon which you need to build your application. In practice, this is often the case when your application works with the database structures also utilized by some other applications.

It is important to understand here that the presence of the underlying database doesn't automatically mean you have the database tier ready to be used. You may need to do a lot of work on the database side before it is actually ready to be utilized within your application. If you recall from the earlier sections, you may need to create views and triggers and even define new database schemas in the underlying database when implementing the database tier of your application. Sometimes, however, modifying the preexisting database is not an option. If this is the case, you will end up with a more complicated entity structure and Java code.

Another issue that may arise if you're dealing with an already existing underlying database is how to learn the exact structure of the database objects being utilized within the application. For example, you have to know for sure the structure of the underlying database tables upon which you want to build JPA entities. Moreover, you need to have all the information about the primary/foreign key pairs in the underlying tables to establish the relationships between the entities you build on those tables.

Suppose you know that all the database objects your application will work with are located in the database schema named usr. The problem is that you don't know for sure what tables and views this schema contains. To find out this, in MySQL you might use the SHOW TABLES statement, which will output the names of both the tables and views belonging to a certain database. For example, if you connect to the MySQL command-line tool as usr and then issue the following commands:

```
use mydb
SHOW TABLES;
```

you might receive the following output:

```
Tables_in_mydb
--------------------
billing_addresses
books
customers
customers_v
employees
orders
orders_v
```

Now that you know what tables and views are in your database, how can you view the structure of those tables and views? The simplest way to look at the structure of a table or view is with the DESCRIBE command. For example, to look at the structure of the orders table, you can issue the following command:

```
DESCRIBE orders;
```

The output of the previous command should tell you the columns' names in the orders table, their types, whether nulls are allowed, whether the column is indexed, and the column's default value. However, it doesn't tell you what columns are foreign keys in the table and what corresponding primary key tables are.

To find out this, you might use the SHOW CREATE TABLE statement. So, by issuing the following command, you can obtain not only names and types of the orders table but also the foreign keys defined on this table:

```
SHOW CREATE TABLE orders;
```

The output of the previous command should look much like the CREATE TABLE orders statement shown in Listing 4-20 earlier in this chapter.

In Oracle, to look through the list of tables and views belonging to the usr schema, you might issue the following statement, being connected as sysdba:

```
SELECT object_name FROM dba_objects ➥
WHERE owner ='USR' AND (object_type='TABLE' OR object_type='VIEW');
```

The output might look like this:

```
OBJECT_NAME
--------------------
billing_addresses
books
customers
customers_v
employees
orders
orders_v
```

Now that you have the list of tables, you might want to look at the structure of a certain table. Like in MySQL, the DESCRIBE command available in SQL*Plus doesn't give you all the information about a table. So, to obtain information about foreign key columns defined in a table, you might query the dba_cons_columns and dba_constraints views predefined in the Oracle Database. For example, issue the following query to obtain information about the constraints defined on the orders table:

```
SELECT column_name, constraint_name FROM dba_cons_columns
WHERE owner ='USR' AND table_name = 'ORDERS';
```

The output generated will look something like this:

```
COLUMN_NAME  CONSTRAINT_NAME
BOOK_ID        SYS_C006515
CUST_ID        SYS_C006514
PONO           SYS_C006513
```

Now that you know what constraints are defined on the orders table, and on which columns they reside, you can learn which of these constraints are foreign keys. This is where the following query may come in handy:

```
SELECT constraint_name, constraint_type FROM dba_constraints
WHERE owner ='USR' AND table_name = 'ORDERS';
```

The output will look like this:

```
CONSTRAINT_NAME  CONSTRAINT_TYPE
SYS_C006513        P
SYS_C006514        R
SYS_C006515        R
```

You may find the values in the constraint_type column a little confusing. According to the Oracle documentation, though, P stands for a primary key constraint, but R means a foreign key constraint.

Thinking of Reusability

After examining the underlying database, the next important task you have to perform in the beginning of the planning stage is determining which Java EE components from other applications might be reused in the application you're planning now.

You might consider reusing EJB components borrowed from other applications. In practice, this means you would reuse enterprise beans already deployed to the application server and currently utilized within other solutions. Thus, an EJB component can be used in more than one application. For example, you can utilize a session bean also used by another application, invoking its business methods from within the client or JSP pages of your application.

As a simplistic example, let's return to the sample application discussed in the "Transaction Considerations" section earlier in this chapter. If you recall, the application consisted of the OrderSessionBean enterprise bean providing the placeOrder method and the client invoking this method. Assuming that the bean has been packed in the order.jar archive and the client in the appclient-order.jar, you might have the application.xml deployment descriptor shown in Listing 4-32 in the application archive.

Listing 4-32. *The Application Deployment Descriptor Used in the Application Discussed in the "Transaction Considerations" Earlier Section*

```
<?xml version="1.0" encoding="UTF-8"?>
<application version="5" xmlns="http://java.sun.com/xml/ns/javaee"
xmlns:xsi="http://www.w3.org/2001/XMLSchema-instance"
xsi:schemaLocation="http://java.sun.com/xml/ns/javaee
http://java.sun.com/xml/ns/javaee/application_5.xsd">
```

```
<display-name>transactions-planning</display-name>
<module>
  <ejb>order.jar</ejb>
</module>
<module>
  <java>appclient-order.jar</java>
</module>
</application>
```

If you recall, you launched the application with the help of the `appclient` command issued from the command line like this:

```
appclient -client transactions-planning.jar 2 1 1 1430209631
```

■Note So far, the book samples have been built along with an application client so that you can launch them with GlassFish's `appclient` command. This approach is particularly handy when you need to perform a quick test of an EJB module deployed to the application server. In practice, though, you will most likely use web modules to utilize EJBs deployed with EJB modules. From the reusability standpoint, the previous approaches are different in how you can reuse EJBs. You don't have to deploy your application archive to the server when the `appclient` is used to launch the application. This means the EJB module included in the application archive and specified in the `application.xml` deployment descriptor will not conflict with this same EJB module already deployed to the server. In contrast, an EAR application archive, in which you pack the EJB module along with the web module utilizing it, has to be deployed to the application server before you can use it. If the EAR archive being deployed contains an EJB module that is already deployed to the server, you will receive an error. To avoid this problem, you might deploy EJB modules and web modules utilizing them, each separately, rather than in an EAR archive, thus providing more room for reusability. This will be discussed in more detail in the "Planning the Steps to Building and Deploying Your Application" section later in this chapter.

In the previous command, the `appclient` command is followed by the name of the application archive, which is followed by a set of parameters passed to the client's main method. In particular, you pass the following parameters: the pono (PO number) of the order being created, the ID of the customer, the number of book copies being purchased, and the ISBN of the book.

Looking at the parameters passed in the previous command line, you may notice that they are just figures presented in a form that is not readily presentable. Let's look at what you can do to improve the situation.

It is fairly obvious that there is no need to change the way in which you specify the number of units and the ISBN of the book ordered (these are the third and fourth parameters, respectively). As for the order number (the first parameter), in a real-world application you most likely won't need to figure it out and then pass it as the argument—the application automatically will do it for you. This will be discussed in more detail in Chapter 6. As for now, however, let's leave it the way it is.

It looks like the only parameter passed to the client's main method that is worth your attention here is the customer ID that you specify as the second argument. Say you want to deal with the customer name rather than its ID. After all, the name is more human-friendly. So, assuming that the updated application is packed in the two-ejbs.jar archive, you might insert a new record into the orders table with the following command:

```
appclient -client two-ejbs.jar 3 "Fast Express" 1 1430209631
```

■**Note** It is important to realize that this approach can be used only if you are sure that no two customers in the customers table are stored with the same name. Otherwise, you run the risk of relating a record being created in the orders table with a wrong record in the customers table.

Now that you know how the updated application should behave, how might you implement it? Another question you might ask is, what components of the existing application might be reused?

To start with, let's take a closer look at the already existing components. If you recall from earlier, there are only two such components: the client packed in the appclient-order.jar archive and the EJB module containing the OrderSessionBean bean packed in the order.jar archive.

In this situation, making some changes to the client sounds obvious, since the way in which the client's main method takes the information about the customer has changed—now you pass the name of a customer instead of its ID. However, you can avoid changing the EJB component used here, because the way in which you insert a new record into the orders underlying table has not changed; you still need to use the ID of a customer when inserting a new record. Therefore, the placeOrder method of the OrderSessionBean bean does not have to be changed, meaning the bean can be reused in the updated application.

As you might guess, the only missing piece of logic so far is the one that defines the process of obtaining the customer's ID based on its name passed as a parameter. (Once again, this approach makes sense only if you are absolutely sure that no two customers in the customers table are stored with the same name.) To implement this functionality, you might define another session bean, say, CustSessionBean, putting it into a separate EJB module packed as, say, cust.jar. Alternatively, you might add this new session bean into the already existing order.jar archive. Although the latter will not affect the functionality of the OrderSessionBean bean already residing in the order.jar archive, it will require you to redeploy the module to the application server.

If you decide on the former and pack the CustSessionBean bean into the separate EJB module cust.jar, then the application.xml deployment descriptor might look like the one shown in Listing 4-33.

Listing 4-33. *The* application.xml *Deployment Descriptor for the Application Utilizing Two EJB Modules*

```
<?xml version="1.0" encoding="UTF-8"?>
<application version="5" xmlns="http://java.sun.com/xml/ns/javaee"
xmlns:xsi="http://www.w3.org/2001/XMLSchema-instance"
```

```
xsi:schemaLocation="http://java.sun.com/xml/ns/javaee
http://java.sun.com/xml/ns/javaee/application_5.xsd">
  <display-name>two-ejbs</display-name>
  <module>
    <ejb>order.jar</ejb>
  </module>
  <module>
    <ejb>cust.jar</ejb>
  </module>
  <module>
    <java>appclient-updated.jar</java>
  </module>
</application>
```

As you can see, order.jar is reused in this application, while cust.jar highlighted in bold is a new EJB module archive.

Now let's look at how the CustSessionBean bean packed in cust.jar might be implemented. Listing 4-34 shows the source code for the CustSessionBean bean implementation.

Listing 4-34. *Source Code for the* CustSessionBean *Bean Containing the* getCustId *Business Method*

```
//import declarations
...
@Stateless
public class CustSessionBean implements CustSession {
    @PersistenceUnit(unitName = "cust-pu")
    private EntityManagerFactory emf;
    public Integer getCustId(String company_name)
    {
     Integer cust_id;
        try {
            EntityManager em = emf.createEntityManager();
            Customer customer = (Customer) em.createQuery("SELECT c ➨
 FROM Customer c WHERE c.company_name = :company_name")
                            .setParameter("company_name", company_name)
                            .getSingleResult();
            cust_id = customer.getCust_id();
        } catch (Exception e) {
            throw new EJBException(e.getMessage());
        }
      return cust_id;
    }
}
```

As you can see, the CustSessionBean bean shown in the listing contains only one method, namely, getCustId, which receives the customer's name as the parameter and returns the corresponding ID. The highlighted code obtains the `Customer` entity instance based on the customer's name passed in and then specified in the `WHERE` clause of the JPQL query used here.

As stated earlier, you also have to modify the client code. Listing 4-35 shows the source code for the updated client, with the lines that have been added or modified in bold.

Listing 4-35. *Source Code for the Updated Client That Utilizes Two EJBs*

```
package ejbjpa.client;
import javax.ejb.EJB;
import ejbjpa.ejb.OrderSession;
import ejbjpa.ejb.CustSession;
public class OrderSessionClient {
     @EJB
     private static OrderSession orderSession;
     @EJB
     private static CustSession custSession;
     public static void main (String[] args)
       {
            Integer pono = Integer.parseInt(args[0]);
            String company_name = args[1];
            Integer units = Integer.parseInt(args[2]);
            String book_id = args[3];
            Integer cust_id = custSession.getCustId(company_name);
            orderSession.placeOrder(pono, cust_id, units, book_id);
       }
}
```

As you can see, the client utilizes both the `CustSessionBean` and `OrderSessionBean` beans. An alternative approach could be to utilize the `CustSessionBean` from within the `OrderSessionBean` bean. However, that would be the worst solution from a reusability standpoint. This is because it would require you to rewrite the source code for the `OrderSessionBean` bean, and even worse, it would make it impossible to continue using that bean in the original application.

The sample discussed here demonstrates quite nicely how EJB components might be reused. In this particular example, you reused the `OrderSessionBean` bean without even redeploying its deployment archive to the application server.

Although reusing EJB components is something that can be easily understood and accomplished, how might you reuse JPA entities implementing the persistence code in Java EE applications? To answer this question, you need to have a clear understanding of the structure of a typical EJB module deployed to an application server.

Usually, an EJB module deployed to an application server contains one or more enterprise beans and a set of JPA entities utilized by those beans. It is fairly obvious that entities included in an EJB module are designed to work with the beans residing within the same module, rather than any other beans. If you want an entity to be reused in a bean residing in another EJB module, you might make a copy of that entity source file, putting it to the appropriate directory within the new EJB module structure. Then, you compile the module sources, package the compiled classes and configuration files into the deployment package, and deploy it to the application server.

Strictly speaking, this second usage described in this scenario is not exactly what is called *reusing*. That way, you actually reuse the source code for the entity, rather than reusing that entity as part of the EJB module already deployed to the application server.

In reality, though, this is not a big problem. The point is, each EJB module, even if it deals with the same underlying database data as some other EJB modules, often utilizes another set of JPA entities, following its own requirements for data access.

Planning the Structure of Your Application

After you have decided what components you need and what role each component will play in the application, you need to figure out how you might put all those components together. In the preceding example, you utilize two EJB components within a single application, where one of those components is also utilized within another application. In reality, though, you may need to develop an application that utilizes tens of EJBs and, therefore, requires careful planning.

As mentioned in the preceding section, you might add a new EJB to an existing EJB module as an alternative to creating a new module. Your decision as to which method to use should not be made spontaneously—you should decide it at the planning stage.

If you are planning a small application whose business logic won't be reused, you might pack all the EJBs and JPA entities being utilized within a single EJB module. However, if you anticipate that some parts of the business logic may be reused, you should organize the EJB components with that in mind. The example in the preceding section illustrated this concept in action. If you recall from that example, the OrderSessionBean bean packed in order.jar and deployed to the application server was then utilized within two different applications.

Although in the preceding example you call the business methods of two different EJBs from within the same client, in a real-world application you might want to utilize several EJBs within a coarser-grained one that will be then utilized within the client code. This approach assumes that a fine-grained EJB can be reused in more than one coarse-grained EJB, thus enhancing reusability and flexibility. Figure 4-9 gives a graphical depiction of this approach.

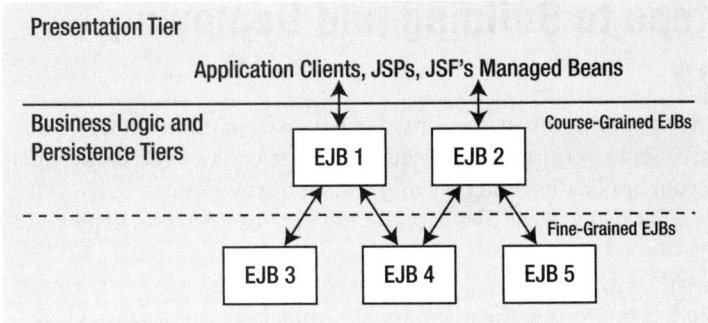

Figure 4-9. *Fine-grained EJBs can be utilized within coarser-grained ones whose business methods are invoked from within the presentation tier.*

When using this approach based on building coarser-grained EJBs upon fine-grained ones, you are not limited to the two-level granularity shown in the figure. Actually, you can choose the level of granularity that suits you best. In most cases, though, using two levels is quite enough.

You might be wondering why you would want to build EJBs upon other EJBs. As stated earlier, this approach allows you to enhance the reusability and flexibility of the EJB components utilized. For example, you may have a set of reusable EJB components, each of which implements a small piece of business logic that potentially will be reused in more than one application. Upon these fine-grained EJBs, you build EJBs that satisfy the requirements of a particular application and, therefore, are application-specific. If the business requirements change, you can modify the coarse-grained EJB involved, while the underlying EJBs will remain unchanged.

The most difficult thing in this approach is to determine how to divide enterprise logic between fine-grained EJBs so that you have a set of reusable components to be then used as building blocks for coarser-grained, solution-specific components. As a general rule of thumb, when planning fine-grained EJBs, avoid including application-specific logic. Whenever possible, you should avoid dependencies between fine-grained EJBs. Typically, a fine-grained EJB should provide functionality for performing a common set of operations on the corresponding entities and should be solution-agnostic.

The `OrderSessionBean` bean discussed in the preceding section is a good example of a solution-agnostic EJB. Its `placeOrder` method simply inserts a new record into the `orders` table through an instance of the `Order` entity, setting that instance's fields to the values passed in as arguments. It is important to note that `placeOrder` doesn't provide any other functionality than that described earlier. So, when you decided to build another application using the `OrderSessionBean` bean, you created the `CustSessionBean` bean and then modified the client code to utilize both the beans, following the application requirements. Although in that particular example you used the application client to implement application-specific logic, in a larger project those specifics might be implemented within a coarse-grained EJB to be then utilized from within one of the following components: a JSP, JSF's managed bean, application client, or another EJB.

Planning the Steps to Building and Deploying Your Application

Before you start developing your application, it is essential to have a clear understanding of the steps you need to take in order to perform the project tasks. Once you've figured out which components will be used in your application and how they will interact with each other, you are ready to outline a plan of what really needs to be done at the development and deployment stages.

Of course, such a plan may vary from project to project—you need to tackle each project individually. To begin with, let's take a look at the major building blocks of a typical Java EE application.

As stated previously, you have several choices when it comes to packaging and deploying components to be utilized within your Java EE application. For example, if you are developing an application consisting of a web application module and EJB module, you can either package both of these modules in an EAR application archive and then deploy it to the server or deploy each module separately. Although the former sounds like common sense—you have all the application modules packed within a single archive—the latter is more appropriate if you are planning to reuse the EJB module utilized within your application in another application; you will have to add only the EJB-JAR module archive to the WAR file of the web application in which you want to reuse that EJB module.

Table 4-3 lists the major components you need to build when developing a Java EE application.

Table 4-3. *Major Components of a Typical Java EE Application*

Component	Description
Underlying database	Represents the database tier of your application and consists of one or more relational databases used to persist the objects belonging to the persistence tier.
EJB module or modules (EJB-JAR)	Each EJB module may contain one or more EJBs implementing the business logic of your application. EJB modules also usually contain the JPA entities implementing the persistence logic of your application. You can deploy an EJB module as part of an enterprise application archive (EAR) or as a stand-alone module. The latter is wise if you are planning to reuse that EJB module in more than one application.
Web application archive	Contains components implementing the presentation tier of your application. Like an EJB module, a web application archive (WAR) may be deployed to the application server as part of an enterprise application archive (EAR) or as a stand-alone unit. In the latter case, you need to make sure to add all the EJB modules' archives being utilized within the web application to its WAR file. Moreover, each of the EJB modules included in the WAR archive must have been deployed to the application server.
Enterprise application archive	This includes an application deployment descriptor(s) and Java EE modules such as web application and EJB modules to be utilized within your application. You deploy this archive to the application server, thus deploying all the Java EE modules included. You should not include an EJB module in an EAR archive if that module has been already deployed to the server as a separate module. If you do so, you will end up with an error occurring during the deployment. The opposite is also true—you should not deploy an EJB module if this same module is included in the EAR archive already deployed to the server. Regardless of the way you deploy an EJB module, it becomes available to all the other modules deployed.

You might be surprised to learn that an EJB module deployed within an EAR archive can be utilized by the other deployed components not included in that EAR archive. As mentioned earlier, regardless of the way you deploy an EJB module (within an EAR or as a stand-alone module), you can utilize it from within any other module deployed to the application server. Let's look at a quick example. Suppose you want to deploy an order.ear EAR that includes an order-ejb.jar archive containing the EJB module to be utilized within the web application packed with the order-war.war archive also included in that EAR. Once the order.ear has been deployed, however, the EJBs packed in the order-ejb.jar module can be utilized not only by the web application packed in order-war.war but also by any other application deployed to the application server.

In practice, though, it might not seem to make a lot of sense to include an EJB module in an EAR application archive if you are planning to reuse that EJB module in another application. In that case, it would be a more elegant solution to deploy such an EJB module as a stand-alone unit, thus making it clear that the EJBs included in that module might be used in any application that needs them.

As you no doubt have realized, deciding what modules to package your application components in is a task that requires careful thought and thorough planning. The most important thing to keep in mind at this stage is that good planning of the application modules will help you not only build a well-structured application but also improve reusability of some of the business logic that you have already implemented.

Now that you have looked at what building blocks your Java EE application may be comprised of, let's take a brief look at how to build each of these components. In the preceding chapters, you saw some examples of building EJB modules. In the later chapters, you will see more examples of how to prepare the previously mentioned, as well as the other, major parts of a Java EE application, which were outlined in Table 4-3. The following sections provide only the general steps to creating these application building blocks, which you have to outline at the planning stage.

The General Steps to Building the Underlying Database

As you learned from the preceding examples, you start the development process with the underlying database. In some cases, you may already have the database upon which you will build your application. If so, you need to check whether you have all the database objects in place and what you have to add.

Follow these general steps when developing the underlying database from scratch:

1. Create one or more database schemas.

2. Build the database objects in the schemas created in step 1.

3. Populate the database tables with data.

However, if you have the underlying database in place, you will need to follow these general steps:

1. Create a database schema through which the application will interact with the database.

2. Build the database objects in the schema created in step 1.

Planning the underlying database is discussed in detail in the next chapter. Then, in Chapter 6, you will look at how to build it to be utilized within your application.

The General Steps to Building an EJB Module

As you have seen in the preceding examples, EJB beans are usually packed with the corresponding JPA entities in EJB modules that are then deployed to the application server.

Here are the general steps you follow when building and deploying an EJB module:

1. Develop JPA entities and EJB beans.

2. Compile the sources.

3. Create the configuration files.

4. Package the classes and configuration files into an EJB-JAR module archive.

5. Deploy the EJB module package to the application server.

Developing JPA entities is discussed in extensive detail in Chapter 8. Then, Chapter 12 covers building EJB components by utilizing JPA entities.

The General Steps to Building a Web Application Module

As stated earlier, most real-world Java EE applications rely on a web tier technology such as JSF or JSP when it comes to the presentation layer. Web application artifacts are usually packed in a WAR file and then deployed to the application server.

Here are the general steps to follow when building and deploying a web application archive:

1. Develop the web pages.

2. Compile the Java classes (if, for example, JSF technology is used).

3. Create the configuration files.

4. Package the web application artifacts into a WAR file.

5. Deploy the WAR package to the application server.

In Chapter 14, I'll discuss how to build the web application to be then utilized as the presentation tier within a Java EE application.

The General Steps to Building an Enterprise Application Module

As an alternative to deploying EJB and web application archives as stand-alone units, you might pack them, as well as archives containing helper classes, into an EAR archive and then deploy it to the application server.

You should perform these general steps to build and deploy an enterprise application:

1. Build the web and EJB archives containing the components to be utilized within the application.

2. Create the `application.xml` deployment descriptor.

3. Package the application modules into an EAR file.

4. Deploy the EAR package to the application server.

As stated earlier, it's wise to keep EJB modules that will be reused in another application as stand-alone units, not including such modules, in the EAR application archive. However, it is good practice to include the web application archive and EJB modules that won't be reused in other applications.

Of course, when you're planning an application that will contain only one EJB module, it is easy to determine whether to include that module in the application archive. But for applications utilizing a number of EJB modules, you're going to think a little harder about which modules to include in the EAR and which ones to deploy as stand-alone units.

Planning the Sample Application

Now that you have gained some useful insights into planning a Java EE application, let's map out a plan for developing the sample application to be built in the next chapters. Without going into all the details, the following sections outline the structure of the sample application and the general steps to be performed to implement that structure.

Planning the Sample Structure

Admittedly, diagrams may worth thousands of words. Providing a visual representation of the components the application will be comprised of and their interactions is an important part of the planning process.

You might start with a simplified graphical representation of the structure of the application being planned. Such a diagram can include only the key components to be utilized within the application. Later, you might draw more detailed diagrams for each tier being utilized within the application.

Figure 4-10 gives a graphical depiction of the structure of the sample application being discussed in the following chapters.

As you can see, the sample application depicted in the figure has a two-layer business logic tier. In the upper layer, you have the JSF bean that will invoke the business methods of the session bean located in the lower layer. In a real-world application, you most likely will have more JSF beans and session beans in the upper layer.

As mentioned earlier, dividing the business logic tier into layers allows you to develop more flexible and reliable solutions utilizing stand-alone pieces of business logic, which get repeated use among applications deployed to the application server.

Another interesting thing to note here is that although both the JSF bean and the EJB bean logically belong to the business logic tier, physically they are packed in different modules. The JSF bean is part of the web application and, therefore, is packed in the WAR archive, whereas the EJB bean is packed into an EJB-JAR module archive.

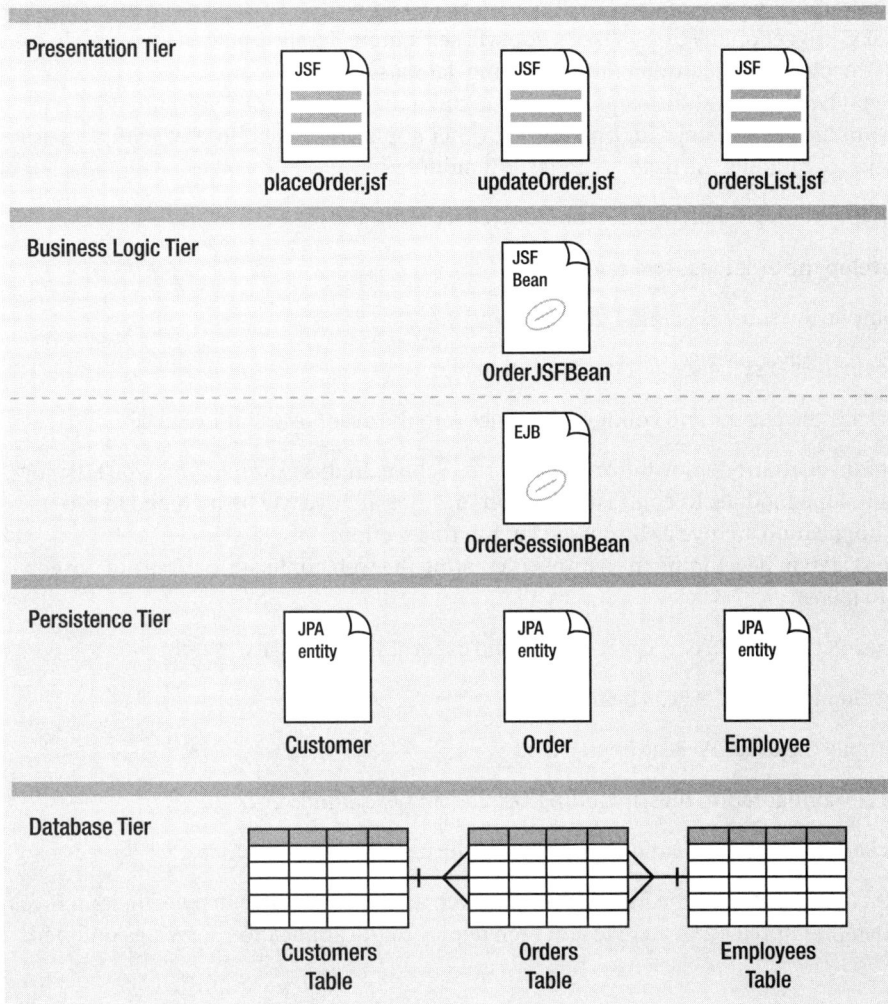

Figure 4-10. *A simplified representation of the structure of the sample application*

Planning the Steps to Building and Deploying the Sample

The next step is to figure out what technically should be done to develop the sample application. You start by planning the general steps to be accomplished. As usual, let's start with planning the steps required to build the underlying database.

1. Create the usr database schema.

2. Build database objects in the usr schema, including the Customers, Employees, and Orders tables.

3. Populate the Customers and Employees database tables with data.

Of course, this is a very rough plan. It doesn't reflect some details, such as creating the BEFORE INSERT trigger on the Orders table. You will see a more detailed plan in the next chapter, which is dedicated to planning the underlying database.

Once you have outlined the steps required to build the database tier, you can move on and figure out the general steps for building the other application tiers. To start with, let's outline the steps for building the order-ejb.jar EJB module:

1. Develop the Customer, Order, and Employee JPA entities.

2. Develop the OrderSessionBean bean.

3. Compile the sources created in steps 1 and 2.

4. Create the persistence.xml configuration file.

5. Package the classes and configuration files into the order-ejb.jar archive.

Note that you didn't deploy the order-ejb.jar archive. In this example, you won't deploy it as a stand-alone module. In contrast, the order-ejb.jar archive will be included in the order.ear application archive as discussed later in this section.

The next step in developing the sample is creating the web application. Here are the general steps to follow:

1. Develop the placeOrder, updateOrder, and ordersList JSF pages.

2. Develop the OrderJSFBean bean.

3. Compile the OrderJSFBean bean class.

4. Create configuration files, including faces-config.xml and web.xml.

5. Package the web application artifacts into the order-war.war archive.

Now that you have both the EJB module and web application, you can pack their archives into the order.ear application archive and then deploy to the application server, as outlined here:

1. Create the application.xml deployment descriptor.

2. Package the order-ejb.jar and order-war.war archives created earlier into the order.ear application archive.

3. Deploy the order.ear package to the application server.

That is it. After performing these steps, you should have your application deployed and ready for use.

Summary

When planning your application, you should make a number of design decisions. This chapter introduces valuable concepts and pulls together some best practices related to planning Java EE applications. Knowing these things should help you make informed decisions at the planning stage.

■ ■ ■

## CHAPTER 5

Planning the Underlying Database

Data is a critical part of almost every Java EE application today. That is why it's important to properly design the database tier of your Java EE solution. Like planning any other application tier, you should consider database tier planning in light of your business needs. Although you may already have an underlying database containing the core data your application will access, you still often need to adjust an existing database structure to address the requirements of the application.

In the preceding chapter, you looked at the issues related to the planning process of all the tiers of a Java EE application. This chapter covers the details related to the planning stage of the database tier of a Java EE application. After reading this chapter, you will have learned how to do the following:

- Map out a plan for building the database tier of a Java EE application

- Plan a Java EE application being built upon an existing, underlying database

- Design an application in which most data processing takes place inside the database

- Make a graphical depiction of the major steps being performed by the application

It is fairly obvious that database planning is a huge topic that cannot be fully covered in one chapter—it would take an entire book to describe it in extensive detail. However, the topics discussed in the following sections focus on the most important issues related to the underlying database design and will help you make informed decisions when planning the database tier of your Java EE application.

Planning the Persistence Tier Upon an Existing, Underlying Database

In practice, it is often the case that a new application is built upon an existing, underlying database. For example, you may need to build an application that will be used for generating sales reports based on the data stored in a number of tables manipulated by some other applications. In such a situation, although you have all the data to be accessed in place, you might want to organize that underlying data in structures that will be easily utilized within your application.

The following sections will discuss some ways of how you can create the intermediate database objects to bridge the gap between the underlying database tables and JPA entities, thus facilitating the existence of multiple applications built upon the same underlying database.

Using Database Views

Often the underlying database upon which you want to build your application is utilized by another already existing application. In such a situation, it is fairly clear that you cannot change the structure of the underlying tables to address the requirements of your application. This is where database views can come in handy.

As you no doubt know, database views provide another representation of the data stored in the underlying tables. If you recall from the "Mapping an Entity to a Database View" section in the preceding chapter, using views built upon more than one table may be a good idea when you need only to access the underlying data, not modify it.

Diagrammatically, using views as an intermediate layer between the underlying tables and JPA entities might look like Figure 5-1.

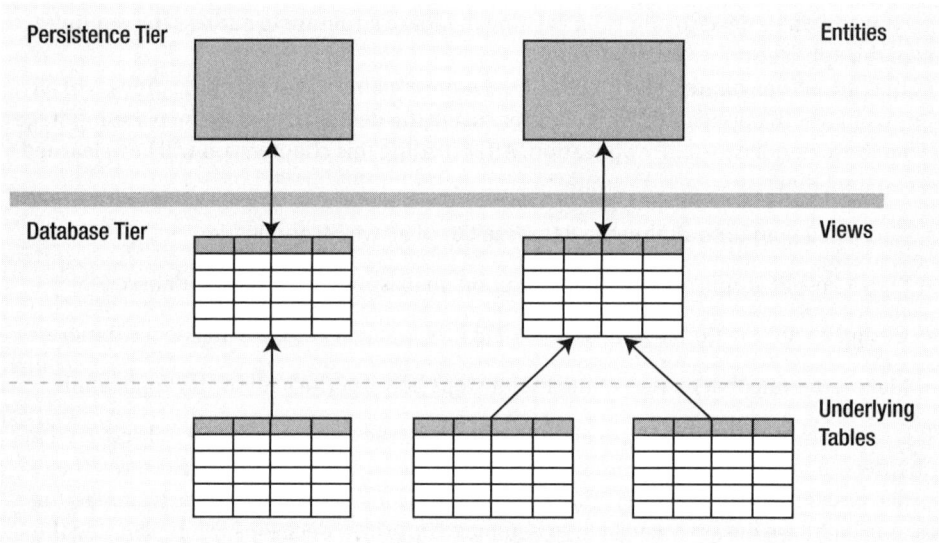

Figure 5-1. *You might want to create a set of views upon which the persistence tier will be based.*

As the diagram illustrates, the views upon which the JPA entities are based can be built on either a set of underlying tables or a single table.

It is interesting to note that hiding some underlying tables' columns containing sensitive information from the application is not the only reason why you might want to utilize views. Another situation where you might want to use views is if there is an existing EJB module containing particular JPA entities and you want to reuse that EJB module. Let's look at a quick example. Suppose your underlying database contains the departments table, which has the following structure:

```
department_id    INTEGER
department_name  VARCHAR(100)
location_id  INTEGER
```

However, the dept EJB module you already have deployed contains the Department entity, which is designed to work with the table called depts, which has a slightly different structure:

```
dept_id     INTEGER
dept_name   VARCHAR(100)
loc_id      INTEGER
```

In that case, you might create a view upon the departments table so that the column names in that view meet the Department entity requirements. Consider the depts view created as follows:

```
CREATE VIEW depts AS
SELECT department_id as dept_id, department_name as dept_name, location_id as loc_id
FROM departments
```

Note that you named the view depts so that you don't need to change the table name used within the EJB module and specified either with the @Table annotation in the Department entity or in a deployment descriptor document.

From a security standpoint, using views is good practice when you need to hide some columns of the underlying tables from the users. For example, you might build a view upon several underlying tables, including just a few columns from those tables. This approach makes sense if the user account through which your application will access the views has the privileges only on the views but no privileges on the underlying tables. This was discussed in extensive detail in Chapter 4 in the section "Planning for Security."

Utilizing New Database Schemas

To make the underlying database more secure and more logically structured, you might think about putting the views built upon the core tables into an intermediate layer built between the underlying database and the application persistence tier, implemented as a separate database schema.

Figure 5-2 graphically illustrates how you might group the views built upon the core tables into separate schemas so that each schema is designed to work with the persistence tier of a particular application.

As you can see in the figure, you can build more than one database schema that will contain views built upon a single schema containing the core underlying tables. In practice, however, the views in such schemas might be based on the database tables located in more than one schema.

Actually, databases may differ in the way they organize custom data and provide access to it. For example, MySQL assumes that you first create a database (schema) that will contain custom objects and then you create a user account, granting it the privileges required to manipulate those schemas' custom objects. Actually, a single user account can be granted the privileges that allow it to access database objects stored in more than one schema.

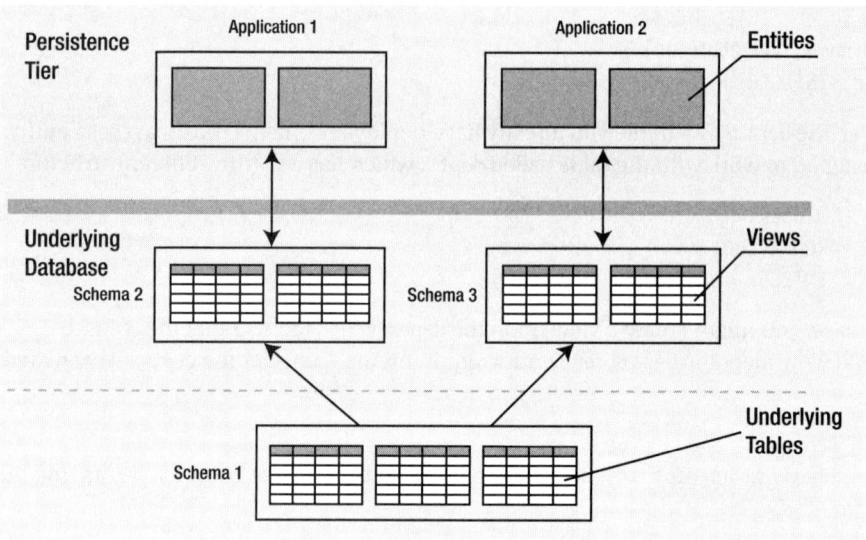

Figure 5-2. *You might group the views, upon which the persistence tier of an application will be built, into a separate database schema for better security and structure of the underlying database.*

■**Note** For additional information on how databases may differ in the way they organize custom data, you can refer to the appendix, specifically, the section "Understanding the Architecture of Your Database."

In Oracle, the schema is automatically defined when you create a user account. Like in MySQL, you can grant a user account privileges that allow it to access database objects stored in more than one schema.

In practical terms, this means you're going to need to create a new schema in Oracle or MySQL, in which you will then create the views being utilized by the persistence tier of an application. In MySQL, you will then need to create a new user account with the privileges to work with that schema's objects. But in Oracle, you will need to create another schema—if you recall from earlier in the chapter, in Oracle the schema is automatically defined when creating a user account. In other words, in the case of Oracle, you will have a redundant, empty schema created just because you needed to create a user account that allows the application to access only those objects that are located in the schema in which you create the views being utilized by the persistence tier of an application.

Figure 5-3 should help you understand these differences between MySQL and Oracle.

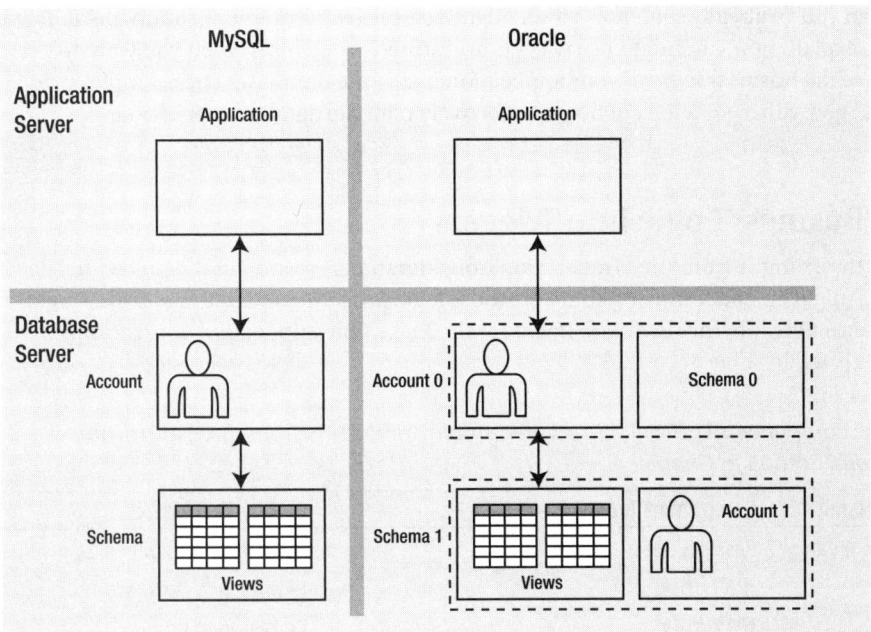

Figure 5-3. *Oracle and MySQL are different in the way they organize user data and provide access to that data. Unlike MySQL, Oracle implicitly defines the schema when creating a user account.*

As you can see in the figure, in the case of Oracle you have a more complicated structure. However, it doesn't seem so complicated when it comes to building it. For an example of how you might organize database schemas and user accounts for better security configuration in both MySQL and Oracle, you can review the section "Planning for Security" in Chapter 4.

Implementing Some Business Logic of an Application Inside the Database

Another important issue you should consider at the beginning of the planning stage is determining how much business logic you might move inside the database. The good news is that both Oracle and MySQL give you the ability to do this by implementing views, stored procedures, and triggers.

■**Caution** Stored procedures and triggers are new MySQL features that first appeared in MySQL 5.0. So, the following discussion assumes you're using version 5 of MySQL or later.

Although you've already seen how views might be utilized in your application, the following sections explain how you might use triggers and stored procedures when you want to move some of the business logic of your application inside the database. The examples provided should give you a good idea of how to effectively plan the database tier of your application.

Moving Business Logic Into Triggers

Continuing the example from the "Transaction Considerations" section in the preceding chapter, you might consider moving some business logic implemented in the business logic and persistence tiers into the database. If you recall, the sample application consists of the components listed in Table 5-1.

Table 5-1. *The Components Utilized Within the Sample Application from the "Transaction Considerations" Section in Chapter 4*

Component Name	Component Type	Application Tier
OrderSessionBean	Session bean	Business logic tier
Order	JPA entity	Persistence tier
Book	JPA entity	Persistence tier
orders	Database table	Database tier
books	Database table	Database tier
newquantity	BEFORE UPDATE trigger on the books table	Database tier

Now, suppose you want to move the logic that is used to calculate the new value of the quantity field in the books table into the database. One way to do this is to define the BEFORE INSERT trigger on the orders table, which will update the quantity field in the books table, reducing the value of the quantity field by the number of units specified in the order being inserted.

So, the updated set of components to be utilized within the sample application will look like the one listed in Table 5-2. The changes column in the table tells you whether you have to modify the component borrowed from the sample discussed in the "Transaction Considerations" section in Chapter 4.

Table 5-2. *The Components to Be Utilized Within the Sample Application Discussed in This Section*

Component Name	Component Type	Application Tier	Changes
OrderSessionBean	Session bean	Business logic tier	Yes
Order	JPA entity	Persistence tier	Yes
orders	Database table	Database tier	No
books	Database table	Database tier	No
newquantity	BEFORE UPDATE trigger on the books table	Database tier	No
neworder	BEFORE INSERT trigger on the orders table	Database tier	New

Not only does Table 5-2 contain one less persistence tier object and one more database tier object, but also the structure of the Order entity has been simplified, since the annotations used to define the relationship between this entity and the Book entity become irrelevant and are removed.

Now let's look at how all these components will interact with each other, by inserting a new record into the orders table. This task is comprised of multiple actions, which diagrammatically might look like Figure 5-4. An explanation of each numbered step is given after the figure.

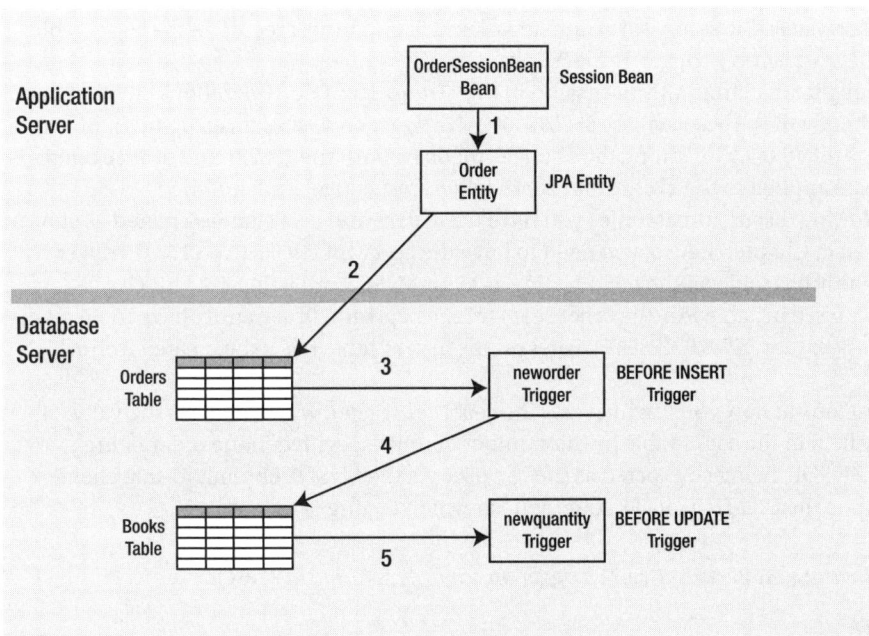

Figure 5-4. *A graphical depiction of the actions performed by the sample application*

Tip It is always a good idea to draw a diagram that depicts the actions performed by the application you're planning. Such a diagram lets you quickly figure out how the components involved in the application development will interact and what can be done to improve the structure of your application.

In Figure 5-4, the actions are numbered in order and can be interpreted as follows:

1. When executed, the placeOrder business method of the OrderSessionBean bean creates an instance of the Order entity and then sets its fields to the appropriate values.

2. The JPA provider persists the Order entity as specified in the placeOrder method of the OrderSessionBean bean, trying to insert a new record into the orders table.

3. The database server fires the neworder BEFORE INSERT trigger, just before inserting the record into the orders table.

4. The `neworder` trigger tries to update the corresponding record in the `books` table by issuing the `UPDATE` statement.

5. The database server fires the `newquantity BEFORE UPDATE` trigger, just before updating the record in the `books` table.

Looking at these steps, you may notice that the event of inserting a record into the `orders` table is followed by the event of firing the `neworder` trigger, which are steps 2 and 3, respectively. In reality, though, the event of firing the trigger is followed by the event of inserting a record, since the `neworder` trigger is a `BEFORE INSERT` one, meaning it fires before the actual inserting takes place. The same is true for steps 4 and 5: updating a record in the `books` table and firing the `newquantity` trigger, respectively.

As you might recall from the discussion in the "Transaction Considerations" section in the preceding chapter, if the `newquantity BEFORE UPDATE` trigger generates an error, then the entire transaction is rolled back, meaning the changes made by both the `INSERT` and `UPDATE` operations that were applied to the `orders` and `books` tables, respectively, are nullified.

The following discussion assumes you have the `orders` and `books` tables created as shown in Listing 4-20 in Chapter 4. Also, you need to have the `newquantity BEFORE UPDATE` trigger defined on the `books` table as shown in Listing 4-23 for MySQL or Listing 4-24 for Oracle.

As you can see in Table 5-2, the `OrderSessionBean` bean and `Order` entity have to be modified, and the `neworder BEFORE INSERT` trigger on the `orders` table has to be created from scratch.

Let's first look at how you might create the `neworder` trigger, which reduces the value of the quantity field in the `books` table by the number of units specified in the order being inserted. In MySQL, being connected as the `usr` user via the MySQL command-line client, you might issue the `CREATE TRIGGER` statement shown in Listing 5-1.

Listing 5-1. *Creating the* `BEFORE INSERT` *Trigger on the* `orders` *Table in MySQL*

```
delimiter //
CREATE TRIGGER neworder
BEFORE INSERT ON orders
FOR EACH ROW
BEGIN
UPDATE books
 SET quantity = quantity - NEW.units
 WHERE isbn = NEW.book_id;
END;
//
delimiter ;
```

In a similar way, you could create the `neworder` trigger in Oracle. Being connected as `usr` within a SQL*Plus session, issue the `CREATE OR REPLACE TRIGGER` command shown in Listing 5-2.

Listing 5-2. *Creating the* `BEFORE INSERT` *Trigger on the* `orders` *Table in Oracle*

```
CREATE OR REPLACE TRIGGER neworder
BEFORE INSERT ON orders
FOR EACH ROW
BEGIN
 UPDATE books
 SET quantity = quantity - :NEW.units
 WHERE isbn = :NEW.book_id;
END;
/
```

With that done, you can switch your focus to the `Order` entity, which has to be modified a little to reflect the changes made in the database tier. Listing 5-3 shows the updated source code for the `Order` entity. The lines of code that were used within the preceding sample but have become unnecessary in this updated version have been commented and highlighted in bold for clarity. The new inserted lines are highlighted in bold too.

Listing 5-3. *Source Code for the Updated* `Order` *Entity*

```
package ejbjpa.entities;
import java.io.Serializable;
import javax.persistence.Column;
import javax.persistence.Entity;
import javax.persistence.Id;
import javax.persistence.Table;
// import javax.persistence.ManyToOne;
// import javax.persistence.JoinColumn;
@Entity
@Table(name = "ORDERS")
public class Order implements Serializable {
    @Id
    @Column(name = "PONO")
    private Integer pono;
    @Column(name = "CUST_ID", nullable = false)
    private Integer cust_id;
    @Column(name = "BOOK_ID", nullable = false)
    private String book_id;
    @Column(name = "UNITS", nullable = false)
    private Integer units;
 // @ManyToOne
 // @JoinColumn(
 //    name="BOOK_ID",
 //    referencedColumnName="ISBN")
 // private Book book;
    public Order() {
    }
    public Integer getPono() {
```

```
        return this.pono;
    }
    public void setPono(Integer pono) {
        this.pono = pono;
    }
    public Integer getCust_id() {
        return this.cust_id;
    }
    public void setCust_id(Integer cust_id) {
        this.cust_id = cust_id;
    }
    public String getBook_id() {
        return this.book_id;
    }
    public void setBook_id(String book_id) {
        this.book_id = book_id;
    }
    public Integer getUnits() {
        return this.units;
    }
    public void setUnits(Integer units) {
        this.units = units;
    }
//  public Book getBook() {
//        return this.book;
//  }
//  public void setBook(Book book) {
//        this.book = book;
//  }
}
```

As you can see in the updated Order entity shown in the listing, you commented the lines of code responsible for establishing the relationship with the Book entity. This is because the Book entity is not used in the application anymore.

The next step in modifying the sample application is to update the placeOrder business method of the OrderSessionBean bean. Listing 5-4 shows the entire source code for the updated OrderSessionBean bean. Just as in the preceding listing, the lines commented and to be removed as well as the newly inserted lines of code are highlighted in bold.

Listing 5-4. *Source Code for the Updated* OrderSessionBean *Bean*

```
package ejbjpa.ejb;
import java.io.Serializable;
import javax.ejb.EJBException;
import javax.ejb.Stateless;
import javax.persistence.EntityManager;
import javax.persistence.EntityManagerFactory;
import javax.persistence.PersistenceUnit;
```

```
import ejbjpa.entities.*;
@Stateless
public class OrderSessionBean implements OrderSession {
    @PersistenceUnit(unitName = "order-pu")
    private EntityManagerFactory emf;
    public void placeOrder(Integer pono,
                           Integer cust_id,
                           Integer units,
                           String book_id)
    {
        try {
            EntityManager em = emf.createEntityManager();
            // Book book = (Book) em.find(Book.class, book_id);
            Order order = new Order();
            order.setPono(pono);
            order.setCust_id(cust_id);
            order.setBook_id(book_id);
            order.setUnits(units);
            // book.setQuantity(book.getQuantity()-units);
            //order.setBook(book);
            em.persist(order);
        } catch (Exception e) {
            throw new EJBException(e.getMessage());
        }
    }
}
```

Since the Book entity has been removed from the application, you comment all the lines of code where there are references to it. Instead, you insert the code line that sets the book_id field of the order instance to the appropriate value.

Once all these changes are applied to the application components, you can recompile these components and then package and deploy them as discussed in extensive detail in Chapter 3. After that, you can test the updated sample application.

If you recall from the examples discussed in the preceding chapter, you can launch the sample application with the appclient command. In this particular example, assuming you packed the client application archive and the EJB module archive within processing-todata. jar, you might issue appclient like this:

```
appclient -client processing-todata.jar 5 1 1 1430209631
```

The previous should insert a new record in the orders table and update the record whose primary key is 1430209631 in the books table, provided that the value of the quantity field in the books's record is not less than or equal to 1. In particular, the orders table should have a new record whose pono is 5, cust_id is 1, units is 1, and book_id is 1430209631. Respectively, the value of the quantity field in the corresponding record in the books table will be reduced by 1.

> ■**Note** When issuing the previous command, you may bump into an error occurring because the value of the `quantity` field in the `books`'s record whose primary key is 1430209631 is less than 1. After you performed the `INSERT` command shown in Listing 4-21 in Chapter 4, you should have that field set to 1. However, if you launched the sample discussed in the section "Planning for Security" in that chapter later, the value of the `quantity` field was reduced to 0. To solve this problem, you have to update the `books`'s record whose primary key is 1430209631, setting the `quantity` field to an integer that is equal to or more than 1. For example, setting it to 10 would be a good idea.

As you can see, the sample application discussed in this section performs the same task as the sample discussed in the section "Planning for Security" in the preceding chapter. From the developer's standpoint, though, these applications are different in how much business logic is implemented in the database tier. Obviously, moving some business logic of your application into the underlying database helps you design more intuitive and simple persistence and business logic tiers. The good news is that you have a lot of flexibility—you can decide what you want to be implemented in the database tier and what you want to be implemented in the other tiers of your application.

Moving Business Logic Into Stored Procedures

Now that you have seen how some business logic of your application can be passed from the business logic and persistence tiers down to the database tier, you might want to go one step further and implement some business logic in the database within stored routines, which could be invoked from within the triggers fired in response to the events triggered from within the persistence tier. This approach greatly enhances your ability to utilize features of the underlying database when implementing the business logic of your application.

A stored routine or subprogram is a named programming block stored in the database that can be invoked with a set of parameters. When implementing a stored routine, you have two choices: a stored procedure or a function. As you might guess, a procedure differs from a function in that the latter returns a computed value, while the former simply performs a specific task.

> ■**Note** It is interesting to note that both stored procedures and stored functions are usually called *stored procedures*.

Figure 5-5 gives a graphical representation of the structure of an application that utilizes stored procedures in the database tier.

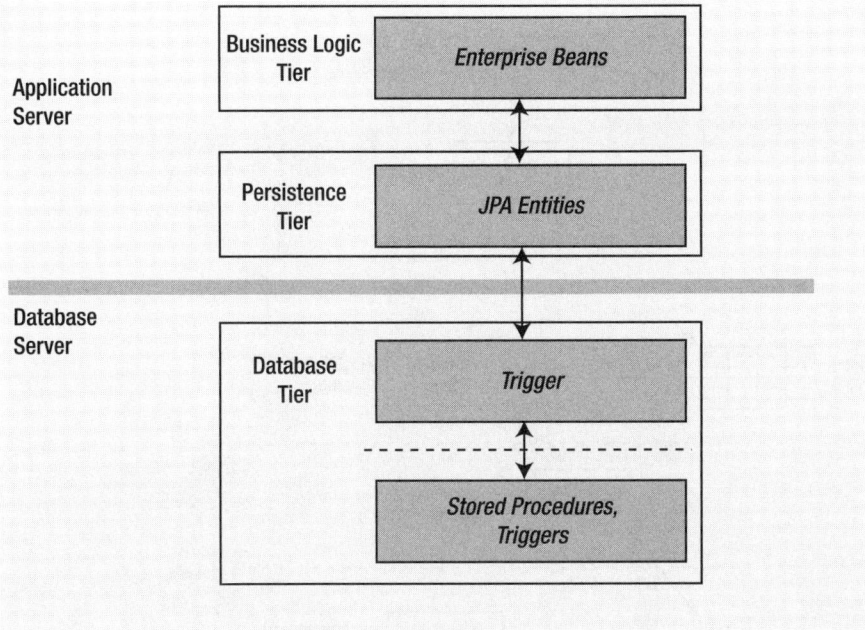

Figure 5-5. *A graphical illustration of how business logic of your application might be divided among application tiers and components*

According to the diagram, stored procedures can be called from within triggers rather than directly from within the persistence tier of the application. This needs a little additional explanation. As you've learned from the examples discussed in this book so far, JPA entities are mapped to specific database tables or views (but not stored procedures) so that you can access and/or manipulate database data from within your Java code. So, when you, for example, persist an instance of an entity to the corresponding database table, you make, among other things, the database server fire an insert trigger, if any, defined on that table. When fired, the trigger in turn may invoke a stored procedure or procedures. In practice, though, you have more options. For example, you may issue a native SQL query from within a business method of an enterprise bean, directly invoking a stored procedure. You will see an example of how you might do this in the "Planning Applications Invoking Stored Procedures Directly from Within the Business Logic Tier" section later in this chapter.

To better organize the logic implemented within a set of triggers and stored procedures, you might divide the database tier into sublayers, thus achieving a good level of reusability, flexibility, and scalability.

Returning to the sample discussed in the preceding section, you might, for example, create the updateBooks stored procedure, which will be called from within the neworder BEFORE INSERT trigger and issue the UPDATE statement against the books table, rather than issuing that statement directly from within the neworder trigger.

Figure 5-6 diagrammatically illustrates the interactions between the components in the updated sample application.

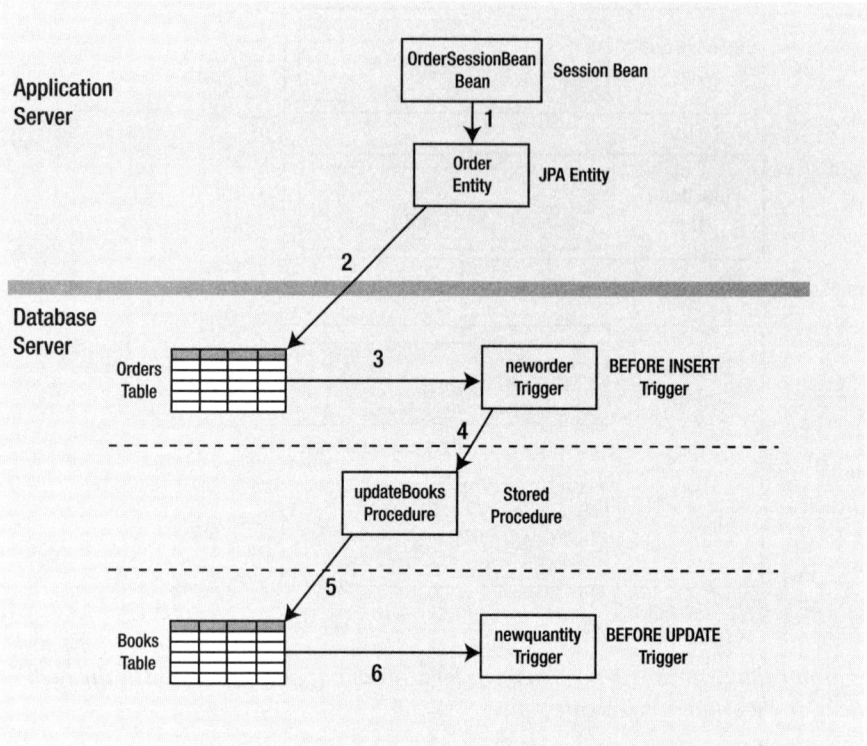

Figure 5-6. *A graphical depiction of the actions performed by the sample application*

Here is the explanation of the steps depicted in the figure:

1. The placeOrder business method of the OrderSessionBean bean creates an instance of the Order entity and then sets its fields to the appropriate values.

2. The JPA provider persists the Order entity, trying to insert a new record into the orders table.

3. The database server fires the neworder BEFORE INSERT trigger before inserting the record into the orders table.

4. The neworder trigger invokes the updateBooks stored procedure.

5. The updateBooks stored procedure tries to update the specified record in the books table by issuing the UPDATE statement.

6. The database server fires the newquantity BEFORE UPDATE trigger before updating the record in the books table.

Returning to the figure, you may notice that this time the database tier is logically divided into three sublayers, thus providing a better level of flexibility. Note that the UPDATE against the books table is not issued directly from within the neworder BEFORE INSERT trigger anymore. What this means in practice is that you won't need to change the upper database tier's sublayer that is interacting with the persistence tier if, for example, you want to change the condition that is handled now in the newquantity BEFORE UPDATE trigger belonging to the bottom sublayer of the database tier. In that case, you most likely will need to change only the middle and bottom sublayers.

It is a good idea to keep the trigger code as simple as possible by implementing business logic with separated stored procedures that will be invoked from within the trigger.

In this particular example, the middle sublayer of the database tier contains only one database object: the updateBooks stored procedure, which will be invoked from within the neworder BEFORE INSERT trigger. The only statement the updateBooks procedure issues is the UPDATE issued against the books table. The procedure takes two input parameters: the book_id identifying the record in the books table to be updated and the units representing the number by which the quantity field in the record being updated must be reduced.

Listing 5-5 shows how you would create the updateBooks stored procedure in MySQL.

Listing 5-5. *Creating the* updateBooks *Stored Procedure in MySQL, Which Will Be Called from Within the* neworder *Trigger Defined in Listing 5-6*

```
delimiter //
CREATE PROCEDURE updateBooks (IN book_id VARCHAR(20), IN units INT)
BEGIN
UPDATE books
 SET quantity = quantity - units
 WHERE isbn = book_id;
END;
//
delimiter ;
```

Now, you need to modify the neworder BEFORE INSERT trigger originally created as shown in Listing 5-1. First you need to drop the original version of the trigger and then create the updated one, as shown in Listing 5-6.

Listing 5-6. *Updating the* neworder BEFORE INSERT *Trigger in MySQL Originally Created in Listing 5-1*

```
DROP TRIGGER neworder;

delimiter //
CREATE TRIGGER neworder
BEFORE INSERT ON orders
FOR EACH ROW
BEGIN
 CALL updateBooks (NEW.book_id, NEW.units);
END;
//
delimiter ;
```

As you can see, the only thing the neworder trigger does is to call the updateBooks stored procedure, passing as parameters the ID of the book record to be updated and the number by which to reduce the quantity of the book.

Now, let's look at how you can create the updateBooks stored procedure in Oracle. Listing 5-7 shows the statement you should issue.

Listing 5-7. *Creating the* updateBooks *Stored Procedure in Oracle, Which Will Be Called from Within the* neworder *Trigger Defined in Listing 5-8*

```
CREATE OR REPLACE PROCEDURE updateBooks (book_id IN VARCHAR2, units IN NUMBER) AS
BEGIN
UPDATE books
 SET quantity = quantity - units
 WHERE isbn = book_id;
END;
/
```

As Listing 5-8 shows, in the case of Oracle you don't have to explicitly drop the original version of the neworder trigger before creating the updated version of it. Instead, you use the CREATE TRIGGER statement with the OR REPLACE clause.

Listing 5-8. *Updating the* neworder BEFORE INSERT *Trigger in Oracle Originally Created As Shown in Listing 5-2*

```
CREATE OR REPLACE TRIGGER neworder
BEFORE INSERT ON orders
FOR EACH ROW
BEGIN
 updateBooks (:NEW.book_id, :NEW.units);
END;
/
```

With that done, you can test the updated application. It is important to note that all the changes made in the database tier in this section do not require you to change anything in the other application layers. So, you can issue the appclient command in the way you did in the "Moving Business Logic Into Triggers" section. Don't forget to increase the ID of the order being inserted to avoid a unique key constraint violation:

```
appclient -client processing-todata.jar 6 1 1 1430209631
```

Just like in the preceding example, the previous should result in inserting a new record into the orders table and reducing the value of the quantity field in the corresponding record in the books table by 1.

Thinking of Reusability

As you no doubt have realized, from the user's standpoint, there is no difference between the applications discussed in this chapter and the application discussed in the "Transaction Considerations" section in the preceding chapter. So, you may be wondering what benefits moving the business logic into the database tier actually brings.

As mentioned earlier, implementing business logic inside the underlying database allows you to simplify the persistence and business logic tiers of your application. Moreover, moving data processing to the data lets you centralize control over business logic. You won't need to duplicate the same code in the other applications working with the same data and performing the same operations on it. For example, if you're going to need to develop another application dealing with the books table, which will automate the process of returning unsold book copies to the publisher, you could rely on the functionality provided by the updateBooks stored procedure and the newquantity trigger, rather than implementing this functionality in the business logic tier of that new application.

You might argue that some business logic implemented in the underlying database might be otherwise implemented within a reusable EJB module or modules, which might be easily utilized within newly created applications dealing with the same underlying data. But what if you want to have some applications implemented using different technologies, not EJB 3? It is fairly obvious that you would not be able to reuse that EJB module or modules if your new application was implemented, say, in PHP.

Figure 5-7 gives a conceptual depiction of how business logic of an application can be divided between the underlying database and Java EE application server or PHP/web server. It illustrates that the logic implemented inside the database can be reused by many applications built upon that database.

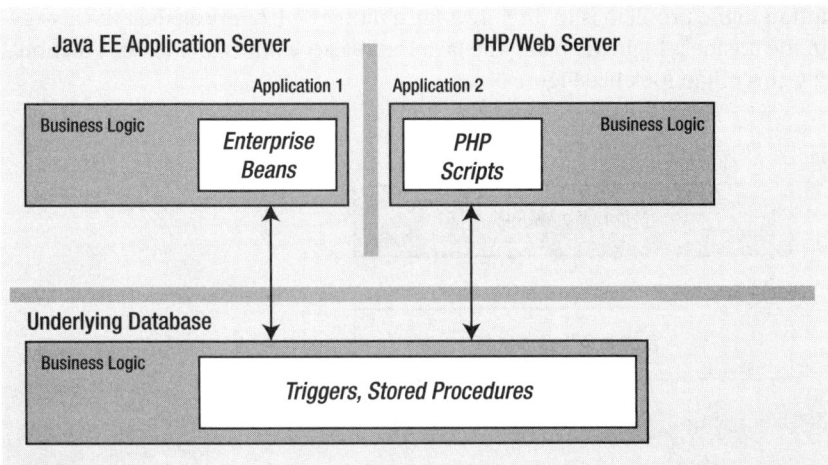

Figure 5-7. *Moving business logic to the data can improve reusability since the logic implemented inside the database can be reused by applications regardless of the technologies on which they are built.*

As you can see, implementing business logic inside the underlying database lets you improve reusability in a scalable and cost-effective way. Once you have a piece of logic sitting in the database, you don't need to reimplement it in the language you chose for building the business logic tier of your application. This is especially useful if you anticipate that logic sitting in the database will be reused by several applications, each of which may be built using different technologies and/or languages.

Knowing When You Might Want to Use Native SQL Queries

As you saw in the preceding sections, moving some business logic of your application into the underlying database simplifies the task of building the persistence and business logic tiers of the application. Moreover, a great thing about implementing business logic inside the database tier is that it lets you centralize control over that logic and improve reusability.

As usual, however, all good things come at a price. Now that you have simplified the Order entity because of removing the code defining a relationship with the Book entity, and now that you don't have the Book entity at all, how are you going to access the books table, if needed? For example, you might want your application to display information about the number of available book copies when a user opens the book's page (long before she might want to purchase a copy, placing an order). To obtain this information, you need to access the books table somehow.

This problem has more than one solution. One possible solution to the problem is to restore the Book entity, while not restoring the original Order entity (since you don't need to establish a relationship between these two entities again). In this particular example, this would be the optimal solution, since all you need here is the value of the quantity field of a certain record in the books table. This value could be easily obtained with the help of the getQuantity getter method of the Book entity. With JPA, you could obtain the required instance of the Book entity through either the entity manager, JPQL, or a native SQL query. All these approaches will be discussed in later chapters of this book.

Another solution to the problem is to directly issue a native SQL query against the books table from within the business logic tier using the Java Database Connectivity (JDBC) technology. Schematically, this might look like Figure 5-8.

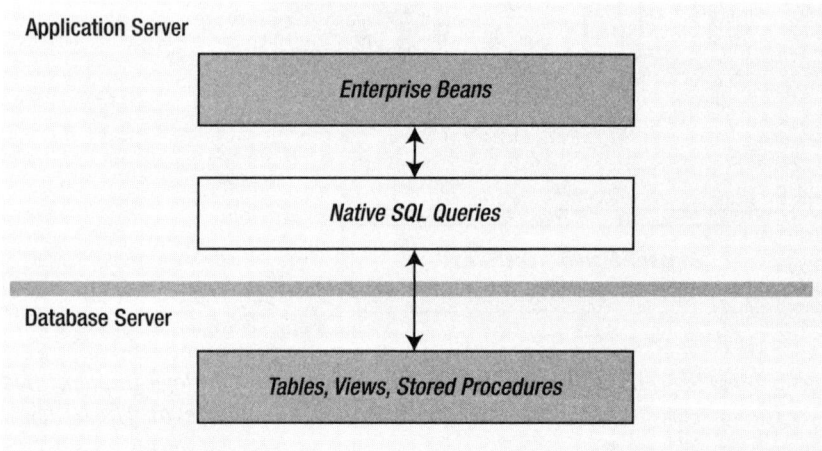

Figure 5-8. *You can access database objects directly from within the business logic tier with the help of the native SQL queries.*

As you can see in the figure, native SQL queries can be issued from within enterprise beans against database tables, views, or stored procedures.

In this particular example, you might create a separate enterprise bean and define a business method within it, which will query the books table with a SELECT query issued through the Persistence Provider. JDBC should be used only in cases where the application developer knows that the Persistence Provider will not be accessed within the same transaction or the transaction is managed by the container and a "managed" datasource is used.

Figure 5-9 identifies the application components involved in the operation of getting the number of copies of a book and depicts the interaction between them.

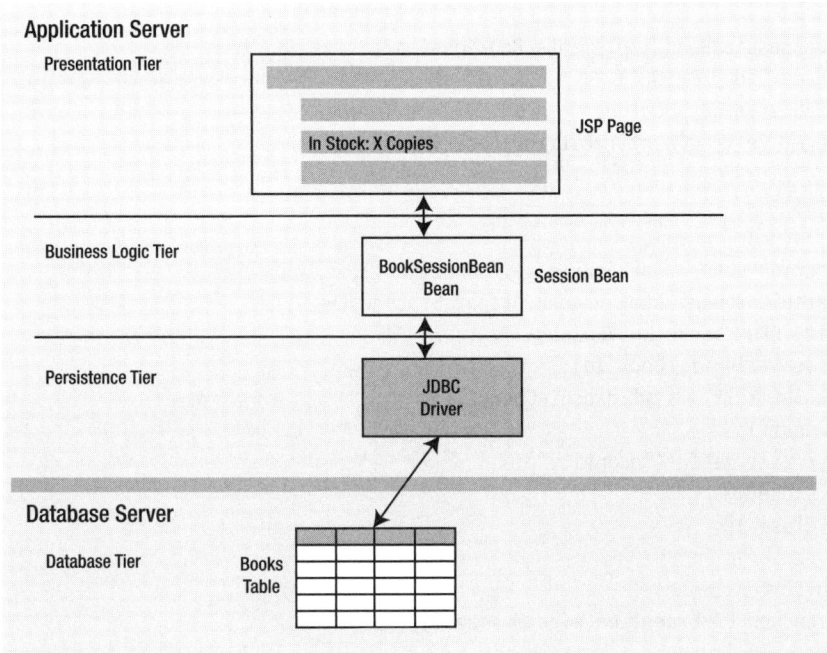

Figure 5-9. *A graphical depiction of how your application gets and then displays the number of available copies of a book when a user opens the page of that book*

As you might guess, the BookSessionBean bean will be invoked from within the JSP page describing a particular book each time that page is loaded.

Note In this particular example, you use the JDBC API from a session bean. In practice, though, you might use it from a JSP directly to access the underlying database, thus moving some business logic of your application to the presentation tier.

Listing 5-9 shows what the source code for the BookSessionBean bean might look like.

Listing 5-9. *Source Code for the* BookSessionBean *Bean Whose* gettingQuantity *Business Method Issues a Direct SQL Query Against the* books *Table Over JDBC*

```
package ejbjpa.ejb;
import java.io.Serializable;
import javax.ejb.EJBException;
import javax.ejb.Stateless;
import javax.annotation.Resource;
```

```
import javax.sql.DataSource;
import java.sql.*;

@Stateless
public class BookSessionBean implements BookSession {
    @Resource(name="jdbc/MySQL")
    private DataSource dataSource;
    public Integer gettingQuantity(String book_id)
    {
    Integer qnty;
        try {
           Connection conn = dataSource.getConnection();
           PreparedStatement stmt = conn.prepareStatement➥
("SELECT quantity FROM books WHERE isbn= ?");
           stmt.setString(1, book_id);
           ResultSet rslt = stmt.executeQuery();
           rslt.next();
           qnty = rslt.getInt("quantity");
           rslt.close();
           stmt.close();
           conn.close();
        } catch (Exception e) {
            throw new EJBException(e.getMessage());
        }
        return qnty;
    }
}
```

In this example, you use the @Resource annotation to inject the data source required to make a connection to the database. Then, you use standard JDBC APIs to retrieve the data of interest from the books table.

Planning Applications Invoking Stored Procedures Directly from Within the Business Logic Tier

You saw how to create a stored procedure in the "Moving Business Logic Into Stored Procedures" section earlier in this chapter. If you recall from that example, the stored procedure was designed to be invoked from within a BEFORE INSERT trigger. In some situations, however, you may need to invoke a stored procedure from within an enterprise bean directly.

Returning to the sample in the preceding section, you might wrap the select statement issued against the books table in a stored function implemented inside the database and then call this function from within the bean code, rather than issuing a direct query against the books table.

■**Note** In this particular example, the decision to move the SELECT statement issued against the books table does not seem to make a lot of sense. After all, you issue a query against a single table, retrieving a single number. However, this approach would make sense if, for example, you needed to calculate that number based on the data received from a set of different database objects. Furthermore, hiding SQL queries within stored procedures improves security since the application does not interact with the underlying tables directly.

To create such a function in MySQL, you might issue the CREATE FUNCTION statement as shown in Listing 5-10.

Listing 5-10. *Creating the* copiesInStock *Stored Function in MySQL*

```
delimiter //
CREATE FUNCTION copiesInStock (book_id VARCHAR(20)) RETURNS INT
BEGIN
 DECLARE qnty INT;
 SELECT quantity INTO qnty FROM books WHERE isbn = book_id;
 RETURN qnty;
END;
//
delimiter ;
```

To create the copiesInStock stored function in Oracle, you might issue the CREATE FUNCTION statement shown in Listing 5-11.

Listing 5-11. *Creating the* copiesInStock *Stored Function in Oracle*

```
CREATE FUNCTION copiesInStock (book_id VARCHAR2) RETURN NUMBER AS
 qnty NUMBER;
BEGIN
 SELECT quantity INTO qnty FROM books WHERE isbn = book_id;
RETURN qnty;
END;
/
```

For a quick test of the copiesInStock function, you might issue the following SELECT statement in both MySQL and Oracle:

```
SELECT copiesInStock('1430209631') as InStock FROM DUAL;
```

If everything is OK, this should produce output that looks like the following:

```
InStock
---------
4
```

Now you can modify the `BookSessionBean` bean shown in Listing 5-9 earlier. In fact, you will need to modify a single line in the code—the one containing the `SELECT` statement. The updated line of code should look like this:

```
PreparedStatement stmt = conn.prepareStatement("SELECT copiesInStock(?) ➡
as quantity FROM DUAL");
```

This is the only change you need to apply to the `BookSessionBean` bean so that it uses the newly created `copiesInStock` stored function.

Planning the Database Tier of the Sample Application

The examples discussed in the preceding sections should have given you some insight into approaches you can take when planning and designing the database tier of your application. Now, let's draw up a plan for developing the database tier of the sample application, which you will start building in the next chapter.

Planning the Structure of the Underlying Database

As explained in the preceding chapter, a visual representation of the components to be utilized within your application, as well as their interactions, is an important part of the planning process. In this section, you will look at the diagram representing database objects to be utilized within the database tier, and interactions between these objects, so that you should have no difficulty following along when it comes to the development.

The diagram includes only the key database objects. Later, you might want to draw up a more detailed diagram as you continue development.

Figure 5-10 gives a graphical representation of the structure of the underlying database, which will be discussed in further detail in the following chapter.

As you can see in the figure, the database tier of the sample application is logically divided into three sublayers. In the upper layer, you have the tables whose data will be directly manipulated from within the application persistence tier. The stored subprograms in the middle layer will be invoked from within the `neworder BEFORE INSERT` trigger. In the lower layer, you have the tables that will be accessed from within the stored subprograms rather than directly from within the persistence tier.

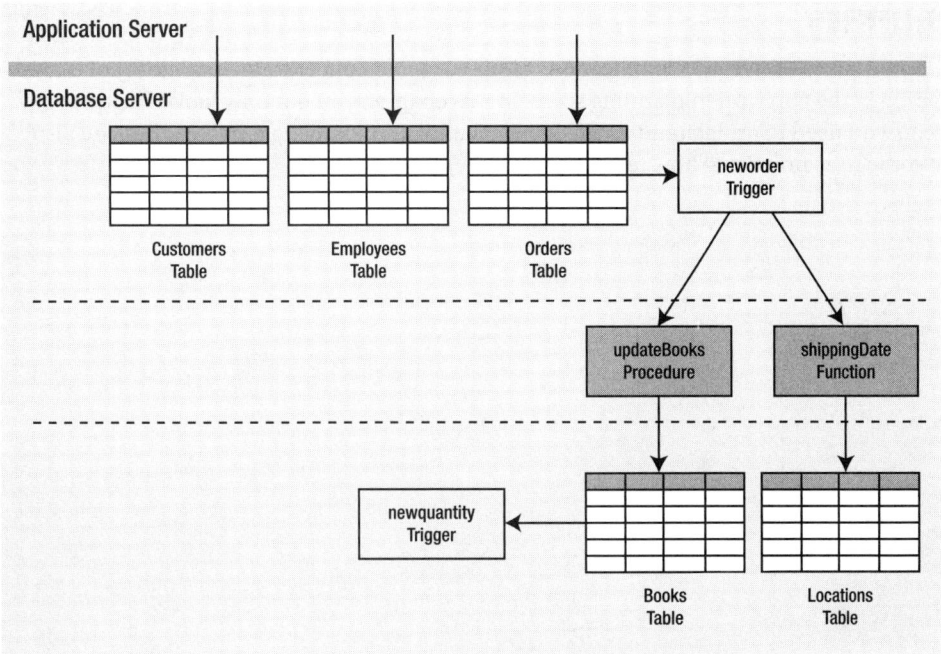

Figure 5-10. *A graphical representation of what components your database tier is comprised of and how these components interact with each other*

Planning the Steps to Building the Database Tier

Now that you have looked at a graphical representation of the structure of the underlying database, you need to think about the steps to be performed to implement the underlying database outlined in the figure. Here are the general steps required to build the underlying database:

1. Create the usr database schema that will be used as the container for the custom database objects being utilized within the sample application.

2. Build the following tables in the usr schema: Customers, Employees, Orders, Books, and Locations.

3. Build the updateBooks stored procedure and shippingDate stored function.

4. Define the neworder BEFORE INSERT trigger on the Orders table and the newquantity BEFORE UPDATE trigger on the Books table.

5. Populate the Customers, Employees, Books, and Locations database tables with data.

Summary

Developing successful Java EE applications requires you to concentrate on a variety of issues beginning in the application planning stage. In this chapter, you not only looked at some key concepts you need to understand to effectively plan your underlying database, but you also spent some time practicing how to put these concepts into action.

## PART 3

Building the Database Tier

CHAPTER 6

■ ■ ■

Implementing the Database Tier

In the preceding chapters, you learned a lot about how to plan and design a relational database to be used as the database tier within a Java EE application. The underlying database is an important part of most applications. Considering the underlying database as a black box used just to store and retrieve information limits your ability to take full advantage of the database features that could help you build a more efficient solution.

Now that you have a good understanding of how to build an underlying database with MySQL or Oracle, let's follow the steps outlined in the "Planning the Steps to Building the Database Tier" section of the preceding chapter and build the database tier for the sample application whose other tiers will be discussed in later chapters of the book. So, as you read this chapter, you will perform the following tasks:

- Create the database schema for the database objects being utilized within the sample application

- Create database tables to store application data

- Populate the database tables with initial data

- Build stored procedures implementing some business logic of the application

- Define triggers on the database tables

- Test the newly created underlying database

If you followed the examples discussed in this book so far, you should already have seen how to perform many of these tasks. In this chapter, however, you will perform them again in a consecutive manner, building the database tier for the sample application.

In case you want to look again at the particular database objects to be created and how these objects will communicate with each other, you might look at Figure 5-10 in the "Planning the Steps to Building the Database Tier" section in the previous chapter. Note, however, that Figure 5-10 gave you only the general shape of the database tier. In this chapter, you will create a few more objects than depicted in the figure.

Creating the Database Schema for the Sample Application

The first thing you typically have to do when building the underlying database for your application is to create the database schema through which the application will interact with that database. Although a real-world application may utilize database objects defined in more than one database schema, in this particular example, for the sake of simplicity, you will create all the underlying database objects being utilized by the application in a single schema.

Creating the Database Schema in MySQL

If you've already read the appendix and, in particular, the "How User Database Objects Are Organized in MySQL" section, you might recall that the task of creating a working area for a new project in MySQL is typically twofold. You first create a database (schema) on the database server, and then you create a database user to interact with the newly created database.

If you followed the examples discussed in the preceding chapters, you already should have the mydb database created, as well as the usr user account that is granted privileges to access and manipulate objects in that database. Of course, you might purge the mydb database, removing all the previously created objects, so that it can be used as the container for the database objects to be utilized within the sample you are working on now. In that case, however, you won't be able to return to the examples discussed in the preceding chapters and build upon database objects currently located in the mydb database. So, to avoid collisions, let's create a new database, say, dbsample. To do this, you have to connect to the MySQL server as root:

```
mysql -u root -p
Enter password: ****
```

Then, you can issue the CREATE DATABASE statement from the mysql prompt, as shown in Listing 6-1.

Listing 6-1. *Creating the* dbsample *Database*

```
CREATE DATABASE dbsample;
```

To make sure you have it, you might issue the SHOW DATABASES statements, as discussed in the "How User Database Objects Are Organized in MySQL" section in the appendix. As a result, among others, you should see the dbsample database in the list displayed.

The next step is to create the user account that will be used to access and manipulate database objects in the dbsample database. To do this, you can issue the statements shown in Listing 6-2.

Listing 6-2. *Creating the* usrsample *Account and Granting It the Privileges Required to Access and Manipulate Objects in the* dbsample *Database*

```
DROP USER 'usrsample'@'localhost';
GRANT CREATE, ALTER, DROP, SELECT, UPDATE, INSERT, DELETE, CREATE ROUTINE, TRIGGER
ON dbsample.*
TO 'usrsample'@'localhost'
IDENTIFIED BY 'pswd';
```

With that done, you can start creating the database objects in the dbsample database using the usrsample user account.

Creating the Database Schema in Oracle

Creating the usr database schema in Oracle is discussed in the "How User Database Objects Are Organized in Oracle" section in the appendix. As explained in that section, Oracle, unlike MySQL, automatically assigns a working area for a new user account. That said, once you have created a new user account and granted required privileges to it, you don't need to worry about the container for the database objects you want to create; Oracle implicitly has taken care of this for you.

Again, if you followed the Oracle-related examples in the preceding chapters, you should already have the usr schema created in your Oracle database, as shown in Listing A-3 in the appendix. However, to avoid collisions with the examples discussed in the preceding chapters, you need to create a new user schema. You can create it as shown in Listing 6-3.

Listing 6-3. *Creating the* usrsample *Account and Granting It the Required Privileges*

```
CONNECT /AS SYSDBA
CREATE USER usrsample IDENTIFIED BY pswd;
GRANT connect, resource TO usrsample;
```

To make sure you have it, you could, being connected as sysdba, issue the following query:

```
SELECT username FROM dba_users;
```

As a result, you should see usrsample in the output list.

It is important to note here that granting the resource and connect roles to a user gives only some basic privileges to that user, allowing them to connect to the database and then create and manipulate database objects of some types in its working area. For example, you will be able to create a table or even a stored procedure, when connected as the user who is granted the resource role. However, if, for example, you need to define a view, you first need to grant the CREATE VIEW privilege to that user.

Creating Database Tables to Store Application Data

Let's first determine which particular tables you need to create and how these tables will be related with each other. So, you might look at Figure 5-10 provided in Chapter 5. However, as mentioned earlier, that figure can give you only the general shape of the database tier being built here.

Figure 6-1 goes a bit further and illustrates the entire set of the tables to be created, as well as the relationships between those tables.

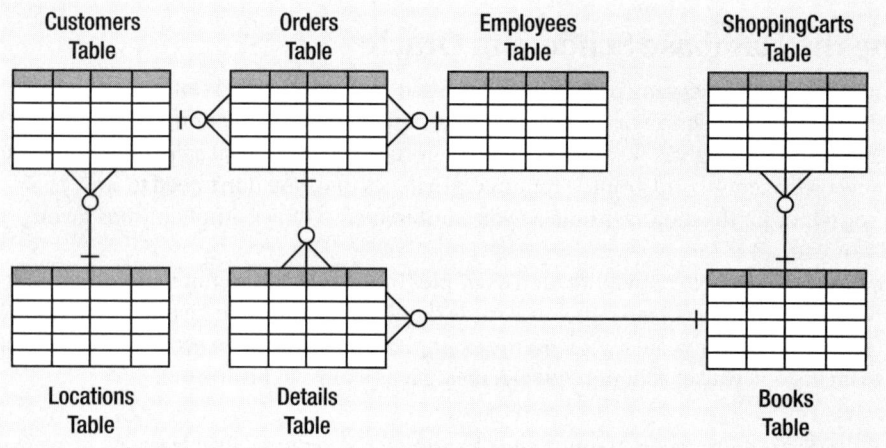

Figure 6-1. *Database tables that will be used within the sample application*

As you can see, we've added two more tables, namely, details and shoppingCarts, in order to make the application look more realistic. The details table will be used to store the line items of orders. It's common practice to store order items in a separate table, since a single order usually has more than one line item. The shoppingCarts table is designed to store the information from the shopping carts of users. Having put one or more books in the shopping cart, a user will be able to then place an order. In that case, the items in the shopping cart are moved from the shoppingCarts table to the details table.

The tables upon which you will build JPA entities are shown in the upper line of the diagram. The tables shown at the bottom will be accessed from within the database tier or business logic tier directly, not through JPA entities.

Building Database Tables in MySQL

This section walks you through the steps to create the tables shown in Figure 6-1, in MySQL. Although some of these tables may already exist in the mydb database because they were used in the previous examples, you have to re-create them in the newly created dbsample database so that they can be used in the sample application.

Before you can follow the SQL commands shown in Listing 6-4, you need to connect to the MySQL server through the MySQL command-line tool as the usrsample user:

```
mysql -u usrsample -p
Enter password: ****
```

Then you can perform the commands shown in the listing.

■**Tip** You can find the batch script shown in the listing in the downloadable archive accompanying this book, specifically, in the `ch6/tablesmysql.sql` file. This can save you lots of time if you use this file as an input parameter of the `mysql` program, as discussed in the "MySQL Command-Line Tool" section in the appendix.

Listing 6-4. *Creating the Tables That Will Be Used in the Sample, in MySQL*

```
USE usrsample;
DROP TABLE IF EXISTS details;
DROP TABLE IF EXISTS shoppingCarts;
DROP TABLE IF EXISTS orders;
DROP TABLE IF EXISTS customers;
DROP TABLE IF EXISTS locations;
DROP TABLE IF EXISTS employees;
DROP TABLE IF EXISTS books;

CREATE TABLE locations (
  loc_id INTEGER PRIMARY KEY,
  area VARCHAR(100)
)
ENGINE = InnoDB;

CREATE TABLE customers (
  cust_id INTEGER PRIMARY KEY,
  cust_name VARCHAR(100),
  loc_id INTEGER,
  email VARCHAR(100),
  phone VARCHAR(20),
  FOREIGN KEY(loc_id) REFERENCES locations(loc_id)
)
ENGINE = InnoDB;

CREATE TABLE employees(
 empno INTEGER PRIMARY KEY,
 firstname VARCHAR(30),
 lastname VARCHAR(30)
)
ENGINE = InnoDB;
```

```
CREATE TABLE books(
  isbn VARCHAR(20) PRIMARY KEY,
  title VARCHAR(150),
  author VARCHAR(150),
  quantity INTEGER,
  price NUMERIC(8,2)
)
ENGINE = InnoDB;

CREATE TABLE orders(
  pono INTEGER PRIMARY KEY,
  cust_id INTEGER,
  empno INTEGER,
  shipping_date DATE,
  delivery_estimate VARCHAR(20),
  FOREIGN KEY(cust_id) REFERENCES customers(cust_id),
  FOREIGN KEY(empno) REFERENCES employees(empno)
)
ENGINE = InnoDB;

CREATE TABLE details(
  ordno INTEGER,
  book_id VARCHAR(20),
  units INTEGER,
  unit_price NUMERIC(8,2),
  PRIMARY KEY(ordno, book_id),
  FOREIGN KEY(ordno) REFERENCES orders(pono),
  FOREIGN KEY(book_id) REFERENCES books(isbn)
)
ENGINE = InnoDB;

CREATE TABLE shoppingCarts(
  cart_id INTEGER,
  book_id VARCHAR(20),
  units INTEGER,
  unit_price NUMERIC(8,2),
  PRIMARY KEY(cart_id, book_id),
  FOREIGN KEY(book_id) REFERENCES books(isbn)
)
ENGINE = InnoDB;
```

If everything is OK, you should see no error messages.

Building Database Tables in Oracle

In this section, you will look at how to create the tables in Oracle. To do this, you first need to connect to the database through SQL*Plus as usrsample:

```
sqlplus usrsample/pswd
```

Then, you can run the batch query shown in Listing 6-5.

■**Tip** You can find the batch script shown here in the `ch6/tablesmysql.sql` file located in the download-able archive accompanying this book. To find out how you can run the entire batch script from within SQL*Plus, refer to the "Oracle SQL*Plus" section in the appendix.

Listing 6-5. *Creating the Tables That Will Be Used in the Sample, in Oracle*

```
DROP TABLE details;
DROP TABLE shoppingCarts;
DROP TABLE orders;
DROP TABLE customers;
DROP TABLE locations;
DROP TABLE employees;
DROP TABLE books;

CREATE TABLE locations (
  loc_id NUMBER PRIMARY KEY,
  area VARCHAR2(100)
);

CREATE TABLE customers (
  cust_id NUMBER PRIMARY KEY,
  cust_name VARCHAR2(100),
  loc_id NUMBER,
  email VARCHAR2(100),
  phone VARCHAR2(20),
  FOREIGN KEY(loc_id) REFERENCES locations(loc_id)
);

CREATE TABLE employees(
 empno NUMBER PRIMARY KEY,
 firstname VARCHAR2(30),
 lastname VARCHAR2(30)
);

CREATE TABLE books(
  isbn VARCHAR2(20) PRIMARY KEY,
  title VARCHAR2(150),
  author VARCHAR2(150),
  quantity NUMBER,
  price NUMBER(8,2)
);
```

```
CREATE TABLE orders(
  pono NUMBER PRIMARY KEY,
  cust_id NUMBER,
  empno NUMBER,
  shipping_date DATE,
  delivery_estimate VARCHAR2(20),
  FOREIGN KEY(cust_id) REFERENCES customers(cust_id),
  FOREIGN KEY(empno) REFERENCES employees(empno)
);

CREATE TABLE details(
  ordno NUMBER,
  book_id VARCHAR2(20),
  units NUMBER,
  unit_price NUMBER(8,2),
  PRIMARY KEY(ordno, book_id),
  FOREIGN KEY(ordno) REFERENCES orders(pono),
  FOREIGN KEY(book_id) REFERENCES books(isbn)
);

CREATE TABLE shoppingCarts(
  cart_id NUMBER,
  book_id VARCHAR2(20),
  units NUMBER,
  unit_price NUMBER(8,2),
  PRIMARY KEY(cart_id, book_id),
  FOREIGN KEY(book_id) REFERENCES books(isbn)
);
```

The DROP TABLE statements at the beginning of this script ensure that the old versions of tables being created, if any, are removed. However, if you run the script for the first time within an empty schema, then each DROP TABLE will generate the following error:

```
ERROR at line 1:
ORA-00942: table or view does not exist
```

The previous, though, doesn't prevent the execution of the subsequent queries in the batch. So, the tables will be created as described in the CREATE TABLE statements.

Populating the Tables with Initial Data

Now that you have the tables created, you can populate them with some data. Of course, you don't have to populate the orders, shoppingCarts, and details tables at this stage; these tables will be implicitly populated later through the application interface. But what you can populate with initial data right now are employees, customers, locations, and books. Listing 6-6 contains the INSERT statements you should perform to populate these tables for both Oracle and MySQL.

In MySQL, before performing the INSERT statements shown in the listing, you should perform the following statements:

```
USE dbsample;
START TRANSACTION;
```

Again, entering the statements in the listing as a batch query could save you a lot of time. To insert data into the tables created in MySQL, you can use the ch6/tablespopulatingmysql.sql file in the code archive. For Oracle, use the ch6/tablespopulatingoracle.sql file.

Listing 6-6. *Populating the Tables with Data*

```
INSERT INTO locations VALUES(1, 'US');
INSERT INTO locations VALUES(2, 'Canada');
INSERT INTO locations VALUES(3, 'Europe');
INSERT INTO locations VALUES(4, 'Other');

INSERT INTO customers VALUES(1, 'John Poplavski', 1, 'joshp@mail.com', ➥
 '(650)777-5665');
INSERT INTO customers VALUES(2, 'Paul Medica', 3, 'paulmed@mail.com', ➥
 '(029)2124-5540');

INSERT INTO employees VALUES(1, 'Serg', 'Oganovich');
INSERT INTO employees VALUES(2, 'Maya', 'Silver');

INSERT INTO books VALUES('1430209631', 'Beginning GlassFish TopLink: ➥
From Novice to Professional', 'Yuli Vasiliev', 10, 44.99);
INSERT INTO books VALUES('1590595300', 'Expert Oracle Database Architecture: ➥
9i and 10g Programming Techniques and Solutions', 'Thomas Kyte', 10, 49.99);

COMMIT;
```

The COMMIT statement you can see at the end makes the changes made by the INSERT statements permanent. Entering all the statements within a single transaction here ensures that either all the changes have been saved in all the tables or none of them has been saved in any table.

Building the Stored Subprograms

According to the plan outlined at the beginning of this chapter, the next step in building the underlying database is creating the stored subprograms. First, though, let's determine the list of the subprograms to be created. Table 6-1 summarizes these subprograms.

Table 6-1. *The Stored Subprograms to Be Utilized Within the Sample Application*

Subprogram Name	Subprogram Type	Description
updateBooks	Procedure	Reduces the number of available book copies stored in the books table by the number of copies specified in the order being placed. This procedure is automatically invoked upon inserting a new row into the details table.
shippingDate	Function	Calculates the shipping date for the order being placed. The function is automatically invoked upon inserting a new row into the orders table.
deliveryEstimate	Function	Calculates the estimate delivery date for the order being placed. Like shippingDate, this function is automatically invoked upon inserting a new row into the orders table.

As you can see, the stored functions shippingDate and deliveryEstimate outlined in the table will be invoked upon inserting a new row into the orders table. In particular, they will be invoked from within the BEFORE INSERT trigger defined on the orders table. In contrast, the updateBooks procedure will be invoked from within the BEFORE INSERT trigger defined on the details table.

Diagrammatically, this might look like Figure 6-2.

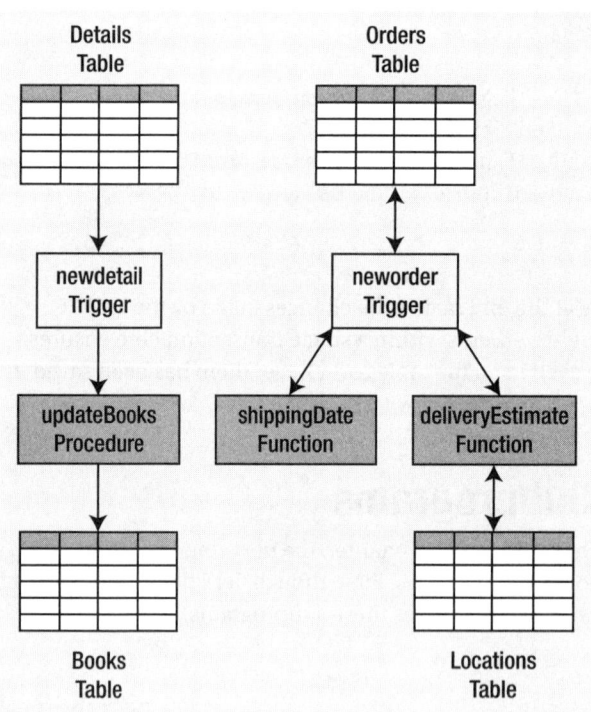

Figure 6-2. *Stored subprograms that will be called from within the* neworder *and* newdetail *BEFORE INSERT triggers that will be discussed in the "Defining the Triggers" section later in this chapter*

As you can see in the figure, the updateBooks procedure and deliveryEstimate function interact with the underlying tables, accessing the books and locations tables, respectively. In contrast, the shippingDate function does its job without accessing any table.

In the following two sections, you will look at how to implement these stored subprograms in both MySQL and Oracle.

Building the Stored Subprograms in MySQL

As mentioned, the updateBooks procedure is to reduce the number of available book copies stored in the books table by the number of copies specified in the item line record being inserted into the details table. Actually, this same procedure might be used when an order is being canceled and, therefore, its line items are being deleted. In these cases, however, the second parameter passed to the procedure must be a negative integer reflecting the number of copies specified in the line item record being deleted.

■Note In real-world applications, the items belonging to an order being canceled are not typically deleted from the details table immediately. Rather, they are simply marked as canceled in a certain column of the details table. In this particular example, however, for the sake of simplicity, the details table does not contain such a column.

Listing 6-7 shows the CREATE PROCEDURE statement you might issue, when connected as usrsample, to create the updateBooks procedure.

Listing 6-7. *Creating the* updateBooks *Stored Procedure in MySQL*

```
USE dbsample
delimiter //
CREATE PROCEDURE updateBooks (IN book_id VARCHAR(20), IN units INT)
BEGIN
UPDATE books
 SET quantity = quantity - units
 WHERE isbn = book_id;
END;
//
delimiter ;
```

As you can see, this is the same procedure you saw in the "Moving Business Logic Into Stored Procedures" section of the preceding chapter. This time, though, this procedure will be invoked from within the BEFORE INSERT trigger defined on the details table rather than the orders table.

Now let's move on to the shippingDate stored function. If you recall, this function doesn't access any table when calculating the shipping data of an order. What it actually does is determine the weekday of the current day, and if this is a weekend day, then it sets the shipping date to the next Monday; otherwise, the shipping date is set to the current date.

Listing 6-8 shows the CREATE FUNCTION statement you should issue to create the shippingDate stored function.

Listing 6-8. *Creating the* shippingDate *Stored Function in MySQL*

```
delimiter //
CREATE FUNCTION shippingDate() RETURNS DATE
BEGIN
 DECLARE dayno INT;
 DECLARE shpdate DATE;
 SELECT WEEKDAY(NOW()) INTO dayno;
 IF dayno < 5 THEN
 SELECT CURDATE() INTO shpdate;
 ELSEIF dayno = 5 THEN
  SELECT DATE_ADD(CURDATE(), INTERVAL 2 DAY) INTO shpdate;
 ELSEIF dayno = 6 THEN
  SELECT DATE_ADD(CURDATE(), INTERVAL 1 DAY) INTO shpdate;
 END IF;
 RETURN shpdate;
END;
//
delimiter ;
```

After performing this statement, you should have the shippingDate function created and stored in your database. As a quick test, you might issue the following statement:

```
SELECT shippingDate() FROM DUAL;
```

The output might look like this:

```
shippingDate();
-------------------
2008-03-17
```

Finally, you need to create the deliveryEstimate stored function, which will return the approximate number of business days required for delivering the order, based on the location of the recipient, as specified in the locations table. In a real application, a similar mechanism could be used to calculate the shipping fee of an order being placed.

Listing 6-9 shows you the statement you need to issue to create the deliveryEstimate function.

Listing 6-9. *Creating the* deliveryEstimate *Stored Function in MySQL*

```
delimiter //
CREATE FUNCTION deliveryEstimate(location_id INT) RETURNS VARCHAR(20)
BEGIN
 DECLARE estimate VARCHAR(20);
 DECLARE location VARCHAR(100);
 SELECT area INTO location FROM locations WHERE loc_id = location_id;
```

```
CASE
WHEN location = 'US' THEN
SET estimate = '2 business days';
WHEN location = 'Canada' THEN
SET estimate = '2-4 business days';
WHEN location = 'Europe' THEN
SET estimate = '4-6 business days';
ELSE
SET estimate = '8-12 business days';
END CASE;
RETURN estimate;
END;
//
delimiter ;
```

In a real-world situation, the logic implemented in this function would be much more complicated, of course. The fact is that the delivery estimate depends on the shipping option the customer chooses. Many online shops provide several shipping options to their customers. To keep things simple, though, this particular example doesn't deal with different shipping options.

Now to test the newly created deliveryEstimate stored function, you might issue the following statement:

```
SELECT deliveryEstimate(1) FROM DUAL;
```

This should produce the following output:

```
deliveryEstimate(1);
-------------------
2 business days
```

Building the Stored Subprograms in Oracle

Now let's look at how the stored subprograms discussed here might be created in Oracle. Let's start with the updateBooks stored procedure.

Listing 6-10 shows the CREATE OR REPLACE PROCEDURE statement you can issue from SQL*Plus, being connected as usrsample, to create the updateBooks procedure.

Listing 6-10. *Creating the* updateBooks *Stored Procedure in Oracle, Which Will Be Called from Within the* newdetail *Trigger Defined As Shown in Listing 5-8*

```
CREATE OR REPLACE PROCEDURE updateBooks (book_id IN VARCHAR2, units IN NUMBER) AS
BEGIN
UPDATE books
 SET quantity = quantity - units
 WHERE isbn = book_id;
END;
/
```

Next, to create the shippingDate stored function in Oracle, you might issue the CREATE OR REPLACE FUNCTION statement shown in Listing 6-11.

Listing 6-11. *Creating the* shippingDate *Stored Function in Oracle*

```
CREATE OR REPLACE FUNCTION shippingDate RETURN DATE IS
  dayno NUMBER;
  shpdate DATE;
 BEGIN
 SELECT TO_NUMBER(TO_CHAR(SYSDATE, 'D')) INTO dayno FROM DUAL;
 IF (dayno>1) AND (dayno<7) THEN
  SELECT SYSDATE INTO shpdate FROM DUAL;
 ELSE
  SELECT NEXT_DAY(SYSDATE, 'MONDAY') INTO shpdate FROM DUAL;
 END IF;
 RETURN shpdate;
END;
/
```

To test the newly created shippingDate function, you might issue the same query you used to test the MySQL version of the function, as discussed in the preceding section.

Next, you can move on and create the deliveryEstimate function returning the approximate number of business days required for delivering the order. Listing 6-12 shows you the statement you need to issue to create the deliveryEstimate function in Oracle.

Listing 6-12. *Creating the* deliveryEstimate *Stored Function in Oracle*

```
CREATE OR REPLACE FUNCTION deliveryEstimate(location_id NUMBER) RETURN VARCHAR2 AS
 estimate VARCHAR2(20);
 location VARCHAR2(100);
BEGIN
 SELECT area INTO location FROM locations WHERE loc_id = location_id;
 estimate :=
 CASE
 WHEN location = 'US' THEN
 '2 business days'
 WHEN location = 'Canada' THEN
  '2-4 business days'
 WHEN location = 'Europe' THEN
 '4-6 business days'
 ELSE
 '8-12 business days'
 END;
 RETURN estimate;
END;
/
```

After performing this statement, you might test the deliveryEstimate function as discussed in the preceding section.

Defining the Triggers

By now you should have all the stored subprograms created and stored in your database. Next you can create the code that will invoke these subprograms. If you recall from the diagram in Figure 6-2, they will be invoked from within the database tier, in particular, from within the triggers defined on the orders and details tables.

In the following two sections, you will look at how to create these triggers, as well as the BEFORE UPDATE trigger defined on the books table, which will generate an error upon trying to update the quantity field to a negative value.

Defining the Triggers in MySQL

Let's first create the newdetail BEFORE INSERT trigger on the details table. This trigger will be invoked each time a new record representing an order line item is inserted into the details table. The only action the trigger performs is to invoke the updateBooks stored procedure that reduces the value of the quantity field in the corresponding record of the books table by the number of units specified in the line item record being inserted. You should have the updateBooks stored procedure created as shown in Listing 6-7 earlier in this chapter.

Listing 6-13 shows the CREATE TRIGGER statement to be issued, being connected as the usrsample user via the MySQL command-line client.

Listing 6-13. *Creating the* BEFORE INSERT *Trigger on the* details *Table in MySQL*

```
delimiter //
CREATE TRIGGER newdetail
BEFORE INSERT ON details
FOR EACH ROW
BEGIN
 CALL updateBooks (NEW.book_id, NEW.units);
END;
//
delimiter ;
```

The next trigger you need to define is the BEFORE INSERT trigger on the orders table. This trigger will invoke the shippingDate and deliveryEstimate functions to determine and then set the shipping_date and delivery_estimate fields, respectively.

Listing 6-14 shows the statement for creating the trigger.

Listing 6-14. *Creating the* BEFORE INSERT *Trigger on the* orders *Table in MySQL*

```
delimiter //
CREATE TRIGGER neworder
BEFORE INSERT ON orders
FOR EACH ROW
BEGIN
 DECLARE location_id INTEGER;
 SELECT loc_id INTO location_id FROM customers WHERE cust_id = NEW.cust_id;
 IF NEW.shipping_date IS NULL THEN
  SET NEW.shipping_date = shippingDate();
```

```
 END IF;
 SET NEW.delivery_estimate = deliveryEstimate(location_id);
END;
//
delimiter ;
```

Finally, you need to define the BEFORE UPDATE trigger on the books table, which will cause an error if the new value of the quantity field is less than 0. The idea behind this trigger is to prevent committing the transaction that should include the operation of inserting a new order and the operations of inserting all its line items, if at least one line item of that order contains an inappropriate quantity of book copies being ordered.

Listing 6-15 shows how you might create this trigger in MySQL.

Listing 6-15. *Creating the* BEFORE UPDATE *Trigger on the* books *Table in MySQL*

```
delimiter //
CREATE TRIGGER newquantity BEFORE UPDATE ON books
FOR EACH ROW
BEGIN
 IF NEW.quantity<0 THEN
  INSERT INTO books VALUES();
 END IF;
END;
//
delimiter ;
```

The trick in this code is that the INSERT statement issued when the new quantity value is less than 0 always fails, generating an error that prevents not only the current update operation from being completed but also makes the database server roll back the entire transaction within which that update is happening. So, if you group all the operations inserting the order and its details into a single transaction, the entire transaction will be rolled back upon the failure of any insert operation. Otherwise, you can safely commit the transaction, making the changes made by the insert operations permanent.

Defining the Triggers in Oracle

This section walks you through the steps required to create the triggers in Oracle. Like in the preceding section, let's start with the newdetail BEFORE INSERT trigger, defining it on the details table.

Listing 6-16 shows the statement you might issue from SQL*Plus when connected as the usrsample user.

Listing 6-16. *Creating the* newdetail BEFORE INSERT *Trigger in Oracle*

```
CREATE OR REPLACE TRIGGER newdetail
BEFORE INSERT ON details
FOR EACH ROW
BEGIN
```

```
 updateBooks (:NEW.book_id, :NEW.units);
END;
/
```

Next, you create the `BEFORE INSERT` trigger on the `orders` table. Listing 6-17 shows how you could do that.

Listing 6-17. *Creating the* neworder `BEFORE INSERT` *Trigger on the* orders *Table in Oracle*

```
CREATE TRIGGER neworder
BEFORE INSERT ON orders
FOR EACH ROW
DECLARE
 location_id INTEGER;
BEGIN
 SELECT loc_id INTO location_id FROM customers WHERE cust_id = :NEW.cust_id;
 IF :NEW.shipping_date IS NULL THEN
  :NEW.shipping_date := shippingDate();
 END IF;
 :NEW.delivery_estimate := deliveryEstimate(location_id);
END;
/
```

Finally, you define the `BEFORE UPDATE` trigger on the `books` table, as shown in Listing 6-18.

Listing 6-18. *Creating the* `BEFORE UPDATE` *Trigger on the* books *Table in Oracle*

```
CREATE OR REPLACE TRIGGER newquantity
BEFORE INSERT OR UPDATE ON books
FOR EACH ROW
WHEN (new.quantity < 0)
BEGIN
 RAISE_APPLICATION_ERROR(-20001, 'Improper quantity');
END;
/
```

You just finished the underlying database that will be used within the sample application whose other layers will be discussed in the later chapters.

Testing the Underlying Database

Now that you have all the database objects in place, you might want to make sure the entire underlying database works as expected. Although you don't have the entire application built yet, you can issue a set of SQL statements against the database, simulating interactions between the application and the underlying database.

To perform such a test, you might accomplish the following steps:

1. Start a new transaction.

2. Insert a new record into the `orders` table.

3. Insert a new record into the `details` table, related to the record inserted in step 2.

4. Insert another new record into the `details` table, related to the record inserted in step 2.

5. Commit or roll back the transaction opened in step 1, depending on whether both steps 3 and 4 were successful.

These steps simulate the behavior of your application. It is important that the previous insert statements are issued within a single transaction. This allows you to roll back the changes made by all the inserts if at least one of them fails.

Figure 6-3 provides a graphical representation of these steps.

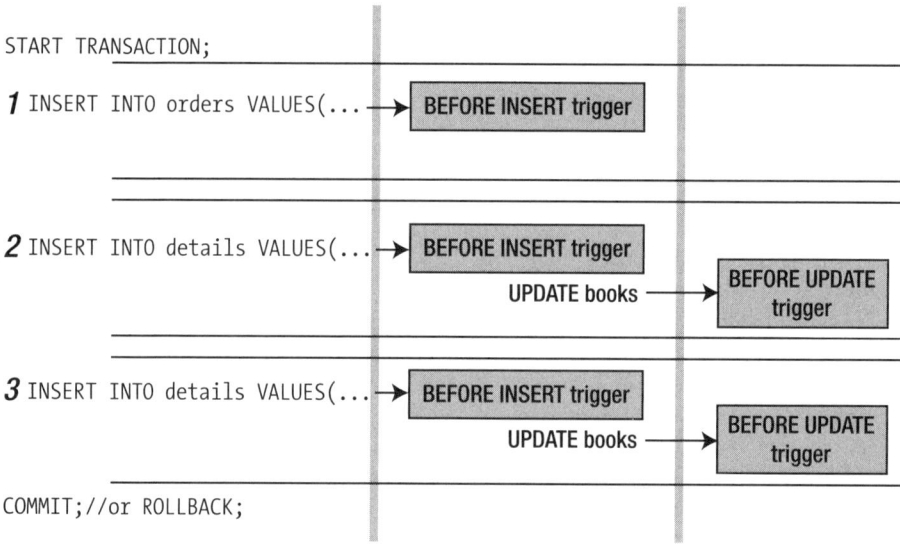

Figure 6-3. *Inserting a new order with its details within a single transaction*

Now let's look at the previous mechanism in action. For that, you will need to connect to your database server as the `usrsample` user and execute the statements discussed next.

In MySQL, you start with explicitly opening a transaction by issuing the following statement:

```
START TRANSACTION;
```

In Oracle, the transaction will be started implicitly, without you doing a thing.

Next, you might want to take a look at the amount of the book copies for each book stored in the `books` table. This can be done with the following statement:

```
SELECT isbn, quantity FROM books;
```

If you filled the books table with data as it was shown in Listing 6-6 earlier in this chapter, this query should produce the following output:

```
isbn       quantity
--------------------------------
1430209631 10
1590595300 10
```

Then, you can insert a new record into the orders table. Here is how you could do that:

```
INSERT INTO orders(pono, cust_id, empno) VALUES(1, 1, 1);
```

You might wonder why you specify only the first three fields when inserting the previous record. The fact is that the other two fields—namely, shipping_date and delivery_estimate— are filled implicitly with the shippingDate and deliveryEstimate functions, respectively, which are invoked from within the neworder BEFORE INSERT trigger.

To make sure that the new record has been successfully inserted, you might issue the following statement:

```
SELECT * FROM orders;
```

This should produce the following output:

```
pono cust_id empno shipping_date delivery_estimate
--------------------------------------------------------------------------
1    1       1     2008-03-17    2 business days
```

This illustrates that both the shippingDate and deliveryEstimate functions work as expected, as well as the neworder BEFORE INSERT trigger that invokes these stored functions.

Now that you have inserted a record in the orders table, you can modify the details table, inserting records representing line items of the newly inserted order. For example, you might insert the following record into the details table:

```
INSERT INTO details VALUES(1, '1430209631', 5, 44.99);
```

You should have no problem when executing this statement. Now, if you query the books table again:

```
SELECT isbn, quantity FROM books;
```

you should see the following output:

```
isbn       quantity
--------------------------------
1430209631 5
1590595300 10
```

As you can see, the number of available copies for the book with the ISBN 1430209631 was reduced by 5. That means the updateBooks stored procedure works fine, as well as the newdetail BEFORE INSERT trigger.

Finally, you need to test the newquantity BEFORE UPDATE trigger. To do this, you might issue the following statement:

```
INSERT INTO details VALUES(1, '1590595300', 15, 49.99);
```

This time, the third parameter representing the number of book copies being ordered is 15, which exceeds the available amount of book copies specified in the books table. So, this statement should fail, outputting an error generated by the newquantity trigger.

Since you failed to insert another record into the details table, you should roll back the changes made by the previous two insert operations. In particular, you should roll back the insert into the orders table and the preceding successful insert into the details table. You can do this with the following statement:

```
ROLLBACK;
```

With that done, you should check all the tables again:

```
SELECT * FROM orders;
```

This should give you the following output:

```
Empty set (0.00 sec)
```

When querying the details table:

```
SELECT * FROM details;
```

you should have the same result:

```
Empty set (0.00 sec)
```

Finally, when querying the books table:

```
SELECT isbn, quantity FROM books;
```

you should see the following output:

```
isbn        quantity
--------------------------------
1430209631  10
1590595300  10
```

This is what you started with. The same is true for the orders and details tables; when the transaction started, these tables were empty.

■**Note** In the previous example, you decided to roll back the transaction based on that the last insert statement has failed, manually entering the ROLLBACK statement. This is a test, however. For an application deployed within an application server, the rollback operation will be automatically performed upon the failure of any operation included into the transaction. This was discussed already in the "Transaction Considerations" section in Chapter 4 and will be discussed in more detail in Chapter 13.

Summary

Without long introductions, this chapter told you exactly what you needed to do to build the underlying database for the sample application. In particular, it walked you through the steps of building all the database objects required for the sample application to work.

In the next chapter, you will look at how to build the data source on your GlassFish application server to be used as the bridge between the underlying database created as discussed here and the other sample application's layers being discussed in the later chapters.

■■■
Setting Up the Data Source

By now you should have the underlying database created as discussed in the preceding chapters. Before you can use it as part of an enterprise application, you have to define the data source in your application server, through which the database will be available to the components deployed to the server.

If you recall, Chapter 2 had a tiny section named "Setting Up the Data Source." In that section, you looked at the steps required to create the data source to be used for establishing a connection with the Java DB database included with the GlassFish application server by default. This chapter provides a more detailed look at the problem of setting up the data source to be utilized by a Java EE application. In particular, you will look at the following:

- An overview of the Java Naming and Directory Interface (JNDI) naming service

- How to install a database driver on your GlassFish application server

- How to set up data sources in your GlassFish server for the underlying database implemented in both MySQL and Oracle

- How to perform a quick test of the newly created data source

As you can see, you will first look at JNDI and how the JNDI naming service is used in the Java EE platform to find and access data sources as well as other resources and components. Then, you will learn how to obtain and then install the database driver on your application server so that you can then define the data source required to connect to the underlying database.

After performing the steps provided in this chapter, you should have the data source to be utilized within the sample application, and its database tier should be already built as discussed in the preceding chapter.

Overview of JNDI

Now that you have the underlying database created, how can you make it available to the other layers of the application? The standard way to do this in the Java EE platform is via the JNDI naming service, which makes it possible for Java EE components to find and access required resources, such as Java Database Connectivity (JDBC) data sources. The JNDI name organizes components in a hierarchical tree structure, called a *JNDI tree* or *JNDI repository*, providing a mechanism to bind a component to a name.

Of course, JNDI is not solely used to deal with JDBC resources, providing applications with a means to connect to their underlying databases. A Java EE application also uses the JNDI feature to locate the components deployed to the application server, as well as the other resources utilized within these components, such as EJB beans and JMS resources. It's important to realize, however, that in EJB 3 you typically do not use JNDI lookups directly in order to obtain a reference to the resource of interest. Instead, you use dependency injection, which provides an abstraction over the JNDI repository.

■**Note** Through Admin Console, you can always look at the JNDI Tree Browsing list, which contains the JNDI names of the resource objects available on the application server. The JNDI Tree Browsing list is displayed in a single window, when you click the JNDI Browsing button in the Application Server dialog box (which you can access by selecting Common Tasks ➤ Application Server).

Figure 7-1 provides a conceptual view of a JNDI tree.

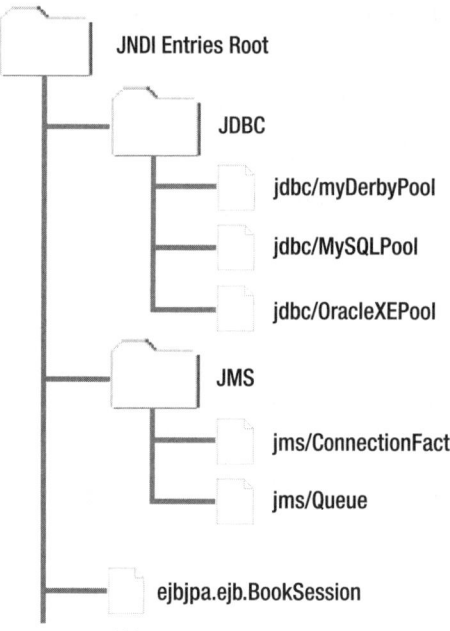

Figure 7-1. *An example of a JNDI tree*

Returning to the task of creating a data source, you start by creating a JDBC connection pool, which you then associate with a JDBC resource. Your application will obtain a database connection from the JDBC connection pool, locating the data source on the JNDI tree and then asking for a connection.

Figure 7-2 shows a simplified diagram of how a Java EE application interacts with its underlying database.

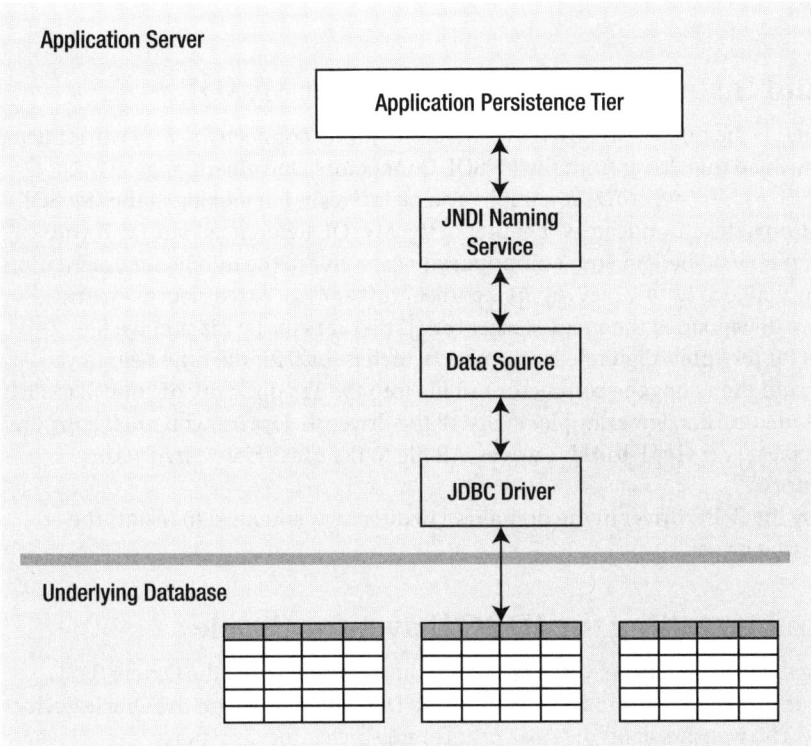

Figure 7-2. *A graphical depiction of the structure through which a Java EE application interacts with its underlying database*

As you can see in Figure 7-2, there are three components between the persistence tier of an application and its underlying database. The upper one, the JNDI naming service, is provided by the application server and, as stated earlier, is used to locate and access the data source associated with the underlying database. Before you can set up a data source, however, you must have the JDBC driver for your database installed in your domain in the application server.

The following section will discuss how to obtain and install JDBC drivers for MySQL and Oracle databases.

Installing a Database Driver on the Application Server

JDBC is a standard way for Java applications to connect and then interact with relational databases. The JDBC drivers implement the standard `java.sql` interfaces and can also implement vendor-specific interfaces.

In GlassFish, installing the JDBC driver for your database is very straightforward. All you need to do is copy the appropriate JDBC driver into the `lib` directory located within the root directory of your domain in the application server. Before you can do that, though, you have to obtain the driver.

Obtaining and Installing the JDBC Driver for MySQL

MySQL Connector/J is the official MySQL JDBC driver providing connectivity for Java applications. You can download this driver from the MySQL Connectors Downloads page at `http://dev.mysql.com/downloads/connector/`. You might also be interested in looking at the "MySQL Connector/J" section in the "Connectors" chapter of the MySQL Reference Manual. If you don't have this manual installed on your computer, you can refer to the online documentation for Connector/J available at `http://dev.mysql.com/doc/refman/5.0/en/connector-j.html`.

Once you have downloaded the `mysql-connector-java-[version]-.zip` archive file (`[version]` stands for the three-digit release number, which is 5.1.6 for the time being), you need to unpack it and then copy the connector JAR file into the `lib` directory of your GlassFish domain, as mentioned earlier. For example, to install the driver in `domain1`, you must copy the `mysql-connector-java-[version]-bin.jar` driver JAR file to the `glassfish_dir/domains/domain1/lib` directory.

After you copy the JDBC driver in the domain's `lib` directory, you need to restart the domain to enable that driver.

Obtaining and Installing the JDBC Driver for Oracle

If your underlying database is Oracle, you need to obtain and then install the Oracle JDBC Thin driver. You can download it from the JDBC Drivers Downloads page on the Oracle Technology Network (OTN) website, at `http://www.oracle.com/technology/software/tech/java/sqlj_jdbc/index.html`. On this page, you can choose the drivers for a certain version of the Oracle Database. Also, you might want to look at the documentation available from the SQLJ JDBC Documentation page at `http://www.oracle.com/technology/docs/tech/java/sqlj_jdbc/index.html`.

Once you have obtained the `ojdbc5.jar` file containing the classes for use with JDK 1.5 or `ojdbc6.jar` for use with JDK 1.6, you simply need to copy it into the `lib` directory of your GlassFish domain.

Just like with the MySQL driver, you need to restart the application server domain to enable the driver.

Setting Up and Configuring the Data Source

Now that you have the JDBC driver integrated with your application server and ready for use, you can move on and create the data source—actually a configuration defined upon that JDBC driver.

When creating a data source, you define a set of parameters to be used with the JDBC driver so that your application can interact with a certain underlying database in the way you want it. In particular, you need to specify the database server name, database name (URL), username, and password, as well as some other settings required to establish a connection and settings that must be in place for it to be used.

Defining a data source in the GlassFish application server implies creating the following two resources:

- JDBC connection pool, which will be associated with the JDBC resource created in the next step

- JDBC resource, which will be utilized by applications in order to establish a database connection with characteristics described in the associated connection pool

---

Note It is interesting to note that the settings you have to establish when creating a JDBC connection pool will depend on the database for which you define the pool. For example, when defining a connection pool for an Oracle database, you have to set the `ServiceName` attribute, which is not required when defining such a pool for another database.

The following sections walk you through the process of setting up the data sources via Admin Console for the underlying MySQL and Oracle databases created as discussed in the preceding chapter.

Setting Up the Data Source to Interact with MySQL

Assuming you have already integrated the MySQL JDBC driver with the application server as discussed in the "Obtaining and Installing the JDBC Driver for MySQL" section earlier, you can perform the following steps to create the JDBC connection pool that defines the aspects of a connection to your MySQL underlying database:

1. Launch the application server's Admin Console by pointing your browser to `http://localhost:4848/login.jsf`.

2. Log in to Admin Console as `admin`.

3. In Admin Console, go to the Resources/JDBC/Connection Pools page by following the corresponding link in the Common Tasks page located on the left side of Admin Console.

4. On the Resources/JDBC/Connection Pools page, click the New button to start the New JDBC Connection Pool Wizard.

5. In the first step of the New JDBC Connection Pool Wizard, set the general settings as follows:

   - Name: `mysqlpool`

   - Resource Type: `javax.sql.DataSource`

   - Database Vendor: `MySQL`

6. Click the Next button to move to the second screen of the wizard.

Figure 7-3 shows what the first screen of the New JDBC Connection Pool Wizard should look like, after you have defined the settings but before you click the Next button.

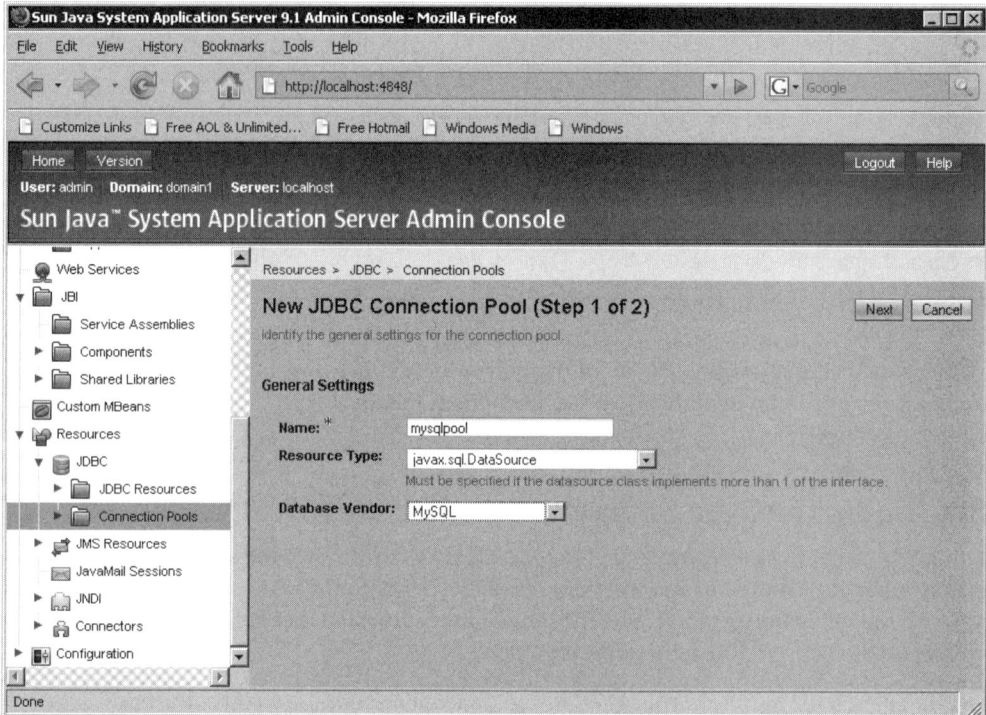

Figure 7-3. *The first screen of the New JDBC Connection Pool Wizard*

The second screen of the wizard displays lots of parameters. You should set some of them to appropriate values, while leaving the others with their default values. The settings are grouped into the following categories:

- General Settings

- Pool Settings

- Connection Validation

- Transaction

- Additional Properties

Note You could use the context help to learn more about settings displayed here. To invoke the Help window, just click the Help button in the top-right corner of the Admin Console window.

7. Now, scroll down to the Additional Properties table, and set up the following five parameters, setting them to appropriate values:

- databaseName: `dbsample`

- user: `usrsample`

- password: `pswd`

- serverName: `localhost`

- portNumber: `3306`

8. Finally, click the Finish button to complete the wizard. As a result, you should see the newly created `mysqlpool` entity in the table located on the Resources/JDBC/Connection Pools page.

Before proceeding any further, it's a good idea to verify the connection pool settings. Assuming that the database server is up and running properly, you can select the `mysqlpool` entity on the Resources/JDBC/Connection Pools page of Admin Console, and then click the Ping button. If everything is OK, the Ping Succeeded message should appear, as shown in Figure 7-4.

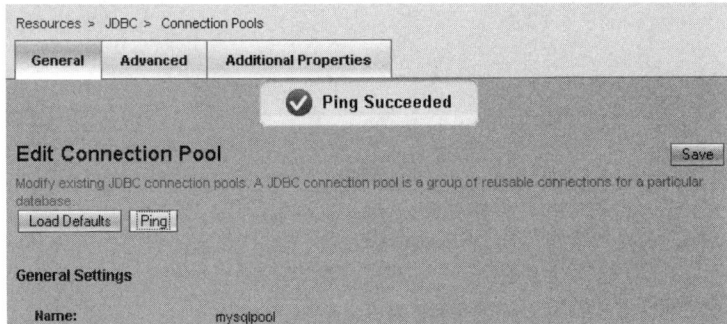

Figure 7-4. *Verifying the connection pool settings*

The next step in defining the data source through which the sample will interact with the underlying database is to create the JDBC resource based on the just-created connection pool. To accomplish this, you should perform these steps:

1. In Admin Console, move on to the Resources/JDBC/JDBC Resources page, and then click the New button.

2. In the New JNDI Resource page, set up the JDBC resource settings as shown here:

- JNDI Name: `jdbc/mysqlpool`

- Pool Name: `mysqlpool`

- Status: `Enabled`

3. Click OK to create the new JDBC resource.

Figure 7-5 shows what the New JDBC Resource page might look like before you click OK to create the resource.

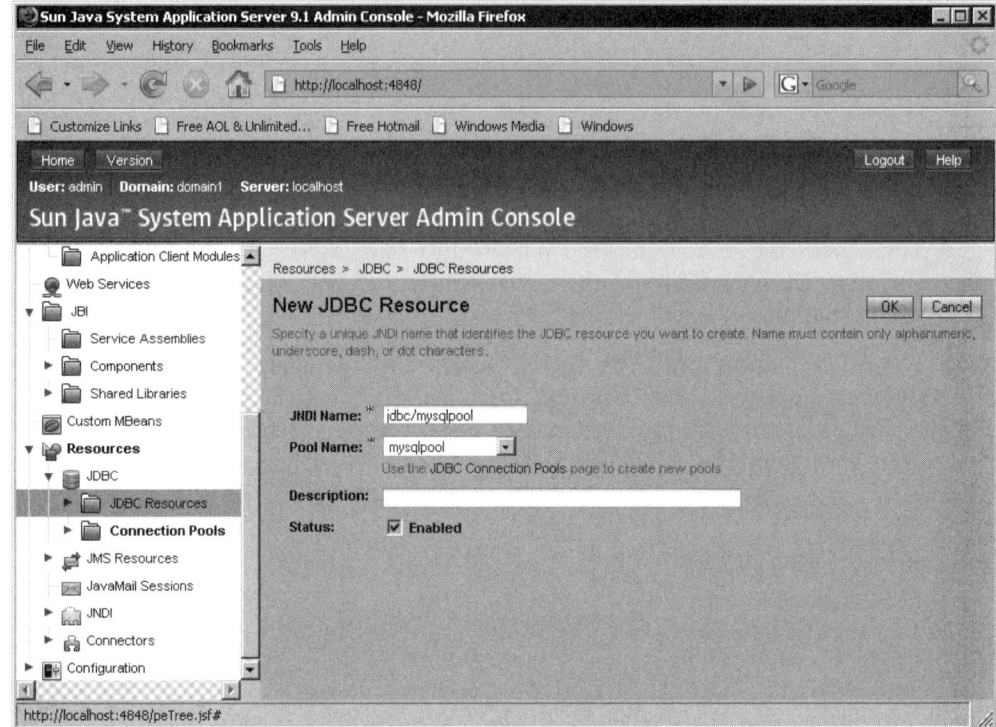

Figure 7-5. *Creating a new JDBC resource with Admin Console*

After you click OK on the New JDBC Resource page, you should see the jdbc/mysqlpool entity appear on the Resources/JDBC/JDBC Resources page. Now you can utilize the newly created JDBC resource in your applications, referring to it by its JNDI name: `jdbc/mysqlpool`. The first example illustrating it is provided in the "Performing a Quick Test of the Data Source" section later in this chapter.

Setting Up the Data Source to Interact with Oracle

If your underlying database is Oracle and you have installed the Oracle JDBC driver as discussed in the "Obtaining and Installing the JDBC Driver for Oracle" section earlier, you should follow the steps in this section to define the data source to be then used by the sample to interact with the underlying database.

First you have to create the JDBC connection pool defining the parameters of a connection to your Oracle database. This can be done as follows:

1. Launch the application server's Admin Console by pointing your browser to
   `http://localhost:4848/login.jsf`.

2. Log in to Admin Console as `admin`.

3. In Admin Console, move on to the Resources/JDBC/Connection Pools page by clicking the corresponding link in the Common Tasks page of Admin Console.

4. On the Resources/JDBC/Connection Pools page, click the New button to launch the New JDBC Connection Pool Wizard.

5. In the first step of the wizard, configure the general settings of the connection pool as follows:

   - Name: `oraclepool`

   - Resource Type: `javax.sql.DataSource`

   - Database Vendor: `Oracle`

6. Click Next to move on to the next screen of the wizard.

7. In the next step of the wizard, scroll down to the Additional Properties table, and make sure to set up the following settings:

   - ServiceName: `XE`

   - User: `usrsample`

   - Password: `pswd`

   - ServerName: `localhost`

   - PortNumber: `1521`

   - URL: `jdbc:oracle:thin:@localhost:1521:XE`

   The only parameter that needs some additional explanation here is `ServiceName`. The fact is that the Oracle JDBC Thin driver interacts with the database server via SQL*Net, which uses alias specified for a connection in the `[ORACLE_HOME]\NETWORK\ADMIN\ tnsnames.ora` configuration file. You have to check out this file to make sure to choose the right value for the `ServiceName` parameter.

8. Click Finish to complete the wizard. As a result, you should see the newly created `oraclepool` entity in the table located on the Resources/JDBC/Connection Pools page.

Now that you have created the JDBC connection pool whose settings characterize connections to be established to the underlying Oracle database, you need to create the JDBC resource associated with this connection pool. To do this, you should perform these steps:

1. In Admin Console, move on to the Resources/JDBC/JDBC Resources page, and then click the New button.

2. On the New JNDI Resource page, set up the JDBC resource settings as shown here:

   - JNDI Name: `jdbc/oraclepool`

   - Pool Name: `oraclepool`

   - Status: `Enabled`

3. Click OK to create the new JDBC resource.

With that done, the jdbc/mysqlpool entity should appear on the Resources/JDBC/JDBC Resources page. That means the newly created jdbc/mysqlpool JDBC resource is ready for use now.

Performing a Quick Test of the Data Source

Now that you have created the data source to be used with the sample application, you might want to perform a quick test of it.

In the sample, you will use the data source created in the preceding section to interact with the underlying database from within enterprise beans. However, you might use it from a servlet or a JSP page as well. So, in this section, you will test the data source with the help of a simple JSP page accessing the database data via that JDBC resource.

Listing 7-1 shows the source code for such a JSP page. You can save this JSP page in a single file, say, testPage.jsp, putting it into any empty directory in your file system.

Listing 7-1. *A Simple JSP Page for Testing a JDBC Resource*

```
<%@ taglib uri="http://java.sun.com/jsp/jstl/sql" prefix="sql" %>
<%@ taglib uri="http://java.sun.com/jsp/jstl/core" prefix="c" %>

<sql:query var="rslt" dataSource="jdbc/mysqlpool">
  select isbn, title, quantity, price from dbsample.books
</sql:query>
<html>
 <head>
   <title>JDBC Connection Test</title>
 </head>
 <body>
  <h1>Available books:</h1>
  <c:forEach var="book" items="${rslt.rows}">
    <b>Isbn:</b> ${book.isbn}<br/>
    <b>Title:</b> ${book.title}<br/>
    <b>Price:</b> $${book.price}<br/>
    <b>In stock:</b> ${book.quantity}<br/>
    <br/>
  </c:forEach>
 </body>
</html>
```

As you can see in the listing, the JSP page uses the jdbc/mysqlpool JDBC resource to connect to the underlying database and then access the books table, displaying the data stored in some fields of that table.

Now that you have the JSP page file, you have to create the deployment descriptors required to deploy that page to the application server.

Listing 7-2 shows what the source code for the web.xml deployment descriptor might look like. You need to store it in the WEB-INF subfolder of the project root directory (the one where you saved the testPage.jsp file shown in Listing 7-1).

Listing 7-2. web.xml *Deployment Descriptor Containing the* resource-ref *Element Declaring the Data Source Defined in the Application Server*

```
<?xml version="1.0" encoding="UTF-8"?>
<web-app xmlns="http://java.sun.com/xml/ns/javaee"
       xmlns:xsi="http://www.w3.org/2001/XMLSchema-instance"
       xsi:schemaLocation="http://java.sun.com/xml/ns/javaee
       http://java.sun.com/xml/ns/javaee/web-app_2_5.xsd" version="2.5">
  <welcome-file-list>
    <welcome-file>
            testPage.jsp
    </welcome-file>
  </welcome-file-list>
  <resource-ref>
      <res-ref-name>jdbc/mysqlpool</res-ref-name>
      <res-type>javax.sql.DataSource</res-type>
      <res-auth>Container</res-auth>
  </resource-ref>
</web-app>
```

Finally, you need to create the sun-web.xml runtime deployment descriptor containing the context root information for the web application being created.

Listing 7-3 shows the source code for the sun-web.xml runtime deployment descriptor. Like web.xml, you need to store it in the WEB-INF folder.

Listing 7-3. sun-web.xml *Runtime Deployment Descriptor*

```
<?xml version="1.0" encoding="UTF-8"?>

<!DOCTYPE sun-web-app PUBLIC "-//Sun Microsystems, Inc.// ➥
DTD Application Server 9.0 Servlet 2.5//EN" ➥
"http://www.sun.com/software/appserver/dtds/sun-web-app_2_5-0.dtd">
<sun-web-app error-url="">
  <context-root>/testPage</context-root>
</sun-web-app>
```

The next step is to package the application so that it can be deployed to the application server. If you recall from Chapter 2 where you built a similar simple web application, you should change directory to the root directory of your application and then issue the following command:

```
#jar cvf testdb.war.
```

This should create the WAR archive that can be deployed to the application server. As you might recall from the discussion in Chapter 2, you have more than one choice when it comes to deploying a web application or EJB module to GlassFish. You might, for example, use the GlassFish's asadmin tool, issuing the following command:

```
#asadmin deploy testdb.war
```

If the deployment process has been successful, you should see the message informing you about that.

Now you can launch the application. You can do this by pointing your browser to `http://localhost:8080/testPage/`. As a result, you should see the page similar to the one in Figure 7-6.

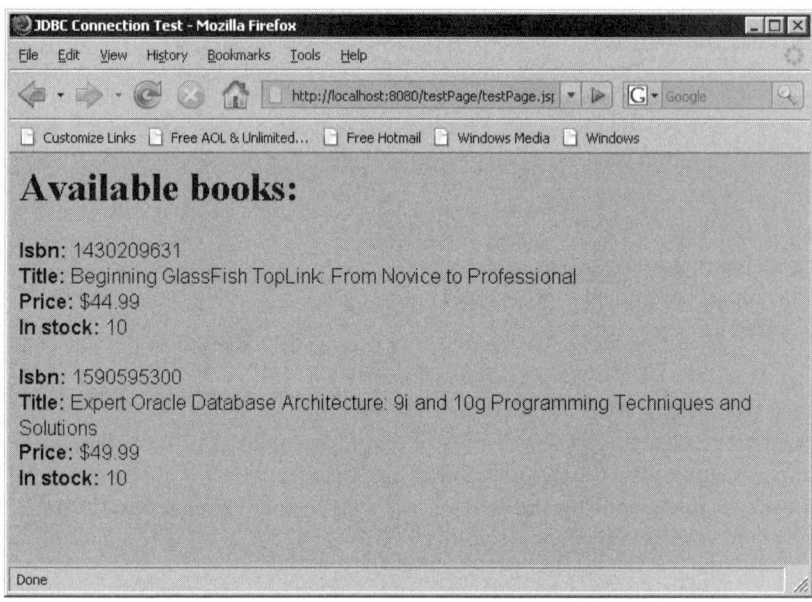

Figure 7-6. *Testing a JDBC connection through a JSP page*

You just tested the `jdbc/mysqlpool` JDBC resource created as discussed in the "Setting Up the Data Source to Interact with MySQL" section earlier. If you need to test `jdbc/mysqlpool` JDBC resource created in the "Setting Up the Data Source to Interact with Oracle" section, you have to change the `sql:query` tag in the JSP page to the following one:

```
<sql:query var="rslt" dataSource="jdbc/oraclepool">
  select isbn, title, quantity, price from books
</sql:query>
```

Then, you need to modify the `res-ref-name` tag in the `web.xml` deployment descriptor as follows:

```
    <res-ref-name>jdbc/oraclepool</res-ref-name>
```

With that done, you have to repackage the application archive so that it contains the updated files and then redeploy that archive. Now, if you launch the application by pointing your browser to `http://localhost:8080/testPage/`, the result page should look like the one shown in Figure 7-6 earlier.

Configuring the Settings of an Existing Data Source

The settings you define when creating a JDBC connection pool can be changed later if necessary. This is handy when the aspects of a connection to the underlying database change. In that case, you won't have to change the code—you will simply need to adjust the settings of the connection pool and then save the changes made.

To edit the settings of an existing connection pool via Admin Console, you need to the Resources/JDBC/Connection Pools page and then choose that connection pool from the list. As a result, a three-tab Edit Connection Pool Properties page should appear. You will most likely need to modify the settings specified on the Additional Properties tag, since it contains some important properties specific to the underlying database, such as the database name, username, and password.

Figure 7-7 shows what the Additional Properties tab of the Edit Connection Pool Properties page might look like.

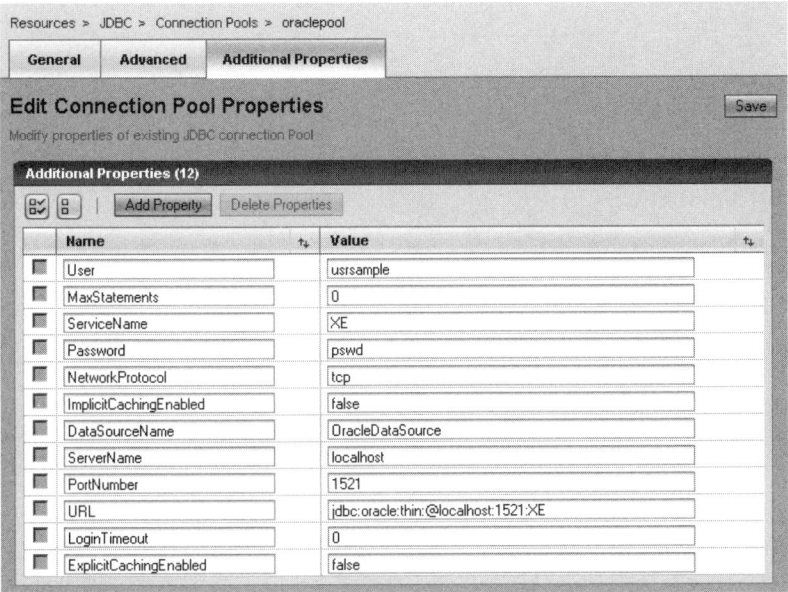

Figure 7-7. *Editing the connection pool properties*

On the Additional Properties tab, you can change one or more settings and then click the Save button to save the changes made. Also, you can add a new setting by clicking the Add Property button or delete one or more settings with the help of the Delete Properties button.

Summary

In this chapter, you looked at how to integrate the JDBC driver with the GlassFish application server and then created the data source upon that driver, defining the aspects of a connection to your underlying database.

Now you're all set to proceed to the next chapters, where you will learn how to build the other layers of the sample application discussed here.

## PART 4

Building the
Persistence Tier

## CHAPTER 8

Designing JPA Entities

Now that you have both the underlying database and the data source allowing the applications deployed to the application server to communicate with that database, you can move on and build the persistence tier, designing the JPA entities through which the sample will actually interact with the underlying database tables.

This chapter describes how to design JPA entities to be utilized within a Java EE application. In particular, over the course of the chapter, you will do the following:

- Create JPA entities that will be utilized within the sample application that you started building in Chapter 6

- Adjust the database tier to be appropriate for the persistence tier

- Perform a quick test of the newly created JPA entities

- Launch a NetBeans project for the sample application

By the time you're done, you should have the persistence tier that will be utilized within the sample application. In the next chapter, you will take a closer look at the object-relational mapping, which makes it possible for you to access and manipulate the underlying data from within enterprise beans. Continuing this theme, Chapters 10 and 11 will discuss how you can employ standard JPA mechanisms to access and manipulate JPA entities, thus accessing and modifying the underlying data via the sample application interface.

Creating JPA Entities Upon the Underlying Database Tables

If you recall from the "Creating Database Tables to Store Application Data" section in Chapter 6, the sample application will access the data stored in the following seven tables: customers, orders, employees, shoppingCarts, locations, details, and books. As stated, you should build JPA entities only upon the first four of these tables.

You might be wondering why you're building a JPA entity upon the orders table while not building it upon the details table. The fact is that there is another table for storing ordered items: shoppingCarts. When a user selects an item for purchasing, an appropriate record appears in the shoppingCarts table rather than in the details table. Then, if the user proceeds to the checkout and places the order, a new record is created in the orders table, and all the appropriate records in the shoppingCarts table are moved to the details table.

This approach makes it unnecessary for the application to utilize a Detail JPA entity, since moving the data from the shoppingCarts table to the details table can be performed at the database tier directly. For example, the following INSERT statement with a subquery might be issued from within the AFTER INSERT trigger defined on the orders table:

```
INSERT INTO details (ordno, book_id, units, unit_price)
    SELECT NEW.pono, book_id, units, unit_price FROM shoppingCarts
    WHERE cart_id=NEW.cust_id;
```

This statement might be followed by this one:

```
DELETE FROM shoppingCarts WHERE cart_id=NEW.cust_id;
```

Or, instead of the previous SQL DELETE statement issued from within the trigger, you might issue the JPQL DELETE statement from within an enterprise bean so that both of the previous statements are issued within the same transaction. The later section "Adjusting the Database Tier" discusses in detail what changes should be applied to the database tier so that it fits the persistence tier being created here.

As an alternative, you might still define and then use a Detail entity, thus making the application more independent of the business logic stored in the underlying database. In that case, however, there will be the additional overhead of making up the instances of the Detail entity on the application server side and then persisting them to the database. Furthermore, the main purpose here is to show you different ways in which the task of persisting details of an order might be implemented.

Diagramming the Persistence Tier

Returning to the entities to be built here, let's first look at the diagram, shown in Figure 8-1, that represents these entities and the relationships between them.

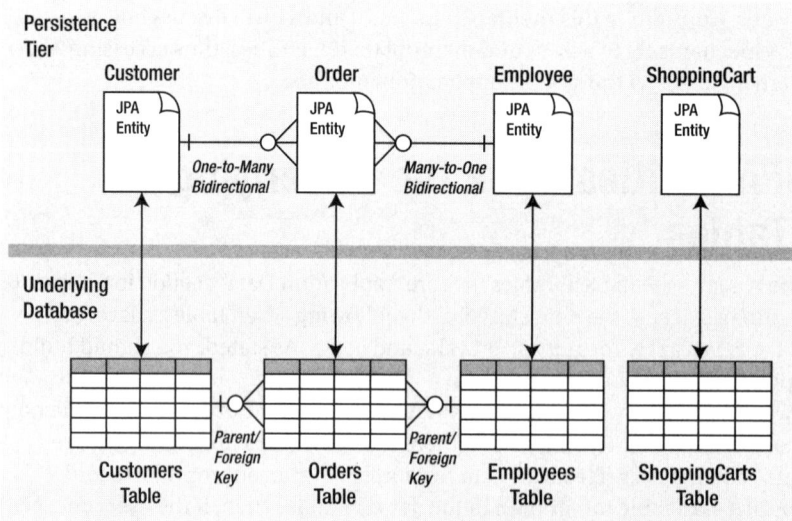

Figure 8-1. *A graphical representation of the entities to be built here and the relationships between them*

As you might notice in the figure, a parent/foreign key relationship established between the underlying tables turns into a bidirectional relationship between the corresponding JPA entities. Of course, that is not a requirement. You can still define no relationship or can define a unidirectional relationship when creating the Customer, Order, and Employee entities. In the case of defining no relationship between the entities, however, an instance of an entity cannot be used to find and then access a corresponding instance or instances of another entity.

If you define a unidirectional relationship, then only one side of the relationship knows about the other, but the opposite is not true. For example, if you define the Order entity so that it has a relationship field to the Customer entity but the latter has no field for the former, then you won't be able to navigate from an instance of the Customer entity to the corresponding instances of the Order entity while still being able to head in the opposite direction. In this particular example, you will define bidirectional relationships to have all options.

Creating the Entities

Now you need to create the JPA entities as depicted in Figure 8-1 earlier. Before moving on, though, you have to create a directory structure for the files of the sample application project. For now, you need to create at least the root directory for the project and the directory structure for the JPA entities. So, Figure 8-2 shows the structure you need to build.

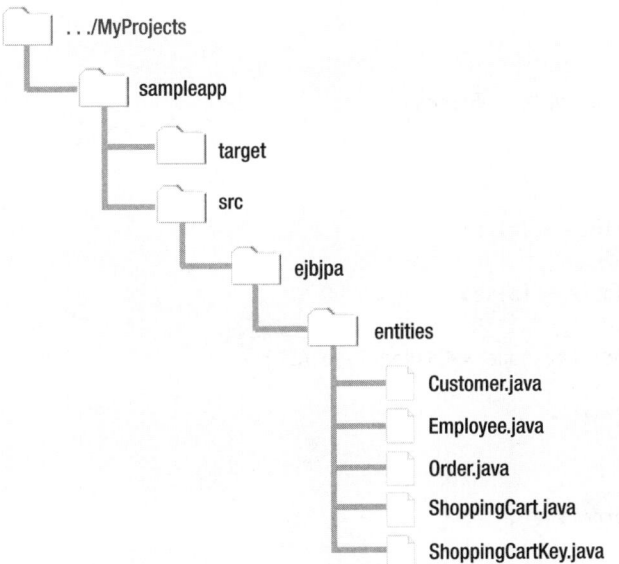

Figure 8-2. *The sample application directory structure for the JPA entities*

Thus, the first thing you need to do now is to create the sampleapp root application directory and then the subdirectories, as shown in Figure 8-2. Once you have created the directories, you can create the entities. Note that the target subdirectory contains nothing for now. The target subdirectory's contents will appear later, when you compile the entity sources.

To begin with, let's look at the Customer and Employee entities defined upon the customers and employees tables, respectively. Listing 8-1 shows what the source code for the Customer entity might look like. It is assumed that you'll save the Customer.java file in the sampleapp/ src/ejbjpa/entities directory, as well as the other three entity files and the ShoppingCartKey composite primary key class, which will be created in this section later.

Listing 8-1. *Source Code for the* Customer *Entity*

```java
package ejbjpa.entities;
import java.io.Serializable;
import javax.persistence.Column;
import javax.persistence.Entity;
import javax.persistence.Id;
import javax.persistence.Table;
import java.util.List;
import javax.persistence.CascadeType;
import javax.persistence.OneToMany;
@Entity
@Table(name = "CUSTOMERS")
public class Customer implements Serializable {
    @Id
    @Column(name = "CUST_ID")
    private Integer cust_id;
    @Column(name = "CUST_NAME", nullable = false)
    private String cust_name;
    @Column(name = "LOC_ID")
    private Integer loc_id;
    @Column(name = "EMAIL", nullable = false)
    private String email;
    @Column(name = "PHONE", nullable = false)
    private String phone;
    @OneToMany(mappedBy="customer", cascade = CascadeType.ALL)
    private List<Order> orders;
    public List<Order> getOrders(){
       return orders;
    }
    public void setOrders(List<Order> orders) {
        this.orders = orders;
    }
    public Customer() {
    }
    public Integer getCust_id() {
        return this.cust_id;
    }
    public void setCust_id(Integer cust_id) {
        this.cust_id = cust_id;
    }
    public String getCust_name() {
```

```
            return this.cust_name;
        }
    public void setCust_name(String cust_name) {
            this.cust_name = cust_name;
        }
    public Integer getLoc_id() {
            return this.loc_id;
        }
    public void setLoc_id(Integer loc_id) {
            this.loc_id = loc_id;
        }
    public String getEmail() {
            return this.email;
        }
    public void setEmail(String email) {
            this.email = email;
        }
    public String getPhone() {
            return this.phone;
        }
    public void setPhone(String phone) {
            this.phone = phone;
        }
}
```

Looking through the source code, you may notice that the Customer entity does not establish a relationship with a Location entity. This is despite that the customers table, as you might recall from Listing 6-4 in Chapter 6, has a foreign key referencing the primary key of the locations table. Note, however, that the underlying locations table will not have a corresponding entity and will be accessed only from within the database tier.

On the other hand, the Customer entity establishes a one-to-many relationship with the Order entity shown in Listing 8-3 later in the chapter. As you will see in Listing 8-3, the Order entity, in turn, establishes a many-to-one relationship with the Customer entity, which makes the relationship between these two entities bidirectional.

Now, let's move on to the Employee entity. Listing 8-2 shows what the source code for the Employee entity looks like.

Listing 8-2. *Source Code for the* Employee *Entity*

```
package ejbjpa.entities;
import java.io.Serializable;
import javax.persistence.Column;
import javax.persistence.Entity;
import javax.persistence.Id;
import javax.persistence.Table;
import java.util.List;
import javax.persistence.CascadeType;
import javax.persistence.OneToMany;
```

```java
@Entity
@Table(name = "EMPLOYEES")
public class Employee implements Serializable {
    @Id
    @Column(name = "EMPNO")
    private Integer empno;
    @Column(name = "FIRSTNAME", nullable = false)
    private String firstname;
    @Column(name = "LASTNAME", nullable = false)
    private String lastname;
    @OneToMany(mappedBy="employee", cascade = CascadeType.ALL)
    private List<Order> orders;
    public List<Order> getOrders(){
        return orders;
    }
    public void setOrders(List<Order> orders) {
        this.orders = orders;
    }
    public Employee() {
    }
    public Integer getEmpno() {
        return this.empno;
    }
    public void setEmpno(Integer empno) {
        this.empno = empno;
    }
    public String getFirstname() {
        return this.firstname;
    }
    public void setFirstname(String firstname) {
        this.firstname = firstname;
    }
    public String getLastname() {
        return this.lastname;
    }
    public void setLastname(String lastname) {
        this.lastname = lastname;
    }
}
```

You may notice that the Employee entity, like the Customer entity, establishes a one-to-many relationship with the Order entity that, in turn, establishes a many-to-one relationship with the Employee entity.

Listing 8-3 shows how you can define the Order entity.

Listing 8-3. *Source Code for the* Order *Entity*

```java
package ejbjpa.entities;
import java.io.Serializable;
import javax.persistence.Column;
import javax.persistence.Entity;
import javax.persistence.Id;
import javax.persistence.Table;
import javax.persistence.Temporal;
import static javax.persistence.TemporalType.DATE;
import javax.persistence.ManyToOne;
import javax.persistence.JoinColumn;
import java.util.Date;
@Entity
@Table(name = "ORDERS")
public class Order implements Serializable {
    @Id
    @Column(name = "PONO")
    private Integer pono;
    @Column(name = "SHIPPING_DATE", nullable = false)
    @Temporal(DATE)
    private Date shipping_date;
    @Column(name = "DELIVERY_ESTIMATE", nullable = false )
    private String delivery_estimate;
    @ManyToOne
    @JoinColumn(
      name="CUST_ID",
      referencedColumnName="CUST_ID")
    private Customer customer;
    @ManyToOne
    @JoinColumn(
      name="EMPNO",
      referencedColumnName="EMPNO")
    private Employee employee;
    public Order() {
    }
    public Customer getCustomer() {
        return this.customer;
    }
    public void setCustomer(Customer customer) {
        this.customer = customer;
    }
    public Employee getEmployee() {
        return this.employee;
    }
    public void setEmployee (Employee employee) {
        this.employee = employee;
    }
```

```
        public Integer getPono () {
            return this.pono;
        }
        public void setPono (Integer pono) {
            this.pono = pono;
        }
        public Date getShipping_date () {
            return this.shipping_date;
        }
        public void setShipping_date (Date shipping_date) {
            this.shipping_date = shipping_date;
        }
        public String getDelivery_estimate () {
            return this.delivery_estimate;
        }
        public void setDelivery_estimate (String delivery_estimate) {
            this.delivery_estimate = delivery_estimate;
        }
}
```

The Order entity establishes many-to-one relationships with the Customer and Employees entities defined, as shown in the preceding listings.

Finally, you have to create the ShoppingCart entity that establishes no relationship with the other entities. Before you can define this entity, however, you have to create the primary key class that will be mapped to the cart_id and book_id fields of the ShoppingCart entity. If you recall, these fields form the composite primary key in the underlying shoppingCarts table.

A composite primary key class must implement the java.io.Serializable interface and override the default equals and hasCode methods. Listing 8-4 shows what the source code for a ShoppingCartKey composite primary key class looks like.

Listing 8-4. *Source Code for the* ShoppingCartKey *Primary Key Class for the* ShoppingCart *Entity*

```
package ejbjpa.entities;
import java.io.Serializable;

public final class ShoppingCartKey implements Serializable {
    public Integer cart_id;
    public String book_id;
    public ShoppingCartKey() {}
    public ShoppingCartKey(Integer cart_id, String book_id) {
      this.cart_id = cart_id;
      this.book_id = book_id;
    }
    public boolean equals(Object obj) {
     if (this == obj) {
      return true;
     }
     if (obj == null) {
```

```
    return false;
   }
   if (!(obj instanceof ShoppingCartKey)) {
    return false;
   }
   ShoppingCartKey other = (ShoppingCartKey) obj;
   if (cart_id != null && other.cart_id!= null && ➥
      this.cart_id.equals(other.cart_id)) {
    return (book_id != null && other.book_id!= null && ➥
        this.book_id.equals(other.book_id));
   }
   return false;
   }
   public int hashCode() {
   if (cart_id!=null && book_id!=null) {
    return (cart_id.hashCode() ^ book_id.hashCode());
   }
   return 0;
  }
}
```

With that in place, you can move on and create the ShoppingCart entity, defining both the cart_id and book_is fields to be used as the composite primary key for the entity. Listing 8-5 shows how you can do this.

Listing 8-5. *Source Code for the* ShoppingCart *Entity*

```
package ejbjpa.entities;
import java.io.Serializable;
import javax.persistence.Column;
import javax.persistence.Entity;
import javax.persistence.Id;
import javax.persistence.IdClass;
import javax.persistence.Table;
@Entity
@Table(name = "SHOPPINGCARTS")
@IdClass(value = ejbjpa.entities.ShoppingCartKey.class)
public class ShoppingCart implements Serializable {
    @Id
    @Column(name = "CART_ID")
    private Integer cart_id;
    @Id
    @Column(name = "BOOK_ID")
    private String book_id;
    @Column(name = "UNITS", nullable = false)
    private Integer units;
    @Column(name = "UNIT_PRICE", nullable = false)
    private Double unit_price;
```

```
    public ShoppingCart() {
    }
    public Integer getCart_id() {
        return this.cart_id;
    }
    public void setCart_id(Integer cart_id) {
        this.cart_id = cart_id;
    }
    public String getBook_id() {
        return this.book_id;
    }
    public void setBook_id(String book_id) {
        this.book_id = book_id;
    }
    public Integer getUnits () {
        return this.units;
    }
    public void setUnits(Integer units) {
        this.units = units;
    }
    public Double getUnit_price() {
        return this.unit_price;
    }
    public void setUnit_price(Double unit_price) {
        this.unit_price = unit_price;
    }
}
```

It is interesting to note that the book_id column defined in the ShoppingCart entity as part of the composite primary key is also a foreign key column in the underlying shoppingCarts table. However, the books table does not have a corresponding entity to be used in this application.

Compiling the Entities

It's always a good idea to test the entities before you move on to creating the enterprise beans that will utilize those entities. Before you can perform any test of the JPA entities created in the preceding section, however, you need to make sure you can successfully compile them.

As you learned in the preceding chapters, you can use the javac command-line tool to compile your Java sources. To compile all the four entities discussed here at once, you first need to change the directory to sampleapp. Aside from the src/ejbjpa/entities directory containing the sources for the entities, the sampleapp directory must contain the empty target directory, as shown in Figure 8-2 earlier in this chapter. Then, you can issue the following command:

```
# javac -cp /glassfish_dir/lib/javaee.jar -d target src/ejbjpa/entities/*.java
```

Note that this command uses the `-cp` (classpath) parameter to explicitly specify the path to the Java EE library, namely, `javaee.jar`, located in the GlassFish's `lib` directory. This is not a requirement, of course, provided that you have this path included in the `CLASSPATH` environment variable. In that case, the previous command might be shortened to the following one:

```
# javac -d target src/ejbjpa/entities/*.java
```

If the compilation process has completed successfully, you should receive no error messages, and the four class files should appear in the generated `sampleapp/target/ejbjpa/entities` directory.

Adjusting the Database Tier

Now that you have created the JPA entities to be utilized within the sample, it is time to look back at the database tier and determine whether some adjustments are required. If you recall from the earlier "Creating JPA Entities Upon the Underlying Database Tables" section, since you did not define a `Detail` entity upon the underlying `details` table, you might want to implement the task of moving the data from the `shoppingCarts` table to the `details` table at the database tier. This task comes up each time a new record is inserted into the `orders` table. As mentioned, you might implement the `AFTER INSERT` trigger on the `orders` table to handle this task.

The following two sections discuss how to implement this trigger in MySQL and Oracle.

Adjusting the Database Tier Implemented with MySQL

To implement the `AFTER INSERT` trigger on the `orders` table in MySQL, you first have to connect to the database as the `usrsample` user via the MySQL command-line tool and then issue the `CREATE TRIGGER` statement shown in Listing 8-6.

Listing 8-6. *Creating the* `AFTER INSERT` *Trigger on the* `orders` *Table in MySQL*

```
delimiter //
use dbsample
CREATE TRIGGER afterinsertorder
AFTER INSERT ON orders
FOR EACH ROW
BEGIN
 INSERT INTO details (ordno, book_id, units, unit_price) SELECT NEW.pono, ➥
book_id, units, unit_price FROM shoppingCarts WHERE cart_id=NEW.cust_id;
 DELETE FROM shoppingCarts WHERE cart_id=NEW.cust_id;
END;
//
delimiter ;
```

As you can see, the trigger, when fired, issues two statements that perform two operations: inserting the data into the `details` table and then deleting this same data from `shoppingCarts`. So, what this trigger actually does is move a user's shopping cart contents from the `shoppingCarts` table to the `details` table when the user places an order.

Looking through the trigger's code, you may notice that the `cart_id` of the shopping cart being processed and the `cust_id` specified in the order being created here are supposed to contain the same value. Of course, this is not the only approach you might apply here. However, by using the customer's ID as the ID for the shopping cart, you simplify the task of associating customers with their shopping carts. Furthermore, this approach implies that customers cannot have more than one shopping cart associated with their records, which forces the application to empty users' shopping carts in a timely manner, rather than keeping a lot of obsolete shopping cart records in the underlying database. As you will learn in Chapter 12's "Designing Session Beans" section, when discussing the `ShoppingCart` session bean, the shopping cart associated with a user is emptied when that user either places the order or explicitly empties the cart.

Adjusting the Database Tier Implemented with Oracle

If your underlying database is implemented with Oracle, you need to connect as `usrsample` via SQL*Plus and then issue the `CREATE OR REPLACE TRIGGER` statement shown in Listing 8-7.

Listing 8-7. *Creating the* `AFTER INSERT` *Trigger on the* `orders` *Table in Oracle*

```
CREATE OR REPLACE TRIGGER afterinsertorder
AFTER INSERT ON orders
FOR EACH ROW
BEGIN
 INSERT INTO details(ordno, book_id, units, unit_price) SELECT :NEW.pono, ➥
book_id, units, unit_price FROM shoppingCarts WHERE cart_id=:NEW.cust_id;
 DELETE FROM shoppingCarts WHERE cart_id=:NEW.cust_id;
END;
/
```

In a real-world situation, of course, you might want to make many more additions to the underlying database when flipping back to the original database tier while building the persistence tier. For example, you might want to create an Oracle sequence generator that will generate unique sequential numbers to be used as IDs for the orders being created. This will be discussed in the next chapter in detail. As for now, though, when performing the test discussed in the "Performing a Quick Test of the Newly Created JPA Entities" section later, you can generate the order IDs on your own.

Testing the Additions

It is good practice to test the components as you add them to the application being built. The simplest way to test the newly created `afterinsertorder` `AFTER INSERT` trigger is to issue the sequence of SQL statements discussed in this section.

To ensure that the data stored in the underlying tables will get back to the state it was in before the test began, you must perform all the statements discussed here within a single transaction. If your underlying database is implemented with Oracle, you have nothing to worry about—as stated earlier, Oracle automatically starts a transaction along with the first executable SQL statement. In MySQL, however, the autocommit mode is enabled by default. Therefore, you have to explicitly start a new transaction by issuing the following statement:

```
START TRANSACTION;
```

Next, you need to populate the shoppingCarts table with some data representing the contents of a user's shopping cart. This could be done as follows, in both MySQL and Oracle:

```
INSERT INTO shoppingCarts VALUES(1, '1430209631', 1, 44.99);
INSERT INTO shoppingCarts VALUES(1, '1590595300', 1, 49.99);
```

If you recall from Listing 6-4 in Chapter 6, the shoppingCarts table contains a multiple-column primary key comprised of the cart_id and book_id columns. This mechanism ensures that a user won't be able to put the same product item in his shopping cart while still being able to increase the number of copies of that product by updating the units field of the corresponding record in the shoppingCarts table. This is a good example of implementing business logic in the database. With this multiple-column primary key in place, you don't need to write any Java code preventing users from putting the same items in the shopping cart, since this task is handled at the database tier.

Now, to make sure that the shoppingCarts table has been successfully modified, you can issue the following query:

```
SELECT * FROM shoppingCarts;
```

This should show the two records created earlier:

CART_ID	BOOK_ID	UNITS	UNIT_PRICE
1	1430209631	1	44.99
1	1590595300	1	49.99

The next step is to insert a new record into the orders table. You could do this by issuing the following command:

```
INSERT INTO orders(pono, cust_id, empno) VALUES(25,1,1);
```

It is important to notice that the value of the cust_id field in the previous INSERT statement must be the same as the value of the cart_id field in the records inserted into the shoppingCarts table earlier. Otherwise, the order being inserted will not be associated with the shopping cart records inserted earlier, and therefore, these records won't be moved from the shoppingCarts table to the details table.

Also, you may notice that the previous INSERT statement specifies values only for the first three fields of the order record. This is because the other two fields—namely, shipping_date and delivery_estimate—are generated automatically with the BEFORE INSERT trigger defined on the orders table as discussed in the "Defining the Triggers" section in Chapter 6.

As you might guess, the previous INSERT statement should have fired not only the neworder BEFORE INSERT trigger but also the afterinsertorder AFTER INSERT trigger. If everything has worked as planned, you should now have a new record in the orders table, two records in the details table, and no records in the shoppingCarts table.

So, if you issue the following query:

```
SELECT * FROM details;
```

you should see the following two rows appear in the details table:

```
ORDNO BOOK_ID    UNITS UNIT_PRICE
------------------------------------------------------------------------------
25      1430209631  1    44.99
25      1590595300  1    49.99
```

Now, if you check the shoppingCarts table like this:

```
SELECT * FROM shoppingCarts;
```

you should receive no rows. If so, this means that the afterinsertorder AFTER INSERT trigger works as expected.

The last thing you might want to check here is the books table. If you recall from the "Defining the Triggers" section in Chapter 6, the newdetail BEFORE INSERT trigger defined on the details table invokes the updateBooks stored procedure every time a new record is inserted into the table. To make sure this has happened, you can issue the following query:

```
SELECT isbn, quantity FROM books;
```

The result returned will depend on the values of the quantity fields that you had at the beginning of the transaction. However, whatever this query returns, you should notice that the values of the quantity fields have been reduced by the number of units specified in the units fields of the corresponding records just inserted into the details table. For example, if the quantity field of each book record was set to 10 before you inserted a new row into the orders table, then the previous query should return the following result:

```
isbn            quantity
-------------------------------
1430209631  9
1590595300  9
```

Now that you know everything is correct, you can roll back all the changes made by the INSERT statements issued in this section. To achieve this, you must issue the following statement, in both MySQL and Oracle:

```
ROLLBACK;
```

After that, if you issue a SELECT statement against orders, details, or shoppingCarts, you should receive no rows. This is the state in which these tables were before the test started. Moreover, if you now reissue the SELECT statement against the books table as shown earlier, this should confirm that the values of the quantity fields have been reinstated to their original values:

```
isbn            quantity
--------------------------------
1430209631 10
1590595300 10
```

These results illustrate that regardless of the way in which a DML statement is issued—explicitly from a SQL prompt tool or implicitly from within a trigger or stored procedure—the changes that statement makes are all rolled back if the transaction it belongs to is rolled back.

Performing a Quick Test of the Newly Created JPA Entities

To make the most of the test you might want to perform on the JPA entities created (as discussed in the earlier section "Creating JPA Entities Upon the Underlying Database Tables"), you should have a good understanding of the purpose of each entity to be tested. The test code you're going to build should do the following:

- Test all the entities you have

- Be compact so you have it all in one source

- Roll back the changes made to the underlying tables upon the completion

You can meet each of these conditions if you decide on a single servlet utilizing the Java Persistence API.

The first thing you need to do is to create a directory structure for the test project discussed here. You might create, say, the directory named entitiestest as the root directory for the test project and then copy into it the /src/ejbjpa/entities directory with its contents from the sampleapp sample application root directory. Then, you're going to need to create the entitiestest/src/ejbjpa/servlets directory into which you will put the servlet performing the test. Finally, you need to create the entitiestest/target/WEB-INF/classes directory for the classes being created and the entitiestest/target/WEB-INF/classes/META-INF directory for the persistence.xml configuration file. As you might guess, the target directory is going to be the root directory for the WAR test application archive that will be then deployed to the application server.

Schematically, the directory structure you need to create for the test project should look like Figure 8-3.

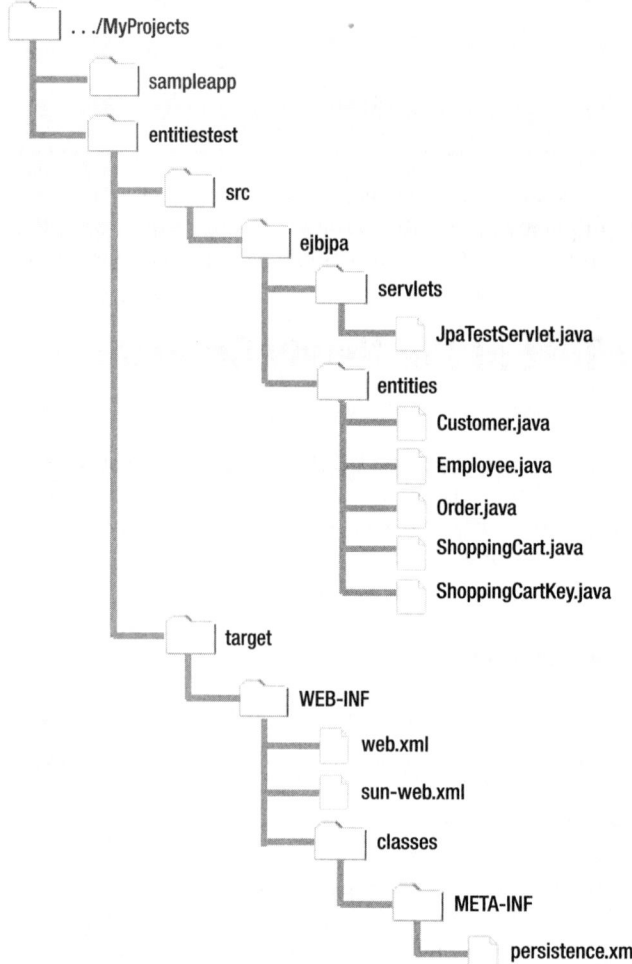

Figure 8-3. *The test application directory structure*

Once you have created the directory structure depicted in the figure, you can start creating the servlet source file as well as the configuration files.

Listing 8-8 shows the source code for the JpaTestServlet.java file, which, according to Figure 8-3, you should save into the entitiestest/src/ejbjpa/servlets directory.

Listing 8-8. *A Servlet for Testing the JPA Entities Created Earlier in This Chapter*

```
package ejbjpa.servlets;
import java.io.*;
import java.util.*;
import java.sql.*;
import javax.servlet.*;
import javax.servlet.http.*;
```

```
import javax.transaction.*;
import javax.annotation.Resource;
import javax.persistence.EntityManager;
import javax.persistence.EntityManagerFactory;
import javax.persistence.PersistenceUnit;
import ejbjpa.entities.*;

public class JpaTestServlet extends HttpServlet {
    @PersistenceUnit
    private EntityManagerFactory emf;
    @Resource
    private UserTransaction userTransaction;

    public void doGet(
        HttpServletRequest request,
        HttpServletResponse response) throws ServletException, IOException {
        response.setContentType("text/html");
        response.setBufferSize(8192);
        PrintWriter out = response.getWriter();
        EntityManager em= emf.createEntityManager();
        //creating ShoppingCart entity instances
        ShoppingCart cart1 = new ShoppingCart();
        cart1.setCart_id(2);
        cart1.setBook_id("1590595300");
        cart1.setUnits(1);
        cart1.setUnit_price(49.99);
        ShoppingCart cart2 = new ShoppingCart();
        cart2.setCart_id(2);
        cart2.setBook_id("1430209631");
        cart2.setUnits(1);
        cart2.setUnit_price(44.99);
        //Creating the order entity instance that will convert the above ➥
         ShoppingCarts into the order's details
        Customer cust1 = (Customer) em.find(Customer.class, 2);
        Employee emp1 = (Employee) em.find(Employee.class, 1);
        Order order1 = new Order();
        order1.setPono(10);
        order1.setCustomer(cust1);
        order1.setEmployee(emp1);
        //Performing transaction
        try{
          userTransaction.begin();
          out.println("Transaction began!"+"<br/>");
          em.persist(cart1);
          em.persist(cart2);
          em.flush();
          em.persist(order1);
```

```
            em.flush();
            out.println("Order shipping date is: " + order1.getShipping_date() + ➥
             "<br/>");
            em.refresh(order1);
            out.println("Order instance has been refreshed from database!" + ➥
             "<br/>");
            out.println("Order shipping date is: " + order1.getShipping_date() + ➥
             "<br/>");
            userTransaction.rollback();
            out.println("Transaction has been rolled back!");
        }
        catch (Exception e){
            e.printStackTrace();
        }
    }
}
```

As you can see, the code in the listing is fairly straightforward. First, you inject an EntityManagerFactory instance into the servlet with the @PersistenceUnit annotation, and you inject the UserTransaction resource with the @Resource.

Next, you set up two ShoppingCart instances, setting their cart_id fields to 2. This means that these instances are associated with the customer whose cust_id is also 2. Then, you set an Order instance, associating it with appropriate Customer and Employee instances.

Finally, you start the transaction within which you first persist the two ShoppingCart instances and call the EntityManager's flush method, and then you persist the Order instance, also calling flush after that. It is important to note here that by calling the flush method you force synchronization of the entities' data to the underlying database, which does not, however, commit the changes made—performing a rollback is still possible. The EntityManager's refresh method applied to the Order instance resets this instance from the database after you have persisted it and called flush to synchronize it to the database.

As you may notice in the code, order1.getShipping_date() is invoked before you refresh the instance from the database, and then you invoke it right after that. The trick is that you didn't set the shipping_date field of the instance explicitly—it is set by the shippingDate stored function automatically invoked from within the neworder BEFORE INSERT trigger, as discussed in Chapter 6. So, the first call of order1.getShipping_date() should receive null, but the second one receives the date generated inside the database for the shipping_date field.

The following steps sum up what the servlet discussed here does, from the point of view of testing the entities:

1. Sets up ShoppingCart and Order instances, obtaining the corresponding Customer and Employee instances

2. Begins a transaction within which the operations upon the entities' instances are performed

3. Persists the ShoppingCart and Order instances, synchronizing them to the database

4. Refreshes the Order instance from the database, thus making it possible to access the instance's fields generated within the database

5. Rolls back the transaction so that all the changes made to the underlying database data are undone

Now that you've seen the internals of the JpaTestServlet servlet, you might want to see the servlet in action. Before you can do that, however, you have to create the required configuration files. In particular, you're going to need to create the web.xml, sun-web.xml, and persistence.xml files, putting them into the directories as shown in Listing 8-3 earlier.

Listing 8-9 shows the source code for the web.xml deployment descriptor, which you should save into the entitiestest/target/WEB-INF directory.

Listing 8-9. *The* web.xml *Configuration File for the* JpaTestServlet *Servlet Application*

```
<?xml version="1.0" encoding="UTF-8"?>
<web-app xmlns="http://java.sun.com/xml/ns/javaee"
 xmlns:xsi="http://www.w3.org/2001/XMLSchema-instance"
 xsi:schemaLocation="http://java.sun.com/xml/ns/javaee ➥
 http://java.sun.com/xml/ns/javaee/web-app_2_5.xsd"
 version="2.5">
    <servlet>
        <servlet-name>JpaTestServlet</servlet-name>
        <servlet-class>ejbjpa.servlets.JpaTestServlet</servlet-class>
    </servlet>
    <servlet-mapping>
        <servlet-name>JpaTestServlet</servlet-name>
        <url-pattern>/jpatestservlet</url-pattern>
    </servlet-mapping>
</web-app>
```

Also, you need to create the sun-web.xml runtime deployment descriptor, in which you should specify the context root of the application. Listing 8-10 shows the source code for this configuration file, which you should save into the entitiestest/target/WEB-INF directory.

Listing 8-10. *The* sun-web.xml *Configuration File for the* JpaTestServlet *Servlet Application*

```
<?xml version="1.0" encoding="UTF-8"?>
<!DOCTYPE sun-web-app PUBLIC "-//Sun Microsystems, Inc.// ➥
DTD Application Server 8.0 Servlet 2.4//➥
EN" "http://www.sun.com/software/appserver/dtds/sun-web-app_2_4-0.dtd">
<sun-web-app>
  <context-root>/jpatest</context-root>
</sun-web-app>
```

Finally, you have to create the persistence.xml configuration file providing information about the data source to be used within the application. The persistence.xml document shown in Listing 8-11 specifies the data source jdbc/mysqlpool, created as discussed in the preceding chapter, assuming your underlying database is implemented with MySQL. If your underlying database is Oracle and you have the `jdbc/oraclepool` data source created as discussed in the preceding chapter, then you have to change `jdbc/mysqlpool` for `jdbc/oraclepool` in the `jta-data-source` element within the `persistence.xml` file shown in the listing.

Listing 8-11. *The* `persistence.xml` *Configuration File for the* `JpaTestServlet` *Servlet Application*

```
<?xml version="1.0" encoding="UTF-8"?>
<persistence xmlns="http://java.sun.com/xml/ns/persistence" ➥
xmlns:xsi="http://www.w3.org/2001/XMLSchema-instance" ➥
xsi:schemaLocation="http://java.sun.com/xml/ns/persistence ➥
http://java.sun.com/xml/ns/persistence/persistence_1_0.xsd" version="1.0">
    <persistence-unit name="jpatestservlet2-pu" transaction-type="JTA">
        <jta-data-source>jdbc/mysqlpool</jta-data-source>
    </persistence-unit>
</persistence>
```

Now you're ready to move on and build the test application. The first step is to compile the entities created as discussed in the "Creating the Entities" earlier section, as well as the `JpaTestServlet` shown in Listing 8-8. To do this, you need to change the directory to the root directory of the project, `entitiestest`, and then issue the following command:

```
javac -cp c:\glassfish\lib\javaee.jar -d target\WEB-INF\classes ➥
src\ejbjpa\entities\*.java src\ejbjpa\servlets\*.java
```

Before you can execute the servlet, you have to package it into a WAR file so that you can deploy it to the application server. With the following commands, you change the directory to `target`, which will be used as the root directory for the WAR archive, and then create that archive:

```
cd target
jar cvf jpatestservlet.war .
```

If you haven't started the application server already, make sure to do it now. This is the command you should issue to start the server:

```
asadmin start-domain domain1
```

Once you've done that, you can deploy the `jpatestservlet.war` application archive to the application server:

```
asadmin deploy jpatestservlet.war
```

If deployment has successfully completed, you can start a test by pointing your browser to `http://localhost:8080/jpatest/jpatestservlet`.

If everything goes right, the output might look like this:

```
Transaction began!
Order shipping date is: null
Order instance has been refreshed from database!
Order shipping date is: Thu Apr 03 00:00:00 PDT 2008
Transaction has been rolled back!
```

As you can see, the order's shipping date (calculated before refreshing the order's instance) is null, while after refreshing it, you have a real date. As mentioned earlier, this happens because the shipping_date field of the order's instance is not set within the servlet code, but it is set by a database stored function, when that instance is persisted to the underlying orders table. So, the previous illustrates that the order's instance created within the servlet has been successfully persisted to the database. Finally, to restore the data to its previous state, you roll back the transaction. This means that if you check the underlying tables after the servlet has completed, you should see no changes.

Looking through the code performing the test, you may notice that it doesn't actually check whether the ShoppingCart instances have been persisted to the database—it simply checks whether the order's instance has been successfully persisted. Although the mechanism of moving the data from the shoppingCarts table to the details table upon inserting an order's record is implemented inside the database, you might still want to make sure that this mechanism works as expected when an order's instance is persisted to the database.

Returning to the JpaTestServlet servlet shown in Listing 8-8 earlier, you might modify the try block within the doGet servlet method so that it implements a little more complicated test.

Listing 8-12 shows how you might update the try block within the doGet servlet method so that it checks whether the ShoppingCart instances have been successfully persisted and they're gone right after the order's instance has been persisted.

Listing 8-12. *Updated* try *Block Within the* doGet *Servlet Method, Allowing You to Perform a More Detailed Test*

```
...
    public void doGet(
...
        int status;
...
        //Performing transaction
        try{
            userTransaction.begin();
            out.println("Transaction began!"+"<br/>");
            em.persist(cart1);
            em.persist(cart2);
            em.flush();
            em.refresh(cart1);
            out.println("cart1 has been refreshed from database!"+ "<br/>");
            out.println("Price of the book in cart1 is: $" + ➥
            cart1.getUnit_price() + "<br/>");
            em.refresh(cart2);
            out.println("cart2 has been refreshed from database!"+ "<br/>");
            out.println("Price of the book in cart2 is: $" + ➥
            cart2.getUnit_price() + "<br/>");
            em.persist(order1);
            em.flush();
            out.println("Order shipping date is: " + ➥
            order1.getShipping_date() + "<br/>");
            em.refresh(order1);
```

```
          out.println("Order instance has been refreshed from database!" + ➥
          "<br/>");
          out.println("Order shipping date is: " + ➥
          order1.getShipping_date() + "<br/>");
          try{
            em.refresh(cart1);
            out.println("Price of the book in cart1 is: $" + ➥
            cart1.getUnit_price() + "<br/>");
            em.refresh(cart2);
            out.println("Price of the book in cart2 is: $" + ➥
            cart2.getUnit_price() + "<br/>");
          }
          catch ( Exception ex){
            out.println("Failed to refresh ShoppingCart ➥
            instances from database!" + "<br/>");
            status = userTransaction.getStatus();
                     if (status==Status.STATUS_MARKED_ROLLBACK){
            out.println("Transaction has been marked for roll back ➥
             due to exception!");
           }
          }
          status = userTransaction.getStatus();
           if (status==Status.STATUS_ACTIVE){
           userTransaction.rollback();
           out.println("Transaction has been rolled back!");
          }
        }
      catch (Exception e){
          e.printStackTrace();
      }
    }
  }
}
```

Examining the try block shown in the listing, you may notice that it contains a nested try block, within which you're trying to refresh the shopping cart instances, after the order instance has been persisted and flushed. However, since the shoppingCarts table's records corresponding to the shopping cart instances discussed here should be gone by now, this refreshing undoubtedly will fail, throwing an exception that will bring the program to a halt. To handle this, you define the catch clause with the nested try block. The code in the catch clause will be executed when the shopping cart entries are not found.

To try the updated servlet, you first need to recompile it and then package and deploy it to the application server as discussed earlier in this section. After this, you can point your browser to http://localhost:8080/jpatest/jpatestservlet to start the test. This is what the browser's output might look like:

```
Transaction began!
cart1 has been refreshed from database!
Price of the book in cart1 is: $49.99
cart2 has been refreshed from database!
Price of the book in cart2 is: $44.99
Order shipping date is: null
Order instance has been refreshed from database!
Order shipping date is: Fri Apr 04 00:00:00 PDT 2008
Failed to refresh ShoppingCart instances from database!
Transaction has been marked for roll back due to exception!
```

If your browser's output matches up with the previous (the shipping date should be different, of course), this means you just completed the test and the JPA entities work as expected.

Building the Sample with the NetBeans IDE

If you want to implement the sample application with the help of the NetBeans IDE, this section explains how to launch a new Enterprise Application project with this visual tool and then incorporate the JPA entities you created as discussed in the earlier section "Creating JPA Entities Upon the Underlying Database Tables" into that IDE project.

In the "Creating and Deploying a Web Application with the NetBeans IDE" section in Chapter 2, you saw how to build and deploy a "Hello World!" application with the NetBeans IDE. In this section, you will launch a more complicated project that will grow as you build the sample application.

With the entities already written, all that's left is to create a new IDE project and then put the entities' sources to an appropriate directory within the root project directory.

The following are the steps to create a new standard NetBeans IDE project for an enterprise application and then incorporate the JPA entities' sources you already have into it:

1. Start the NetBeans IDE from the Start menu of your operating system.

2. In the NetBeans IDE, select File ➤ New Project to start the New Project Wizard.

3. On the Choose Project screen of the New Project Wizard, choose Enterprise in the Categories box and Enterprise Application in the Project box, and then click Next.

4. On the Name and Location screen of the New Project Wizard, type **sampleappIDE** in the Project Name box, and set the project location to the directory in which you want to save the project files. Leave the other settings at their defaults, and click Finish. As a result, the following three nodes should appear in the Projects window:

   - sampleappIDE

   - sampleappIDE-ejb

   - sampleappIDE-war

   Next, you need to create a persistence unit that will be used within the sampleappIDE-ejb project.

5. In the Projects window, right-click sampleappIDE-ejb, and choose New ➤ Persistence Unit.

6. In the Provider and Database dialog box, select a data source from the drop-down menu, say, jdbc/mysqlpool. Then, select None for Table Generation Strategy, and click Finish, leaving the other settings at their defaults. As a result, the `persistence.xml` document should appear under the sampleappIDE-ejb/Configuration Files node.

Next, you need to incorporate the entities' sources into the project.

7. In your file system, go to the sampleappIDE project root directory that was just generated by the IDE. Once you're there, move on to the `sampleappIDE-ejb/src/java` directory.

8. Within the `sampleappIDE/sampleappIDE-ejb/src/java` directory, create the `ejbjpa/entities` directory, and copy the JPA entities' sources created as discussed in the earlier section "Creating the Entities." So, you should copy five files: `Customer.java`, `Employee.java`, `Order.java`, `ShoppingCartKey.java`, and `ShoppingCart.java`.

9. Return to the IDE, and extend the sampleappIDE-ejb/Source Packages node in the Projects window. You should see that the `ejbjpa.entities` package has appeared.

10. Double-click the ejbjpa.entities package node. You should see that the package contains the entities' sources you copied into the `sampleappIDE/sampleappIDE-ejb/src/java/ejbjpa/entities` directory in step 6.

11. Right-click the ejbjpa.entities package node, and choose Compile Package. If everything goes right, the last message you should see in the Output window is `BUILD SUCCESSFUL`.

12. Close the IDE by choosing File ➤ Exit.

You'll return to this project in Chapter 12, where you will design the enterprise beans utilizing the JPA entities created in this chapter.

Summary

In this chapter, you built JPA entities upon the underlying database tables created earlier, as discussed in Chapter 6. The entities created and tested in this chapter form the persistence tier of the sample application.

In the next three chapters, you will take a closer look at object-relational mapping, the EntityManager API, and Java Persistence Query Language (JPQL). Armed with this knowledge, you will then build the enterprise beans that will manipulate the JPA entities discussed in this chapter.

CHAPTER 9

■■■

Object/Relational Mapping

It's hardly possible to show all the features provided by the Java Persistence API with a single sample application. So, in this chapter, I'll temporarily digress from the sample you started building in the preceding chapters and give you a closer look at the object/relational mapping of Java objects to relational database data, investigating this facility with many examples.

The chapter starts with an overview of the object/relational mapping facility, briefly reviewing what you've already learned about it in the preceding chapters of this book. Then, it moves on to some interesting topics explaining how to seamlessly bridge the gap between Java objects and the underlying database tables with the help of object/relational mapping. In particular, this chapter discusses the following:

- Specifying object/relational mapping metadata with annotations

- Using XML deployment descriptors instead of mapping annotations

- Navigating related entities over their relationships

- Cascading operations performed on related entities

- Defining composite primary keys that include foreign key mappings

- Generating values for identity columns

Of course, object/relational mapping is a very broad topic that can't be covered in full detail in a single chapter. The main purpose of this chapter, however, is to show you that although object/relational mapping offers a fairly wide variety of features, it can still be quite easy to use and understand.

Mapping Java Objects to the Underlying Database

If you have followed the examples discussed in the preceding chapters, you should already have at least a cursory knowledge of object/relational mapping. To recap, the Java Persistence API uses an object/relational mapping approach when it comes to managing relational data. With this approach, you can associate a regular Java class with a relational database table, mapping each field of the class to a column in the underlying table. To turn a Java class into a JPA entity representing a table in a relational database, you can use object/relational mapping annotations or XML, specifying the exact details of the mapping applied.

The following two sections provide a brief overview of the JPA's object/relational mapping approach, followed by the sections that provide some examples of mapping the entity data to the underlying database.

Object-Oriented and Relational Paradigms

As you no doubt know, there are significant differences in the ways data is handled in Java and in a relational database. In Java, like in any other object-oriented language, you use classes as building blocks when developing an application. Classes are patterns used for creating objects through which you can access and manipulate application data. When defining a class, actually a blueprint for the class objects (instances), you describe both attributes for holding data and methods to access and manipulate that data. Once a class is defined, you can create as many instances as you need. However, when it comes to entity instances found within the same persistence context, you cannot have two instances of the same entity class, if the values of their primary key attributes are equal.

Often, application data is distributed across many objects. In most cases, these objects are related to each other, following the relationships defined in the underlying relational structures. However, unlike relational structures containing underlying data, Java objects have methods to access and manipulate their data. Also, you can navigate from one object to another if you have established a relationship between those objects. Since many objects are related with other ones with a parent/child relationship (one-to-many or many-to-one), these objects form a tree that you can move up and down, navigating from one object to another. Figure 9-1 shows an example of this.

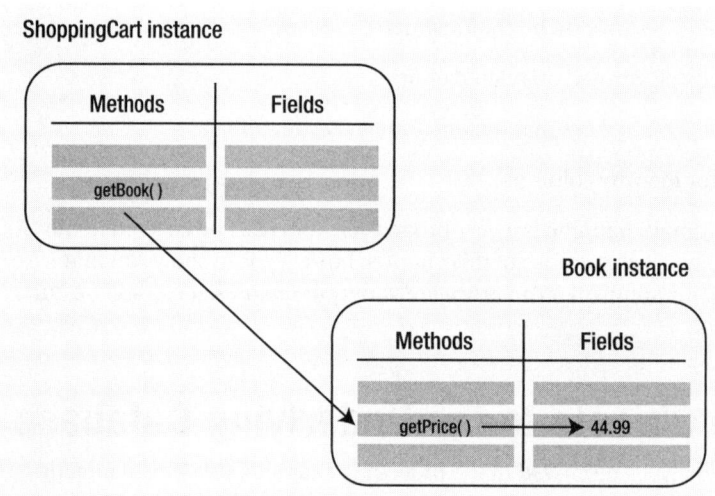

Figure 9-1. *A graphical representation of how you can access data from within a related JPA entity*

As you can see in the figure, the getBook method of a ShoppingCart instance is used to obtain the corresponding Book instance so that you can access the data held within the fields of the latter. Here is what this might look like in the code:

```
...
Double book_price;
book_price = cart1.getBook().getPrice();
```

You will see this approach in action in the later sections in this chapter.

Now let's look at how things work in a relational database. As you learned in Chapter 6, relational data is stored in tables that can be related to other tables with primary/foreign key relationships. A relational table typically holds a set of records, each of which, like a Java object, represents a business entity. Unlike Java objects, however, a table's records do not contain a mechanism to access their data or navigate to the data stored in other records, following the primary/foreign key relationships defined. As discussed in the "Using SQL Database Language" section in the appendix, the primary tool to access and manipulate data in any modern relational database is SQL. For example, when you need information from related rows stored in more than one table, you use a SQL join query, extracting information from these related tables as specified in the select list and WHERE clause of that join query.

Figure 9-2 shows how you can obtain data stored in two different tables related with a primary/foreign key relationship.

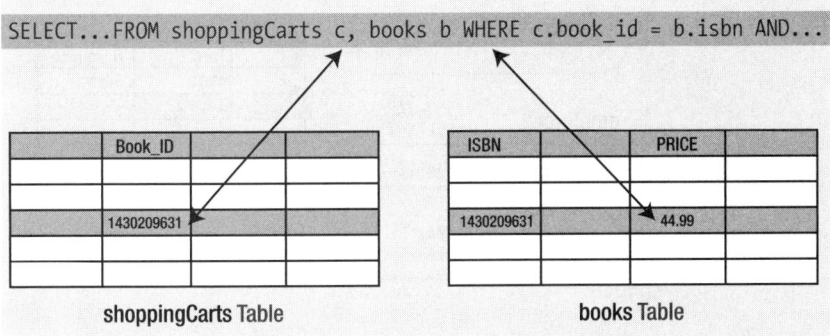

Figure 9-2. *A graphical representation of how you can extract information from related records stored in different database tables*

As you can see, there are several significant differences in the way data is structured and accessed in Java and in a relational database in which the underlying data resides. To smooth the difficulties that arise from these differences, the Java Persistence API uses an object/relational mapping approach, hiding the complexity of what actually occurs behind the scenes. This allows Java programmers to deal with Java objects mapped to the underlying tables, rather than dealing with those tables directly via SQL/JDBC.

The Big Picture

The concept behind object/relational mapping is simple. You start by creating Java classes called *JPA entities* or just *entities*, building them upon the underlying database tables. In a simple entity, you define persistent instance variables, one per column in the underlying table, as well as the getter and setter methods for these variables.

Next, using either object/relational annotations or deployment descriptor elements in an object/relational mapping XML file named `orm.xml`, you provide the persistence provider with the details of the mapping being applied. These approaches will be discussed in more detail in the next two sections.

Given object/relational mapping metadata, the persistence provider can figure out what SQL statement to implicitly issue in response to a certain operation performed upon an entity instance. Note, however, that when developing an entity, you do not need to define methods performing database-related operations, such as persist, merge, refresh, or remove. The fact is that all these methods, as well as some others designed to interact with the persistence context, are available through the `EntityManager` standard interface whose instance is injected in the code dealing with entities.

Figure 9-3 gives a graphical illustration of how relational data mapped to a JPA entity can be accessed from your application code via an `EntityManager` instance.

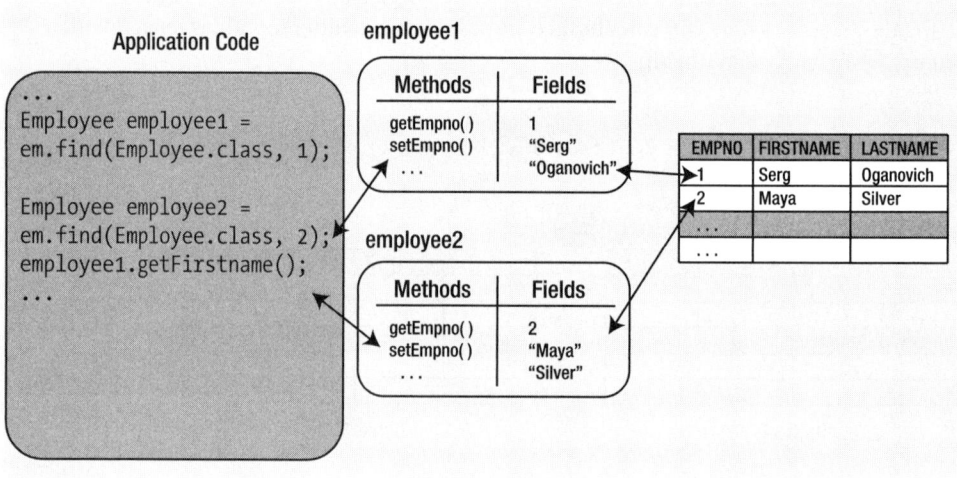

Figure 9-3. *A graphical representation of how application code accesses underlying data mapped to JPA entities*

In short, to take advantage of the object/relational mapping approach in your application, you need to accomplish the following tasks:

- Build entity classes upon those underlying tables that store the data needed by your application

- Create a persistence unit by defining the `persistence.xml` configuration file within which you specify the data source along with some other information to be used by the persistence provider

- Inject an `EntityManager` instance into the application component that will manipulate entity instances

As you saw in the book examples so far, an `EntityManager` instance required to handle dealing with entities can be injected into an enterprise bean or a web component such as a servlet.

Specifying Object/Relational Mapping Metadata

As mentioned, you can specify object/relational mapping metadata in two ways, providing the persistence provider with the details of the mapping being applied. You can use mapping annotations, object/relational mapping for the XML file `orm.xml`, or a combination of both. Although you should be already familiar with the first method, the second one has not been covered in this book yet, so it will be discussed in more detail here.

Using Mapping Annotations

As you saw in many examples discussed earlier in this book, object/relational mapping annotations are used to specify the mapping between an entity and its underlying relational table. For example, you use the `@Table` annotation to specify the name of the underlying database table, and you use `@Column` to specify the column name in that table. You apply the column mapping annotations to either an entity's persistent fields or an entity's getter methods, thus specifying the way in which the persistence provider will access entity's data.

If you create two entities built upon the tables related to each other through a parent key/foreign key association, you may define a relationship between these entities using either appropriate relationship annotations, such as `@OneToOne` and `@OneToMany`, as you saw in the book examples discussed so far, or mapping metadata in `orm.xml`, as you will see in the "Specifying Mapping Metadata in orm.xml" section later.

For a quick refresher on using mapping annotations, you might take a peek back at the "Planning JPA Entities" section in Chapter 4. For a detailed list of the annotations used to perform object/relational mapping, you can refer to the Enterprise JavaBeans 3.0 Specification Java Persistence API document, which is part of the Enterprise JavaBeans 3.0 Specification (JSR-220) available at `http://jcp.org/en/jsr/detail?id=220`.

Specifying Mapping Metadata in orm.xml

If you recall from the "XML Deployment Descriptors vs. Annotations" section in Chapter 4, you can use XML deployment descriptors to specify the application metadata as an alternative to using annotations or as an overriding mechanism for them. In that section, you looked at the pros and cons for both approaches. In particular, you learned that the main advantage of using deployment descriptors is that it enables you to keep the code of your application separate from the application's metadata, thus increasing maintainability and component reusability. Also, you saw an example of how to replace annotations with deployment descriptor XML elements when developing an enterprise bean.

In this section, you will look at an example of moving object/relational mapping metadata from an entity annotation to the `orm.xml` configuration file. Based on the test project discussed in the "Performing a Quick Test of the Newly Created JPA Entities" section from the preceding chapter, you create a new project that will demonstrate how to specify mapping metadata in an `orm.xml` configuration file instead of using mapping annotations.

You might create a new directory—say, `ormxmltest`—to be used as the root directory for the project. The directory structure for this new project might be the same as the one used for the test project in the preceding chapter. You can omit the `ShoppingCart.java` and `ShoppingCartKey.java` files in the `/src/ejbjpa/entities` directory and also add the `orm.xml` file to the `target/WEB-INF/classes/META-INF` directory. Listing 9-1 shows what the source code for this configuration file might look like.

Listing 9-1. *Source Code for the* `orm.xml` *Configuration File*

```
<?xml version="1.0" encoding="UTF-8"?>
<entity-mappings xmlns="http://java.sun.com/xml/ns/persistence/orm"
    xmlns:xsi="http://www.w3.org/2001/XMLSchema-instance"
    xsi:schemaLocation="http://java.sun.com/xml/ns/persistence/orm orm_1_0.xsd"
    version="1.0">
  <package>ejbjpa.entities</package>
  <access>FIELD</access>
  <entity class = "Employee">
    <table name = "EMPLOYEES" />
    <attributes>
      <id name = "empno">
        <column name = "EMPNO"/>
      </id>
      <basic name="firstname">
        <column name="FIRSTNAME" nullable = "false"/>
      </basic>
      <basic name="lastname">
        <column name="LASTNAME" nullable = "false"/>
      </basic>
      <one-to-many name="orders" mapped-by="employee">
          <cascade>
              <cascade-all/>
          </cascade>
      </one-to-many>
    </attributes>
  </entity>
</entity-mappings>
```

As you can see, the `orm.xml` file shown in the listing contains only one `entity` element, which provides the mapping metadata for the `Employee` entity. Actually, you might include as many `entity` elements in this file as there are entities being used in your application. In this particular example, however, the other `entity` elements are omitted to save space.

If you want, you can write the rest of the `entity` elements in the `orm.xml` file discussed here on your own. In that case, you're going to need to look at a detailed list of the XML elements that you can use in an object/relational mapping XML file. This information can be found in the Enterprise JavaBeans 3.0 Specification Java Persistence API document, which is part of JSR-220 available at `http://jcp.org/en/jsr/detail?id=220`.

> ■**Note** It is interesting to note that you can use both the deployment descriptor and mapping annotations in the same application. For example, you can specify mapping metadata for the `Employee` entity in the `orm.xml` file, while still using mapping annotations in the `Order` and `Customer` entities—the way it is done in this example. Also, you can specify mapping metadata for an entity using both methods. In that case, however, the deployment descriptor will override annotations. If you find it difficult to deal with XML elements for now, you can still use annotations until you are ready to take on building an `orm.xml` configuration file on your own.

Now that you have defined mapping metadata for the `Employee` entity in the `orm.xml` file, you might completely remove the annotations specified in the `Employee` entity file. After that, the source code for the `Employee` entity will look like Listing 9-2. You can compare the updated `Employee.java` with the original one shown in Listing 8-2 in the preceding chapter.

Listing 9-2. *Source Code for the* Employee *Entity Without Object/Relational Mapping Annotations*

```java
package ejbjpa.entities;
import java.io.Serializable;
import java.util.List;

public class Employee implements Serializable {
    private Integer empno;
    private String firstname;
    private String lastname;
    private List<Order> orders;
    public List<Order> getOrders(){
       return orders;
    }
    public void setOrders(List<Order> orders) {
        this.orders = orders;
    }
    public Employee() {
    }
    public Integer getEmpno() {
        return this.empno;
    }
    public void setEmpno(Integer empno) {
        this.empno = empno;
    }
    public String getFirstname() {
        return this.firstname;
    }
    public void setFirstname(String firstname) {
        this.firstname = firstname;
    }
    public String getLastname() {
```

```
        return this.lastname;
    }
    public void setLastname(String lastname) {
        this.lastname = lastname;
    }
}
```

As you can see, there are no annotations anymore. Removing the annotations was not a requirement, though. As mentioned earlier, you could have both mapping metadata in orm.xml and annotations. In that case, however, the deployment descriptor elements override the annotations.

Next, check out the Order.java and Customer.java files implementing the Order and Customer entities, respectively. These entities still have to contain mapping annotations since you do not define mapping metadata for them in the orm.xml file, and they should look like they were presented in Listing 8-3 and Listing 8-1 in the preceding chapter, respectively.

Finally, you need to create a servlet with the help of which you could make sure that replacing annotations with the deployment descriptor does not cause any problem at run-time. So, move on to the src/ejbjpa/servlets directory, and replace the JpaTestServlet.java file with the OrmXMLTestServlet.java file shown in Listing 9-3.

Listing 9-3. *Source Code for the* OrmXMLTestServlet *Servlet You Might Use to Test the* Employee *Entity Implemented Without Mapping Annotations*

```
package ejbjpa.servlets;
import java.io.*;
import java.util.*;
import java.sql.*;
import javax.servlet.*;
import javax.servlet.http.*;
import javax.transaction.*;
import javax.annotation.Resource;
import javax.persistence.EntityManager;
import javax.persistence.EntityManagerFactory;
import javax.persistence.PersistenceUnit;
import ejbjpa.entities.*;
public class OrmXMLTestServlet extends HttpServlet {
    @PersistenceUnit
    private EntityManagerFactory emf;
    @Resource
    private UserTransaction userTransaction;
    public void doGet(
        HttpServletRequest request,
        HttpServletResponse response) throws ServletException, IOException {
        response.setContentType("text/html");
        response.setBufferSize(8192);
        PrintWriter out = response.getWriter();
```

```
        EntityManager em= emf.createEntityManager();
        Customer cust = (Customer) em.find(Customer.class, 2);
        Employee emp = (Employee) em.find(Employee.class, 2);
        Order order1 = new Order();
        order1.setPono(10);
        order1.setCustomer(cust);
        order1.setEmployee(emp);
        Order order2 = new Order();
        order2.setPono(11);
        order2.setCustomer(cust);
        order2.setEmployee(emp);
        //Performing transaction
        try{
           userTransaction.begin();
           out.println("Transaction began!"+"<br/>");
           em.persist(order1);
           em.persist(order2);
           em.flush();
           em.refresh(emp);
           out.println("order " + emp.getOrders().get(0).getPono()+ " placed ➥
              via: " + emp.getOrders().get(0).getEmployee().getLastname() + "<br/>");
           out.println("order " + emp.getOrders().get(1).getPono()+ " placed ➥
              via: " + emp.getOrders().get(1).getEmployee().getLastname() + "<br/>");
           userTransaction.rollback();
           out.println("Transaction has been rolled back!");
        }
        catch (Exception e){
           e.printStackTrace();
        }
     }
}
```

In the `OrmXMLTestServlet` servlet shown in the listing, you find `Employee` and `Customer` entity instances by the primary keys specified and define two `Order` entity instances, which you then persist to the database. Next, you refresh the `Employee` entity from the database. Finally, to make sure everything works as expected, you obtain the employee's last name for each order just persisted using the following calls to the `Employee` entity:

```
emp.getOrders().get(0).getEmployee().getLastname()
emp.getOrders().get(1).getEmployee().getLastname()
```

Now that you have the sources ready, all that's left is to compile them, package them into a WAR archive, and finally deploy the package to the application server. After that, you can run the servlet shown in the listing by pointing your browser to `http://localhost:8080/ormxmltest/ormxmltestservlet` (the actual URL will depend on the settings you specified in the `web.xml` and `sun-web.xml` files, of course). If everything is right, you should see the following output:

```
Transaction began!
order 10 placed via: Silver
order 11 placed via: Silver
Transaction has been rolled back!
```

Note that, like the preceding test, this one is also performed within a transaction that is rolled back at the end to ensure that all changes made to the underlying tables during the test are canceled.

Utilizing Entity Relationships

Taking a quick peek at the "Using Unidirectional Relationships Between Entities" and "Using Bidirectional Relationships Between Entities" sections in Chapter 4, you might recall that when defining two entities upon two underlying tables related with a primary/foreign key relationship, you can and often should define a relationship between those entities. A relationship between two entities may be one-to-one, one-to-many, many-to-one, or many-to-many established with @OneToOne, @OneToMany, @ManyToOne, or @ManyToMany relationship modeling annotation, respectively.

In the following two sections, you will look at how you can navigate from one entity to another through the relationship established between them and how cascading operations are performed on related entities.

Navigating Over Relationships

As mentioned, you've already seen how to establish both unidirectional and bidirectional relationships in Chapter 4. To recap, to define a relationship between two entities, you apply an appropriate relationship modeling annotation to the corresponding persistent field or property in the referencing entity. In the case of a bidirectional relationship, an appropriate annotation is applied to each side of the relationship.

The example discussed in this section illustrates how you can navigate from one related entity to the other via a one-to-many/many-to-one bidirectional relationship, using the relationship between the Customer and Order entities discussed in the preceding examples.

Like in the example in the earlier "Specifying Mapping Metadata in orm.xml" section, you might use the test project discussed in the "Performing a Quick Test of the Newly Created JPA Entities" section in the preceding chapter as a starting point for the new project being discussed here. Again, you might borrow the directory structure from the test project, adjusting the configuration details in the XML files and implementing, this time, the RelationshipTestServlet servlet in the src/ejbjpa/servlets directory.

Before you start coding the RelationshipTestServlet servlet, though, let's do a little planning and look at the steps it is supposed to perform:

1. Get a Customer instance from a database, as well as an Employee instance, using the find method of the EntityManager instance injected into the servlet.

2. Create two Order instances, and then set their Customer and Employee fields to the instances obtained in step 1.

3. Persist the Order instances created in step 2.

4. Synchronize the Order instances to the database with flush.

5. Refresh the Customer instance from the database.

6. Create an ArrayList, and then populate it with the Order instances, using the getOrders method of the Customer instance refreshed from the database in step 5.

7. Make sure that the Order instances created in step 2 have been successfully obtained through the Customer instance, accessing those Order instances via the ArrayList created in step 6.

Now that you know what exactly the RelationshipTestServlet servlet is going to do, you can start writing the code. Listing 9-4 shows what the source code for this servlet might look like.

Listing 9-4. *Source Code for a Servlet That Illustrates How You Can Navigate from One Entity to Another Through the Relationship Established Between Them*

```java
package ejbjpa.servlets;
import java.io.*;
import java.util.*;
import java.sql.*;
import javax.servlet.*;
import javax.servlet.http.*;
import javax.transaction.*;
import javax.annotation.Resource;
import javax.persistence.EntityManager;
import javax.persistence.EntityManagerFactory;
import javax.persistence.PersistenceUnit;
import java.util.List;
import ejbjpa.entities.*;
public class RelationshipTestServlet extends HttpServlet {
    @PersistenceUnit
    private EntityManagerFactory emf;
    @Resource
    private UserTransaction userTransaction;
    public void doGet(
        HttpServletRequest request,
        HttpServletResponse response) throws ServletException, IOException {
        response.setContentType("text/html");
        response.setBufferSize(8192);
        PrintWriter out = response.getWriter();
        EntityManager em= emf.createEntityManager();
        //Creating the order entity instances
        Customer cust = (Customer) em.find(Customer.class, 2);
        Employee emp = (Employee) em.find(Employee.class, 1);
        List<Order> orders = new ArrayList<Order>();
        Order order1 = new Order();
```

```
    order1.setPono(10);
    order1.setCustomer(cust);
    order1.setEmployee(emp);
    Order order2 = new Order();
    order2.setPono(11);
    order2.setCustomer(cust);
    order2.setEmployee(emp);
    //Performing transaction
    try{
        userTransaction.begin();
        out.println("Transaction began!"+"<br/>");
        em.persist(order1);
        em.persist(order2);
        em.flush();
        em.refresh(cust);
        orders = cust.getOrders();
        for (int i = 0; i < orders.size(); i++) {
          out.println("order "+ orders.get(i).getPono()+ " placed by: " + ➥
            orders.get(i).getCustomer().getCust_name() + "<br/>");
        }
        userTransaction.rollback();
        out.println("Transaction has been rolled back!");
    }
    catch (Exception e){
        e.printStackTrace();
    }
  }
}
```

After you are done with compiling, packaging, and deploying the servlet, you can run it. If everything is OK, the results should look as follows:

```
Transaction began!
order 10 placed by: Paul Medica
order 11 placed by: Paul Medica
Transaction has been rolled back!
```

The next run should give the same results, since all the operations performed against the data in the servlet got rolled back.

Cascading Operations Performed on Related Entities

When defining a relationship between two entities with a @OneToOne, @OneToMany, @ManyToOne, or @ManyToMany annotation, you can use the cascade annotation element to describe how the effect of an operation will be propagated to instances of the associated entity.

Table 9-1 summarizes the cascade types you can use when setting up the cascade annotation element.

Table 9-1. *The Cascade Types to Which You Can Set the Cascade Annotation Element*

Cascade Type	Description
MERGE	EntityManager's merge operations will be cascaded to the target of the association.
PERSIST	EntityManager's persist operations will be cascaded to the target of the association.
REFRESH	EntityManager's refresh operations will be cascaded to the target of the association.
REMOVE	EntityManager's remove operations will be cascaded to the target of the association.
ALL	Any the previous operations will be cascaded to the target of the association.

In fact, you've already seen an example of using the cascade annotation element in the Customer and Employee entities utilized in most of the preceding examples. As a quick recap, Listing 9-5 shows a fragment of Customer.java, illustrating the use of the cascade annotation element.

Listing 9-5. *An Example of Using the Cascade Annotation Element*

```
...
import javax.persistence.CascadeType;
...
public class Customer implements Serializable {
...
    @OneToMany(mappedBy="customer", cascade = CascadeType.ALL)
    private List<Order> orders;
    public List<Order> getOrders(){
        return orders;
    }
    public void setOrders(List<Order> orders) {
        this.orders = orders;
    }
...
}
```

Let's now create a servlet that illustrates how cascading of, say, the persist operation performed against a Customer instance works. For example, you could implement a servlet that accomplishes the following steps:

1. Obtain a Customer instance from a database, as well as an Employee instance, with the help of the find method of the EntityManager.

2. Set up two Order instances, setting their Customer and Employee fields to the instances obtained in step 1.

3. Define an ArrayList, and then add the Order instances created in step 2 to this structure.

4. Associate the `ArrayList` defined in step 3 with the `Customer` instance obtained in step 1, using the `setOrders` method of the latter.

5. Persist the `Customer` instance. Actually, this step is optional. This is because the `Customer` instance, unlike `Order` instances created in step 2, is in the `EntityManager`'s persistence context from the beginning and, therefore, will be automatically synchronized to the database in the next step with the `flush EntityManager`'s method.

6. Synchronize the `Customer` instance to the database with `flush`. Since you have the `cascade` element of the `@OneToMany` annotation in the `Customer` entity set to `ALL`, the `Order` instances associated with the `Customer` instance will also be persisted to the database.

7. Refresh the `Customer` instance from the database.

8. Make sure that the `Order` instances associated with the `Customer` instance in step 4 have been persisted. To obtain these instances, you use the `getOrders` method of the refreshed `Customer` instance, looping through the array returned by the `getOrders` method.

Now let's look at the source code for a servlet that performs these steps. In Listing 9-6 showing the code, the import declarations, as well as some other code lines unimportant here, have been omitted to save space.

Listing 9-6. *Source Code for a Servlet That Shows How Cascading of the Persist Operation Performed Against a* `Customer` *Instance Works*

```
//import declarations
...
public class CascadingTestServlet extends HttpServlet {
...
    public void doGet(
        HttpServletRequest request,
        HttpServletResponse response) throws ServletException, IOException {
...
        Customer cust = (Customer) em.find(Customer.class, 2);
        Employee emp = (Employee) em.find(Employee.class, 2);
        Order order1 = new Order();
        order1.setPono(10);
        order1.setCustomer(cust);
        order1.setEmployee(emp);
        Order order2 = new Order();
        order2.setPono(11);
        order2.setCustomer(cust);
        order2.setEmployee(emp);
        List<Order> orders = new ArrayList<Order>();
        orders.add(order1);
        orders.add(order2);
        cust.setOrders(orders);
        //Performing transaction
```

```
        try{
            userTransaction.begin();
            out.println("Transaction began!"+"<br/>");
            em.persist(cust); //can be omitted
            em.flush();
            em.refresh(cust);
            orders = cust.getOrders();
            for (int i = 0; i < orders.size(); i++) {
              out.println("order "+ orders.get(i).getPono()+ " placed by: " + ➥
              orders.get(i).getCustomer().getCust_name() + "<br/>");
            }
            userTransaction.rollback();
            out.println("Transaction has been rolled back!");
        }
      catch (Exception e){
          e.printStackTrace();
      }
   }
}
```

The most interesting thing about the code shown in the listing is that you don't have to explicitly persist the Order instances created there to the database. The persistence provider does it implicitly when the Customer instance with which those Order instances have been associated is persisted. It's important to realize that the previous is not the default behavior. As you might recall from Table 9-1, the persistence provider does it that way here because the cascade element of the @OneToMany annotation in the Customer entity is set to ALL, which means all operations performed against a Customer instance will be cascaded to the associated Order instances.

By default, the cascade element is not set at all. This means that if you modify the Customer entity as shown in the snippet in Listing 9-7, then the CascadingTestServlet servlet shown in Listing 9-6 will end up with an error, providing no output after the "Transaction began!" message appears.

Listing 9-7. *The One-to-Many Relationship Defined in the* Customer *Entity, Without the Cascade Annotation Element*

```
...
public class Customer implements Serializable {
...
    @OneToMany(mappedBy="customer")
    private List<Order> orders;
    public List<Order> getOrders(){
        return orders;
    }
    public void setOrders(List<Order> orders) {
        this.orders = orders;
    }
...
}
```

Now, to make the CascadingTestServlet servlet shown in Listing 9-6 work again and produce the same results, you might change its source code as shown in Listing 9-8.

Listing 9-8. *The Updated* CascadingTestServlet *Servlet That Will Work with the* Customer *Entity Modified As Shown in Listing 9-7*

```
//import declarations
...
public class CascadingTestServlet extends HttpServlet {
...
    public void doGet(
        HttpServletRequest request,
        HttpServletResponse response) throws ServletException, IOException {
...
        Customer cust = (Customer) em.find(Customer.class, 2);
        Employee emp = (Employee) em.find(Employee.class, 2);
        List<Order> orders = new ArrayList<Order>();
        Order order1 = new Order();
        order1.setPono(10);
        order1.setCustomer(cust);
        order1.setEmployee(emp);
        Order order2 = new Order();
        order2.setPono(11);
        order2.setCustomer(cust);
        order2.setEmployee(emp);
        //Performing transaction
        try{
            userTransaction.begin();
            out.println("Transaction began!"+"<br/>");
            em.persist(order1);
            em.persist(order2);
            em.flush();
            em.refresh(cust);
            orders = cust.getOrders();
            for (int i = 0; i < orders.size(); i++) {
              out.println("order "+ orders.get(i).getPono()+ " placed by: " + ➥
                orders.get(i).getCustomer().getCust_name() + "<br/>");
            }
            userTransaction.rollback();
            out.println("Transaction has been rolled back!");
        }
        catch (Exception e){
            e.printStackTrace();
        }
    }
}
```

As you can see, the servlet shown in the listing works in a similar manner as the one shown in Listing 9-6 earlier. This time, however, you explicitly persist the Order instances to the database. This is because the @OneToMany annotation used in the Customer entity to define a relationship with the Order entity doesn't set the cascade element anymore. As a result, the persistence provider will no longer cascade any operations performed against a Customer instance to the associated Order instances.

Dealing with Entity Primary Keys

Like relational tables, entities use primary keys to uniquely identify entity instances. If you recall, you can use the @Id annotation to specify the primary key property or field when creating an entity.

In the following sections, you will look at some practical examples of how to define primary key entity fields, including how to deal with composite primary keys that include foreign key mappings and how to instruct the persistence provider to automatically generate values for the primary key fields.

Dealing with Composite Primary Keys

If you recall from the discussion in the "Creating the Entities" section in Chapter 8, you can declare a composite primary key using the @IdClass annotation. A more complex example assumes that one of the composite primary key fields is also a foreign key through which you establish a relationship with a related entity. The following example shows what you can do in this situation.

Let's create a new project for this example. Again, to save time, you can borrow the directory structure from the test project discussed in the "Performing a Quick Test of the Newly Created JPA Entities" section in the preceding chapter. This time, however, you must not remove the ShoppingCart.java and ShoppingCartKey.java files from the /src/ejbjpa/entities directory. Instead, you can remove the Customer.java and Employee.java files. Also, for this example, you're going to need to create a Book entity and modify the ShoppingCart entity, establishing a bidirectional relationship between these entities. As you might recall from Chapter 6, the shoppingCarts table is defined with the composite primary key that includes the book_id column, which is also a foreign key to the primary key of the books table.

Listing 9-9 shows the code you might use to create the Book entity.

Listing 9-9. *Source Code for the* Book *Entity*

```
package ejbjpa.entities;
import java.util.List;
import javax.persistence.CascadeType;
import java.io.Serializable;
import javax.persistence.Column;
import javax.persistence.Entity;
import javax.persistence.Id;
import javax.persistence.Table;
import javax.persistence.OneToMany;
@Entity
```

```java
@Table(name = "BOOKS")
public class Book implements Serializable {
    @Id
    @Column(name = "ISBN")
    private String isbn;
    @Column(name = "TITLE", nullable = false)
    private String title;
    @Column(name = "AUTHOR", nullable = false)
    private String author;
    @Column(name = "PRICE", nullable = false)
    private Double price;
    @Column(name = "QUANTITY", nullable = false)
    private Integer quantity;
    @OneToMany(mappedBy="book", cascade = CascadeType.ALL)
    private List<ShoppingCart> shoppingCarts;
    public List<ShoppingCart> getShoppingCarts(){
       return shoppingCarts;
    }
    public void setShoppingCarts(List<ShoppingCart> shoppingCarts) {
        this.shoppingCarts = shoppingCarts;
    }
    public Book() {
    }
    public String getIsbn() {
        return this.isbn;
    }
    public void setIsbn(String isbn) {
        this.isbn = isbn;
    }
    public String getTitle() {
        return this.title;
    }
    public void setTitle(String title) {
        this.title = title;
    }
    public String getAuthor() {
        return this.author;
    }
    public void setAuthor(String author) {
        this.author = author;
    }
    public Double getPrice() {
        return this.price;
    }
    public void setPrice(Double price) {
        this.price = price;
    }
```

```
    public Integer getQuantity() {
        return this.quantity;
    }
    public void setQuantity(Integer quantity) {
        this.quantity = quantity;
    }
}
```

Now you can move on and modify the ShoppingCart entity, defining an association to the Book entity. Listing 9-10 shows the updated ShoppingCart entity.

Listing 9-10. *Source Code for the Updated* ShoppingCart *Entity*

```
package ejbjpa.entities;
import java.io.Serializable;
import javax.persistence.Column;
import javax.persistence.Entity;
import javax.persistence.Id;
import javax.persistence.IdClass;
import javax.persistence.Table;
import javax.persistence.ManyToOne;
import javax.persistence.JoinColumn;

@Entity
@Table(name = "SHOPPINGCARTS")
@IdClass(value = ejbjpa.entities.ShoppingCartKey.class)
public class ShoppingCart implements Serializable {
    @Id
    @Column(name = "CART_ID")
    private Integer cart_id;
    @Id
    @Column(name = "BOOK_ID", insertable=false, updatable=false)
    private String book_id;
    @Column(name = "UNITS", nullable = false)
    private Integer units;
    @Column(name = "UNIT_PRICE", nullable = false)
    private Double unit_price;
    @ManyToOne
    @JoinColumn(
      name="BOOK_ID",
      referencedColumnName="ISBN")
    private Book book;
    public ShoppingCart() {
    }
    public Book getBook() {
        return this.book;
    }
```

```java
    public void setBook(Book book) {
        this.book = book;

    }
    public Integer getCart_id() {
        return this.cart_id;
    }
    public void setCart_id(Integer cart_id) {
        this.cart_id = cart_id;
    }
    public Integer getUnits () {
        return this.units;
    }
    public void setUnits(Integer units) {
        this.units = units;
    }
    public Double getUnit_price() {
        return this.unit_price;
    }
    public void setUnit_price(Double unit_price) {
        this.unit_price = unit_price;
    }
}
```

Note that in the ShoppingCart entity shown in the listing, the BOOK_ID column is mapped twice: first as a primary key field, book_id, and then as a relationship field, book. However, since the persistence provider cannot allow you to have two writable entity fields mapped to the same underlying table column, you have to define one of them as read-only. That is why you set insertable=false and updatable=false when defining the book_id entity field. Otherwise, you will end up with the following error:

```
Multiple writable mappings exist for the field [SHOPPINGCARTS.BOOK_ID]. ➥
Only one may be defined as writable, all others must be specified read-only.
```

Now that you have the entities, it's time to put them to use. The CompositeKeyTestServlet servlet shown in Listing 9-11 illustrates how you might create some ShoppingCart entities, persist them to the database, and then obtain them from the database again. The servlet assumes that in addition to the ShoppingCart.java and Book.java files discussed earlier, you also have the ShoppingCartKey.java in the /src/ejbjpa/entities directory, created as shown in Listing 8-4 in Chapter 8.

Listing 9-11. *Source Code for the* CompositeKeyTestServlet *Servlet*

```java
package ejbjpa.servlets;
import java.io.*;
import java.util.*;
import java.sql.*;
```

```java
import javax.servlet.*;
import javax.servlet.http.*;
import javax.transaction.*;
import javax.annotation.Resource;
import javax.persistence.EntityManager;
import javax.persistence.EntityManagerFactory;
import javax.persistence.PersistenceUnit;
import ejbjpa.entities.*;
public class CompositeKeyTestServlet extends HttpServlet {
    @PersistenceUnit
    private EntityManagerFactory emf;
    @Resource
    private UserTransaction userTransaction;
    public void doGet(
        HttpServletRequest request,
        HttpServletResponse response) throws ServletException, IOException {
        response.setContentType("text/html");
        response.setBufferSize(8192);
        PrintWriter out = response.getWriter();
        EntityManager em= emf.createEntityManager();
        //creating ShoppingCart entity instances
        ShoppingCart cart1 = new ShoppingCart();
        cart1.setCart_id(2);
        Book book1 = (Book) em.find(Book.class, "1590595300");
        cart1.setBook(book1);
                cart1.setUnits(3);
        cart1.setUnit_price(49.99);
        out.println("Price of the book in book1 is: $" + book1.getPrice() + "<br/>");
        ShoppingCart cart2 = new ShoppingCart();
        cart2.setCart_id(2);
        Book book2 = (Book) em.find(Book.class, "1430209631");
        cart2.setBook(book2);
        cart2.setUnits(2);
        cart2.setUnit_price(44.99);
        out.println("Price of the book in book2 is: $" + book2.getPrice() + "<br/>");
        //Performing transaction
        try{
            userTransaction.begin();
            out.println("Transaction began!"+"<br/>");
            em.persist(cart1);
            em.persist(cart2);
            em.flush();
            out.println("cart instances have been persisted to database!"+ "<br/>");
            ShoppingCart  cart3 = (ShoppingCart) em.find(ShoppingCart.class, ➥
              new ShoppingCartKey(2, "1590595300"));
            out.println("Price of the book in cart3 is: $" + ➥
             cart3.getBook().getPrice() + "<br/>");
```

```
        ShoppingCart cart4 = (ShoppingCart) em.find(ShoppingCart.class, ➥
        new ShoppingCartKey(2, "1430209631"));
        out.println("Price of the book in cart4 is: $" +➥
        cart4.getBook().getPrice() + "<br/>");
        userTransaction.rollback();
        out.println("Transaction has been rolled back!");
      }
      catch (Exception e){
        e.printStackTrace();
      }
    }
  }
}
```

If everything goes right, the CompositeKeyTestServlet servlet shown in the listing should produce the following output:

```
Price of the book in book1 is: $49.99
Price of the book in book2 is: $44.99
Transaction began!
cart instances have been persisted to database!
Price of the book in cart3 is: $49.99
Price of the book in cart4 is: $44.99
Transaction has been rolled back!
```

These results indicate that the ShoppingCart entities have been successfully persisted to the database and then obtained again from it with the help of the composite primary key specified. As usual, you finish by rolling back the transaction.

Generating Values for Primary Key Columns

Databases are different from one another. Frameworks like TopLink Essentials are designed to smooth all the major differences between databases, providing Java developers with a unified interface to the underlying data. However, there are of course still things that work differently for different underlying databases. One of those things is generating values for primary key columns.

Table 9-2 lists the types of primary key generation strategies.

Table 9-2. *The Types of Primary Key Generation*

Generation Type	Description
TABLE	Instructs the persistence provider to store the sequence name and its current value in a table in the underlying database, increasing the current value each time a new instance of the annotated entity is persisted.
SEQUENCE	Can be used if your underlying database supports sequences. The persistence provider will utilize the sequence specified, which you must have created in the database.

Generation Type	Description
IDENTITY	Can be used if your underlying database supports generating a unique identity for new rows.
AUTO	The persistence provider chooses an appropriate strategy, based on the type of the underlying database.

In the next three sections, you will look at each of the first three primary key generation strategies outlined in the table.

Generating Primary Keys Using the TABLE Strategy

The main advantage of the TABLE primary key generation strategy over the others is that it can be used with an underlying database of any type—no special features are required. To start with, you create a two-column table in the same database schema where you have created the other underlying tables. In this table, you will store information about custom sequences so that the first column stores a sequence name and the second stores its current value.

Listing 9-12 shows how you might create such a table.

Listing 9-12. *An Underlying Table to Store Information About User-Defined Sequences*

```
CREATE TABLE pono_gen_table(
gen_name VARCHAR(20) PRIMARY KEY,
gen_value NUMERIC(10)
);
```

To set up a new sequence, you have to insert a new row into the previous table. For example, you might insert the following row:

```
INSERT INTO pono_gen_table VALUES('pono_gen', 10);
```

With that done, you have a custom sequence named pono_gen whose initial value is set to 10.

Now that you have defined a custom sequence for generating primary keys, you can start using it. Once again, you can create a new project, borrowing the structure from the test project discussed in the "Performing a Quick Test of the Newly Created JPA Entities" section in Chapter 8. Then, modify the Order entity source as shown in Listing 9-13.

Listing 9-13. *The* Order *Entity Updated to Use the* TABLE *Primary Key Generation Strategy*

```
package ejbjpa.entities;
import java.io.Serializable;
import javax.persistence.Column;
import javax.persistence.Entity;
import javax.persistence.Id;
import javax.persistence.Table;
import javax.persistence.Temporal;
import static javax.persistence.TemporalType.DATE;
import javax.persistence.ManyToOne;
import javax.persistence.JoinColumn;
```

```java
import javax.persistence.GeneratedValue;
import javax.persistence.GenerationType;
import javax.persistence.TableGenerator;
import java.util.Date;
@Entity
@Table(name = "ORDERS")
public class Order implements Serializable {
    @TableGenerator(name = "ponoGen",
                    table = "PONO_GEN_TABLE",
                    pkColumnName = "GEN_NAME",
                    valueColumnName = "GEN_VALUE",
                    pkColumnValue = "PONO_GEN",
                    allocationSize = 1)
    @Id
    @GeneratedValue(strategy=GenerationType.TABLE, generator = "ponoGen")
    @Column(name = "PONO")
    private Integer pono;
    @Column(name = "SHIPPING_DATE", nullable = false)
    @Temporal(DATE)
    private Date shipping_date;
    @Column(name = "DELIVERY_ESTIMATE", nullable = false)
    private String delivery_estimate;
    @ManyToOne
    @JoinColumn(
      name="CUST_ID",
      referencedColumnName="CUST_ID")
    private Customer customer;
    @ManyToOne
    @JoinColumn(
      name="EMPNO",
      referencedColumnName="EMPNO")
    private Employee employee;
    public Order() {
    }
...
//The Order entity setter and getter methods
...
}
```

To test the generator defined in the Order entity, you might create the
GeneratingKeyTestServlet servlet as shown in Listing 9-14.

Listing 9-14. *Source Code for a Servlet That Tests the* Order *Entity Updated to Use Automatically Generated Primary Keys*

```java
//import declarations
...
public class GeneratingKeyTestServlet extends HttpServlet {
```

```
@PersistenceUnit
private EntityManagerFactory emf;
@Resource
private UserTransaction userTransaction;
public void doGet(
    HttpServletRequest request,
    HttpServletResponse response) throws ServletException, IOException {
    response.setContentType("text/html");
    response.setBufferSize(8192);
    PrintWriter out = response.getWriter();
    EntityManager em= emf.createEntityManager();
    Customer cust = (Customer) em.find(Customer.class, 2);
    Employee emp = (Employee) em.find(Employee.class, 2);
    Order order1 = new Order();
    order1.setCustomer(cust);
    order1.setEmployee(emp);
    Order order2 = new Order();
    order2.setCustomer(cust);
    order2.setEmployee(emp);
    //Performing transaction
    try{
        userTransaction.begin();
        out.println("Transaction began!"+"<br/>");
        em.persist(order1);
        em.persist(order2);
        em.flush();
        em.refresh(order1);
        em.refresh(order2);
        out.println("order "+ order1.getPono()+ " placed by: " + ➥
           order1.getCustomer().getCust_name() + "<br/>");
        out.println("order "+ order2.getPono()+ " placed by: " + ➥
           order2.getCustomer().getCust_name() + "<br/>");
        userTransaction.rollback();
        out.println("Transaction has been rolled back!");
    }
    catch (Exception e){
        e.printStackTrace();
    }
  }
}
```

Note that in the GeneratingKeyTestServlet servlet shown in the listing, you don't set pono fields of the Order instances, since the persistence provider will do it for you.

When executed, the GeneratingKeyTestServlet servlet should output the following messages:

```
Transaction began!
order 11 placed by: Paul Medica
order 12 placed by: Paul Medica
Transaction has been rolled back!
```

As mentioned, the main advantage of using the TABLE primary key generation strategy is that it can be easily adopted for any underlying database. However, this strategy has some disadvantages. The main disadvantage is that the current value of the sequence used for generating subsequent numbers is stored in a regular table. That means this value may be changed in several ways, not necessarily through the persistence provider.

Generating Primary Keys Using the IDENTITY Strategy

Another downside to the TABLE strategy is that the value of the pono field can still be set via the setPono method or directly with an INSERT statement, and the current value of the pono_gen sequence stored in the pono_gen_table table will not change. Furthermore, if the generated value happens to be already present in the pono field of an existing record in the orders table, then an error will occur upon trying to persist that new Order instance. Even worse, if such an error occurs, you won't be able to overcome it by retrying to perform the persist operation on the same Order instance. Each new attempt will fail, causing the transaction to be rolled back. Therefore, the current value of the table generator used here will never be increased, unless you manually change the pono field of the instance being inserted or change the current value of the table generator by directly updating the pono_gen_table table.

Using the IDENTITY primary key generation strategy lets you avoid all these problems (at least, this is true when your underlying database is MySQL). This strategy implies that the persistence provider actually exploits the primary key generation mechanism provided by the database server, which will handle all the data integrity issues using its built-in functionality.

Unfortunately, not all databases support the IDENTITY strategy. MySQL is one of those that support it. If your underlying database is MySQL, you can now alter the orders table created as shown in Listing 6-4 in Chapter 6. To do this, you need to connect to the database server as usrsample user and then issue the ALTER statement shown in Listing 9-15.

Listing 9-15. *Setting the* AUTO_INCREMENT *Attribute to the* pono *Column of the* orders *Table*

```
use dbsample;
ALTER TABLE orders MODIFY pono INTEGER AUTO_INCREMENT;
```

■**Caution** Although the examples discussed in this chapter are implemented in separate projects, and as stated in the beginning of the chapter, you temporarily digressed from the main book sample project that you started building in the preceding chapters, altering the orders underlying table will, of course, affect the sample discussed throughout the book. So, if you're implementing the underlying database in MySQL, you must modify the Order.java file shown in Listing 8-3 and used in the main book sample, as shown in Listing 9-16 in this section.

It is important to note that later you can always remove the AUTO_INCREMENT attribute, returning the orders table to its original state as follows:

```
ALTER TABLE orders MODIFY pono INTEGER;
```

Listing 9-16 shows how you have to update the Order.java file so that it can utilize the IDENTITY primary key generation strategy. As mentioned in the previous caution block, in case your underlying database is implemented in MySQL, you also have to update the Order.java file used in the main book sample project and shown in Listing 8-3 in Chapter 8.

Listing 9-16. *The* Order *Entity Updated to Utilize the* IDENTITY *Primary Key Generation Strategy*

```java
package ejbjpa.entities;
import java.io.Serializable;
import javax.persistence.Column;
import javax.persistence.Entity;
import javax.persistence.Id;
import javax.persistence.Table;
import javax.persistence.Temporal;
import static javax.persistence.TemporalType.DATE;
import javax.persistence.ManyToOne;
import javax.persistence.JoinColumn;
import javax.persistence.GeneratedValue;
import javax.persistence.GenerationType;
import java.util.Date;
@Entity
@Table(name = "ORDERS")
public class Order implements Serializable {
    @Id
    @GeneratedValue(strategy=GenerationType.IDENTITY)
    @Column(name = "PONO")
    private Integer pono;
    @Column(name = "SHIPPING_DATE", nullable = false)
    @Temporal(DATE)
    private Date shipping_date;
    @Column(name = "DELIVERY_ESTIMATE", nullable = false)
    private String delivery_estimate;
    @ManyToOne
    @JoinColumn(
      name="CUST_ID",
      referencedColumnName="CUST_ID")
    private Customer customer;
    @ManyToOne
    @JoinColumn(
      name="EMPNO",
      referencedColumnName="EMPNO")
    private Employee employee;
    public Order() {
```

```
    }
...
//The Order entity setter and getter methods
...
}
```

It is interesting to note that when using the IDENTITY strategy, you don't need to worry about specifying an initial value with which the generator starts producing sequence numbers—the database server will do it for you, figuring out a new sequence number based on the maximum value of the pono field within existing records in the orders underlying table. So, when you now run the GeneratingKeyTestServlet servlet for the first time, you should see that the value generated for the pono field of the first entity is the number that is right next to the maximum value of the pono field within already existing records. For example, if the orders table already has some records and the maximum value of the pono field within those records is 5, then you should see the following output when executing the GeneratingKeyTestServlet servlet for the first time:

```
Transaction began!
order 6 placed by: Paul Medica
order 7 placed by: Paul Medica
Transaction has been rolled back!
```

Each new load of the servlet will show increased results, regardless of whether the transaction has been rolled back or committed.

From now on, even if you explicitly specify the value for the pono field of an Order instance, as shown in the following snippet:

```
...
        Order order1 = new Order();
        order1.setPono(25);
        order1.setCustomer(cust);
        order1.setEmployee(emp);
...
```

the specified value, if any, will be disregarded, and the generated value will take effect.

Generating Primary Keys Using the SEQUENCE Strategy

In the case of Oracle, you can use the SEQUENCE primary key generation strategy as an alternative to the TABLE strategy discussed earlier.

To start with, you must create a sequence to be used. To do this, you need to connect to the database server as usrsample user and then issue the ALTER statement shown in Listing 9-17.

Listing 9-17. *Creating a Sequence in Oracle*

```
CREATE SEQUENCE pono_gen_sequence START WITH 10 INCREMENT BY 1;
```

Next, you can change the Order.java file as shown in Listing 9-18. Also, make sure to update the Order.java file used in the main book sample project, provided you're going to use an Oracle underlying database in this project.

Listing 9-18. *The* Order *Entity Updated to Utilize the* SEQUENCE *Primary Key Generation Strategy*

```
package ejbjpa.entities;
import java.io.Serializable;
import javax.persistence.Column;
import javax.persistence.Entity;
import javax.persistence.Id;
import javax.persistence.Table;
import javax.persistence.Temporal;
import static javax.persistence.TemporalType.DATE;
import javax.persistence.ManyToOne;
import javax.persistence.JoinColumn;
import javax.persistence.GeneratedValue;
import javax.persistence.GenerationType;
import javax.persistence.SequenceGenerator;
import java.util.Date;
@Entity
@Table(name = "ORDERS")
public class Order implements Serializable {
    @SequenceGenerator(name = "ponoGen",
                    sequenceName = "PONO_GEN_SEQUENCE",
                    initialValue = 10,
                    allocationSize = 1)
    @Id
    @GeneratedValue(strategy=GenerationType.SEQUENCE, generator = "ponoGen")
    @Column(name = "PONO")
    private Integer pono;
    @Column(name = "SHIPPING_DATE", nullable = false)
    @Temporal(DATE)
    private Date shipping_date;
    @Column(name = "DELIVERY_ESTIMATE", nullable = false)
    private String delivery_estimate;
    @ManyToOne
    @JoinColumn(
      name="CUST_ID",
      referencedColumnName="CUST_ID")
    private Customer customer;
    @ManyToOne
    @JoinColumn(
      name="EMPNO",
      referencedColumnName="EMPNO")
    private Employee employee;
    public Order() {
    }
```

```
...
//The Order entity setter and getter methods
...
}
```

In Oracle, each time a sequence is accessed, its current value is incremented immediately and won't be set back even if you roll back the transaction within which you access the sequence. This is similar to the IDENTITY strategy on this point. However, if you now explicitly specify the value for the pono field when defining an Order instance in the way you saw in the snippet shown at the end of the preceding section, then the specified value will be given priority over the generated one. To be exact, the generator will not even generate a value in this situation, so the current sequence number will not be increased.

Summary

As you no doubt have realized, the Java Persistence API provides an efficient way of mapping between object-oriented and relational data storage, removing the burden from Java developers to access the underlying database via SQL/JDBC. However, there is still a lot to learn to be able to efficiently map the entity data to the underlying database.

In this chapter, you looked at some practical examples on object/relational mapping, including how to specify mapping metadata, utilize entity relationships, and deal with primary keys in entities.

CHAPTER 10

■■■

Using EntityManager

As you learned in the preceding chapter, the idea behind object/relational mapping is to provide the persistence provider with detailed information on how to associate entities with the corresponding underlying database tables and also to describe relationships between entities and how the operations performed on related entities should work. The object/relational mapping facility, however, has nothing to do with managing entity instances and their life cycles.

In this chapter, you will take a close look at the EntityManager, a Java Persistence API interface providing all the methods for manipulating entities mapped to relational tables. The chapter starts with an overview of the EntityManager and then talks about the different ways in which you can use it. After reading this chapter, you will have learned how to do the following:

- Manage the life cycles of entity instances

- Obtain an instance of the EntityManager

- Deal with container-managed and application-managed EntityManagers

- Use Java Transaction Architecture (JTA) and resource-local EntityManagers

- Utilize EntityManager methods to manipulate entities

- Use entity life-cycle callback methods

Over the course of this chapter, you will look at some basic examples that tackle these operations, helping you understand the mechanics behind the EntityManager tool.

Managing Entities

Now that you know how to use ORM metadata to tell the persistence provider how to map entities to underlying database tables, what persistence mechanism might you use to manipulate those entities?

The following sections address this question while taking a look at the EntityManager, the tool through which you can manage the entity instances' life cycles.

The Big Picture

In a nutshell, if ORM metadata provides the persistence provider with the exact details of how to map the entities to the underlying database, then the EntityManager interface methods provide a standard way to manipulate instances of those entities from within application components, such as enterprise beans and servlets.

Diagrammatically, this might look like Figure 10-1.

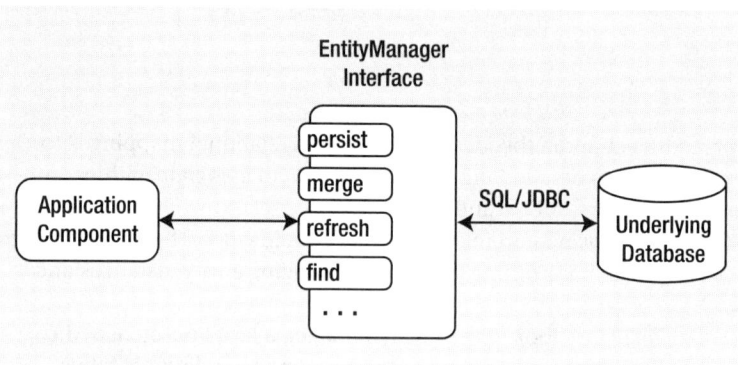

Figure 10-1. *Application components employ the EntityManager interface to manipulate entities mapped to the underlying database data.*

As you can see in the figure, an application component can interact with the underlying database through the EntityManager interface, which is similar to JDBC in that it provides a set of standard methods allowing you to perform all operations on relational data. Unlike JDBC, however, EntityManager methods operate with JPA entities mapped to the underlying tables with object/relational mapping, as discussed in the preceding chapter.

■**Note** It's interesting to note that behind the scenes the EntityManager relies on a set of JDBC drivers used by the persistence provider to interact with the underlying databases of different types. So, each time you invoke an EntityManager method, the persistence provider generates and then implicitly issues an appropriate SQL statement through the corresponding JDBC driver (sometimes, though, cached data is used).

The EntityManager can be used in both Java EE and Java SE environments. In Java EE environments, the EntityManager can be used in EJB components, Java EE web components, and Java EE application clients.

To take advantage of the EntityManager interface in your application, you have to accomplish the following key steps:

1. Create entities upon the underlying tables as necessary.

2. Define a persistence unit upon an appropriate JDBC resource defined in the application server.

3. In case you want to obtain an application-managed EntityManager, you first have to obtain an instance of `EntityManagerFactory` created upon a certain persistence unit. In the case of a container-managed EntityManager, the container will create the `EntityManagerFactory` implicitly.

4. Obtain an EntityManager instance.

5. Access and manipulate the entities through the EntityManager instance.

Whether explicitly or not, an EntityManager instance is obtained from an `EntityManagerFactory` associated with a certain persistence unit. There cannot be more than one `EntityManagerFactory` per persistence unit available simultaneously. Graphically, this might look like Figure 10-2.

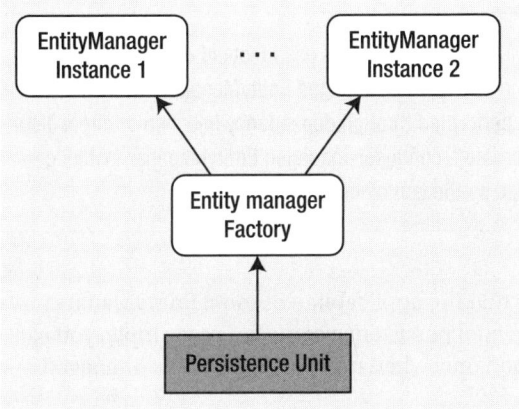

Figure 10-2. *An EntityManager instance is obtained from an* `EntityManagerFactory` *associated with a certain persistence unit.*

Actually, you've already seen the EntityManager in practice in the preceding chapter, where you used the EntityManager APIs to manipulate entity instances from within a servlet. In this chapter, in the later "Uses of EntityManager" section, you will see some examples of using the EntityManager in EJB components.

Persistence Contexts

As mentioned, you have to obtain an instance of EntityManager before you can use its methods to access and manipulate entities available within your application. Not surprisingly, each instance of the EntityManager is associated with a certain context, which is called the *persistence context* of that EntityManager instance.

So, you might think of an EntityManager instance as an object of a class that implements the EntityManager interface and allows you to operate on a certain persistence context.

Note In the object-oriented world, it is most common that an instance of a class manipulates the data specific to that instance and held in its variables. Note, however, that EntityManager is not a regular class but an interface and, thus, has no variables for holding data. Creating an object that lets you manipulate a certain persistence context through the EntityManager interface methods occurs behind the scenes with the help of an entity manager factory. Such an object is typically called an *EntityManager instance*.

It's important to realize that a single persistent context may be associated with more than one EntityManager reference, provided all those EntityManager references are obtained from the same entity manager factory.

Note You may be wondering why the term *EntityManager reference* is used instead of *EntityManager instance* here. As you will learn in the later "Obtaining a Container-Managed EntityManager" section, obtaining a container-managed EntityManager instance is performed through dependency injection or direct JNDI lookup of the EntityManager. So, you don't actually create a container-managed EntityManager instance—rather, you obtain a reference to the instance provided by the container.

Another important thing to remember is that the applicability of some EntityManager methods is dependent upon the type of associated persistence context. For example, you can call the EntityManager interface's close method only when using an application-managed EntityManager.

The EntityManager instance operating on a persistence context is obtained from an entity manager factory associated with a certain persistence unit. As you will learn a bit later in this chapter, you won't need to explicitly deal with the EntityManagerFactory interface in the case of a container-managed EntityManager, since the container does it for you implicitly.

The following sections explain the concept behind the persistence context in more detail.

EntityManager and Its Persistence Context

The persistence context of an EntityManager instance defines the scope within which you can use that EntityManager instance to access and manipulate particular entity instances. Within a certain persistence context, any persistent entity identity may be represented by a single instance.

Figure 10-3 illustrates that a persistence context consists of a set of entity instances manipulated by a certain EntityManager instance.

As stated earlier, an EntityManager instance uses its methods to access and manipulate the entity instances in the associated persistent context. You can find the list of the most commonly used EntityManager interface methods in Table 10-2 later in this chapter.

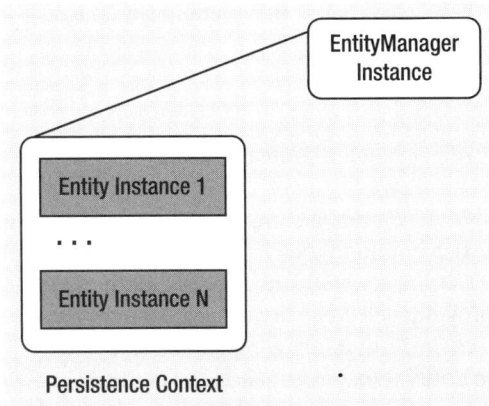

Figure 10-3. *A persistence context consists of a set of entity instances managed by an EntityManager instance.*

The life cycle of a persistence context depends on its type. As you will learn in the following sections, there are two major types of persistence contexts: container-managed and application-managed. A container-managed persistent context in turn can be either transaction-scoped or extended, depending on whether the context is scoped to a single transaction or might span multiple transactions, respectively. In both cases, though, the life cycle of the persistent context is automatically managed by the Java EE container. In contrast, the life cycle of an application-managed persistence context is explicitly managed by the application.

Container-Managed Persistence Context

In EJB components, you will normally use EntityManagers associated with container-managed persistence contexts. As its name implies, the container manages a container-managed persistence context. What this means in practice is that it is the responsibility of the Java EE container to manage the life cycle of such a persistence context. The scope of a container-managed persistence context is defined upon creating the EntityManager instance and, by default, corresponds to the scope of an active JTA transaction or can be defined as extended so that it can survive multiple transactions.

■**Note** A JTA transaction is one that is controlled by the Java EE transaction manager and may include invocations across multiple application components. The alternative to JTA is resource-local transactions that are controlled by the application. The type of transactions to be used is defined in the persistence unit whose factory was used when creating the EntityManager instance. An EntityManager whose underlying transactions are JTA is called a *JTA EntityManager*. The underlying transactions of a container-managed EntityManager instance are always JTA transactions. You will see an example of using an application-managed EntityManager whose underlying transactions are resource-local in the "An Example of Using an Application-Managed EntityManager" section later in this chapter. Then, the "An Example on Persistence Context Propagation" section provides an example of using an EntityManager whose persistence context is propagated with the JTA transaction.

The following two sections will touch upon these two types of the container-managed persistence context: transaction-scoped and extended.

Transaction-Scoped Persistence Context

As mentioned, the lifetime of a container-managed persistence context defaults to the scope of a single transaction.

When you inject a container-managed EntityManager into a component, you obtain an EntityManager instance whose persistence context is bound to the JTA transaction. If there is no existing persistent context defined upon the JTA transaction by the time one of the Entity-Manager's methods is invoked, the persistence provider will create a new persistence context. After the JTA transaction ends, the container closes the EntityManager instance associated with it, detaching all managed entities within the EntityManager's persistence context.

As you might guess, this mechanism enables a single persistent context to be shared between more than one application component, as shown in Figure 10-4.

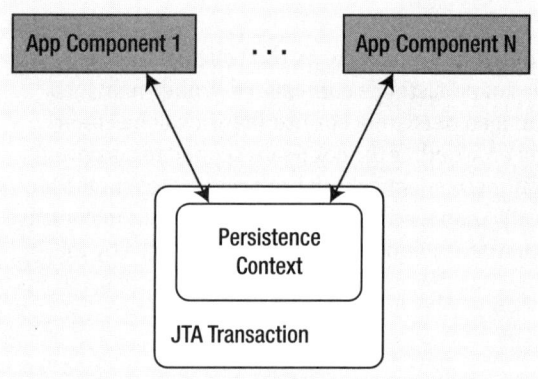

Figure 10-4. *A transaction-scoped persistence context is bound to a single JTA transaction that can be shared between more than one application component.*

Each application component interacts with the persistence context bound to the JTA transaction through an EntityManager reference injected into that component via the `javax.persistence.PersistenceContext` annotation.

Extended Persistence Context

An extended persistence context can be bound only to the scope of a stateful session bean. To achieve this, you have to explicitly set the `type` element of the `PersistenceContext` annotation to `PersistenceContextType.EXTENDED`. An extended persistence context can survive more than one transaction, as depicted in Figure 10-5.

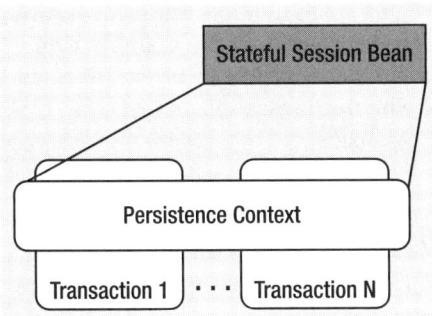

Figure 10-5. *An extended persistence context can survive more than one transaction.*

An extended persistence context bound to a stateful session bean begins when an instance of that stateful bean is created and ends just before the container removes the bean's instance.

Application-Managed Persistence Context

When using an application-managed EntityManager, the application explicitly manages the life cycle of the persistence context. Application-managed persistence contexts are not bound to the scope of a transaction and may actually survive multiple transactions, as depicted in Figure 10-6.

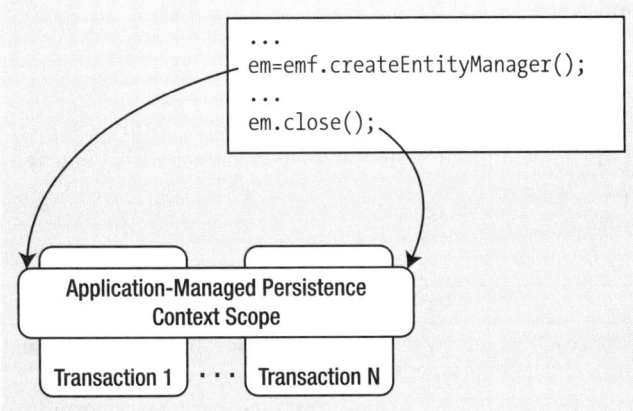

Figure 10-6. *An application-managed persistence context starts when the associated Entity-Manager is explicitly created and ends when it is closed. It may survive several transactions.*

As you can see in the figure, an application-managed persistence context begins when you obtain an EntityManager instance by invoking the createEntityManager method of the EntityManagerFactory interface and is closed when the associated EntityManager instance is closed with the close method. If the EntityManager instance being closed is associated with an active transaction, the persistence context is closed when the transaction completes.

Although the persistence context depicted in the figure spans multiple transactions, this is not always the case with an application-managed persistence context. For example, if an application-managed JTA EntityManager is created within the scope of the current JTA transaction, then the persistence context will be associated with the transaction. In that case, however, you will still need to explicitly close the EntityManager.

Note If you recall from the note on JTA in the "Container-Managed Persistence Context" section, a JTA EntityManager is one whose underlying `EntityManagerFactory` is based on a persistence unit where the type of transactions to be used is set to JTA. In practical terms, in the `persistence.xml` file that defines the persistence unit, you have to set the `transaction-type` attribute of the `persistence-unit` element to JTA.

In practice, though, application-managed EnityManagers are often used to deal with resource-local transactions controlled by the application through the EntityTransaction interface. You will see an example of using a resource-local EntityManager in the "An Example of Using an Application-Managed EntityManager" section later.

Managing the Life Cycle of Entity Instances

Now that you know how the life cycle of persistence contexts is managed, how can you manage the life cycle of a certain entity instance within a persistence context? The following two sections briefly address this question.

States of Entity Instances

You use an appropriate EntityManager instance to manage the life cycle of an entity instance. An entity instance can be in one of the following states: new, managed, detached, or removed. Table 10-1 summarizes these states.

Table 10-1. *Possible States of an Entity Instance*

Method	Description
New	When you create an instance of an entity with the new operator, it is not yet associated with a persistence context, and its state is set to new.
Managed	When you perform the persist operation on an entity instance in the new state or obtain an entity instance by the find method of the EntityManager within a transaction context, that instance becomes managed and is associated with the persistence context. A detached instance becomes managed when you perform the merge operation on it.
Detached	When a persistence context ends, all its entity instances become detached—not managed and not associated with a persistence context anymore. Also, when you obtain an entity by the find method or query outside the scope of a transaction, the state of that entity is set to detached.
Removed	When you perform the remove operation on an entity instance in the managed state, its state changes to removed. A removed entity is then removed from the database when the persistence context is synchronized to the database.

The most important thing to understand here is that some EntityManager operations cause a change in the state of the entity instances to which they apply. If you want an entity instance's data to be synchronized to the database, you first have to make it managed.

Attaching Entities to the Persistence Context

As explained earlier, an entity instance becomes managed when you perform one of the EntityManager operations that associate that instance with a persistence context. The particular method to use depends on the current state of the entity instance you want to make managed.

For example, when you have an entity instance in the new state, you can use the EntityManager's persist method to make it managed, associating it with the EntityManager's persistence context. If you have an entity instance in the detached state, you can use the merge method to attach it to the persistence context.

You don't need to worry about explicitly attaching an entity instance to the persistence context if you are obtaining that instance by the find method invoked within the scope of a transaction.

Figure 10-7 shows a graphical depiction of how an entity instance can be attached to a persistence context.

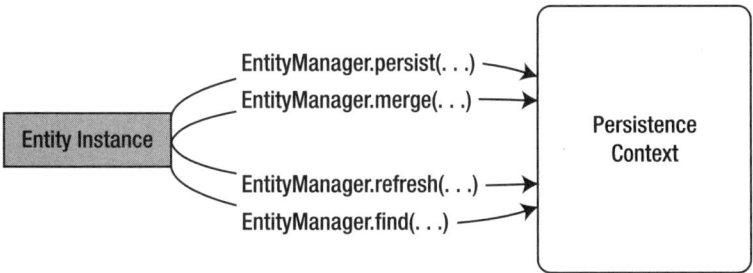

Figure 10-7. *A graphical representation of how an entity can be attached to the EntityManager persistence context*

An important thing to remember when dealing with entity instances is that only managed entity instances are synchronized to the database (to be exact, the state of the entities scheduled for removal from the database is synchronized too—they are removed).

The problem is that, in many cases, a persistence context to which entity instances are attached ends implicitly, because of an operation performed by the container behind the scenes, making all the managed entity instances detached. For example, say the container commits the underlying transaction with which the persistence context is associated.

As a quick example, let's look at a stateless session bean that uses container-managed transactions. As a matter of fact, all the entity instances you attach to a transaction-scoped persistence context within a business method of such a bean become detached when method execution ends. So, when calling another method of that bean, you have to reattach those entity instances, provided you want to continue to synchronize their state to the database.

EntityManager Interface

As stated earlier, the EntityManager interface provides the methods through which you can interact with the persistence context associated with a certain EntityManager instance.

Table 10-2 summarizes the most commonly used EntityManager interface methods.

Table 10-2. *The Most Commonly Used EntityManager Interface Methods*

Method	Description
`public <T> T find(Class<T> entityClass, Object primaryKey)`	Finds an entity by its primary key and then sends it to the EntityManager's persistence context
`public void persist(Object entity)`	Makes an instance managed, sending it to the EntityManager's persistence context
`public <T> T merge(T entity)`	Merges an instance into the EntityManager's persistence context
`public void remove(Object entity)`	Schedules an instance for removal from the EntityManager's persistence context
`public void refresh(Object entity)`	Refreshes an instance in the EntityManager's persistence context from the database
`public void flush()`	Synchronizes the EntityManager's persistence context to the underlying database
`public boolean isOpen()`	Determines whether the EntityManager is open; returns true if the EntityManager has not been closed
`public void clear()`	Clears the EntityManager's persistence context, detaching all managed entities
`public void close()`	Used to close an application-managed EntityManager
`public EntityTransaction getTransaction()`	Used with a resource-local EntityManager to obtain the resource-level transaction object through which you can then begin and commit multiple transactions
`public void joinTransaction()`	Associates an application-managed EntityManager with the current JTA transaction

Note that this table doesn't include EntityManager methods with which you can create a Java Persistence Query Language (JPQL) or native SQL statement. These methods will be listed and discussed in the next chapter.

You can find the full list of the EntityManager interface methods in the section entitled "EntityManager Interface" in the Enterprise JavaBeans 3.0 Specification Java Persistence API document, part of JSR-220, available at `http://jcp.org/en/jsr/detail?id=220`.

Using EntityManager to Manipulate Entities

Now that you have a grasp of the ideas behind the EntityManager API, it's time to look at how you can put the API into action.

In the following sections, you'll start by looking at how you can obtain an EntityManager instance. Then, you will take a look at some examples of using the EntityManager API.

Obtaining an Instance of EntityManager

The ways in which you can obtain an EntityManager instance vary, depending on whether you want a container-managed or application-managed EntityManager instance.

Obtaining a Container-Managed EntityManager

The container-managed EntityManager is the most commonly used type of EntityManager in Java EE environments. Using a container-managed EntityManager simplifies development, since the life cycle of it is controlled by the container rather than by the code you write. So, when designing an EJB component, you will most likely want to utilize a container-managed EntityManager.

The simplest way to obtain a container-managed EntityManager instance is to inject it into the component with the help of the `javax.persistence.PersistenceContext` annotation like this:

```
import javax.persistence.EntityManager;
import javax.persistence.PersistenceContext;
...
@PersistenceContext
EntityManager em;
```

If you have more than one persistence unit available, you have to explicitly specify which one will be used, with the `unitName` element of the `PersistenceContext` annotation:

```
@PersistenceContext(unitName="containeremtest-pu")
EntityManager em;
```

If you need to inject a container-managed EntityManager of type `PersistenceContextType.EXTENDED` into a stateful session bean, you might do it like this:

```
@PersistenceContext(type=PersistenceContextType.EXTENDED)
EntityManager em;
```

The alternative to injection is JNDI lookup, which can be done as follows:

```
...
import javax.annotation.Resource;
import javax.ejb.SessionContext;
...
@PersistenceContext(name="containeremtest")
public class TestSessionBean implements TestSession {
  @Resource SessionContext ctx;
  public void testMethod() {
   EntityManager em = (EntityManager)ctx.lookup("containeremtest");
   ...
  }
}
```

Obtaining an Application-Managed EntityManager

In a Java EE environment, obtaining an application-managed EntityManager is a two-step process. First, you inject an `EntityManagerFactory` like this:

```
...
import javax.persistence.EntityManager;
import javax.persistence.EntityManagerFactory;
import javax.persistence.PersistenceUnit;
...
@PersistenceUnit
EntityManagerFactory emf;
```

Then, you can obtain an EntityManager instance as follows:

```
EntityManager em = emf.createEntityManager();
```

If you have more than one persistence unit available, you have to use the `unitName` element of the `PersistenceUnit` annotation to explicitly specify which one will be used:

```
@PersistenceUnit(unitName="appemtest-pu")
EntityManagerFactory emf;
```

Uses of EntityManager

The following sections provide examples using the EntityManager API. In particular, you will look at some uses of container-managed and application-managed EntityManagers in EJB components.

An Example of Using a Container-Managed EntityManager

Let's start with a simple example of using a container-managed EntityManager. To illustrate the concept, you might create a stateless session bean with a single business method, within which you utilize the EntityManager instance injected into the bean with the `@PersistenceContext` annotations.

Take a look at the `OrderTestBean` bean shown in Listing 10-1. This bean assumes you will use the `Customer` and `Employee` entities defined as shown in Listing 8-1 and Listing 8-2 in Chapter 8, respectively. As for the `Order` entity, it should be defined as discussed in Chapter 9 and shown in Listing 9-16 for an underlying MySQL database or in Listing 9-18 for Oracle.

Listing 10-1. *An Example of Stateless Session Bean That Uses a Container-Managed EntityManager*

```
package ejbjpa.ejb;
import java.io.Serializable;
import javax.ejb.EJBException;
import javax.ejb.Stateless;
import javax.persistence.EntityManager;
import javax.persistence.PersistenceContext;
import ejbjpa.entities.*;
```

```
@Stateless
public class OrderTestBean implements OrderTest {
    @PersistenceContext
    private EntityManager em;
    public Integer setOrder(Integer cust_id, Integer empno) {
        Integer order_pono;
        try {
          Customer cust = (Customer) em.find(Customer.class, cust_id);
          Employee emp = (Employee) em.find(Employee.class, empno);
          Order order1 = new Order();
          order1.setCustomer(cust);
          order1.setEmployee(emp);
          em.persist(order1);
          em.flush();
          em.refresh(order1);
          order_pono = order1.getPono();
        } catch (Exception e) {
            throw new EJBException(e.getMessage());
        }
        return order_pono;
    }
}
```

The first step you perform here is injecting a container-managed EntityManager instance with the PersistenceContext annotation. Then you use the obtained EntityManager instance in the setOrder business method of the OrderTestBean session bean.

In particular, the setOrder business method performs the following steps:

1. Obtains a Customer and an Employee instance with the help of the find method of the EntityManager

2. Creates a new Order instance and then sets its Customer and Employee fields to the instances obtained in step 1

3. Persists the Order instance created in step 2, attaching it to the EntityManager's persistence context

4. Synchronizes the Order instance to the database with flush

5. Refreshes the Order instance from the database

6. Obtains the generated pono with the getPono method of the Order instance

Now, to test the OrderTestBean session bean, you might use the servlet shown in Listing 10-2.

Listing 10-2. *A Servlet That Might Be Used to Test the* OrderTestBean *Session Bean*

```
package ejbjpa.servlets;
import java.io.*;
import javax.servlet.*;
```

```
import javax.servlet.http.*;
import javax.ejb.EJB;
import ejbjpa.entities.*;
import ejbjpa.ejb.*;
public class EmEjbTestServlet extends HttpServlet {
    @EJB private OrderTest orderTest;
    public void doGet(
        HttpServletRequest request,
        HttpServletResponse response) throws ServletException, IOException {
        response.setContentType("text/html");
        response.setBufferSize(8192);
        PrintWriter out = response.getWriter();
        try{
            out.println("Created order: "+orderTest.setOrder(2,1)+"<br/>");
        }
        catch (Exception e){
            e.printStackTrace();
        }
    }
}
```

The EmEjbTestServlet servlet shown in the listing simply calls the OrderTestBean's setOrder business method, passing in 2 and 1 as the customer ID and employee ID, respectively. This method returns the generated order's pono, which is then sent to the browser's output.

This is a simple example of using a container-managed EntityManager. It simply demonstrates how you can obtain and then utilize a container-managed EntityManager instance.

Now, suppose you deploy the OrderTestBean session bean discussed here with the persistence.xml configuration file that defines two persistence units rather than one. The point of utilizing two persistence units here is to get some practice using EntityManager instances created with different factories to deal with common problems.

Listing 10-3 shows what such a persistence.xml configuration file might look like.

Listing 10-3. *An Example of the* persistence.xml *Configuration File Containing More Than One Persistence Unit Element*

```
<?xml version="1.0" encoding="UTF-8"?>
<persistence xmlns="http://java.sun.com/xml/ns/persistence" ➥
xmlns:xsi="http://www.w3.org/2001/XMLSchema-instance" ➥
xsi:schemaLocation="http://java.sun.com/xml/ns/persistence ➥
http://java.sun.com/xml/ns/persistence/persistence_1_0.xsd" version="1.0">
    <persistence-unit name="containeremtest1-pu" transaction-type="JTA">
        <jta-data-source>jdbc/mysqlpool</jta-data-source>
    </persistence-unit>
    <persistence-unit name="containeremtest2-pu" transaction-type="JTA">
        <jta-data-source>jdbc/mysqlpool</jta-data-source>
    </persistence-unit>
</persistence>
```

If you try to use the `persistence.xml` configuration file with the `OrderTestBean` bean shown in Listing 10-1 earlier, you will get the following deployment error message:

```
Could not resolve a persistence unit corresponding to the persistence-context➥
-ref-name [ejbjpa.ejb.OrderTestBean/em] in the scope of the module called ...
```

So, you might update the `OrderTestBean` session bean as shown in Listing 10-4. (To save space, the body of `setOrder` is not shown in this listing.)

Listing 10-4. *The* `OrderTestBean` *Session Bean Updated to Use Two Persistence Contexts*

```java
package ejbjpa.ejb;
import java.io.Serializable;
import javax.ejb.EJBException;
import javax.ejb.Stateless;
import javax.persistence.EntityManager;
import javax.persistence.PersistenceContext;
import ejbjpa.entities.*;
@Stateless
public class OrderTestBean implements OrderTest {
    @PersistenceContext(unitName="containeremtest1-pu")
    private EntityManager em;
    @PersistenceContext(unitName="containeremtest2-pu")
    private EntityManager em2;
    public Integer setOrder(Integer cust_id, Integer empno) {
...
    //The code of this method is shown in Listing 10-1
...
    }
    public String changeOrderEmpTest(Integer pono, Integer empno) {
        String order_details;
        try {
          Employee emp = (Employee) em.find(Employee.class, empno);
          Order order1 = (Order) em.find(Order.class, pono);
          order1.setEmployee(emp);
          order_details = "order "+ order1.getPono()+ " placed via: " + ➥
          order1.getEmployee().getLastname()+"<br/>";
          Order order2 = (Order) em2.find(Order.class, pono);
          order_details = order_details+"order "+ order2.getPono()+ " placed ➥
           via: " + order2.getEmployee().getLastname()+"<br/>";
          order_details = order_details+"order "+ order1.getPono()+ " placed ~CC
           via: " + order1.getEmployee().getLastname();
        } catch (Exception e) {
            throw new EJBException(e.getMessage());
        }
        return order_details;
    }
}
```

As you can see, the updated version of the bean includes another business method called changeOrderEmpTest. This method illustrates using two different persistence contexts within a single method. In particular, it shows you that employing two different persistence contexts makes it possible for you to have two different entity instances running simultaneously and representing the same record in the underlying table.

To test the updated OrderTestBean session bean, you also need to update the EmEjbTestServlet servlet, as shown in Listing 10-5.

Listing 10-5. *The Updated* EmEjbTestServlet *Servlet to Test the* OrderTestBean *Session Bean Utilizing Two Persistence Contexts*

```
//import declarations
...
public class EmEjbTestServlet extends HttpServlet {
    @EJB private OrderTest orderTest;
    public void doGet(
        HttpServletRequest request,
        HttpServletResponse response) throws ServletException, IOException {
        response.setContentType("text/html");
        response.setBufferSize(8192);
        PrintWriter out = response.getWriter();
        try{
            Integer pono = orderTest.setOrder(2,1);
            out.println("Created order "+ pono +"<br/>");
            out.println(orderTest.changeOrderEmpTest(pono,2));
        }
        catch (Exception e){
            e.printStackTrace();
        }
    }
}
```

The updated EmEjbTestServlet servlet first calls the OrderTestBean's setOrder method and then the changeOrderEmpTest method.

The output of the EmEjbTestServlet servlet shown in the listing might look like this:

```
Created order 11
order 11 placed via: Silver
order 11 placed via: Oganovich
order 11 placed via: Silver
```

An Example of Using an Application-Managed EntityManager

Unlike a container-managed EntityManager whose life cycle is managed by the container, an application-managed EntityManager is controlled by the code you write. As stated earlier, an application-managed EntityManager can be either JTA or resource-local, depending on the type of underlying transactions, as specified in the corresponding persistence unit.

Listing 10-6 shows the `persistence.xml` configuration file defining two persistence units—both of which are resource-local.

Listing 10-6. *An Example of the* `persistence.xml` *Configuration File Defining Persistence Units Whose Transaction Type Is Resource-Local*

```
<?xml version="1.0" encoding="UTF-8"?>
<persistence xmlns="http://java.sun.com/xml/ns/persistence" ➥
xmlns:xsi="http://www.w3.org/2001/XMLSchema-instance" ➥
xsi:schemaLocation="http://java.sun.com/xml/ns/persistence ➥
http://java.sun.com/xml/ns/persistence/persistence_1_0.xsd" version="1.0">
    <persistence-unit name="appemtest1-pu" transaction-type="RESOURCE_LOCAL">
        <jta-data-source>jdbc/mysqlpool</jta-data-source>
    </persistence-unit>
    <persistence-unit name="appemtest2-pu" transaction-type="RESOURCE_LOCAL">
        <jta-data-source>jdbc/mysqlpool</jta-data-source>
    </persistence-unit>
</persistence>
```

Returning to the `OrderTestBean` session bean discussed in the preceding section, you might update it now as shown in Listing 10-7.

Listing 10-7. *The* `OrderTestBean` *Session Bean Updated to Use an Application-Managed EntityManager*

```
package ejbjpa.ejb;
import java.io.Serializable;
import javax.ejb.EJBException;
import javax.ejb.Stateless;
import javax.persistence.EntityManager;
import javax.persistence.EntityManagerFactory;
import javax.transaction.UserTransaction;
import javax.persistence.PersistenceUnit;
import javax.annotation.Resource;
import ejbjpa.entities.*;
@Stateless
public class OrderTestBean implements OrderTest {
    @PersistenceUnit(unitName="appemtest1-pu")
    private EntityManagerFactory emf;
    @PersistenceUnit(unitName="appemtest2-pu")
    private EntityManagerFactory emf2;
    public Integer setOrder(Integer cust_id, Integer empno) {
        Integer order_pono;
        try {
          EntityManager em = emf.createEntityManager();
          Customer cust = (Customer) em.find(Customer.class, cust_id);
          Employee emp = (Employee) em.find(Employee.class, empno);
          Order order1 = new Order();
```

```java
            order1.setCustomer(cust);
            order1.setEmployee(emp);
            em.getTransaction().begin();
            em.persist(order1);
            em.flush();

            em.refresh(order1);
            order_pono = order1.getPono();
            em.getTransaction().commit();
            em.close();
        } catch (Exception e) {
            throw new EJBException(e.getMessage());
        }
        return order_pono;
    }
    public String changeOrderEmpTest(Integer pono, Integer empno) {
        String order_details;
        try {
            EntityManager em = emf.createEntityManager();
            em.getTransaction().begin();
            Employee emp = (Employee) em.find(Employee.class, empno);
            Order order1 = (Order) em.find(Order.class, pono);
            order1.setEmployee(emp);

            order_details = "order "+ order1.getPono()+ " placed via: " + ➥
            order1.getEmployee().getLastname()+"<br/>";
            EntityManager em2 = emf2.createEntityManager();
            Order order2 = (Order) em2.find(Order.class, pono);
            order_details = order_details+"order "+ order2.getPono()+ " placed ➥
             via: " + order2.getEmployee().getLastname()+"<br/>";
            em.getTransaction().commit();
            em2.refresh(order2);
            order_details = order_details+"order "+ order2.getPono()+ " placed ➥
             via: " + order2.getEmployee().getLastname();
            em.close();
            em2.close();
        } catch (Exception e) {
            throw new EJBException(e.getMessage());
        }
        return order_details;
    }
}
```

When executed, the previous servlet should produce output like the following:

```
Created order 14
order 14 placed via: Silver
order 14 placed via: Oganovich
order 14 placed via: Silver
```

You might want to spend some time practicing how to use transactions with resource-local EntityManagers. The first thing to note here is that each call to the EntityManager's flush method must be explicitly wrapped in a transaction. Not following this rule will cause the javax.persistence.TransactionRequiredException to be thrown. To understand why it works this way, you need to recall that the flush method is used to synchronize the persistence context to the underlying database. So, you cannot call flush outside a transaction context. For example, if you change the try block in the setOrder business method as follows:

```
...
        EntityManager em = emf.createEntityManager();
        Customer cust = (Customer) em.find(Customer.class, cust_id);
        Employee emp = (Employee) em.find(Employee.class, empno);
        Order order1 = new Order();
        order1.setCustomer(cust);
        order1.setEmployee(emp);
        em.persist(order1);
        em.getTransaction().begin();
        em.flush();
        em.refresh(order1);
        order_pono = order1.getPono();
        em.getTransaction().commit();
        em.close();
...
```

this will still work, despite that the persist method is invoked out of the transaction. However, if you put the call to the flush method outside the scope of the transaction like this:

```
...
        EntityManager em = emf.createEntityManager();
        Customer cust = (Customer) em.find(Customer.class, cust_id);
        Employee emp = (Employee) em.find(Employee.class, empno);
        Order order1 = new Order();
        order1.setCustomer(cust);
        order1.setEmployee(emp);
        em.persist(order1);
        em.flush();
        em.getTransaction().begin();
        em.refresh(order1);
        order_pono = order1.getPono();
        em.getTransaction().commit();
        em.close();
...
```

this will cause the persistence provide to throw a javax.persistence.TransactionRequired➥ Exception exception.

In practice, however, it's always a good idea to explicitly include any call to persist, merge, remove, or refresh in a transaction. The fact is that the flush default mode is set to AUTO, which means the persistence provider will automatically perform synchronization with the database when it needs to ensure that the results of a query being issued are correct. For example, look at the following try block in the setOrder business method:

```
EntityManager em = emf.createEntityManager();
Customer cust = (Customer) em.find(Customer.class, cust_id);
Employee emp = (Employee) em.find(Employee.class, empno);
Order order1 = new Order();
order1.setCustomer(cust);
order1.setEmployee(emp);
em.getTransaction().begin();
em.persist(order1);
List orderList = em.createQuery("SELECT o FROM Order o")
                        .getResultList();
em.refresh(order1);
em.flush();
em.refresh(order1);
order_pono = order1.getPono();
em.getTransaction().commit();
em.close();
```

Within the resource transaction used here, you added calls to the createQuery and refresh methods of the EntityManager instance—both are highlighted in bold. Although the refresh method applied to order1 is called before the call to flush, the previous code works OK. As mentioned earlier, the default flush mode of the Query object is set to AUTO. That is why the call to the createQuery method here will force the persistence provider to implicitly perform the flush operation, synchronizing the state of the EntityManager instance persistence context to the database. This is like explicitly making a call to the flush method before calling createQuery.

So, if you remove the call to the createQuery method, you will get the following error caused by the call to the refresh method before the flush operation has been performed:

Entity no longer exists in the database:

In this particular case, though, you should take it as saying "The entity has not been persisted to the database yet."

But what happens if the call to the createQuery method is made outside the transaction scope?

```
EntityManager em = emf.createEntityManager();
Customer cust = (Customer) em.find(Customer.class, cust_id);
Employee emp = (Employee) em.find(Employee.class, empno);
Order order1 = new Order();
order1.setCustomer(cust);
order1.setEmployee(emp);
```

```
em.persist(order1);
List orderList = em.createQuery("SELECT o FROM Order o")
                    .getResultList();
em.getTransaction().begin();
em.refresh(order1);
em.flush();
em.refresh(order1);
order_pono = order1.getPono();
em.getTransaction().commit();
em.close();
```

Again, the call to the refresh method highlighted in bold here will cause an error. This is because in this example the order1 instance has not been synchronized to the database.

An Example on Persistence Context Propagation

Returning to container-managed EntityManagers, it might be interesting to look at an example of how a persistence context is propagated by the container across component calls.

Listing 10-8 shows the source code for the PropagationTestBean stateless session bean whose checkShoppingCart method will be invoked from another bean, ShoppingCartTestBean, shown in Listing 10-9 later. These beans illustrate the concept behind persistence context propagation.

The beans discussed here utilize the Book and ShoppingCart entities from Chapter 9, shown in Listing 9-9 and Listing 9-10, respectively. Also, you're going to need the ShoppingCartKey composite primary key class from Chapter 8, shown in Listing 8-4.

Listing 10-8. *The* PropagationTestBean *Session Bean Whose* checkShoppingCart *Method Will Be Invoked from a Business Method of Another Bean Within the Same Persistence Context*

```
package ejbjpa.ejb;
import java.io.Serializable;
import javax.ejb.EJBException;
import javax.ejb.Stateless;
import javax.persistence.EntityManager;
import javax.persistence.PersistenceContext;
import ejbjpa.entities.*;
@Stateless
public class PropagationTestBean implements PropagationTest {
    @PersistenceContext
    private EntityManager em;
    public void checkShoppingCart(Integer cart_id, String book_id) {
        try {
            ShoppingCart testcart = (ShoppingCart) em.find(ShoppingCart.class, ➥
            new ShoppingCartKey(cart_id, book_id));
            testcart.setUnits(testcart.getUnits()+1);
```

```
        } catch (Exception e) {
            throw new EJBException(e.getMessage());
        }
    }
}
```

As you can see, the checkShoppingCart business method performs the following operations: it retrieves a specified ShoppingCart entity instance, and it changes the value of the units field in the retrieved ShoppingCart instance.

Now, take a look at the ShoppingCartTestBean session bean whose setShoppingCart method invokes the PropagationTestBean's checkShoppingCart method.

Listing 10-9. *The* ShoppingCartTestBean *Session Bean Whose* setShoppingCart *Method Makes a Call to the* checkShoppingCart *Method of* PropagationTestBean, *Sharing the Same Persistence Context*

```
package ejbjpa.ejb;
import java.io.Serializable;
import javax.ejb.EJBException;
import javax.ejb.Stateless;
import javax.persistence.EntityManager;
import javax.persistence.PersistenceContext;
import javax.ejb.EJB;
import ejbjpa.entities.*;
@Stateless
public class ShoppingCartTestBean implements ShoppingCartTest {
    @PersistenceContext
    private EntityManager em;
    @EJB private PropagationTest test;
    public String[] setShoppingCart(Integer cart_id, String book_id, ➥
                                     Integer units, Double unit_price) {
        String[] cart_details = new String[8];
        try {
          Book book = (Book) em.find(Book.class, book_id);
          ShoppingCart cart = new ShoppingCart();
          cart.setCart_id(cart_id);
          cart.setBook(book);
          cart.setUnits(units);
          cart.setUnit_price(unit_price);
          em.persist(cart);
          cart_details[0] = cart.getCart_id().toString();
          cart_details[1] = cart.getBook().getIsbn();
          cart_details[2] = cart.getUnits().toString();
          cart_details[3] = cart.getUnit_price().toString();
          test.checkShoppingCart(cart_id, book_id);
          cart_details[4] = cart.getCart_id().toString();
          cart_details[5] = cart.getBook().getIsbn();
          cart_details[6] = cart.getUnits().toString();
```

```
            cart_details[7] = cart.getUnit_price().toString();
            em.remove(cart);
        } catch (Exception e) {
            throw new EJBException(e.getMessage());
        }
        return cart_details;
    }
}
```

To make sure that the persistence context created by the container when the setShoppingCart method is invoked is then propagated along with the JTA transaction that includes the call to the checkShoppingCart method, you might use the servlet shown in Listing 10-10.

Listing 10-10. *The* EmEjbTestServlet *Servlet Making a Call to the* setShoppingCart *Method of* ShoppingCartTestBean

```
package ejbjpa.servlets;
import java.io.*;
import javax.servlet.*;
import javax.servlet.http.*;
import javax.ejb.EJB;
import ejbjpa.entities.*;
import ejbjpa.ejb.*;
public class EmEjbTestServlet extends HttpServlet {
    @EJB private ShoppingCartTest cartTest;
    public void doGet(
        HttpServletRequest request,
        HttpServletResponse response) throws ServletException, IOException {
        response.setContentType("text/html");
        response.setBufferSize(8192);
        PrintWriter out = response.getWriter();
        try{
            String[] details = new String[8];
            details = cartTest.setShoppingCart(2,"1430209631", 1, 44.99);
            out.println("Cart id : "+ details[0] +"<br/>");
            out.println("Book id : "+ details[1] +"<br/>");
            out.println("Units : "+ details[2] +"<br/>");
            out.println("Unit_price: "+ details[3] +"<br/>");
            out.println("-------------------"+"<br/>");
            out.println("Cart id : "+ details[4] +"<br/>");
            out.println("Book id : "+ details[5] +"<br/>");
            out.println("Units : "+ details[6] +"<br/>");
            out.println("Unit_price: "+ details[7] +"<br/>");
        }
        catch (Exception e){
            e.printStackTrace();
```

```
        }
    }
}
```

When executed, the servlet shown in the listing should output the following results:

```
Cart id : 2
Book id : 1430209631
Units : 1
Unit_price: 44.99
------------------
Cart id : 2
Book id : 1430209631
Units : 2
Unit_price: 44.99
```

This proves that the called checkShoppingCart method used the same persistence context as the calling setShoppingCart method. In other words, the persistence context started upon invocation of the ShoppingCartTestBean's setShoppingCart method was then propagated to the PropagationTestBean session bean upon calling its checkShoppingCart method.

Using Entity Life-Cycle Callback Methods

The concept behind entity life-cycle callback methods is the same as the concept of triggers in relational databases. Like a database trigger defined for each row on a certain table, an entity life-cycle callback method is invoked for each instance of the entity in response to a certain event. Also, like triggers, entity callback methods are invoked as part of the corresponding operation—before or after it. So, there are Pre and Post entity callback methods.

You can define an entity life-cycle event callback method directly in an entity class or in an entity listener class. To do this, you can decorate a method of interest with an appropriate annotation. Table 10-3 lists the annotations you can use to designate life-cycle event callback methods.

Table 10-3. *The Annotations Used for Entity Life-Cycle Event Callback*

Annotation	Description
PrePersist	Marks a method to be invoked for an entity before the EntityManager executes the persist operation for that entity. This is also invoked on all entities to which this operation is cascaded.
PostPersist	Marks a method to be invoked for an entity after it has been persisted. Generated primary keys are available in this method. This is also invoked on all entities to which this operation is cascaded.
PreUpdate	Marks a method to be invoked before the operation that triggers a database update operation performed against a given entity. Depending on the implementation, it may be invoked at the time the entity state is updated in the persistence context or at the time the context is flushed to the database.
PostUpdate	Marks a method to be invoked after the operation that triggers a database update operation performed against a given entity. Depending on the implementation, it may be invoked at the time the entity state is updated in the persistence context or at the time the context is flushed to the database.

Annotation	Description
PreRemove	Marks a method to be invoked for an entity before the EntityManager executes the remove operation for that entity. This is also invoked on all entities to which this operation is cascaded.
PostRemove	Marks a method to be invoked after an entity has been removed. This is also invoked on all entities to which this operation is cascaded.
PostLoad	Marks a method to be invoked after an entity is loaded or refreshed from the underlying database.

The easiest way to see how entity event callback methods work is by example. Suppose you want to define the PrePersist method on the Order entity class discussed in some examples earlier in this book. For example, you might want this PrePersist method to check whether the shipping_date field of the Order instance is set and to set it if it is null. As you might guess, the PrePersist method discussed here overrides some functionality of the neworder BEFORE INSERT trigger defined on the orders underlying table as discussed in Chapter 6.

Figure 10-8 gives a graphical depiction of the process of persisting an Order entity.

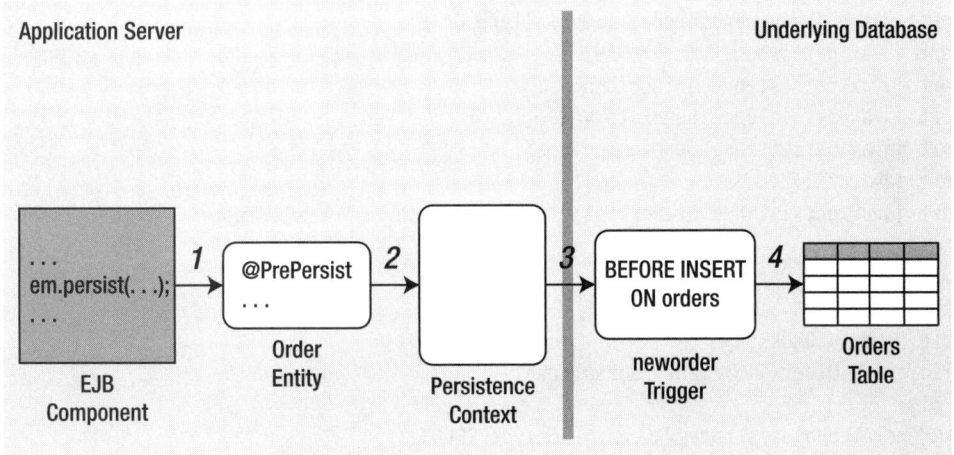

Figure 10-8. *A graphical representation of the steps that occur during the process of persisting an order entity to the underlying database*

Here is the explanation of the steps in the figure:

1. You start the process of persisting an Order entity by calling the persist method of an EntityManager instance. If you have a method decorated with @PrePersist defined in the Order entity, then this method is invoked.

2. The Order instance being persisted is then added to the EntityManager's persistence context.

3. Upon flushing the persistence context, the Order instance is sent to the underlying database in the form of the appropriate INSERT statement issued against the orders table. So, if the BEFORE INSERT trigger is defined on the orders table, it is fired.

4. The Order instance data is saved to the orders table.

Now you're ready to update the Order entity class. In particular, you need to add the PrePersist life-cycle event callback method to it.

Listing 10-11 shows the source code for the updated Order entity class.

Listing 10-11. *The Updated* Order *Entity Class Containing the* PrePersist *Life-Cycle Event Callback Method*

```java
package ejbjpa.entities;
import java.io.Serializable;
import javax.persistence.Column;
import javax.persistence.Entity;
import javax.persistence.Id;
import javax.persistence.Table;
import javax.persistence.Temporal;
import static javax.persistence.TemporalType.DATE;
import javax.persistence.ManyToOne;
import javax.persistence.JoinColumn;
import javax.persistence.GeneratedValue;
import javax.persistence.GenerationType;
import java.util.*;
import javax.persistence.PrePersist;

import java.util.Date;
@Entity
@Table(name = "ORDERS")
public class Order implements Serializable {
    @Id
    @GeneratedValue(strategy=GenerationType.IDENTITY)
    @Column(name = "PONO")
    private Integer pono;
    @Column(name = "SHIPPING_DATE", nullable = false)
    @Temporal(DATE)
    private Date shipping_date;
    @Column(name = "DELIVERY_ESTIMATE", nullable = false)
    private String delivery_estimate;
    @ManyToOne
    @JoinColumn(
      name="CUST_ID",
      referencedColumnName="CUST_ID")
    private Customer customer;
    @ManyToOne
    @JoinColumn(
```

```
   name="EMPNO",
   referencedColumnName="EMPNO")
private Employee employee;
@PrePersist
private void setShippingDate() {
 if (this.getShipping_date() == null)
 {
    Calendar calendar = new GregorianCalendar();
    long weekday = calendar.get(Calendar.DAY_OF_WEEK);
    long days;
    if (weekday == 6) {
        days = 3;
    } else if (weekday == 7) {
        days = 2;
    } else {
        days =1;
    }
    Date date = new Date();
    long msDay = 1000 * 60 * 60 * 24;
    date.setTime(date.getTime() + msDay * days);
    this.setShipping_date(date);
 }
}
public Order() {
}
public Customer getCustomer() {
    return this.customer;
}
public void setCustomer(Customer customer) {
    this.customer = customer;
}
public Employee getEmployee() {
    return this.employee;
}
public void setEmployee (Employee employee) {
    this.employee = employee;
}
public Integer getPono () {
    return this.pono;
}
public void setPono (Integer pono) {
    this.pono = pono;
}
public Date getShipping_date () {
    return this.shipping_date;
}
public void setShipping_date (Date shipping_date) {
```

```
            this.shipping_date = shipping_date;
        }
        public String getDelivery_estimate () {
            return this.delivery_estimate;
        }
        public void setDelivery_estimate (String delivery_estimate) {
            this.delivery_estimate = delivery_estimate;
        }
    }
```

To test the updated Order entity, you might rewrite the OrderTestBean session bean, as shown in Listing 10-12.

Listing 10-12. *The* OrderTestBean *Session Bean Rewritten to Test the Updated* Order *Entity*

```
package ejbjpa.ejb;
import java.io.Serializable;
import javax.ejb.EJBException;
import javax.ejb.Stateless;
import javax.persistence.EntityManager;
import javax.persistence.PersistenceContext;
import java.util.Date;
import ejbjpa.entities.*;
@Stateless
public class OrderTestBean implements OrderTest {
    @PersistenceContext
    private EntityManager em;
    public String[] setOrder(Integer cust_id, Integer empno, ➥
                            Date shipping_date, String delivery_estimate) {
        String[] order_details = new String[2];
        try {
          Customer cust = (Customer) em.find(Customer.class, cust_id);
          Employee emp = (Employee) em.find(Employee.class, empno);
          Order order1 = new Order();
          order1.setCustomer(cust);
          order1.setEmployee(emp);
          order1.setShipping_date(shipping_date);
          order1.setDelivery_estimate(delivery_estimate);
          em.persist(order1);
          Date date = order1.getShipping_date();
          order_details[1] = date.toString();
          em.flush();
                    em.refresh(order1);
order_details[0] = order1.getPono().toString();
        } catch (Exception e) {
            throw new EJBException(e.getMessage());
        }
```

```
        return order_details;
    }
}
```

Finally, to perform a test, you might use a servlet shown in Listing 10-13.

Listing 10-13. *The* EmEjbTestServlet *Servlet Rewritten to Test the Updated* OrderTestBean *Session Bean*

```java
package ejbjpa.servlets;
import java.io.*;
import javax.servlet.*;
import javax.servlet.http.*;
import javax.ejb.EJB;
import ejbjpa.entities.*;
import ejbjpa.ejb.*;
public class EmEjbTestServlet extends HttpServlet {
    @EJB private OrderTest orderTest;
    public void doGet(
        HttpServletRequest request,
        HttpServletResponse response) throws ServletException, IOException {
        response.setContentType("text/html");
        response.setBufferSize(8192);
        PrintWriter out = response.getWriter();
        try{
            String[] details = new String[2];
            details = orderTest.setOrder(2,1, null, null);
            out.println("Created order pono: "+ details[0] +"<br/>");
            out.println("Order shipping date: "+ details[1] +"<br/>");
        }
        catch (Exception e){
            e.printStackTrace();
        }
    }
}
```

The results generated by the servlet shown in the listing might look like this:

```
Created order pono: 21
Order shipping date: Sat Apr 26 15:02:26 PDT 2008
```

It is important to remember that the PrePersist life-cycle event callback method defined in the Order entity class will set the shipping_date field only if it is not null. So, you can still set the shipping_date field explicitly when dealing with an Order entity instance. Listing 10-14 shows how you might do it from within a servlet.

Listing 10-14. *The Version of the* `EmEjbTestServlet` *Servlet That Illustrates That the* `shipping_date` *Field Can Still Be Set Explicitly*

```
//import declarations
...
import java.util.Date;

public class EmEjbTestServlet extends HttpServlet {
    @EJB private OrderTest orderTest;
    public void doGet(
...
        try{
            long days =5;
            Date date = new Date();
            long msDay = 1000 * 60 * 60 * 24;
            date.setTime(date.getTime() + msDay * days);
            String[] details = new String[2];
            details = orderTest.setOrder(2,1, date, null);
            out.println("Created order pono: "+ details[0] +"<br/>");
            out.println("Order shipping date: "+ details[1] +"<br/>");
        }
...
}
```

In this servlet, you call the `setOrder` method of `OrderTest`, specifying the `date` parameter set to a particular date—five days forward from the current date.

Summary

In this chapter, you looked at the EntityManager interface whose methods are used to manage entity instances. You saw some basic examples of using the EntityManager interface in different scenarios, helping you understand the mechanics behind this Java Persistence tool.

In the next chapter, you will look at the EntityManager methods that allow you to use the Query API for retrieving entities.

Using Java Persistence Query Language (JPQL)

In the preceding chapter, you saw how you can find and retrieve an entity instance by primary key with the help of the EntityManager's find method. This method of retrieving entities has at least two serious limitations, however. First, you are limited to using primary keys only. Second, you can retrieve only a single entity instance at a time. In practice, however, you may need to retrieve a set of entity instances, based on a condition defined over entity attributes. This is where Java Persistence Query Language (JPQL) comes to the rescue.

Of course, this is not the only situation where you might need to use JPQL. You will come to JPQL when, for example, you need to perform join queries on the entities related to each other with a relationship. The applicability of JPQL is further discussed in the "When You Might Want to Use JPQL" section later in this chapter.

This chapter covers the details related to using JPQL as well as native SQL. After reading this chapter, you will have learned how to do the following:

- Use JPQL and native SQL queries

- Create static and dynamic queries

- Utilize the Query API

As you will see in this chapter, the JPQL syntax appears to be very similar to the syntax of SQL. So, it is assumed that you are already somewhat familiar with SQL.

Defining Queries Over Entities

To illustrate the scope of JPQL, the chapter starts with a brief overview of this query language. This overview explains what JPQL is and when you might want to use it. Also, it covers the operations you can perform with JPQL and gives you the basics of how to deal with JPQL statements.

What Is JPQL?

In many ways, JPQL is similar to SQL, a standard tool to interact with a relational database. Both are used to interact with a relational database, accessing and manipulating data with the help of *nonprocedural statements*, which are commands recognized by a special interpreter.

Furthermore, JPQL is similar to SQL in its syntax. The JPQL statements and their clauses are similar to those used in SQL.

The key difference between JPQL and SQL lies in the objects you specify in the statements and the objects returned by those statements. In SQL statements, you define directly the database objects to operate on, specifying, for example, a certain table or view to be queried or modified. In contrast, in JPQL statements, you deal with entities. The same is true for the results retrieved by JPQL queries; they are entity instances, whereas the results returned by SQL queries are usually table or view records. To summarize, JPQL deals with entities mapped to underlying database structures, rather than dealing with those database structures directly.

Another thing that distinguishes JPQL from SQL is that it is a database vendor–independent language. What this means in practice is that, to JPQL, it does not make any difference to what type of underlying database the entities being manipulated are mapped.

Of course, if there were no JPQL, you could still query the underlying data with SQL/JDBC and then create entity instances, manually setting their fields. Then, you would need to make these entity instances managed, performing the persist operation over them. That would require a lot of extra coding, though.

JPQL simplifies the task of retrieving entity instances a lot. All the entity instances returned become automatically managed, provided the query method is invoked within a transaction context. So, you don't need to perform the merge operation over such instances.

Figure 11-1 provides a high-level view of interactions between a persistence context and the underlying database performed via JPQL.

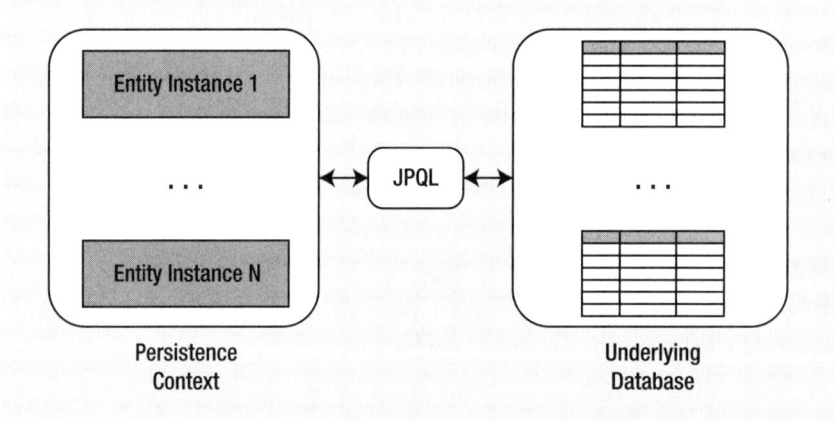

Figure 11-1. *When you query the underlying database with JPQL, the retrieved entity instances become automatically managed—when retrieved within a transaction context, of course.*

While Figure 11-1 gives a very high-level view of how JPQL is used in the process of inter-action between a persistence context and the underlying database, Figure 11-2 provides a more detailed depiction of how an application component may interact with the underlying database through JPQL.

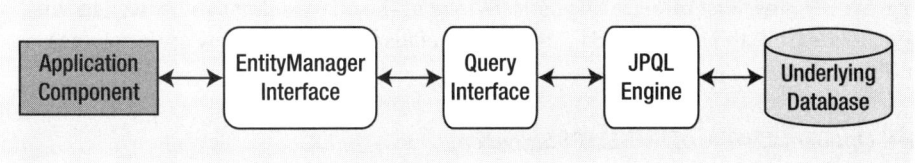

Figure 11-2. *An application component issues a JPQL statement via the EntityManager and Query interfaces.*

As you can see in the figure, an application component interacts with the JPQL engine through the EntityManager and Query interfaces. For further details on how the EntityManager and Query interfaces can be utilized when it comes to JPQL, you can refer to the later "Dealing with JPQL Statements" section. Then, in the "Retrieving Entities with JPQL" section, you will look at some examples that should help to clear it all up.

For detailed information on JPQL, you can refer to the documentation chapter "Query Language" in the Enterprise JavaBeans 3.0 Specification Java Persistence API document, part of JSR-220, which is available at `http://jcp.org/en/jsr/detail?id=220`.

When You Might Want to Use JPQL

When developing an application that utilizes the Java Persistence API (JPA), you have strong reason to choose JPQL over SQL. This is because JPQL is specifically designed to deal with JPA entities and, therefore, is ideally suited for use in Java applications utilizing JPA.

As mentioned at the beginning of the chapter, JPQL is perfectly appropriate when you need to retrieve a set of entity instances, based on a condition defined over a nonprimary key column or columns. Like SQL, JPQL lets you restrict the results returned by a query, specifying a condition or conditions in the WHERE clause of the JPQL SELECT statement. GROUP BY, HAVING, and ORDER BY are also allowed. Also, you will be able to perform join queries on the entities related to each other with a relationship.

With JPQL, not only can you issue select queries, but you can also perform bulk delete and update operations, applying them to entities of a certain entity class or inheritance hierarchy.

Being a database vendor–independent language, JPQL lets you create portable solutions. Although JPQL uses a SQL-like syntax, JPQL queries are portable across different underlying databases. So, the ability to create database platform–independent queries is another good reason to choose JPQL over SQL.

Operations Supported in JPQL

Now that you have a rough idea of what JPQL is and when you might want to use it, it's time to look at what statements are supported in this query language. The list of statements supported in JPQL contains three items. A JPQL statement may be one of the following:

- SELECT
- UPDATE
- DELETE

Since SELECT is of most interest this list, let's look at the clauses that can be used in this statement. Aside from the SELECT and FROM required clauses, there are a few optional ones, as listed in Table 11-1.

Table 11-1. *Optional Clauses of the* SELECT *Statement*

Clause	Description
WHERE	Conditions specified in this clause are used to restrict the result set of the query.
GROUP BY	A set of the retrieved entity instances is divided into groups based on the values of the entity field specified in this clause.
HAVING	Used in conjunction with GROUP BY to restrict the groups of the retrieved entities to those groups that satisfy the specified condition.
ORDER BY	A set of the retrieved entity instances is ordered based on the sorting applied to the entity field specified in this clause.

Also, JPQL provides a set of operators and functions that you can use in query clauses. The syntax and use of most of them are similar to those used in SQL. For further information, you can look at chapter "Query Language" in the Enterprise JavaBeans 3.0 Specification Java Persistence API document.

Dealing with JPQL Statements

The EntityManager interface provides two methods that you can use in conjunction with the Query interface methods to create, bind, and execute JPQL statements. Table 11-2 summarizes these EntityManager methods.

Table 11-2. *The EntityManager Interface Methods for Creating a Query Instance for Executing a JPQL Query*

Method	Description
public Query createQuery(String jpql_stmt)	Creates a dynamic query defined within business logic code. It takes a JPQL statement string as the parameter and returns a Query instance for executing that JPQL statement.
public Query createNamedQuery(String query_name)	Creates a static query defined in meta-data. It takes the name of either a JPQL query defined with the NamedQuery annotation or a native SQL query defined with the NamedNativeQuery annotation applied to an entity and returns a Query instance for executing that named query.

The createQuery and createNamedQuery methods return a Query instance that lets you execute that query using either the getResultList or getSingleResult methods for a SELECT query or the executeUpdate method for an UPDATE or DELETE query.

■**Note** The EntityManager interface methods that can be used to create a Query instance for executing a
native SQL query are listed in Table 11-4, which can be found in the "Dealing with Native SQL Queries" later
section.

Here is an example of creating and executing a SELECT query:

```
Query query = em.createQuery("SELECT e FROM Employee e");
List<Employee> employees = (List<Employee>)query.getResultList();
```

In practice, however, you might want to use the following syntax instead:

```
List<Employee> employees = (List<Employee>)em.createQuery(➥
   "SELECT e FROM Employee e")
                           .getResultList();
```

As you can see, this alternate syntax eliminates the need for you to explicitly import the
javax.persistence.Query interface.

In the later "Retrieving Entities with JPQL" section, you will look at some more complicated examples of SELECT queries. In particular, you will see how to bind an argument to a
named parameter of a query, set a vendor-specific hint, and fetch entity associations with
JPQL join fetch.

Figure 11-3 provides a graphical representation of how a List object returned by the
Query's getResultList method is then cast to a List of instances of a certain type.

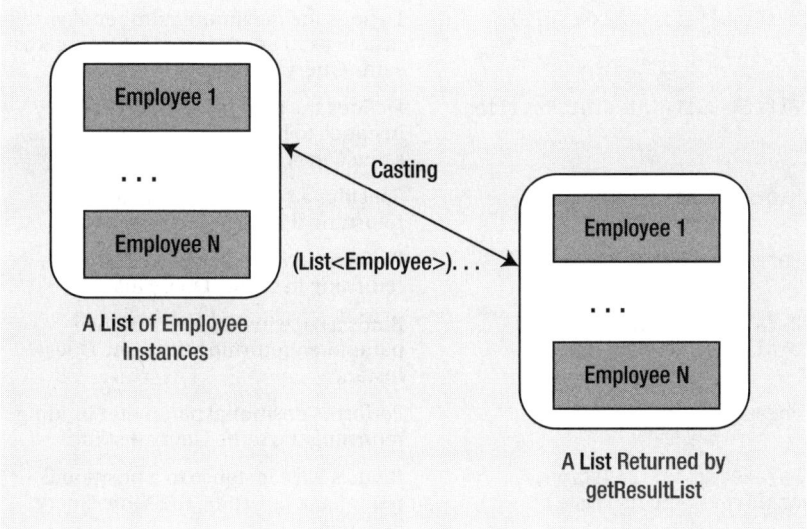

Figure 11-3. *A Query instance returned by an EntityManager's create query method lets you
invoke the* getResultList *method that returns a List castable to a List of a certain type.*

Both the `getResultList` and `getSingleResult` methods belong to the Query API, which is discussed in the next section.

Using Query API

Once you have created a `Query` instance with the `createQuery` or `createNamedQuery` method, you then need to execute the query and retrieve the results. These tasks, as well as the tasks of parameter binding and pagination control are handled with the Query interface methods.

By and large, the Query interface provides methods used to control execution of JPQL and native SQL queries. Table 11-3 lists the most commonly used Query interface methods.

Table 11-3. *The Most Commonly Used Query Interface Methods*

Method	Description
`public List getResultList()`	Executes a `SELECT` query created by the EntityManager's `createQuery` or `createNamedQuery` method and retrieves a set of entities as a list
`public Object getSingleResult()`	Executes a `SELECT` query created by the EntityManager's `createQuery` or `createNamedQuery` method and retrieves a single entity as the result
`public int executeUpdate()`	Executes an `UPDATE` or `DELETE` query created by the EntityManager's `createQuery` or `createNamedQuery` method and returns the number of entities affected
`public Query setMaxResults(int maxResult)`	Defines the maximum number of entity instances to be retrieved, returning the same Query instance
`public Query setFirstResult(int startPosition)`	Defines the position of the first entity instance to be retrieved, returning the same Query instance
`public Query setHint(String hintName, Object value)`	Specifies a vendor-specific hint, returning the same Query instance
`public Query setParameter(String name, Object value)`	Performs named parameter binding, returning the same Query instance
`public Query setParameter(String name, Date value, TemporalType temporalType)`	Binds a `Date` instance to a named parameter, returning the same Query instance
`public Query setParameter(int position, Object value)`	Performs positional parameter binding, returning the same Query instance
`public Query setParameter(int position, Date value, TemporalType temporalType)`	Binds a `Date` instance to a positional parameter, returning the same Query instance

In the rest of this chapter, you will look at several examples of using some of the Query interface methods listed in the table.

Retrieving Entities with JPQL

As you learned earlier, JPQL lets you perform select, update, and delete operations over entities. In practice, however, select operations are most commonly used ones.

The following sections provide several examples of how you can perform select operations with JPQL.

A Simple Example of JPQL in Action

Let's start with a simple example. In the getEmployees business method of the JpqlTestBean session bean shown in Listing 11-1, you create and execute the JPQL query that retrieves all the employee entity instances.

Listing 11-1. *A Session Bean That Illustrates How You Can Retrieve a Set of Entity Instances with a Single JPQL Statement*

```
package ejbjpa.ejb;
import java.io.Serializable;
import javax.ejb.EJBException;
import javax.ejb.Stateless;
import javax.persistence.EntityManager;
import javax.persistence.PersistenceContext;
import java.util.List;
import ejbjpa.entities.*;
@Stateless
public class JpqlTestBean implements JpqlTest {
    @PersistenceContext
    private EntityManager em;
    public List<Employee> getEmployees() {
        List<Employee> employees = null;
        try {
          employees = (List<Employee>)em.createQuery("SELECT e FROM Employee e")
                              .getResultList();
        } catch (Exception e) {
            throw new EJBException(e.getMessage());
        }
        return employees;
    }
}
```

As you can see, all the JpqlTestBean's getEmployees method does is create a SELECT JPQL query with the EntityManager's createQuery method and then execute the query with the Query's getResultList method. Next, the retrieved list is cast to a list of employee instances, which is then returned by the getEmployees method.

To test the JpqlTestBean session bean, you might create a servlet that calls the bean's getEmployees method. Consider the JpqlTestServlet servlet shown in Listing 11-2.

Listing 11-2. *A Servlet That You Might Use to Test the* JpqlTestBean *Session Bean Shown in Listing 11-1*

```
package ejbjpa.servlets;
import java.io.*;
import javax.servlet.*;
import javax.servlet.http.*;
import javax.ejb.EJB;
import java.util.List;
import java.util.Iterator;
import ejbjpa.entities.*;
import ejbjpa.ejb.*;
public class JpqlTestServlet extends HttpServlet {
    @EJB private JpqlTest jpqlTest;
    public void doGet(
        HttpServletRequest request,
        HttpServletResponse response) throws ServletException, IOException {
        response.setContentType("text/html");
        response.setBufferSize(8192);
        PrintWriter out = response.getWriter();
        try{
            List<Employee> employees = jpqlTest.getEmployees();
            Iterator i = employees.iterator();
            Employee employee;
            while (i.hasNext()) {
                employee = (Employee) i.next();
                out.println("Employee id: "+ employee.getEmpno() +"<br/>");
                out.println("First name: "+ employee.getFirstname() +"<br/>");
                out.println("Last name: "+ employee.getLastname() +"<br/>");
                out.println("----------"+ "<br/>");
            }
        }
        catch (Exception e){
            e.printStackTrace();
        }
    }
}
```

In the JpqlTestServlet servlet, you make a call to the JpqlTestBean's getEmployees method and then use an Iterator instance to navigate through the retrieved list of employee entity instances, displaying the values of their fields.

If you have populated the employees table with data as shown in Listing 6-5 back to Chapter 6, the previous servlet should generate the following output:

```
Employee id: 1
First name: Serg
Last name: Oganovich
----------
```

```
Employee id: 2
First name: Maya
Last name: Silver
----------
```

Are Retrieved Entities Managed?

The last example brings up an interesting question: do entity instances retrieved by a JPQL query become automatically managed?

The JPA specification has the answer to this question, of course. According to the JPA specification, regardless of the way you retrieve entities, they are automatically attached to the current persistence context, provided you execute the query in a transactional context. To look at how all this works in practice, you might perform the test discussed in this section. For that, you're going to need to add a checkIfManaged method to the JpqlTestBean bean shown in Listing 11-1 earlier.

Listing 11-3 shows what the source code for the checkIfManaged method might look like.

Listing 11-3. *The* JpqlTestBean *Bean Originally Shown in Listing 11-1 with the* checkIfManaged *Method*

```java
//import declarations
...
import java.util.Iterator;
@Stateless
public class JpqlTestBean implements JpqlTest {
    @PersistenceContext
    private EntityManager em;
    public List<Employee> getEmployees() {

       ...

    }
    public boolean checkIfManaged(){
        List<Employee> employees = null;
        try {
          employees = (List<Employee>)em.createQuery("SELECT e FROM Employee e")
                            .getResultList();
          Employee employee;
          Iterator i = employees.iterator();
          while (i.hasNext()) {
             employee = (Employee) i.next();

           if (!em.contains(employee)) {
              return false;
            }
          }
        }
```

```
    } catch (Exception e) {
        throw new EJBException(e.getMessage());
    }
    return true;
  }
}
```

In the `checkIfManaged` business method shown in the listing, you check to see whether each `employee` entity instance retrieved belongs to the current persistence context, using the EntityManager's `contains` method. The `checkIfManaged` business method returns true only if all of the retrieved `employee` entity instances are in the managed state.

■Note You might be wondering why it is important to know in what state the entities you are dealing with are. If you recall from the discussion on entity states in the preceding chapter, only managed entities are attached to a persistence context and can be manipulated within it as necessary. For example, you can perform the remove operation against a managed entity, thus changing its state to removed. It is important to realize, however, that all managed entities become automatically detached when their persistence context is closed. In this particular example, the persistence context associated with the `checkIfManaged` business method is closed when method execution ends. To make a detached entity managed again, you should call the EntityManager's `merge` method on it.

Now, to perform the test, you might update the `JpqlTestServlet` servlet so that it makes a call to the `checkIfManaged` method. The added code line in which you call the `checkIfManaged` method is highlighted in bold in Listing 11-4.

Listing 11-4. *The* `JpqlTestServlet` *Servlet Updated to Make a Call to the* `checkIfManaged` *Method of the* `JpqlTestBean` *Session Bean*

```
//import declarations
...
public class JpqlTestServlet extends HttpServlet {
    @EJB private JpqlTest jpqlTest;
    public void doGet(
...
        try{
...
          out.println("All employee entities were managed during the ➥
          checkIfManaged call: "+ jpqlTest.checkIfManaged() +"<br/>");
        }
        catch (Exception e){
            e.printStackTrace();
        }
    }
}
```

The highlighted line should output `true` since all the `employee` entity instances retrieved by a JPQL query created and executed within the `checkIfManaged` method must be in the managed state.

Navigating Over Relationships in the Retrieved Entities

Now that you've seen that entity instances retrieved by a JPQL query are automatically managed, what about their associations? Do they become automatically managed upon retrieving the query results too?

Although this question will be addressed in the next section, the example in this section is going to show you that in the most common cases the answer to this question is irrelevant.

It is important to understand that the entity instances related to the entity instances retrieved by a JPQL query are not necessarily returned with the query execution. Whether or not the instances of the related entity are retrieved along with the entity instance returned by a query depends on the fetch mode of the relationship defined between those entities.

■Note You can explicitly set the fetch mode when defining a relationship between entities using the OneToOne, OneToMany, ManyToOne, or ManyToMany annotation, setting the fetch element to either EAGER or LAZY. By default, the fetch mode is set to LAZY for one-to-many and many-to-many relationships, while one-to-one and many-to-one are defaulted to EAGER.

In most cases, however, it doesn't make any difference whether associated entities have been retrieved with the query. The following example illustrates that when you start accessing associated entities, they automatically become managed.

Listing 11-5 shows the `JpqlTestBean`'s `checkIfManaged` method updated to check not only the `employee` instances retrieved by the query but also the `order` instances associated with those `employee` instances. If at least one instance is not in the managed state, `checkIfManaged` will return false. The added code is highlighted in bold.

Listing 11-5. *The* `JpqlTestBean` *Session Bean Updated to Illustrate That Entities Related to Entities Retrieved by a Query Automatically Become Managed the First Time They Are Accessed*

```
//import declarations
...
@Stateless
public class JpqlTestBean implements JpqlTest {
    @PersistenceContext
    private EntityManager em;
    public List<Employee> getEmployees() {
      ...
    }
    public boolean checkIfManaged(){
        List<Employee> employees = null;
        List<Order> orders =null;
        try {
```

```
        employees = (List<Employee>)em.createQuery("SELECT e FROM Employee e")
                        .getResultList();
        Employee employee;
        Order order;
        Iterator i = employees.iterator();
        Iterator j;
        while (i.hasNext()) {
            employee = (Employee) i.next();

            if (!em.contains(employee)) {
              return false;
             }
            orders = (List<Order>)employee.getOrders();
            j= orders.iterator();
            while (j.hasNext()) {
                order = (Order) j.next();
                if (!em.contains(order)) {
                  return false;
                }
            }
        }
    } catch (Exception e) {
        throw new EJBException(e.getMessage());
    }
    return true;
  }
}
```

To test the updated bean, you might use the JpqlTestServlet servlet shown in Listing 11-4 in the preceding section. Like in the previous example, the checkIfManaged method called within the servlet should return true, thereby proving the order instances are managed by the time they are accessed through an iterator.

■**Note** If an employee instance has no associated order instances, the nested while loop will not be executed. However, if you followed the examples from the preceding chapter, you should have some orders associated with employees.

Now if you modify the checkIfManaged method so that it, for example, removes an order entity before checking its status, the EntityManager's contains method will then return false when called on that order entity.

To see this in action, you might modify the nested while loop in the checkIfManaged method as follows:

```
        while (j.hasNext()) {
            order = (Order) j.next();
            em.remove(order);
            if (!em.contains(order)) {
              return false;
            }
        }

    }
```

To make sure that the remove operation will not actually affect the underlying data in the orders table, you might wrap a call to the checkIfManaged method in a transaction that is then rolled back.

Listing 11-6 shows the updated JpqlTestServlet servlet. Again, the added code is highlighted in bold.

Listing 11-6. *The* JpqlTestServlet *Servlet Updated to Call the* checkIfManaged *Method Within a Transaction*

```
//import declarations
...
import javax.annotation.Resource;
import javax.transaction.UserTransaction;
public class JpqlTestServlet extends HttpServlet {
    @EJB private JpqlTest jpqlTest;
    @Resource
    UserTransaction utx;
    public void doGet(
        HttpServletRequest request,
        HttpServletResponse response) throws ServletException, IOException {
        response.setContentType("text/html");
        response.setBufferSize(8192);
        PrintWriter out = response.getWriter();
        try{
            List<Employee> employees = jpqlTest.getEmployees();
            Iterator i = employees.iterator();
            Employee employee;
            while (i.hasNext()) {
                employee = (Employee) i.next();
                out.println("Employee id: "+ employee.getEmpno() +"<br/>");
                out.println("First name: "+ employee.getFirstname() +"<br/>");
                out.println("Last name: "+ employee.getLastname() +"<br/>");
                out.println("----------"+ "<br/>");
            }
            utx.begin();
            out.println("All employee entities were managed during the ➥
             checkIfManaged call: "+ jpqlTest.checkIfManaged() +"<br/>");
            utx.rollback();
        }
```

```
            catch (Exception e){
                e.printStackTrace();
            }
        }
    }
}
```

As mentioned earlier, this time the checkIfManaged method called in the JpqlTestServlet servlet shown in the listing should return false.

Using JPQL Fetch Joins

The previous example doesn't answer the question of whether the entity instances related to the entity instances retrieved by a JPQL query become immediately managed upon retrieving the query results. As stated in the beginning of the preceding section, the answer to this question depends on the fetch mode defaulted or explicitly set when defining a relationship between entities. If the LAZY mode is used, then the associations are not retrieved. Sometimes, however, you might want to retrieve them along with the query results. This is where using JPQL FETCH JOINS may come in very handy.

Let's look at an example that makes it possible for you to look at the state of the associations of the entity instances returned by a regular query and a join query, immediately after retrieving. Say you create a JpqlJoinsTestBean session bean whose countOrders business method implements the logic required to perform this test.

For testing purposes, you could employ several EntityManager instances, each of which is based on a separate persistence unit. In particular, you might define three independent EntityManager instances to execute three JPQL queries, each in a separate persistence context, and then evaluate the results of those queries.

The following steps summarize the tasks you might want the JpqlJoinsTestBean's countOrders business method to perform:

1. Inject three independent EntityManager instances.

2. With em0, create and execute a SELECT JPQL query retrieving the employee instance with the specified empno.

3. With em1, create and execute a SELECT JPQL FETCH JOIN query retrieving the employee instance with the specified empno, along with the associated order instances.

4. With em2, create and execute a SELECT JPQL query retrieving the employee instance with the specified empno.

5. Obtain the order entities related to the employee retrieved by the first query performed in step 2. Count the number of those orders.

6. Increase the number of orders for the employee retrieved by the first query by 1, and commit the change.

7. Obtain the order entities related to the employee retrieved by the second query performed in step 3. Count the number of those orders.

8. Obtain the order entities related to the employee retrieved by the third query performed in step 4. Count the number of those orders.

The idea behind this test is to make sure that a SELECT JPQL FETCH JOIN query returns the associated order instances together with the employee instance retrieved. To find out this, you first create and execute three queries associated with three different persistence contexts, in steps 2, 3, and 4, respectively. Then, you compare the numbers of the order instances obtained in steps 5, 7, and 8.

Since the number of orders calculated in step 5 is obtained before a new order is added (in step 6), this number should be the same as you got when the test started.

After adding a new order associated with the employee and synchronizing this change to the database, you, in step 7, calculate the number of the orders associated with the employee returned by the SELECT JPQL FETCH JOIN query executed in step 3. In fact, the number of orders calculated in step 7 should be equal to the number calculated in step 5. This is because the orders associated with the employee returned by the FETCH JOIN query have been obtained upon the query execution in step 3 and immediately attached to the persistence context.

However, this is not the case for the SELECT JPQL query executed in step 4. When, in step 8, calculating the number of orders associated with the employee returned by this query, you should have the number of orders increased by 1. This is because the associated orders were obtained when you first time accessed them, rather than upon query execution. Since you first time accessed those orders after a new order had been added and the transaction had been committed, you got the number of orders increased by 1.

Listing 11-7 shows what the source code for the JpqlJoinsTestBean session bean implementing this test might look like.

Listing 11-7. *An Example of a Session Bean That Illustrates a JPQL Join Query in Action*

```
package ejbjpa.ejb;
import java.io.Serializable;
import javax.ejb.EJBException;
import javax.ejb.Stateless;
import javax.persistence.EntityManager;
import javax.persistence.EntityManagerFactory;
import javax.persistence.PersistenceUnit;
import java.util.List;
import ejbjpa.entities.*;
@Stateless
public class JpqlJoinsTestBean implements JpqlJoinsTest {
    @PersistenceUnit(unitName="jpqljoins0-pu")
    private EntityManagerFactory emf0;
    @PersistenceUnit(unitName="jpqljoins1-pu")
    private EntityManagerFactory emf1;
    @PersistenceUnit(unitName="jpqljoins2-pu")
    private EntityManagerFactory emf2;
    public Integer[] countOrders(Integer empno){
        List<Order> orders0 = null;
        List<Order> orders1 = null;
        List<Order> orders2 = null;
        EntityManager em0 = emf0.createEntityManager();
        EntityManager em1 = emf1.createEntityManager();
        EntityManager em2 = emf2.createEntityManager();
```

```
Integer[] numOfOrders= new Integer[3];
try {
  //perform queries
  Employee employee0 = (Employee)em0.createQuery("SELECT e ➡
    FROM Employee e WHERE e.empno=:empno")
                      .setHint("toplink.refresh", "true")
                      .setParameter("empno", empno)
                      .getSingleResult();
  Employee employee1 = (Employee)em1.createQuery("SELECT DISTINCT e ➡
      FROM Employee e LEFT JOIN FETCH e.orders WHERE e.empno=:empno")
                      .setHint("toplink.refresh", "true")
                      .setParameter("empno", empno)
                      .getSingleResult();
  Employee employee2 = (Employee)em2.createQuery("SELECT e ➡
      FROM Employee e WHERE e.empno=:empno")
                      .setHint("toplink.refresh", "true")
                      .setParameter("empno", empno)
                      .getSingleResult();
  //count the number of orders for the employee retrieved with ➡
    the first query
  orders0 = (List<Order>)employee0.getOrders();
  numOfOrders[0] = orders0.size();
  //increase the number of orders for the employee by 1 and commit➡
    the change
  Order order = new Order();
  order.setEmployee(employee0);
  em0.getTransaction().begin();
  em0.persist(order);
  em0.getTransaction().commit();
  //count the number of orders for the employee retrieved with the ➡
    second and third queries
  orders1 = (List<Order>)employee1.getOrders();
  numOfOrders[1] = orders1.size();
  orders2 = (List<Order>)employee2.getOrders();
  numOfOrders[2] = orders2.size();
} catch (Exception e) {
    throw new EJBException(e.getMessage());
}
em0.close();
em1.close();
em2.close();
return numOfOrders;
  }
}
```

To use the JpqlJoinsTestBean session bean shown in the listing, you might create a servlet that will make a call to the bean's countOrders business method. The JpqlJoinsTestServlet servlet shown in Listing 11-8 is designed for this purpose.

Listing 11-8. *A Servlet That Might Be Used to Test the Session Bean Shown in Listing 11-7*

```
package ejbjpa.servlets;
import java.io.*;
import javax.servlet.*;
import javax.servlet.http.*;
import javax.ejb.EJB;
import ejbjpa.entities.*;
import ejbjpa.ejb.*;
public class JpqlJoinsTestServlet extends HttpServlet {
    @EJB private JpqlJoinsTest jpqlJoinsTest;
    public void doGet(
        HttpServletRequest request,
        HttpServletResponse response) throws ServletException, IOException {
        response.setContentType("text/html");
        response.setBufferSize(8192);
        PrintWriter out = response.getWriter();
        Integer[] numOfOrders= new Integer[3];
        numOfOrders=jpqlJoinsTest.countOrders(1);
        try{
            out.println("Number of orders associated with employee 1 before ➥
                increasing: "+numOfOrders[0] +"<br/>");
            out.println("Number of orders returned by the JOIN query after ➥
                increasing: "+numOfOrders[1] +"<br/>");
            out.println("Number of orders you actually got after ➥
                increasing: "+numOfOrders[2] +"<br/>");
        }
        catch (Exception e){
            e.printStackTrace();
        }
    }
}
```

When executed, the servlet shown in the listing should output the results that might look like this:

```
Number of orders associated with employee 1 before increasing: 25
Number of orders returned by the JOIN query after increasing: 25
Number of orders you actually got after increasing: 26
```

The actual numbers may vary of course. However, the first two figures should be always equal, while the last one should greater by 1.

Using Native SQL Queries

When developing a Java application that utilizes the Java Persistence API, you can still express queries in native SQL. You might want to choose SQL over JPQL in the cases where you need, for example, to exploit database-specific features that cannot be leveraged with JPQL.

The following two sections provide a brief look at how you might use native SQL queries in your Java applications utilizing JPA.

Dealing with Native SQL Queries

Like with JPQL, you use special EntityManager methods to create a query expressed in native SQL.

There are some EntityManager methods to deal with native SQL queries. Table 11-4 summarizes these EntityManager methods.

Table 11-4. *The EntityManager Interface Methods That Can Be Used to Create a Query Instance for Executing a Native SQL Query*

Method	Description
`public Query createNamedQuery(String query_name)`	Creates a static query defined in metadata with either the `NamedQuery` annotation or the `NamedNativeQuery` annotation applied to an entity and returns a Query instance for executing that named query.
`public Query createNativeQuery(String sql_stmt)`	Creates a dynamic query defined within business logic code. It takes a native SQL statement: `UPDATE` or `DELETE` as the parameter and returns a Query instance for executing that SQL statement.
`public Query createNativeQuery(String sql_stmt, Class result_class)`	Creates a dynamic query defined within business logic code. It takes two parameters, a `SELECT` SQL statement and the entity class of the resulting instance or instances, and it returns a Query instance for executing the SQL statement specified.
`public Query createNativeQuery(String sql_stmt, String result_SetMapping)`	Creates a dynamic query defined within business logic code. It takes two parameters, a `SELECT` SQL statement and the name of the result set mapping defined in metadata with the `SqlResultSetMapping` annotations, and it returns a Query instance for executing the SQL statement specified.

As you might notice, the `createNamedQuery` method listed at the top of the table can also be found in Table 11-2 (in the "Dealing with JPQL Statements" section earlier). The fact is that this method is used to create a static query based on either a JPQL statement or a SQL statement.

A Simple Example of Native SQL Query

The most important thing to understand about native SQL queries created with the Entity-Manager methods listed in Table 11-4 is that they, like JPQL queries, are typically used to return entity instances, rather than table records.

Listing 11-9 illustrates a simple use of a dynamic native SQL query in a stateless session bean.

Listing 11-9. *A Session Bean Providing a Simple Example of Using a Dynamic Native SQL Query*

```
package ejbjpa.ejb;
import java.io.Serializable;
import javax.ejb.EJBException;
import javax.ejb.Stateless;
import javax.persistence.EntityManager;
import javax.persistence.PersistenceContext;
import java.util.List;
import ejbjpa.entities.*;
@Stateless
public class NativeQueryTestBean implements NativeQueryTest {
    @PersistenceContext
    private EntityManager em;
    public List<Employee> getEmployees() {
        List<Employee> employees = null;
        try {
            employees = (List<Employee>)em.createNativeQuery("SELECT * FROM➥
            employees", ejbjpa.entities.Employee.class)
                        .getResultList();
        } catch (Exception e) {
            throw new EJBException(e.getMessage());
        }
        return employees;
    }
}
```

It's interesting to note that to test the NativeQueryTestBean session bean shown in the listing you might use the same servlet you used to test the JpqlTestBean session bean discussed in the earlier "A Simple Example of JPQL in Action" section. The only thing you will have to change is the name of the bean injected with the EJB annotation.

Summary

As you learned in this chapter, JPQL provides a powerful way to access and manipulate entity instances. JPQL is database vendor–independent language. To JPQL, it does not make any difference what underlying database the entities being manipulated are mapped to. However, when you need to take advantage of a database-specific feature that cannot be leveraged with JPQL, you can still use native SQL to create and execute queries over JPA entities.

This chapter completes our discussion of the Java Persistence API features. Now you're all set to return to the sample application discussed throughout the book, the one from which you temporarily digressed in Chapter 9. In the next chapter, you will learn how to build the business logic tier of the sample.

PART 5

■■■

Building the Business Logic Tier

CHAPTER 12

■■■

Designing Session Beans

In the past three chapters, you learned a lot about the Java Persistence API, which you can utilize as a standards-based persistence solution in your Java EE and even Java SE applications. You're now ready to take a closer look at how you can utilize the Java Persistence API from enterprise beans.

Returning to the sample application in Chapter 9, you can now take the next step and develop the business logic tier, building the session beans that implement the business logic of the sample application.

In particular, through the course of the chapter, you will do the following:

- Create session beans to be utilized within the sample application

- Perform a quick test of the newly created session beans

- Continue with the NetBeans project started in Chapter 8

After performing these steps, you should have the business logic tier in the sample application. Then, after looking at transactions in the next chapter, you will be guided through the process of creating the sample presentation tier discussed in Chapter 14.

Creating Session Beans Implementing the Sample Application Logic

Now that you have the underlying database tables and JPA entities defined upon them, it's time to develop the session bean that implements the business logic of the sample.

For simplicity, the sample application discussed here will use just a couple of session beans—the first one, OrderBean, will be stateless, and the other one, CartBean, will be stateful. In the following three sections, you will look at how you can implement these beans.

Planning the Business Logic Tier

Before proceeding to building the beans, however, it's important to take some time for planning. Normally, you need to answer the following questions at this stage:

- What beans should you build?

- What operations will each bean perform?

- Does the bean you're building need to contain a conversational state between its method invocations?

As mentioned, in this particular example you might have just two beans: OrderBean and CartBean. Let's take a little closer look at each of them.

The OrderBean session bean will be used to deal with orders. At the least, this bean might have two business methods: placeOrder and getOrdersList. You might want to create the OrderBean bean stateless because there is no need for it to contain a conversational state between its method invocations. When a user places an order, the OrderBean bean's placeOrder business method is invoked, resulting in the creation of the new record in the underlying orders table and possibly a few related records in the details table. This doesn't mean, however, that the placeOrder method directly manipulates the underlying data. Instead, it deals with the corresponding JPA entities, of course.

The other bean to be created is the CartBean stateful session bean. Unlike OrderBean, CartBean should maintain its conversational state. This is because each instance of this stateful bean will be associated with a certain client's shopping cart whose state should be maintained during the entire client's session.

■**Note** It's important to understand, however, that creating a bean implementing a shopping cart as stateful is not a requirement. For example, you might have a stateless shopping cart bean whose state is synchronized with the database as required upon its business method invocations. In that case, you would need to track sessions in the applications utilizing such a stateless bean. In particular, you would need to pass the client's ID to each bean's method so that it can access or manipulate the data related to this particular client. In a stateful bean, such information is usually contained in an instance's variable.

The CartBean bean discussed here will have the following methods: initialize, addItem, removeItem, getItems, and emptyCart. The names of the previous business methods are self-explanatory. In the "Creating the Stateful Session Beans" section, you will look at how these methods are implemented.

Creating the Stateless Session Beans

In this section, you will look at how to build the OrderBean stateless session mentioned earlier. The business methods of this bean will access and manipulate the JPA entities created as discussed in Chapter 8.

Listing 12-1 shows what the source code for the OrderBean stateless session bean might look like. You should continue with the project started in Chapter 8, so you need to create the sampleapp/src/ejbjpa/ejb directory, in which you should save the OrderSample.java and OrderBean.java files. As you can see in the listing, OrderSample is the business interface implemented by OrderBean.

Listing 12-1. *Source Code for the* OrderBean *Stateless Session Bean*

```
package ejbjpa.ejb;
import java.io.Serializable;
import javax.ejb.EJBException;
import javax.ejb.Stateless;
import javax.persistence.EntityManager;
import javax.persistence.PersistenceContext;
import java.util.List;
import ejbjpa.entities.*;
@Stateless
public class OrderBean implements OrderSample {
    @PersistenceContext
    private EntityManager em;
    public void placeOrder(Integer cust_id,
                           Integer empno) {
        try {
            Customer cust = (Customer) em.find(Customer.class, cust_id);
            Employee emp = (Employee) em.find(Employee.class, empno);
            Order order = new Order();
            order.setCustomer(cust);
            order.setEmployee(emp);
            em.persist(order);
        } catch (Exception e) {
            throw new EJBException(e.getMessage());
        }
    }
    public List<Order> getOrdersList() {
     List<Order> orders = null;
        try {
          orders = (List<Order>)em.createQuery("SELECT o FROM Order o")
                    .getResultList();
        } catch (Exception e) {
            throw new EJBException(e.getMessage());
        }
      return orders;
    }
}
```

Let's take a close look at the placeOrder business method of the OrderBean stateless session bean shown in the listing. You may wonder why this method doesn't deal with an order's details. How are an order's details persisted to the database then? At first glance, it may seem that you still need another business method to deal with the details of an order.

Actually, all work on an order's details is performed behind the scenes after placeOrder is invoked. For details, you can refer to the "Adjusting the Database Tier" section in Chapter 8.

To recap, here is what is going on when you invoke the `placeOrder` business method:

1. The `placeOrder` business method starts by obtaining instances of the `Customer` and `Employee` entities, based on the `cust_id` and `empno` incoming parameters.

2. Then it creates an instance of the `Order` entity and sets its fields to the appropriate values.

3. Next, it calls the `persist` EntityManager method. As a result, the JPA provider persists the `Order` entity, trying to insert a new record into the `orders` table.

4. The database server fires the `neworder` `BEFORE INSERT` trigger before inserting the record into the `orders` table. This trigger will automatically populate the `shipping_date` and `delivery_estimate` fields of the order record being inserted.

5. The database server fires the `afterinsertorder` `AFTER INSERT` trigger also defined on the `orders` table. The `afterinsertorder` trigger moves the records associated with the customer placing the order, from the `shoppingCarts` table to the `details` table.

6. The database server fires the `newdetail` trigger defined on the `details` table. The `newdetail` trigger invokes the `updateBooks` stored procedure. The `updateBooks` stored procedure tries to update the specified record in the `books` table by issuing the `UPDATE` statement.

7. The database server fires the `newquantity` `BEFORE UPDATE` trigger before updating the record in the `books` table. This trigger will cause an error if the new value of the `quantity` field of the updated record in the `books` table is less than 0.

As you can see, the `placeOrder` business method, when invoked, starts a complex sequence of invocations that take place inside the database.

Creating the Stateful Session Beans

As mentioned, there's no state to keep track of in instances of the `OrderBean` session bean. That is why you created that bean as stateless. In contrast, you might want to keep track of the state of an instance of the `CartBean` session bean. This is because instances of this stateful bean will be maintained for each client's session.

Within the same client's session, each time the `ShoppingCart` JSP page is accessed, the container will provide access to the same `CartBean` instance. The `custId` instance variable is initialized within the `initialize` business method you should invoke upon creating each bean instance. In particular, you might want to invoke the `initialize` method the first time you access the `ShoppingCart` JSP page within a client's session.

The values of the instance variables of a stateful bean instance are preserved between invocations within the same client session. So, all business methods of a `CartBean` instance will use the value of the `custId` instance variable initialized in the `initialize` method at the beginning.

Listing 12-2 shows how you might implement the `CartBean` stateful session bean discussed here. Like the `OrderSample.java` and `OrderBean.java` files, you save the `CartBean.java` and `Cart.java` files in the `sampleapp/src/ejbjpa/ejb` directory.

Listing 12-2. *Source Code for the* CartBean *Stateful Session Bean*

```
package ejbjpa.ejb;
import java.util.List;
import javax.ejb.Remove;
import javax.ejb.Stateful;
import javax.ejb.EJBException;
import javax.persistence.EntityManager;
import javax.persistence.PersistenceContext;
import javax.persistence.PersistenceContextType;
import ejbjpa.entities.*;
@Stateful
public class CartBean implements Cart {
@PersistenceContext(type=PersistenceContextType.EXTENDED)
EntityManager em;
Integer custId;
List<ShoppingCart> items;
public void initialize(Integer cust_id) {
 if (cust_id == null) {
  throw new EJBException("Null cust_id provided.");
 } else {
    custId = cust_id;
  }
 }
 public void addItem(String item_id, Integer quantity, Double price) {
    ShoppingCart cart = (ShoppingCart) em.find(ShoppingCart.class, ➥
    new ShoppingCartKey(custId, item_id));
      if(cart != null)
      {
        em.remove(cart);
        em.flush();
      }
      cart = new ShoppingCart();
      cart.setCart_id(custId);
      cart.setBook_id(item_id);
      cart.setUnits(quantity);
      cart.setUnit_price(price);
      em.persist(cart);
 }
 public void removeItem(String item_id) {
    ShoppingCart cart = (ShoppingCart) em.find(ShoppingCart.class, ➥
    new ShoppingCartKey(custId, item_id));
    if(cart == null){
      throw new EJBException("This item is not in cart.");
     } else {
      em.remove(cart);
     }
 }
```

```java
public List<ShoppingCart> getItems() {
    items = (List<ShoppingCart>)em.createQuery("SELECT s FROM ➡
            ShoppingCart s WHERE s.cart_id =:cust_id")
                        .setParameter("cust_id", custId)
                        .getResultList();
    em.clear();
    return items;
}
@Remove
public Integer emptyCart() {
    Integer num =0;
    num = em.createQuery("DELETE FROM ShoppingCart s WHERE s.cart_id =:cust_id")
                        .setParameter("cust_id", custId)
                        .executeUpdate();
    return num;
}
 @Remove
 public void clearCartInstance() {
 }
}
```

In the bean's listing, note the use of the @Remove annotation, which has not been used in the preceding examples. With this annotation, you decorate a bean's method whose invocation should cause the removal of the bean instance upon the method completion.

As you might notice, there are two remove methods in the CartBean stateful session bean shown in the listing. The first one is called emptyCart and is designed to empty the customer's cart, deleting all the shoppingCarts table's rows associated with that customer. The emptyCart method returns the number of rows deleted.

The other remove method, clearCartInstance, does nothing and should be called when you simply want to destroy the bean's instance. Alternatively, you might rely on that the container automatically removes an instance of a stateful session bean when its lifetime expires. However, this approach is inefficient in terms of memory consumption, since a bean's instance remains in the application server memory even after the client's session within which that instance has been utilized closes.

Compiling, Packaging, and Deploying the Session Beans

Now that you have created the session beans that will be utilized in the sample application, you need to compile, package, and finally deploy them to the application server.

You might compile the beans along with the JPA entities created as discussed in Chapter 8. For that, in a terminal prompt, you should go to the sample project directory, namely, sampleapp, and then issue the following command:

```
# javac -d target src/ejbjpa/entities/*.java src/ejbjpa/ejb/*.java
```

If the entities and beans have been compiled successfully, you should receive no error messages, and the class files should appear in the sampleapp/target/ejbjpa/entities and sampleapp/target/ejbjpa/ejb directories.

The next step is to package the compiled classes in the deployment archive. Before you can do this, though, you have to create the `sampleapp/target/META-INF` directory and put the `persistence.xml` file in it. Listing 12-3 shows what the source for `persistence.xml` might look like.

Listing 12-3. *Source Code for the* `persistence.xml` *Configuration File*

```
<?xml version="1.0" encoding="UTF-8"?>
<persistence xmlns="http://java.sun.com/xml/ns/persistence" ➥
xmlns:xsi="http://www.w3.org/2001/XMLSchema-instance" ➥
xsi:schemaLocation="http://java.sun.com/xml/ns/persistence ➥
http://java.sun.com/xml/ns/persistence/persistence_1_0.xsd" version="1.0">
    <persistence-unit name="sampleapp-pu" transaction-type="JTA">
        <jta-data-source>jdbc/mysqlpool</jta-data-source>
    </persistence-unit>
</persistence>
```

Once you're done, you can then proceed to creating the deployment archive. This can be done with the following commands:

```
cd target
jar cvf appejb.jar .
```

Finally, you can deploy the archive to the application server as follows:

```
asadmin deploy appejb.jar
```

If everything is OK, you should receive the following message:

```
Command deploy executed successfully
```

Testing the Newly Created Session Beans

Before proceeding to the presentation tier of the sample, it's a good idea to test the newly created and deployed session beans discussed in the preceding sections.

If you recall from the preceding discussions, the `OrderSessionBean` bean was first introduced in the "Transaction Considerations" section in Chapter 4, where you performed a quick test of this bean. Although the `OrderBean` bean discussed in this chapter is a little different from the `OrderSessionBean` bean discussed in Chapter 4, each of these beans contains the `placeOrder` business method that triggers the underlying mechanism of the stored procedure invocations inside the database. So, if you want to look at how to perform a simple test of the `OrderBean` bean, you can refer to Chapter 4.

In the following section, you will look at the servlets designed to test the `CartBean` stateful session bean.

Testing Session Beans with Servlets

Although the presentation of the sample will be built using the JSF technology, this section illustrates how you might perform a quick test of deployed session beans with servlets. As far as a stateful session bean is concerned, it is a good idea to perform a test that illustrates how an instance of that bean might be used within the duration of a certain client session.

To achieve this, you might create two servlets that will be launched one after another so that the second servlet uses the CartBean instance created and used during the invocation of the first servlet. Diagrammatically, this might look like Figure 12-1.

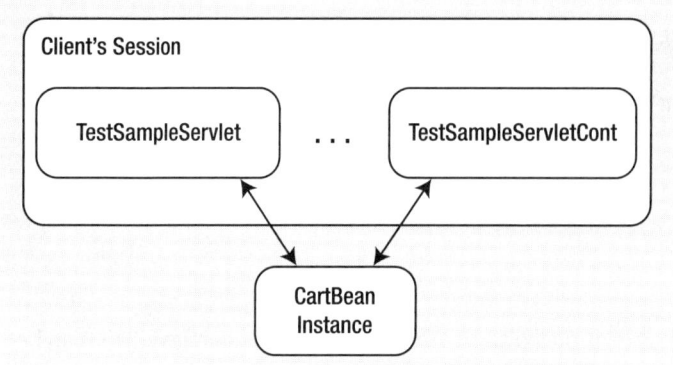

Figure 12-1. *The same* CartBean *instance can be used within the duration of a certain client session.*

Here are the tasks the first servlet might accomplish:

1. Obtains a CartBean bean instance and associates it with the HttpSession object, binding that bean instance to a session parameter

2. Adds a couple of items to the cart instance obtained in step 1

3. Iterates through the cart, displaying the items added in step 2

4. Only if an exception occurs, removes the cart instance from the session

---

■**Note** When testing a session bean, it is important to take into account that an uncaught exception thrown from within a business method of a session bean changes the state of that bean to "does not exist."

Listing 12-4 shows what the source code for the TestSampleServlet servlet might look like.

Listing 12-4. *Source Code for the* TestSampleServlet *Servlet That Might Be Used to Test the* CartBean *Stateful Session Bean*

```
package ejbjpa.servlets;
import java.io.*;
import javax.servlet.*;
import javax.servlet.http.*;
import javax.ejb.EJB;
```

```java
import javax.naming.InitialContext;
import java.util.List;
import java.util.Iterator;
import ejbjpa.entities.*;
import ejbjpa.ejb.*;
public class TestSampleServlet extends HttpServlet {
    @EJB(name="ejb/CartBean", beanInterface=Cart.class)
    public void doGet(
        HttpServletRequest request,
        HttpServletResponse response) throws ServletException, IOException {
        response.setContentType("text/html");
        response.setBufferSize(8192);
        PrintWriter out = response.getWriter();
        HttpSession session = request.getSession();
        Cart cart = (Cart)session.getAttribute("cartatt");
        try{
        if (cart == null) {
          cart = (Cart) (new ➥
InitialContext()).lookup("java:comp/env/ejb/CartBean");
            session.setAttribute("cartatt", cart);
            cart.initialize(2);
            out.println("Cart initialized" +"<br/>");
            }
            cart.addItem("1430209631", 1, 29.69);
            cart.addItem("1590595300", 2, 32.99);
            List<ShoppingCart> items = cart.getItems();
            Iterator i = items.iterator();
            ShoppingCart shoppingCart;
            while (i.hasNext()) {
                shoppingCart = (ShoppingCart) i.next();
                out.println("Cart id: "+ shoppingCart.getCart_id() +"<br/>");
                out.println("Book id: "+ shoppingCart.getBook_id() +"<br/>");
                out.println("Quantity: "+ shoppingCart.getUnits() +"<br/>");
                out.println("Unit price: "+ shoppingCart.getUnit_price() +"<br/>");
                out.println("----------"+ "<br/>");
            }
        }
        catch (Exception e){
            e.printStackTrace();
            session.removeAttribute("cartatt");
        }
    }
}
```

Of special interest here is the code responsible for obtaining an instance of the CartBean bean and associating it with the HttpSession object. You start by creating a session object using the HttpServletRequest's getSession method. Then you try to obtain the CartBean instance bound to the session. If the cart instance is null, you obtain it through JNDI lookup and then bind it to the session. Finally, you invoke the cart's `initialize` method, passing the ID of a customer as the parameter.

▪**Note** JNDI lookup is used here because a servlet's instance may be shared by several clients simultaneously, thus making the use of dependency injection impossible.

Note that you remove the cart instance from the session only if an exception occurs. If this is not the case, the `CartBean` instance obtained in this servlet is not destroyed after servlet execution completion and stays available for further uses.

It is interesting to note that if you execute the `TestSampleServlet` servlet discussed here two or more times, one after another, the second or subsequent execution will result in an error generated when calling the cart's `addItem` method. This is caused by the database server in response to the attempt to insert the same records into the `shoppingCarts` table. As a result, an exception will be thrown, and `HttpSession`'s `removeAttribute` method will be called in the `catch` block, removing the cart instance from the session. In this situation, you don't need to worry about destroying the cart instance, since the container will do it for you.

To avoid errors, however, you should not perform another execution of the `TestSampleServlet` servlet immediately after it has been executed. Instead, you should launch the `TestSampleServletCont` servlet that, among other things, will handle the task of destroying the `CartBean` instance obtained in the `TestSampleServlet` servlet earlier.

Here are the tasks the `TestSampleServletCont` servlet might accomplish:

1. Obtains a `CartBean` bean instance and associates it with the `HttpSession` object, binding that bean instance to a session parameter

2. Removes one of those cart items added during the execution of the `TestSampleServlet` servlet discussed earlier

3. Iterates through the cart, displaying the items currently available in the cart

4. Empties the cart and destroys its instance

5. Removes the cart instance from the session

Listing 12-5 shows what the source code for the `TestSampleServletCont` servlet might look like.

Listing 12-5. *Source Code for the* `TestSampleServletCont` *Servlet That Might Be Used to Test the* `CartBean` *Stateful Session Bean, When Called After the* `TestSampleServlet` *Servlet in Listing 12-4*

```
package ejbjpa.servlets;
import java.io.*;
import javax.servlet.*;
import javax.servlet.http.*;
import javax.ejb.EJB;
import javax.naming.InitialContext;
import java.util.List;
```

```java
import java.util.Iterator;
import javax.ejb.EJBException;
import ejbjpa.entities.*;
import ejbjpa.ejb.*;
public class TestSampleServletCont extends HttpServlet {
    @EJB(name="ejb/CartBean", beanInterface=Cart.class)
    public void doGet(
        HttpServletRequest request,
        HttpServletResponse response) throws ServletException, IOException {
        response.setContentType("text/html");
        response.setBufferSize(8192);
        PrintWriter out = response.getWriter();
        HttpSession session = request.getSession();
        Cart cart = (Cart)session.getAttribute("cartatt");
        try{
        if (cart == null) {
          cart = (Cart) (new InitialContext()).lookup("java:comp/env/ejb/CartBean");
          session.setAttribute("cartatt", cart);
          cart.initialize(2);
          out.println("Cart initialized" +"<br/>");
         }
         out.println("Remove the first item from the cart "+ "<br/>");
         cart.removeItem("1430209631");
         cart.removeItem("1590595300");
         cart.addItem("1590595300", 2, 32.99);
         List<ShoppingCart> items = cart.getItems();
         ShoppingCart shoppingCart;
         Iterator i = items.iterator();
         while (i.hasNext()) {
                shoppingCart = (ShoppingCart) i.next();
                out.println("Cart id: "+ shoppingCart.getCart_id() +"<br/>");
                out.println("Book id: "+ shoppingCart.getBook_id() +"<br/>");
                out.println("Quantity: "+ shoppingCart.getUnits() +"<br/>");
                out.println("Unit price: "+ shoppingCart.getUnit_price() +"<br/>");
                out.println("----------"+ "<br/>");
         }
         Integer num = cart.emptyCart();
         out.println(num + " item(s) removed " + "<br/>");
        }
        catch (Exception e){
             e.printStackTrace();
        }
        finally {
             session.removeAttribute("cartatt");
        }
    }
}
```

As you can see, the `TestSampleServletCont` servlet shown in the listing uses the same mechanism of obtaining a `CartBean` instance as you saw in the `TestSampleServlet` servlet shown in Listing 12-4 earlier.

Note that the `HttpSession`'s `removeAttribute` method is called in the `finally` block in the previous servlet. This guarantees that the operation of removing the cart instance from the session will take place under all circumstances.

The deployment descriptor to be used with the servlets discussed here should, among other elements such as `servlet` and `servlet-mapping`, contain the `ejb-ref` element highlighted in bold in the snippet shown in Listing 12-6.

Listing 12-6. *You Have to Include the* `ejb-ref` *Element in the* `web.xml` *Deployment Descriptor to Declare* `CartBean` *References*

```
<web-app
...
    <ejb-ref>
        <ejb-ref-name>ejb/CartBean</ejb-ref-name>
        <ejb-ref-type>Session</ejb-ref-type>
        <remote>ejbjpa.ejb.Cart</remote>
    </ejb-ref>
</web-app>
```

After you are done with compiling, packaging, and deploying the test application discussed in this section, you can launch the `TestSampleServlet` servlet. If everything is OK, it should produce the following output:

```
Cart initialized
Cart id: 2
Book id: 1430209631
Quantity: 1
Unit price: 29.69
----------
Cart id: 2
Book id: 1590595300
Quantity: 2
Unit price: 32.99
----------
```

As you can see, the cart instance has been initialized and two items have been added to the cart. Now, you can launch the `TestSampleServletCart` servlet. This should produce the following results:

```
Remove the first item from the cart
Cart id: 2
Book id: 1590595300
Quantity: 2
```

```
Unit price: 32.99
----------
1 item(s) removed
```

This time, the `Cart initialized` message does not appear. This simply means the `TestSampleServletCart` servlet launched here used the cart instance created by the `TestSampleServlet` servlet launched previously. The output also shows that the `TestSampleServletCart` servlet successfully removed one item from the cart, then it displayed what was left, and finally it emptied the cart.

If you want, you can repeat the test by making another run of the `TestSampleServlet` servlet and then the `TestSampleServletCart` servlet. You should see the same results.

If Something Goes Wrong . . .

If you have managed to deploy your bean on the application server and received no error messages but you get an error when starting the application invoking that bean, it is always a good idea to look at the JNDI Tree Browsing list, which contains the JNDI names of the resource objects available on the server.

If the bean you deployed is missing in the JNDI tree, the next place to go is the `glassfish_dir/domains/domain1/generated/xml/j2ee-modules/your_ejb_name/META-INF` directory, where you can find the deployment descriptors actually used by the application server. The application server automatically generates these descriptors during the deployment stage, based on the metadata found in the annotations and custom deployment descriptors.

Continuing with the Sample Project in the NetBeans IDE

You may find the information provided in this section useful if you implement the sample application discussed here with the help of the NetBeans IDE. In the "Building the Sample with the NetBeans IDE" section in Chapter 8, you started a new standard NetBeans IDE project for an enterprise application and then incorporated the JPA entities discussed in that chapter into the project.

In this chapter, you will look at how you can add the session beans created in this chapter into the IDE project created as discussed in Chapter 8. Here are the steps to accomplish this:

1. In your file system, go to the `sampleappIDE` project root directory generated by the IDE when you created the `sampleappIDE` project as discussed in Chapter 8. Once you're there, move on to the `sampleappIDE-ejb/src/java` directory.

2. Within the `sampleappIDE/sampleappIDE-ejb/src/java/ejbjpa` directory, create the `ejb` directory, and copy the session bean sources created as discussed in the earlier sections "Creating the Stateless Session Beans" and "Creating the Stateful Session Beans." In particular, you should copy four files: `Cart.java`, `CartBean.java`, `OrderSample.java`, and `OrderBean.java`.

3. Launch the IDE from the Start menu of your operating system.

4. In the Projects window, extend the sampleappIDE-ejb/Source Packages node. You should see two packages there: `ejbjpa.entities` and `ejbjpa.ejb`.

5. In the Projects window, double-click the ejbjpa.ejb package node. You should see that the package contains the session beans sources you copied into the `sampleappIDE/sampleappIDE-ejb/src/java/ejbjpa/ejb` directory in step 2.

6. In the Projects window, right-click the sampleappIDE-ejb node, and choose Build Project. If everything is OK, the last message you should see in the Output window is `BUILD SUCCESSFUL`.

7. In the Projects window, right-click the sampleappIDE-ejb node, and choose Deploy Project. If everything is OK, the last message you should see in the Output window is `BUILD SUCCESSFUL`.

8. Close the IDE by choosing File ➤ Exit.

Now that you have deployed the deployment archive, you can test the session beans included in that archive. For this, you might create a servlet application as discussed earlier in this section.

Summary

Following the instructions provided in this chapter, you built the session beans to be utilized within the sample application discussed throughout the book. You looked at both stateless and stateful session beans.

In the next chapter, you will take a close look at transaction management. Then, in Chapter 14 you will return to the sample discussed here and learn how to build the presentation tier of it.

■■■

Managing Transactions

Transactions are an important part of any enterprise system. When your Java EE application performs operations affecting the underlying data, the changes are done within the scope of a transaction, ensuring the data you're dealing with is always in a consistent state.

This chapter discusses choices you have when it comes to transactions in your Java EE application. The material provided will help you better understand how transactions are managed and find the best transaction scenario for your application, out of many alternatives. In particular, you will learn how to do the following:

- Develop transactional enterprise beans and client applications

- Use different types of transaction demarcation

- Deal with resource-local transactions

- Implement an appropriate transaction scenario when developing a stateless or stateful session bean

Although the discussion in this chapter does not affect directly the sample discussed throughout the book, it may give you some ideas on how you might modify the sample and move some sample's business logic from the database to the business logic tier, relying on the transactional behavior of the components implemented in the business logic tier.

Using Transactions in Java EE Applications

Usually a Java EE application accesses and manipulates the data stored in one or more underlying databases, which may be simultaneously accessed by other applications. The operations an enterprise application performs on the data are typically grouped in logical units of work, each of which corresponds to an indivisible business operation, for example, transferring money from a savings account to a checking account.

Since the underlying data a typical enterprise application deals with is crucial for a business, there must be a reliable mechanism ensuring that the data is kept consistent, accurate, and current, regardless of the operations you perform on it and the number of applications concurrently accessing it. In enterprise environments, all these problems are solved with the help of transactions.

JTA Transactions

In most cases, when developing a Java EE application, you will have to deal with Java Transaction API (JTA) transactions, which are managed by the container. To recap, JTA provides a set of interfaces to the underlying transaction manager used by the application server.

In practice, however, the only JTA interface you may need to know about is `javax.transaction.UserTransaction`, which allows you to control transaction boundaries programmatically. This interface will be discussed in the "Demarcating Transactions Programmatically" section later in this chapter. For more detailed information on JTA, you can refer to JTA specifications at `http://java.sun.com/products/jta/`.

To instruct the container to use JTA when dealing with a `DataSource` object defined upon the underlying database, you have to define that data source in `persistence.xml` using the `jta-data-source` element, as you did in many preceding examples. As a quick recap, look at the following snippet:

```
<persistence ...>
    <persistence-unit name="sampleapp-pu" transaction-type="JTA">
        <jta-data-source>jdbc/mysqlpool</jta-data-source>
    </persistence-unit>
</persistence>
```

It's interesting to note that when dealing with JTA transactions, you don't necessarily have to use the `javax.transaction.UserTransaction` interface. If you choose container-managed transaction demarcation, it will be the container's responsibility to demarcate transaction boundaries. The next section outlines the types of transaction demarcation you can choose when developing a Java EE component. Each of these types is then discussed in more detail in the subsequent sections.

As an alternative to JTA transactions, you can use resource-local transactions, which are controlled by the application rather than the container. Resource-local transactions will be further discussed in the "Dealing with Resource-Local Transactions" section later in this chapter.

Types of Transaction Demarcation

If you look through any technical article on transactions, you should notice that, from the application developer's perspective, the most important thing when developing transactional code is defining transaction boundaries. Even if explicit transaction demarcation is not required, the developer should clearly understand where a transaction starts and where it completes.

Table 13-1 summarizes the types of transaction demarcation you can use in a Java EE application.

Table 13-1. *The Transaction Attribute Can Be Set to One of These Values*

Demarcation Type	Description
Declarative transaction demarcation	Known as *container-managed transaction demarcation*. With it, the container controls transaction demarcation declaratively, based on the value of the transaction attribute that you can specify using the `TransactionAttribute` annotation applied to an entire bean class or a certain bean's business method. As an alternative to the `TransactionAttribute` annotation, you can specify the transaction attributes in the deployment descriptor.
Programmatic transaction demarcation	Often called *bean-managed transaction demarcation*. When using this type of demarcation, you explicitly demarcate transaction boundaries in the bean's business methods, using the `UserTransaction` interface.
Client-managed transaction demarcation	Like bean-managed transaction demarcation, client-managed transaction demarcation implies using the `UserTransaction` interface methods to explicitly demarcate transactions. In this case, though, you define a transaction in a client program that invokes an enterprise bean's business method.

When developing enterprise bean transactional code, you can choose between using container-managed and bean-managed transaction demarcation. When developing transactional client application code, you can demarcate transactions programmatically.

It's interesting to note, however, a business method of an enterprise bean may be a client to a business method of another bean. If this is the case, the client may still use container-managed transaction demarcation, which is discussed in more detail the next section.

Using Declarative Transaction Demarcation

When declarative transaction demarcation is used, the EJB container will control transactions without you having to explicitly invoke `begin` and `commit`. In this case, it's the responsibility of the container to demarcate transactions.

However, you can still affect the way the container will demarcate transactions by setting the transaction attribute to an appropriate value or programmatically demarcating the transaction. That is, the transaction attribute is used to control the scope of a transaction. You can set the transaction attribute through the `TransactionAttribute` metadata annotation or in the deployment descriptor, setting the `trans-attribute` element used within the `container-transaction` element.

Table 13-2 lists the possible values of the transaction attribute.

Table 13-2. *The Transaction Attribute Can Be Set to One of These Values*

TransactionAttribute Annotation	trans-attribute Element	Description
NOT_SUPPORTED	NotSupported	The container will not start a transaction if the transaction attribute of the enterprise bean's business method being invoked is set to this value. If the client code is running within a transaction context, then the client's transaction is suspended until the called business method completes.
REQUIRED	Required	The container invokes the business method with a transaction context. If the client is associated with a transaction context, the business method runs within the client's transaction. Otherwise, the container creates a new transaction for the method.
SUPPORTS	Supports	If the client is associated with a transaction context, the business method runs within the client's transaction. Otherwise, the container invokes the business method without a transaction context.
REQUIRES_NEW	RequiresNew	The container invokes the business method with a new transaction, regardless of whether the client is executed within a transaction. If the client is running within a transaction, that transaction is temporarily suspended and then resumed when the called business method ends.
MANDATORY	Mandatory	The container invokes the business method within the client's transaction context. If the client has no transaction context, a TransactionRequired➥ Exception exception is thrown.
NEVER	Never	The container invokes the business method without a transaction context. If the client is running within a transaction context, a RemoteException is thrown.

By default, the transaction attribute is set to REQUIRED. This means that by default a business method is executed in a transaction context, regardless of whether the client is executed in a transaction context.

Figure 13-1 illustrates both of these situations. A call to a business method of an enterprise bean from a transactional client is depicted at the left side of the figure, and a nontransactional client scenario is shown on the right.

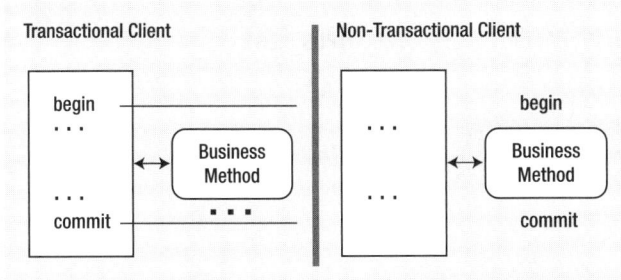

Figure 13-1. *If the transaction attribute is set to* REQUIRED, *a business method called will be executed in the context of the client's transaction, if any. Otherwise, the method is executed in a new transaction context.*

Don't be misled by begin and commit shown in the scenario involving a nontransactional client in the figure (the diagram shown on the right). In fact, you don't need to explicitly invoke these methods there. Since you use container-managed transaction demarcation, everything will be done by the container behind the scenes. In particular, the container will start a new transaction just before the business method executes and completes it immediately after execution of the method.

An important thing to note here is that the EJB architecture does not support nested transactions—only flat transactions are allowed. For example, if the transaction attributes of the bean's methods being invoked from a transactional client are set to REQUIRED and all calls to those methods are made within a single client's transaction, all these methods will be executed within that single transaction, as depicted in the transactional client scenario in the figure (shown on the left).

■**Note** Even if you set the transaction attribute to REQUIRES_NEW for the business methods invoked from a transactional client, the client's transaction is suspended during invocations of those methods. So, at any given moment, there is only one active transaction and no nested transactions.

Container-managed transaction demarcation is best understood by example. Say you have two session beans, where one acts as the client to the other one. Listing 13-1 shows the snippet of the client.

Listing 13-1. *Snippet of the* ShoppingCartBean *Stateless Session Bean Whose* placeOrder *Business Method Is Executed in a New Transaction*

```
...
@Stateless
public class ShoppingCartBean
    implements ShoppingCart {
    @EJB
    private OrderSession neworder;
```

```
...
  @TransactionAttribute(TransactionAttributeType.REQUIRES_NEW)
  public void placeOrder() {
    ...
      pono = neworder.createOrder(cust_id);
      neworder.addOrderDetails(pono, items);
    ...
   }
  ...
}
```

As you can see, the `placeOrder` business method of the `ShoppingCartBean` stateless session bean shown in the snippet will be always executed with a new transaction, since its transaction attribute is set to `REQUIRES_NEW`. So, the calls to the `OrderSessionBean`'s `createOrder` and `addOrderDetails` methods made from within `placeOrder` are performed in a single transaction.

Listing 13-2 shows the structure of the `OrderSessionBean` session bean whose `createOrder` and `addOrderDetails` methods are called from the client.

Listing 13-2. *Snippet of the* `OrderSessionBean` *Stateless Session Bean Whose Transaction Attribute Is Set to* `REQUIRED`

```
...
@TransactionAttribute(TransactionAttributeType.REQUIRED)
@Stateless
public class OrderSessionBean
    implements OrderSession {
  ...
  public Integer createOrder() {
    ...
   return pono;
  }
  public Integer addOrderDetails(Integer pono, List items) {
    ...
  }
  ...
}
```

As you can see in the listing, the `OrderSessionBean` stateless session bean uses the `REQUIRED` transaction attribute for the entire class, meaning the `REQUIRED` transaction attribute is applied to all the `OrderSessionBean`'s methods.

Demarcating Transactions Programmatically

In some situations, you might want to programmatically demarcate transaction boundaries. In such cases, you might take advantage of the `javax.transaction.UserTransaction` interface used to interact with the underlying JTA transaction manager controlling transactions. This interface can be used in client programs and enterprise beans.

Table 13-3 lists the methods of the `javax.transaction.UserTransaction` interface.

Table 13-3. *The Methods of the* UserTransaction *Interface*

Method	Description
void begin()	Begins a new transaction, associating it with the current thread
void commit()	Completes the transaction attached to the current thread, making the effects of all operations performed within the transaction permanent
void rollback()	Rolls back the transaction attached to the current thread, undoing the effects of all operations within the transaction
void setRollbackOnly()	Instructs the container that the only possible outcome for the transaction is to roll back it.
int getStatus()	Obtains the status of the transaction attached to the current thread
void setTransactionTimeout(int secs)	Modifies the timeout for the transactions started by the current thread

In the example shown in Listing 13-3, you use the UserTransaction's begin and commit to delimit transaction boundaries in the placeOrder business method of the ShoppingCartBean bean whose structure was originally shown in Listing 13-1.

Listing 13-3. *The* ShoppingCartBean *Stateless Session Bean Modified to Delimit Transaction Boundaries Programmatically*

```
...
@Stateless
@TransactionManagement(TransactionManagementType.BEAN)
public class ShoppingCartBean
    implements ShoppingCart {
    @Resource
    javax.Transaction.UserTransaction ut;
    @EJB
    private OrderSession neworder;
    ...
    public void placeOrder() {
      ...
        ut.begin();
        pono = neworder.createOrder(cust_id);
        neworder.addOrderDetails(pono, items);
        ut.commit();
      ...
    }
    ...
}
```

The main difference between the snippet shown in Listing 13-1 earlier and the one shown here is that in the former the transaction associated with the placeOrder business method automatically starts by the container before the method execution and commits immediately after it, while in the latter you manually define transaction boundaries. So, the latter is more flexible in that it allows you to include only part of the business method code in a transaction or define more than one transaction within a single business method.

Using Transaction Demarcation in Client Code

The example in the preceding section illustrated how you might use the UserTransaction's begin and commit to delimit transaction boundaries in an enterprise bean when using bean-managed transaction demarcation. However, the use of the UserTransaction interface is not limited to enterprise beans. You can also use it to demarcate a JTA transaction in web components, such as servlets and JSP pages.

The snippet shown in Listing 13-4 illustrates how you might wrap calls to the OrderSessionBean's createOrder and addOrderDetails methods in a transaction defined in a servlet.

Listing 13-4. *An Example of Using the* UserTransaction *Interface to Demarcate Transaction Boundaries in a Servlet*

```
...
public class placeOrder extends HttpServlet {
 @Resource
 UserTransaction utx;
 public void doGet(HttpServletRequest request,
 HttpServletResponse response) {
 ...
  try {
   utx.begin();
    pono = neworder.createOrder(cust_id);
    neworder.addOrderDetails(pono, items);
   utx.commit();
  } catch (Exception ex) {
   try {
    utx.rollback();
   } catch(Exception e) {
    e.printStackTrace();
   }
  }
 }
 ...
}
```

In the servlet shown in the listing, you call the rollback method of the UserTransaction interface if something goes wrong, calling this method from within the try block nested in the catch block executed if createOrder or addOrderDetails fails.

Dealing with Resource-Local Transactions

Aside from JTA transactions, there are resource-local transactions controlled by the application through the `EntityTransaction` interface. Normally, you might want to use resource-local transactions in Java SE environments, since JTA is not supported in such environments.

You can obtain a reference to the `EntityTransaction` instance by calling the `getTransaction` method of a resource-local EntityManager. Before moving on to an example, however, let's first look at the `EntityTransaction` interface methods listed in Table 13-4.

Table 13-4. *The Methods of the* `EntityTransaction` *Interface*

Method	Description
`void begin()`	Begins a new resource transaction
`void commit()`	Completes the current transaction, making the effects of all operations performed within the transaction permanent
`void rollback()`	Rolls back the current transaction, undoing the effects of all operations within the transaction
`void setRollbackOnly()`	Marks the current transaction to be rolled back
`boolean getRollbackOnly()`	Checks to see whether the current transaction has been marked to be rolled back
`boolean isActive()`	Checks to see whether there is a transaction in progress

To use resource-local transactions, you have to set the `transaction-type` attribute of the `persistence-unit` element in `persistence.xml` to `RESOURCE_LOCAL`. Then you should use the `non-jta-data-source` element to define a non-JTA data source to be used in the application. Listing 13-5 shows what a resource-local data source in `persistence.xml` might look like.

Listing 13-5. *An Example of* `persistence.xml` *Configuration File Defining a Persistence Unit Upon a Resource-Local Data Source Object*

```xml
<?xml version="1.0" encoding="UTF-8"?>
<persistence xmlns="http://java.sun.com/xml/ns/persistence" ➥
xmlns:xsi="http://www.w3.org/2001/XMLSchema-instance" ➥
xsi:schemaLocation="http://java.sun.com/xml/ns/persistence ➥
http://java.sun.com/xml/ns/persistence/persistence_1_0.xsd" version="1.0">
    <persistence-unit name="app-pu" transaction-type="RESOURCE_LOCAL">
        <non-jta-data-source>jdbc/mysqlpool</non-jta-data-source>
    </persistence-unit>
</persistence>
```

Listing 13-6 provides an example of how you might use the `EntityTransaction` interface to define resource-local transactions in a POJO.

Listing 13-6. *An Example of Using Resource-Local Transactions in a Regular Java Class*

```java
public class OrderClass {
 private EntityManagerFactory emf;
 private EntityManager em;
```

```
 private Order order;
 private Part part;
 public OrderClass() {
  emf = Persistence.createEntityManagerFactory("app-pu");
  em = emf.createEntityManager();
 }
 public void getOrder(int pono) {
  order = em.find(Order.class, pono);
 }
 public void getPart(String partid) {
  part = em.find(Part.class, partid);
 }
 public void addLineItem(int quantity) {
  em.getTransaction().begin();
  LineItem lineItem = new LineItem(order, part, quantity);
  order.getLineItems().add(lineItem);
  em.getTransaction().commit();
 }
 public void destroy() {
  em.close();
  emf.close();
 }
}
```

In the constructor of OrderClass shown in the listing, you create an entity manager factory as it is created in Java SE environments, and then you obtain a resource-local Entity-Manager. In the addLineItem method, you use the EntityManager's getTransaction method to obtain the EntityTransaction interface used then to create a resource-local transaction.

Some Transaction Scenarios

Now that you have a good grasp of how transactions can be utilized in your Java EE application, it's time to look at some transaction scenarios.

In the next section, you will look at how transactions work in a business method performing persistence operations with the help of two container-managed entity managers. Then, you will look at an example of using transactions in a stateful session bean utilizing an entity manager of type PersistenceContextType.EXTENDED.

Transactional Behavior of a Business Method Involving Operations of More Than One Container-Managed EntityManager

You already saw some examples of using several entity managers within a single business method. In particular, in the "An Example of Using a Container-Managed EntityManager" section in Chapter 10, you saw an example of using two container-managed entity managers of type PersistenceContextType.TRANSACTION. Returning to that example, let's now take a closer look at the code used there, from the standpoint of transactions.

First, though, let's look at Listing 13-7 illustrating the persistence.xml configuration file that might be used to define two persistence units upon which the container will configure and create entity manager factories used then for creating container-managed entity managers.

Listing 13-7. persistence.xml *Defining Two Persistence Units*

```xml
<?xml version="1.0" encoding="UTF-8"?>
<persistence xmlns="http://java.sun.com/xml/ns/persistence" ➥
xmlns:xsi="http://www.w3.org/2001/XMLSchema-instance" ➥
xsi:schemaLocation="http://java.sun.com/xml/ns/persistence ➥
http://java.sun.com/xml/ns/persistence/persistence_1_0.xsd" version="1.0">
    <persistence-unit name="contaneremtest1-pu" transaction-type="JTA">
        <jta-data-source>jdbc/mysqlpool</jta-data-source>
    </persistence-unit>
    <persistence-unit name="contaneremtest2-pu" transaction-type="JTA">
        <jta-data-source>jdbc/mysqlpool</jta-data-source>
    </persistence-unit>
</persistence>
```

Now, let's return to the OrderTestBean session bean utilizing two container-managed entity managers, as it was originally shown in Listing 10-4 in Chapter 10. Listing 13-8 shows the source code for OrderTestBean with comments in the changeOrderEmpTest business method to help you better understand how this method is working from the standpoint of transactions.

Listing 13-8. *The* OrderTestBean *Stateless Session Bean Whose* changeOrderEmpTest *Method, When Executed, Is Associated with Two Transactions*

```java
//import declarations
...
@Stateless
public class OrderTestBean implements OrderTest {
    @PersistenceContext(unitName="contaneremtest1-pu")
    private EntityManager em1;
    @PersistenceContext(unitName="contaneremtest2-pu")
    private EntityManager em2;
    public Integer setOrder(Integer cust_id, Integer empno) {
        Integer order_pono;
        try {
          Customer cust = (Customer) em1.find(Customer.class, cust_id);
          Employee emp = (Employee) em1.find(Employee.class, empno);
          Order order1 = new Order();
          order1.setCustomer(cust);
          order1.setEmployee(emp);
          em1.persist(order1);
          em1.flush();
          em1.refresh(order1);
```

```
            order_pono = order1.getPono();
        } catch (Exception e) {
            throw new EJBException(e.getMessage());
        }
        return order_pono;
    }
    public String changeOrderEmpTest(Integer pono, Integer empno, Integer custid) {
        String order_details;
        try {
            //finds the order
            Order order1 = (Order) em1.find(Order.class, pono);
            //shows the original order
            order_details = "order "+ order1.getPono()+ " emp: " + ➥
             order1.getEmployee().getLastname()+" cust: " + ➥
             order1.getCustomer().getCust_name()+"<br/>";
            //updates order1 and synchronize it to the database
            Employee emp = (Employee) em1.find(Employee.class, empno);
            order1.setEmployee(emp);
            em1.flush();
            em1.refresh(order1);
            //shows the change in order1 obtained from the database
            order_details = order_details+"order "+ order1.getPono()+ " emp: " + ➥
             order1.getEmployee().getLastname()+" cust: " + ➥
             order1.getCustomer().getCust_name()+"<br/>";
            //obtains the same order with the other EntityManager
            Order order2 = (Order) em2.find(Order.class, pono);
            //change order2 and synchronize it to the database
            Customer cust = (Customer) em1.find(Customer.class, custid);
            order2.setCustomer(cust);
            em2.flush();
            em2.refresh(order2);
            //shows the change in order2 obtained from the database
            order_details = order_details+"order "+ order2.getPono()+ " emp: " + ➥
               order2.getEmployee().getLastname()+" cust: " + ➥
               order2.getCustomer().getCust_name()+"<br/>";
        } catch (Exception e) {
            throw new EJBException(e.getMessage());
        }
        return order_details;
    }
}
```

As you can see, the OrderTestBean stateless session bean shown in the listing contains two business methods: setOrder and changeOrderEmpTest. The first one creates and persists an order, while the second one allows you to change the employee and customer fields of an already existing order to another value.

Of special interest here is the changeOrderEmpTest method, where you deal with two different container-managed entity managers. The method illustrates that a change applied to the order instance with the first entity manager appears at the instance associated with the same order record but obtained with the other entity manager after you have performed the flush operation with the first entity manager. It is important to realize that although the two entity managers used here are associated with two different persistence contexts, they both operate in the same transaction. That is why changes made by the first entity manger can be seen when using the other manager, after the first manager synchronizes those changes to the database.

To test the OrderTestBean's business methods, you might use the EmEjbTestServlet servlet shown in Listing 13-9.

Listing 13-9. *The* EmEJBTestServlet *Servlet Can Be Used to Test the* OrderTestBean *Stateless Session Bean*

```
//import declarations
...
public class EmEjbTestServlet extends HttpServlet {
    @EJB private OrderTest orderTest;
    public void doGet(
        HttpServletRequest request,
        HttpServletResponse response) throws ServletException, IOException {
        response.setContentType("text/html");
        response.setBufferSize(8192);
        PrintWriter out = response.getWriter();
        Integer custid1=1;
        Integer custid2=2;
        Integer empno1=1;
        Integer empno2=2;
        try{
            Integer pono = orderTest.setOrder(custid1,empno1);
            out.println("Created order "+ pono +"<br/>");
            out.println(orderTest.changeOrderEmpTest(pono,empno2, custid2));
        }
        catch (Exception e){
            e.printStackTrace();
        }
    }
}
```

In the EmEJBTestServlet servlet shown in the listing, you first call the setOrder method to create a new order and then invoke the changeOrderEmpTest method that changes the value of the employee and customer fields and outputs the values of the changed fields in the context of each of the two entity managers. This output might look like this:

```
Created order 21
order 21 emp: Oganovich cust: John Poplavski
order 21 emp: Silver cust: John Poplavski
order 21 emp: Silver cust: Paul Medica
```

The first line in the previous output tells you that the new order whose pono is 21 has been created. All the other output lines are generated in the changeOrderEmpTest method. The second line shows the values of the employee and customer fields of the order entity instance obtained with the first manager, before applying any changes to that order. In the third output line, you can see that the employee field of the order has been changed. This is done with the first manager. Then, with the help of the second manager, you change the customer field of the order and synchronize this change to the database. The last line of the output shows the employee and customer fields you finally have when obtaining the order with the second manager. As you can see, the changes made by the first manager and flushed to the database can be seen when using the second manager.

It's interesting to note that flushing changes to the database in this example does not automatically mean committing the transaction in the context for which these changes are made. As mentioned earlier, both the entity managers used here operate in the same transaction. So, if you mark the transaction for rollback, then all the changes made by both the managers will be rolled back upon completion of the method.

Listing 13-10 shows the code you need to add to the changeOrderEmpTest method so that it rolls back the changes made within it.

Listing 13-10. *The* OrderTestBean *Stateless Session Bean Modified to Roll Back the Changes Made by Both the Entity Managers Used in the* changeOrderEmpTest *Method*

```
//import declarations
...
import javax.annotation.Resource;
import javax.ejb.SessionContext;
@Stateless
public class OrderTestBean implements OrderTest {
  ...
    @Resource
    private SessionContext ctx;
  ...
    public String changeOrderEmpTest(Integer pono, Integer empno) {
...
          ctx.setRollbackOnly();
        } catch (Exception e) {
           throw new EJBException(e.getMessage());
        }
        return order_details;
    }
}
```

The simplest way to make sure the transaction has been rolled back is to connect to the underlying database directly with a command-line tool and issue the query retrieving the record of interest from the orders table. So, the query might look like this:

```
SELECT o.pono, e.lastname, c.cust_name FROM orders o, employees e, customers c ➥
WHERE o.pono = 21 AND o.empno=e.empno AND o.cust_id=c.cust_id;
```

This should produce the following output:

```
pono lastname    cust_name
------------------------------------------
21    Oganovich  John Poplavski
```

As you can see, the employee and customer have not been changed. This is because the transaction started during the changeOrderEmpTest method execution is rolled back.

Defining Transactions in Stateful Session Beans

Another interesting case is defining a transaction in a stateful session bean that has an extended persistence context.

Listing 13-11 illustrates an example of such a stateful session bean. In particular, you can see the ShoppingCartBean stateful bean that uses bean-managed transaction demarcation.

Listing 13-11. *An Example of How You Can Define a Transaction in a Stateful Session Bean, So That It Survives Several Client Calls*

```
...
@Stateful
@TransactionManagement(TransactionManagementType.BEAN)
public class ShoppingCartBean
    implements ShoppingCart {
    @Resource
    javax.Transaction.UserTransaction ut;
    @PersistenceContext(type=EXTENDED)
    EntityManager em;
    private Order order;
    ...
    public void newOrder(Integer pono) {
        ut.begin();
        order = em.find(Order.class, pono);
    }
    public void addLineItem(LineItem lineItem) {
        order.getLineItems.add(lineItem);
    }
    public void placeOrder() {
        ut.commit();
    }
    ...
}
```

When you call the ShoppingCartBean's newOrder business method, a new transaction begins. The transaction is then retained across all calls to the addLineItem method. Finally, it commits when the placeOrder method is invoked.

Summary

In this chapter, you looked at how transactions work in Java EE environments. You learned that there are several types of transaction demarcation to choose from when it comes to building Java EE components. You looked at JTA and resource-local transactions and at how they can be explicitly and implicitly utilized in stateless and stateful session beans and servlets.

In the next chapter, you will return to the sample application discussed throughout the book and learn how to build the presentation tier of the sample.

PART 6

■ ■ ■

Building the Presentation Tier and Testing

■ ■ ■

Building the Presentation Tier

Having the database, persistence, and business logic tiers of your application would not make sense without implementing, at some point, the presentation tier, also referred to as the *front-end layer* of the application. As its name implies, the presentation tier implements the application's presentation logic, making it possible for the users of the application to take advantage of all this functionality implemented in the other application layers.

This chapter describes how you might build the presentation tier for the sample application discussed throughout the book, using the JavaServer Faces (JSF) technology. This is the final stage in development of the sample application. Following the instructions provided in the chapter, you will do the following:

- Build JSF beans through which you will access the session beans already in place

- Develop JSF pages upon the JSF beans

- Secure your web application

- Configure your web application

- Deploy your web application to the application server

As you can see, the way in which this chapter is going to deal with JSF doesn't assume using JBoss Seam, the framework allowing you to effectively integrate EJB 3.0 and JSF components that is quickly gaining popularity among Java EE developers. In a nutshell, JBoss Seam lets you refer to EJB session beans directly from within JSF UI components, eliminating the need for JSF managed beans and thus simplifying development of the front-end layer of a Java EE application. However, a discussion of the JBoss Seam framework could fill an entire book by itself and is beyond the scope of this book.

Accessing Java EE Functionality from a Presentation Tier

As you might recall from the examples discussed in the first chapters, you don't necessarily have to build web components to access EJB and JTA components. For example, you might create an application client to access enterprise beans using the `appclient` command-line tool.

In most situations, however, you might want to build an application client only to test the EJB and JTA components built to be eventually utilized in a web application. So, building the presentation tier of a Java EE application means building a web application utilizing the Java EE components that provide the business logic for the application.

Choosing a Web Tier Technology

In the preceding chapter, you saw how the sample's enterprise beans might be utilized within servlets. Since the purpose of those servlets was to perform a quick test of the beans, many parameters were simply hard-coded into the servlet code. In reality, though, you would need a solution that interacts with the user and deals with dynamic parameters. In this chapter, you will look at how to build the sample's presentation tier using the JavaServer Faces technology.

Of course, JavaServer Faces is not the only technology to choose from when it comes to implementing a Java EE web application. For example, it's still possible to build the web tier of a Java EE application using the JSP technology and invoking enterprise bean's business methods directly from within JSP pages.

However, the JavaServer Faces technology provides many advantages over JSP, where the most important one is a clean separation between business logic and presentation.

Actually, you don't necessarily have to utilize enterprise beans when developing a JSF application. Instead, you might use JSF managed beans. However, since you already have the enterprise beans built, you might want to develop the JSF beans that will utilize the functionality of those enterprise beans, rather than implementing the application's business logic from scratch. This means the JSF beans to be used in your application won't need to deal directly with the JPA entities built upon the underlying database; they deal with the enterprise beans instead. So, the enterprise beans act as the facade built upon the persistence tier, uncoupling the client from the entity model. Figure 14-1 gives a graphical depiction of this approach.

The solution depicted in the figure is known as the Facade pattern. To learn more about the Facade pattern, you can refer to the "Using a Model Facade" document available at `https://blueprints.dev.java.net/bpcatalog/ee5/persistence/facade.html` and the "Using an EJB Session Bean as a Model Facade" document at `https://blueprints.dev.java.net/bpcatalog/ee5/persistence/ejbfacade.html`.

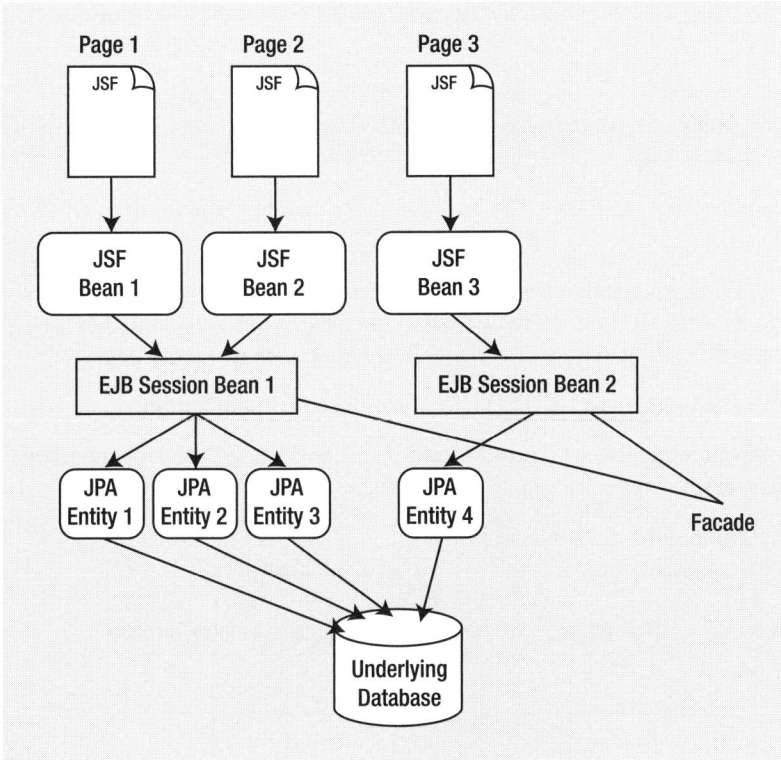

Figure 14-1. *A Java EE application based on the Facade pattern*

Planning the Presentation Tier

What you are going to build here is not, of course, a full-functional application. The idea is to illustrate how you can utilize EJB components from within JSF managed beans, using the Facade pattern.

Now let's try to figure out how the JSF application to be built in the next sections might be organized. Since you want to see the CartBean and OrderBean enterprise beans in action, you're going to need at least the following two pages:

- A page that displays all the books available for purchasing and allows the user to add a book of interest to the shopping cart. This can be the page being loaded first and called index.jsp.

- A page that shows the shopping cart items and allows the user to delete unnecessary items from the cart and eventually place an order. This page could be called showcart.jsp, for example.

You might want to create the following JSF managed beans to be referred to from within these two pages:

- A JSF managed bean that will be used to interact with the CartBean and OrderBean enterprise beans created as discussed in Chapter 12. This managed bean might be called OrderJSFBean.

- A managed bean to access the data in the books underlying table. You might call it BookJSFBean.

Another important thing you need to think about is security. In the next section, you will look at the JAAS-based security mechanism to be used in the sample in more detail. For the time being, however, it's interesting to note that you will need to create two more pages:

- A login authentication page, say, login.jsp, for form-based authentication.

- An error page to which the user will be redirected if authentication fails. This might be called, say, login_error.jsp.

The resulting diagram might look like Figure 14-2.

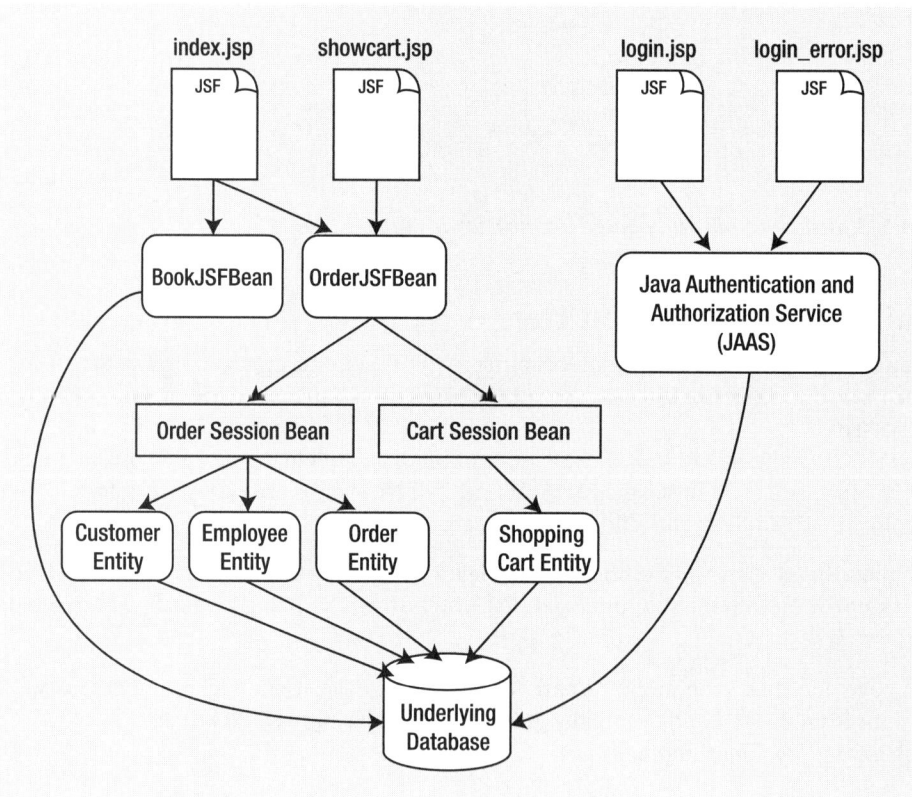

Figure 14-2. *A high-level view of the sample application*

As you can see in the figure, the sample is going to employ the Java Authentication and Authorization Service (JAAS), a set of APIs that enable user authentication and authorization. Although it's not a requirement, in this particular example you will authenticate users against account information stored in the underlying database.

You might also notice that the BookJSFBean managed bean doesn't refer to the facade beans, dealing with the underlying database directly. As you will learn a bit later in this chapter, the BookJSFBean managed bean establishes a JDBC connection to the database and obtains information from the books underlying table.

Using JAAS to Secure Java EE Applications

Since the sample discussed here is going to manipulate sensitive information, you need to employ a security mechanism that enables user authentication and authorization. Once authenticated, the user credentials will determine the security context of the sample instance, allowing it to associate the shopping cart with the authenticated user.

The JAAS provides a standard way to achieve these goals. To take advantage of JAAS in GlassFish, you first need to set up a security realm, organizing users into security groups. Once the security realm is set up in the application server, you will need to add a login page to your application, where the user will enter its credentials. A properly authenticated user will be authorized to use only those resources that are allowed for the group to which that user belongs.

In the following section, you will create a JDBC security realm in your GlassFish application server so that users of the sample are authenticated against the data stored in the underlying database. Then, in the "Creating Security Pages" section, you will create the login.jsp and login_error.jsp pages.

Creating a JDBC Realm in GlassFish

GlassFish ships with the following three predefined security realms: admin-realm, file realm, and certificate realm. The admin-realm is used to control user's access to the application server resources. So, you use users defined in this realm to connect to the Admin Console, a GlassFish's browser interface to perform administration and configuration tasks.

Unlike the admin-realm, the file realm and certificate realm can be used to authenticate users of the applications deployed to the application server. The file-realm stores users' authentication information in the local file keyfile. You can manipulate file-realm users from within Admin Console. The certificate realm stores user credentials in a certificate database using certificates with the HTTPS protocol for authenticating users.

Aside from these three preconfigured GlassFish's realms, you can create the following ones:

- A LDAP realm stores authentication information in a LDAP database.

- A JDBC realm stores authentication information in a relational database.

- A Solaris realm can be used only on the Solaris operating system.

In the following sections, you will look at how to create a JDBC realm holding authentication information in the underlying database.

Creating the Database Tables to Store Account Information

Before you can create a JDBC realm in your application server, you need to create the database tables to store users' account information. In particular, you will need to set up the following three tables:

- A table holding user credentials. For that, you might use the already existing customers table created as discussed in Chapter 6 (specifically Listing 6-4). However, you will need to modify the customers table's structure, adding a password column for storing users' passwords.

- A table holding information about groups of users.

- A join table of the many-to-many relationship between these two tables.

Once you have these three tables in place, you might want to create a view upon these tables so that the JDBC realm you're going to create will use only one database contact point. Listing 14-1 shows a set of the SQL commands you have to perform on your MySQL server when connected as usrsample user:

Listing 14-1. *Creating the Database Structure in MySQL to Be Used by the JDBC Security Realm*

```
use dbsample;
ALTER TABLE customers ADD COLUMN password CHAR(32);

CREATE TABLE groups(
group_id VARCHAR(25) PRIMARY KEY,
group_desc VARCHAR(100)
);

CREATE TABLE customergroups(
cust_id INTEGER,
group_id VARCHAR(25),
PRIMARY KEY(cust_id, group_id),
FOREIGN KEY(cust_id) REFERENCES customers(cust_id),
FOREIGN KEY(group_id) REFERENCES groups(group_id)
);

CREATE VIEW login_v
AS SELECT c.cust_id, c.password, g.group_id FROM ➥
customers c, groups g, customergroups r
WHERE c.cust_id = r.cust_id AND g.group_id = r.group_id;
```

You might notice that the password column added to the customers table is defined as CHAR(32). The fact is that the MD5 is the default algorithm in GlassFish to encrypt users passwords, and a MD5 hash is a 32-character string.

■**Note** If you're using Oracle as the underlying database, you have to modify it in a similar way, choosing appropriate types for the columns in the tables being created.

The next step is populating the tables created here with data. Also, you have to populate the password column added to the customers table. Of course, real-world applications usually offer a form where new users may register. For simplicity, however, in this particular example you will populate the security tables directly. Listing 14-2 shows the SQL statements you might perform to insert authentication information for the two customer records you should already have in the customers table (from Listing 6-5 in Chapter 6).

Listing 14-2. *Populating the Tables Containing Information About Users and Groups*

```
INSERT INTO groups VALUES('testRole', 'Security group for users of the sample app');

INSERT INTO customergroups VALUES(2, 'testRole');

UPDATE customers
SET password = '42766beab1dc267fbf26df32e1addfff'
WHERE cust_id = 1;

UPDATE customers
SET password = '0f8031d929f89ecb1d251f0f8bc9d9f9'
WHERE cust_id = 2;
```

In the first UPDATE statement in the listing, you set the password field of the customer whose cust_id is 1 to the MD5 hash corresponding to the password poplavskipswd. The second UPDATE sets the password of the second customer record to the MD5 hash of medicapswd.

Creating the JDBC Realm

Now that you have set up the database to store user credentials, you can move on and create a JDBC realm in your application server.

To start with, connect to Admin Console as admin, and then move on to the Configuration/Security/Realm page, which is shown in Figure 14-3.

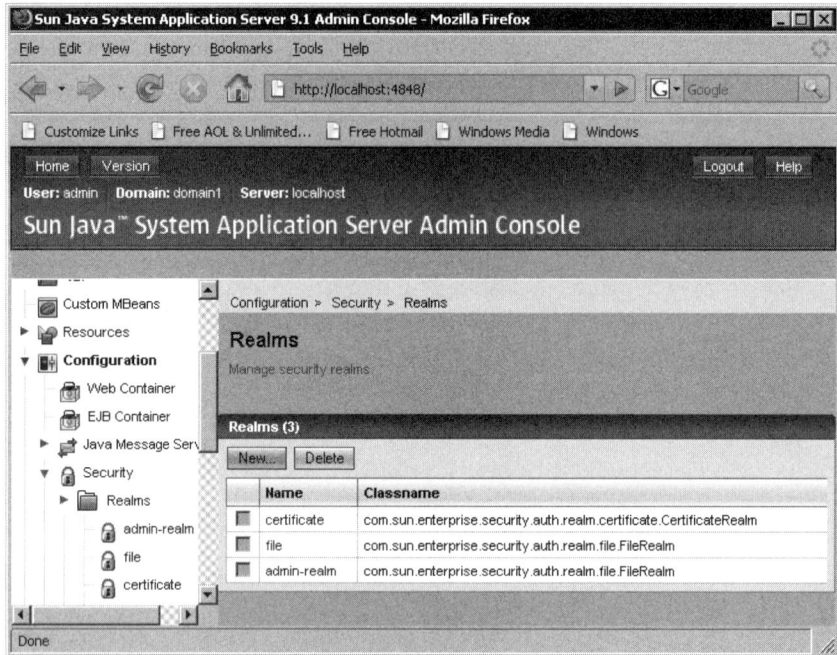

Figure 14-3. *The Realms page in Admin Console*

In the Realms page shown in the figure, click the New button. As a result, the New Realm dialog box will appear. To start with, type in the name in the Name field, say, myjdbc, and then choose com.sun.enterprise.security.auth.realm.jdbc.JDBCRealm in the Class Name box.

Next, move on to the Properties Specific to This Class section of the dialog box, and fill in the fields as described in Table 14-1.

Table 14-1. *Setting Up the JDBC Realm Properties*

Property Name	Property Value	Description
JAAS context	jdbcRealm	Type of login module to use, defaulted to jdbcRealm.
JNDI	jdbc/mysqlpool	JNDI name of the data source through which the security tables can be accessed.
User Table	login_v	Table containing information about users to be used. In this example, you use a view derived from both the customers and groups tables.
User Name Column	cust_id	The username column in the user table.
Password Column	password	The password name column in the user table.
Group Table	login_v	Table containing information about security groups. In this example, you use a view derived from both the customers and groups tables.
Group Name Column	group_id	The username column in the group table.

Once you are done with setting up the properties, click the OK button in the New Realm dialog box. As a result, a new JDBC realm will be created.

Building the Sample's Presentation Tier with JSF

Now you are ready to start building the sample's presentation tier. In the following sections, you will build it using the JavaServer Faces technology.

Diagramming the Project

As usual, let's first create a diagram representing the directory structure of the project, including files to be created. Figure 14-4 shows what actually needs to be done.

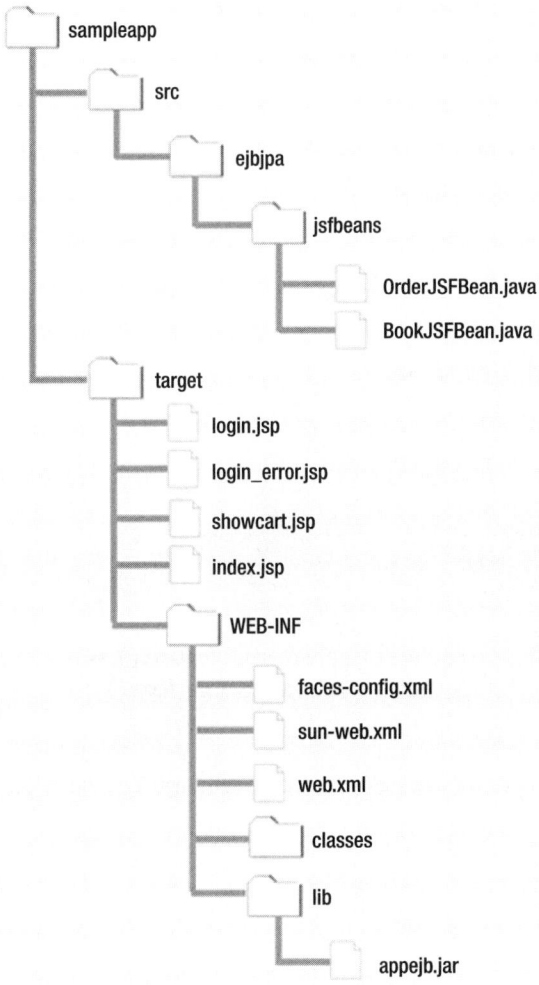

Figure 14-4. *The structure of the sample project*

To begin with, you need to create the directory structure for the project as shown in the figure, and then you can create the files as discussed in the following sections.

Developing JSF Managed Beans

As mentioned earlier, in a JSF application, managed beans encapsulate the application's business logic so that JSF pages can refer to beans properties.

In the sample discussed here, however, you already have some business logic implemented in the enterprise beans created as discussed in Chapter 12. So, to utilize that logic in the enterprise beans, you will need to create a managed bean that will act as a bridge between JSF pages and the logic in those enterprise beans. For this purpose, you will create the OrderJSFBean managed bean shown in Listing 14-3.

Listing 14-3. *Source Code for the* OrderJSFBean *Managed Bean*

```
package ejbjpa.jsfbeans;
import javax.ejb.EJB;
import javax.naming.InitialContext;
import javax.faces.context.FacesContext;
import javax.servlet.http.HttpSession;
import java.util.List;
import java.util.Map;
import ejbjpa.ejb.*;
import ejbjpa.entities.*;

@EJB(name="ejb/CartBean", beanInterface=Cart.class)
public class OrderJSFBean {
    private Cart cart;
    @EJB
    private OrderSample order;
    private List<ShoppingCart> cartItems;
    private Integer custId;
    public OrderJSFBean() {
        custId = Integer.parseInt(
                    FacesContext.getCurrentInstance().getExternalContext().➥
                                        getUserPrincipal().getName());
      try{
        if (cart == null) {
           cart = (Cart) (new InitialContext()).lookup("java:comp/env/ejb/CartBean");
        }
        cart.initialize(custId);
      } catch (Exception e) {
            e.printStackTrace();
      }
    }
```

```java
    public Integer getCustId() {
        return custId;
    }
    public List<ShoppingCart> getCartItems() {
        cartItems = null;
        try {
            cartItems = cart.getItems();
        } catch (Exception e) {
            e.printStackTrace();
        }
        return cartItems;
    }
    public void addToCart() {
        try {
         FacesContext cxt = FacesContext.getCurrentInstance();
         Map params = cxt.getExternalContext().getRequestParameterMap();
         String isbn = (String)params.get("isbn");
         String price_str = (String)params.get("price");
         Double price =new Double(price_str);
         cart.addItem(isbn, 1, price);
        } catch (Exception e) {
            e.printStackTrace();
        }
    }
    public void removeFromCart() {
        try {
         FacesContext cxt = FacesContext.getCurrentInstance();
         Map params = cxt.getExternalContext().getRequestParameterMap();
         String itemId = (String)params.get("itemId");
         cart.removeItem(itemId);
        } catch (Exception e) {
            e.printStackTrace();
        }
    }
    public String ProceedToCheckout() {
        try {
          order.placeOrder(custId, 1);
        } catch (Exception e) {
            e.printStackTrace();
        }
      return "continue";
    }

}
```

Unlike the OrderJSFBean managed bean, BookJSFBean shown in Listing 14-4 has no references to the enterprise beans. Instead, the BookJSFBean managed bean directly connects to the underlying database through a JDBC connection and retrieves all the records from the books table.

Listing 14-4. *Source Code for the* BookJSFBean *Managed Bean*

```
package ejbjpa.jsfbeans;
import javax.ejb.EJB;
import javax.naming.InitialContext;
import javax.faces.context.FacesContext;
import javax.servlet.http.HttpSession;
import java.util.List;
import ejbjpa.ejb.*;
import ejbjpa.entities.*;
import java.sql.*;
import javax.sql.DataSource;
public class BookJSFBean {
    private Connection connDb;
    public void openConnection() throws Exception {
      if(connDb != null)
        return;
      DataSource dataSource = (DataSource) (new ➡
                  InitialContext()).lookup("java:comp/env/jdbc/mysqlpool");
      connDb = dataSource.getConnection();
    }
    public ResultSet getAllBooks() throws Exception {
    ResultSet rslt = null;
      this.openConnection();
      Statement stmt = connDb.createStatement();
      rslt = stmt.executeQuery("SELECT * FROM books");
      return  rslt;
    }
    }

}
```

As you can see, the BookJSFBean managed bean doesn't even utilize JPA entities, illustrating a JDBC way of interacting with the underlying database from within a JSF managed bean.

Now that you have created the source files for the managed beans, you can compile them. For that, you can change the directory for sampleapp and then issue the following command:

```
# javac -cp target/WEB-INF/lib/appejb.jar;yourglassfishdir/lib/javaee.jar ➡
-d target/WEB-INF/classes src/ejbjpa/jsfbeans/*.java
```

As a result, the ejbjpa/jsfbeans directory should appear within the sampleapp/target/WEB-INF/classes directory and the BookJSFBean.class and BookJSFBean.class files should appear in it.

Developing JSF Pages

The next step in building the application is to create the JSF pages. Listing 14-5 shows the source code for the index.jsp page that refers to the allBooks property of the BookJSFBean managed bean.

Listing 14-5. *Source Code for the* index.jsp *Page*

```
<%@ taglib uri="http://java.sun.com/jsf/html" prefix="h" %>
<%@ taglib uri="http://java.sun.com/jsf/core" prefix="f" %>
<f:view>
<head>
 <link href="stylesheet.css" rel="stylesheet" type="text/css"/>
</head>
<h:form>
 <h2>List of books</h2>
 <br/>
 <h:dataTable value="#{book.allBooks}" var ="book"
   headerClass= "header"
   columnClasses="evenCol, oddCol">
   <h:column>
    <f:facet name="header">
      <h:outputText value="ISBN"/>
    </f:facet>
    <h:outputText value="#{book.isbn}"/>
   </h:column>
   <h:column>
    <f:facet name="header">
      <h:outputText value="Title"/>
    </f:facet>
    <h:outputText value="#{book.title}"/>
   </h:column>
   <h:column>
    <f:facet name="header">
      <h:outputText value="Author"/>
    </f:facet>
    <h:outputText value="#{book.author}"/>
   </h:column>
   <h:column>
    <f:facet name="header">
      <h:outputText  value="Price"/>
    </f:facet>
    <h:outputText value="#{book.price}"/>
   </h:column>
   <h:column>
    <f:facet name="header">
      <h:outputText  value="Copies left"/>
    </f:facet>
```

```
    <h:outputText value="#{book.quantity}"/>
   </h:column>
   <h:column>
    <h:commandLink action="#{OrderJSFBean.addToCart}" value="Add to cart">
      <f:param name = "isbn" value = "#{book.isbn}"/>
      <f:param name = "price" value = "#{book.price}"/>
    </h:commandLink>
   </h:column>
 </h:dataTable>
 <p/>
 <h:commandButton action="showcart" value="Move to cart"/>
 </h:form>
</f:view>
```

As you can see in the listing, the index.jsp page will display the entire list of the book records, allowing the user to add books of interest to the shopping cart.

Listing 14-6 shows the source for the showcart.jsp page that can be launched from within the index.jsp.

Listing 14-6. *Source Code for the* showcart.jsp *Page*

```
<%@ taglib uri="http://java.sun.com/jsf/html" prefix="h" %>
<%@ taglib uri="http://java.sun.com/jsf/core" prefix="f" %>
<f:view>
<head>
 <link href="stylesheet.css" rel="stylesheet" type="text/css"/>
</head>
<h:form>
 <h2>Your shopping cart items to buy now</h2>
 <br/>
 <h:dataTable value="#{OrderJSFBean.cartItems}" var ="shoppingCart"
   headerClass= "header"
   columnClasses="evenCol, oddCol">
   <h:column>
    <f:facet name="header">
      <h:outputText value="Book isbn"/>
    </f:facet>
    <h:outputText value="#{shoppingCart.book_id}"/>
   </h:column>
   <h:column>
    <f:facet name="header">
      <h:outputText value="Quantity"/>
    </f:facet>
    <h:outputText value="#{shoppingCart.units}"/>
   </h:column>
   <h:column>
    <f:facet name="header">
      <h:outputText value="Unit price"/>
```

```
      </f:facet>
      <h:outputText value="#{shoppingCart.unit_price}"/>
    </h:column>
    <h:column>
      <h:commandLink action="#{OrderJSFBean.removeFromCart}" value="Delete">
        <f:param name = "itemId" value = "#{shoppingCart.book_id}"/>
      </h:commandLink>
    </h:column>
  </h:dataTable>
<p/>
  <h:commandButton action="#{OrderJSFBean.ProceedToCheckout}" value=➡
                                "Proceed to checkout"/>
  <h:commandButton action="continue" value="Continue shopping"/>
</h:form>
</f:view>
```

As you can see, the `showcart.jsp` shown in the listing lets you look through the contents of the shopping cart and remove an item or items if necessary. Then, you can place the order, which will automatically empty the cart.

Creating Security Pages

Now, let's create pages required to perform form-based authentication. Listing 14-7 shows the source for the `login.jsp` page.

Listing 14-7. *Source Code for the* `login.jsp` *Page*

```
<%@ taglib uri="http://java.sun.com/jsp/jstl/core" prefix="c" %>
<%@ taglib uri="http://java.sun.com/jsp/jstl/functions" prefix="fn" %>
<html>
 <head><title>Login Page</title></head>
 <h2>Please login:</h2>
 <form method="POST" action="j_security_check">
  <p>Enter Customer ID: <input type="text" name="j_username" size="25"></p>
  <p>Enter Password:<input type="password" size="15" name="j_password"></p>
  <input type="submit" value="Submit">
  <input type="reset" value="Reset">
 </form>
</html>
```

If authentication fails, the `login_error.jsp` page should appear. Listing 14-8 shows the source for this page.

Listing 14-8. *Source Code for the* `login_error.jsp` *Page*

```
<%@ taglib uri="http://java.sun.com/jsp/jstl/core" prefix="c" %>
<html>
 <head><title>Login error page</title></head>
 <body>
```

```
    <c:url var="url" value="index.faces"/>
    <h2>User name or password is wrong.</h2>
    <p>Please enter a valid user name and password. ➥
            Click here to <a href="${url}"> ➥
            try again.</a></p>
  </body>
</html>
```

As you can see, the login_error.jsp page informs the user that authentication has failed and offers to try again by clicking at the try again link.

Configuring the Application

Before you can package the application into the deployment archive, you need to create the deployment descriptors: sun-web.xml and web.xml, as well as the configuration resource file: faces-config.xml.

Listing 14-9 shows the source for the faces-config.xml configuration file.

Listing 14-9. *Source Code for the* faces-config.xml *Configuration File*

```
<?xml version="1.0"?>
<faces-config xmlns="http://java.sun.com/xml/ns/javaee"
              xmlns:xsi="http://www.w3.org/2001/XMLSchema-instance"
              xsi:schemaLocation="http://java.sun.com/xml/ns/javaee ➥
                     http://java.sun.com/xml/ns/javaee/web-facesconfig_1_2.xsd"
              version="1.2">
 <managed-bean>
        <managed-bean-name>OrderJSFBean</managed-bean-name>
        <managed-bean-class>ejbjpa.jsfbeans.OrderJSFBean
        </managed-bean-class>
        <managed-bean-scope>session</managed-bean-scope>
 </managed-bean>
 <managed-bean>
        <managed-bean-name>book</managed-bean-name>
        <managed-bean-class>ejbjpa.jsfbeans.BookJSFBean
        </managed-bean-class>
        <managed-bean-scope>session</managed-bean-scope>
 </managed-bean>
 <navigation-rule>
    <navigation-case>
        <description>
           By clicking the "Move to cart" button on the index.jsp page ➥
                      you move to showcart.jsp
        </description>
        <from-outcome>showcart</from-outcome>
      <to-view-id>/showcart.jsp</to-view-id>
    </navigation-case>
    <navigation-case>
```

```
        <description>
            Clicking the "Continue shopping" turns you back to index.jsp ➥
                    showing the list of books available
        </description>
        <from-outcome>continue</from-outcome>
      <to-view-id>/index.jsp</to-view-id>
    </navigation-case>
  </navigation-rule>
</faces-config>
```

Listing 14-10 shows what the web.xml web application deployment descriptor might look like.

Listing 14-10. *Source Code for the* web.xml *Configuration File*

```
<?xml version="1.0" encoding="UTF-8"?>
<web-app xmlns="http://java.sun.com/xml/ns/javaee"
          xmlns:xsi="http://www.w3.org/2001/XMLSchema-instance"
          xsi:schemaLocation="http://java.sun.com/xml/ns/javaee ➥
                              http://java.sun.com/xml/ns/javaee/web-app_2_5.xsd"
          version="2.5">
  <security-constraint>
    <web-resource-collection>
      <web-resource-name>testing web app</web-resource-name>
      <url-pattern>/*</url-pattern>
      <http-method>POST</http-method>
      <http-method>GET</http-method>
    </web-resource-collection>
    <auth-constraint>
      <role-name>testRole</role-name>
    </auth-constraint>
    <user-data-constraint>
      <transport-guarantee>NONE</transport-guarantee>
    </user-data-constraint>
  </security-constraint>
  <login-config>
    <auth-method>FORM</auth-method>
    <realm-name>myjdbc</realm-name>
    <form-login-config>
      <form-login-page>/login.jsp</form-login-page>
      <form-error-page>/login_error.jsp</form-error-page>
    </form-login-config>
  </login-config>
  <security-role>
    <role-name>testRole</role-name>
  </security-role>
  <servlet>
        <display-name>FacesServlet</display-name>
```

```
                <servlet-name>FacesServlet</servlet-name>
                <servlet-class>javax.faces.webapp.FacesServlet</servlet-class>
                <load-on-startup>1</load-on-startup>
    </servlet>
    <servlet-mapping>
                <servlet-name>FacesServlet</servlet-name>
                <url-pattern>*.faces</url-pattern>
    </servlet-mapping>
    <welcome-file-list>
                <welcome-file>index.faces</welcome-file>
    </welcome-file-list>
     <ejb-ref>
                <ejb-ref-name>ejb/CartBean</ejb-ref-name>
                <ejb-ref-type>Session</ejb-ref-type>
                <remote>ejbjpa.ejb.Cart</remote>
     </ejb-ref>
   <resource-ref>
     <res-ref-name>jdbc/mysqlpool</res-ref-name>
     <res-type>javax.sql.DataSource</res-type>
     <res-auth>Container</res-auth>
     <res-sharing-scope>Shareable</res-sharing-scope>
   </resource-ref>
</web-app>
```

Finally, Listing 14-11 shows the source for the `sun-web.xml` runtime deployment descriptor.

Listing 14-11. *Source Code for the* `sun-web.xml` *Configuration File*

```
<?xml version="1.0" encoding="UTF-8"?>
<!DOCTYPE sun-web-app PUBLIC "-//Sun Microsystems, Inc.//➥
DTD Application Server 8.0 Servlet 2.4//EN" ➥
"http://www.sun.com/software/appserver/dtds/sun-web-app_2_4-0.dtd">
<sun-web-app>
  <context-root>/sampleapp</context-root>
   <security-role-mapping>
       <role-name>testRole</role-name>
       <group-name>testRole</group-name>
   </security-role-mapping>
</sun-web-app>
```

Now that you have all the files in place, you can move on and pack them into a deployment package. To achieve this, you have to change directory for `sampleapp\target` and issue the following command:

```
jar cvf jsfapp.war .
```

Then, you can deploy the archive as follows:

```
asadmin deploy jsfapp.war
```

Summary

In this chapter, you completed the sample discussed throughout the book. You saw how the JavaServer Faces technology might be used to implement the presentation tier of a Java EE application, utilizing enterprise beans encapsulating the application's business logic.

In the next chapter, you will test the sample application completed here, figuring out what might be changed to improve efficiency.

Testing the Application

The final step involved in the development cycle is to test the application to make sure everything works as expected. After performing a test, you may want to make some changes or additions to the application to improve its functionality.

In this chapter, you will test the sample built throughout the book. For that, you will need to perform a set of steps typically carried out at the testing stage. In particular, during the course of the chapter, you will do the following:

- Launch the sample application

- Test the sample's functionality

- Modify some of the sample's components to improve their functionality

Put simply, in this chapter you will test the functionality and behavior of the sample and then modify some application components as necessary.

Launching the Sample Application

Now that you have built the sample, you need to test it. The first step in this process is launching the application.

Before you can launch the application, make sure your application server is running. Otherwise, you need to start it. As you might recall from the first chapters of this book, you can do this with the following command issued from the command line:

```
asadmin start-domain domain1
```

Assuming you have deployed the sample as discussed at the end of the preceding chapter, you can now launch it by pointing your browser here:

```
http://localhost:8080/sampleapp/index.faces
```

You might be wondering why index.faces is specified in the URL instead of index.jsp, which is actually used in the application. The .faces extension is used here to activate the JSF servlet, which then replaces faces with jsp behind the scenes. Returning to Listing 14-10 in the preceding chapter, take a closer look at the servlet-mapping element in the web.xml deployment descriptor file. To recap, it should look as follows:

```
<servlet-mapping>
    <servlet-name>FacesServlet</servlet-name>
    <url-pattern>*.faces</url-pattern>
</servlet-mapping>
```

As you can see, a suffix mapping is used here.

Log In to the Sample

It's interesting to note, however, that pointing your browser to `http://localhost:8080/` `sampleapp/index.faces` won't lead to loading the `index.jsp` page. Instead, you first will be taken to the `login.jsp` page, as shown in Figure 15-1.

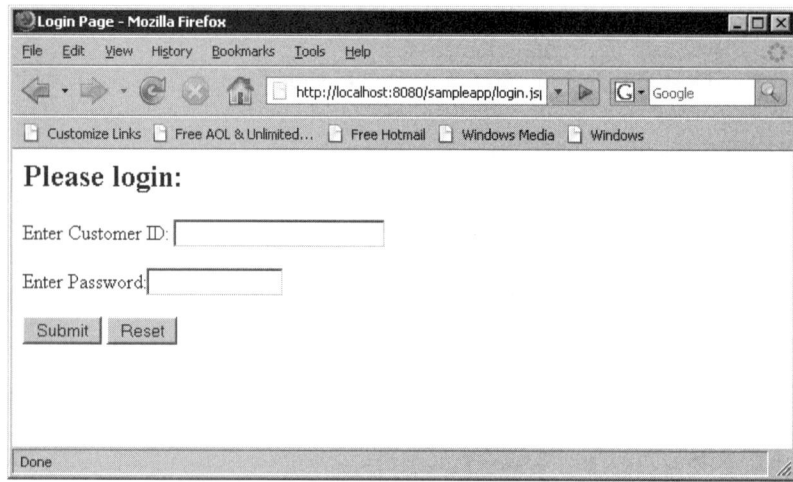

Figure 15-1. *The login page of the sample*

The `login.jsp` page is loaded because you specified it as the login form in the `web.xml` descriptor, back in Listing 14-10:

```
<login-config>
  <auth-method>FORM</auth-method>
  <realm-name>myjdbc</realm-name>
  <form-login-config>
    <form-login-page>/login.jsp</form-login-page>
    <form-error-page>/login_error.jsp</form-error-page>
  </form-login-config>
</login-config>
```

Also note that the `login_error.jsp` page is specified as the error page that will be displayed upon authentication failure. If authentication is successful, you will be taken to the `index.jsp` page.

Now that you know how the authentication mechanism used here works, let's try it. In the Enter Customer ID field, type **2**, and in the Enter Password field, type **medicapswd**. Then click the Submit button.

Filling Up the Shopping Cart

If authentication was successful, you should see the `index.jsp` page shown in Figure 15-2.

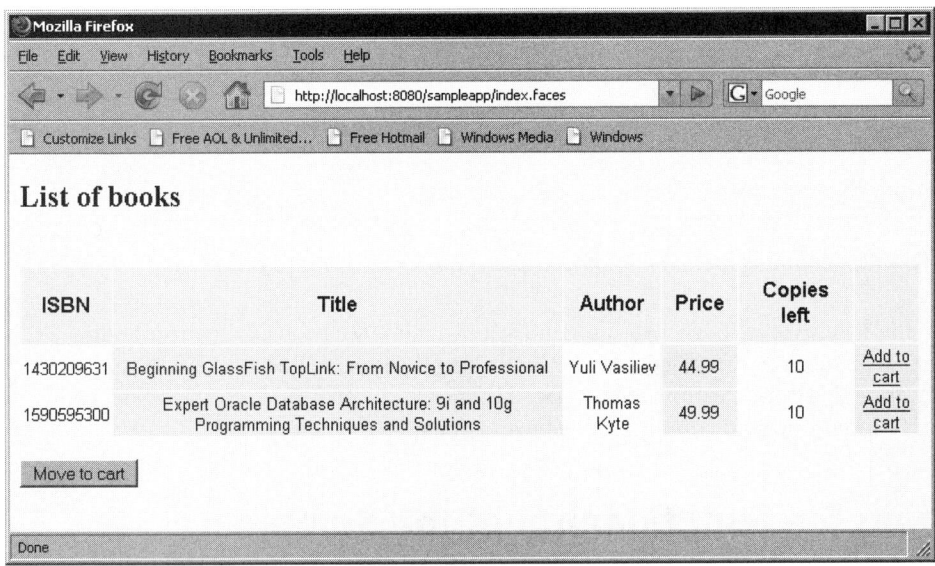

Figure 15-2. *The index page of the sample, showing all the books available*

In this page, you can look through the entire list of books and move the book or books of interest to the shopping cart.

Looking Through the Cart Items and Placing an Order

After you have filled up the cart, you can move on to the cart page by clicking the Move to Cart button on the `index.jsp` page. When loaded, the `showcart.jsp` page might look like Figure 15-3.

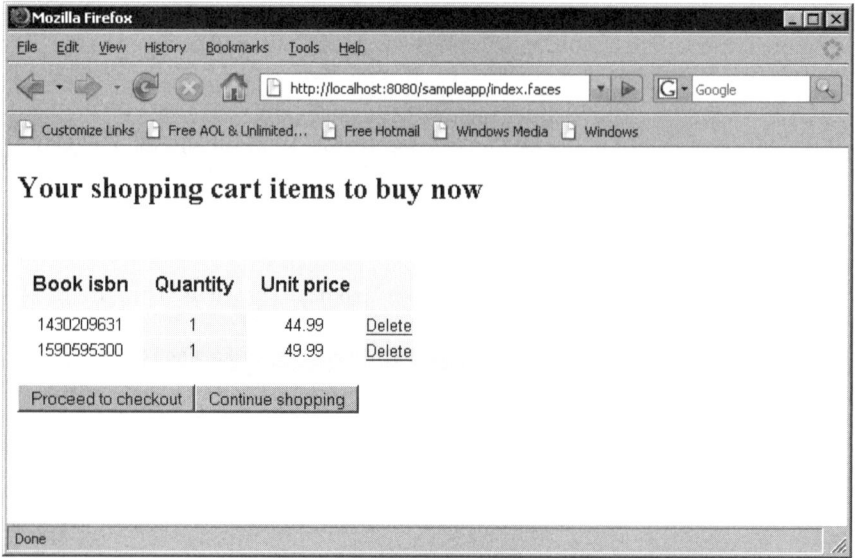

Figure 15-3. *The shopping cart page of the sample, showing the items selected*

On the showcart.jsp page, you can remove a cart item by clicking the corresponding Delete link. Finally, you can place an order by clicking the Proceed to Checkout button. Since this is a simplified example, the order is placed immediately after the Proceed to Checkout button is clicked—no confirmation dialog boxes appear.

Testing the Functionality of the Sample

Unfortunately, some application components, when utilized within the application, may behave differently from what you expect, and this is hard to predict in advance.

In the following section, you will take a closer look at the sample behavior, trying to identify weaknesses in the design and implementation.

Finding Weaknesses

A more detailed test of the sample shows the following weaknesses:

- If an item is already in the cart and you click its Add to Cart link on the index.jsp page, then all the items shown in showcart.jsp will disappear.

- After clicking the Proceed to Checkout button, you won't be able to choose an item that was in the cart when you started placing the order.

Let's take a closer look at what the application is actually doing and why it encounters these troubles. A simple analysis shows that a problem arises when you try to add the same item to the cart for the second time. It's interesting to note that even if you have placed an order, which automatically removes the corresponding records from the shoppingcarts underlying table, it doesn't empty the persistence context associated with the CartBean stateful session bean instance being employed by the application.

Fixing the Problems

To fix the problems outlined in the preceding section, you will need to make some changes to the CartBean enterprise bean originally created as discussed in Chapter 12.

Listing 15-1 shows the updated CartBean stateful session bean. For your convenience, the code added or modified is highlighted in bold.

Listing 15-1. *Source Code for the Updated* CartBean *Stateful Session Bean*

```java
package ejbjpa.ejb;
import java.util.List;
import javax.ejb.Remove;
import javax.ejb.Stateful;
import javax.ejb.EJBException;
import javax.persistence.EntityManager;
import javax.persistence.PersistenceContext;
import javax.persistence.PersistenceContextType;
import ejbjpa.entities.*;
@Stateful
public class CartBean implements Cart {
@PersistenceContext(type=PersistenceContextType.EXTENDED)
EntityManager em;
Integer custId;
List<ShoppingCart> items;
public void initialize(Integer cust_id) {
 if (cust_id == null) {
  throw new EJBException("Null cust_id provided.");
 } else {
    custId = cust_id;
  }
}
 public void addItem(String item_id, Integer quantity, Double price) {
    ShoppingCart cart = (ShoppingCart) em.find(ShoppingCart.class, ➥
    new ShoppingCartKey(custId, item_id));
      if(cart != null)
      {
        em.remove(cart);
        em.flush();
      }
      cart = new ShoppingCart();
      cart.setCart_id(custId);
      cart.setBook_id(item_id);
      cart.setUnits(quantity);
      cart.setUnit_price(price);
      em.persist(cart);
 }
 public void removeItem(String item_id) {
    ShoppingCart cart = (ShoppingCart) em.find(ShoppingCart.class, ➥
```

```
    new ShoppingCartKey(custId, item_id));
    if(cart == null){
      throw new EJBException("This item is not in cart.");
    } else {
      em.remove(cart);
    }
  }
public List<ShoppingCart> getItems() {
    items = (List<ShoppingCart>)em.createQuery("SELECT s FROM ShoppingCart s ➥
    WHERE s.cart_id =:cust_id")
                        .setParameter("cust_id", custId)
                        .getResultList();
    em.clear();
    return items;
}
@Remove
public Integer emptyCart() {
  Integer num =0;
  num = em.createQuery("DELETE FROM ShoppingCart s WHERE s.cart_id =:cust_id")
                        .setParameter("cust_id", custId)
                        .executeUpdate();
  return num;
}

 @Remove
 public void clearCartInstance() {
 }
}
```

Now you should recompile the `CartBean.java` file, re-create the `appejb.jar` deployment package, and redeploy it to the application server. Also, make sure to re-create the `jsfapp.war` web application package, replacing the `appejb.jar` lib file with the newly created one. Then, you will need to redeploy `jsfapp.war`.

Once you're done with it, you can launch the sample again. This time everything should work as expected.

Summary

In this chapter, you looked at the sample application in action. However, the first test showed that the application does not always behave as expected. So, you had to return to the `CartBean` stateful enterprise bean and make some slight changes to it to fix the situation.

PART 7

■ ■ ■

Appendix

Getting Familiar with Relational Databases

The last example in Chapter 3 shows how the EJB 3 and JPA technologies can be used together, providing a standard yet easy-to-use way of interacting with the underlying database from within a Java EE application. In that example, you use a simple Derby database containing a single table. It is fairly obvious, however, that real-world applications utilize much more complicated relational database structures built on popular open source and commercial RDBMS platforms.

In this appendix, you first will look at why databases are different from one another and why you might prefer one over another. Then, you will look at the SQL database language, which provides the most common way of interacting with relational databases. Finally, you will learn some interesting details about using management tools shipped with your databases, which allows you to improve your experience of using these tools.

To summarize, here is a list of what you will have learned after reading this appendix:

- How to choose an appropriate database for your application

- Why databases are different

- What SQL is and how to use this database language

- How to use management tools shipped with your database

Although there are dozens of databases, the examples provided in this appendix are based on perhaps the most popular two: MySQL and Oracle. If you have already gotten your feet wet with relational databases and perhaps have had a project or two with both MySQL and Oracle, you may not be interested in the material provided here.

The appendix assumes you have already installed MySQL and Oracle Database XE or any other edition of Oracle Database. If not, you can refer to Chapter 1 for the installation instructions.

What Database to Choose?

When choosing a database platform for your application, you should clearly understand the following:

- The underlying database is an integral part of your application.

- Databases are different in architecture they implement.

- Each database offers a different set of features and has different capabilities.

It's interesting to note that each of these statements could be followed by this sentence: therefore, you should choose the database that suits the needs of your application best. The following sections explain these statements in more detail.

The Underlying Database Is Part of the Entire Solution

When designing an application interacting with a database, an important thing to understand is that the underlying database is an integral part of the entire solution being designed.

This is best understood by example. Suppose your application operates on purchase orders stored in two tables: `orders` and `items`, generating reports and printed forms of orders based on the information stored in these tables. One of the common tasks performed by the application when preparing the printed form of an order is calculating the total sum of that order based on the quantities, item prices, and shipping and handling figures. Actually, there are several ways in which you can accomplish this task. The most significant two scenarios are discussed in this section.

Scenario 1 assumes that the application obtains the required figures from the database, calculating the results in Java. Using JPA, you will need to establish a one-to-many relationship between the `Order` and `Item` entities. Then, you will loop through the `Item` entities representing the items of an order of interest, getting the cumulative result at the end. The problem of mapping JPA entities is discussed in Chapter 9. Then, Chapter 10 explains in detail how to manipulate entities with EntityManager.

Scenario 2 assumes that all the computing takes place inside the database, returning the resultant figure to the calling Java code. To make the database server perform this computing, you might issue a complex SQL query employing the `SUM` SQL aggregate function and a subquery. Another approach to this problem is to create a stored function performing all the required computation within the database. The problem of moving key business logic of an application into the database is further discussed in Chapter 4 and Chapter 5.

Both of these scenarios are depicted in Figure A-1, which illustrates that a significant part of the business logic in a database-based application can be moved inside the underlying database:

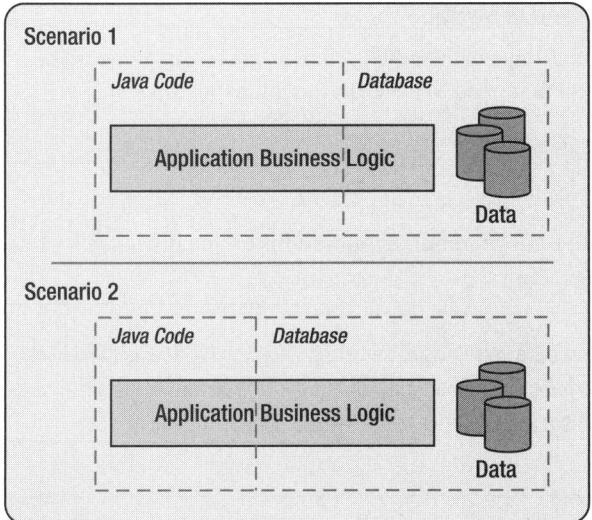

Figure A-1. *A significant part of the business logic in a database-backed application may be implemented inside the database.*

This figure shows you that some business logic of your application interacting with a database may be and often should be moved to the database tier, thus making the underlying database an integral part of the entire solution.

Understanding the Architecture of Your Database

Nowadays, when the SQL database language is used as a standard and is the most popular way to interact with a relational database whatever platform it belongs to, you might assume all databases implement a similar architecture and are different only in a set of features provided.

This would be a false assumption, though. Of course, in the case of GlassFish, you generally don't have to worry about the specifics of the underlying database you're using with your application. This is because the TopLink framework used in GlassFish smoothes out all the major differences between databases. For example, you don't have to worry about how your application establishes a connection to the underlying database. Once you have set the data source, the application server will be responsible for establishing and pooling database connections, without you doing a thing. However, there are still several issues arising from the architectural differences between databases. What this means in practice is that it is still highly recommended that you understand the architecture of the database of your choice.

Returning to MySQL and Oracle, let's look at a simple example illustrating some differences between these databases, which you need to know about. In particular, let's look at the ways in which database objects created by a user are logically organized in each of these databases.

How User Database Objects Are Organized in MySQL

When you want to define custom database objects in MySQL, such as tables and views to be then utilized within your application, you first need to perform the following three steps:

1. Create a database (schema) on the server.

2. Create a user to interact with the database.

3. Grant the privileges to the user to perform required operations on the database.

▓**Note** The following discussion assumes you have your MySQL server up and running. This is most likely the case if you agreed to start the server automatically at boot time, during the MySQL server installation. For more details, you can refer to Chapter 1. Also, you can refer to the MySQL documentation at `http://www.mysql.com/doc/en/index.html`.

The first step is to connect to the running server via the MySQL command-line client, logging in as the `root` user. Assuming you are in the `mysql/bin` directory or that this directory is included in the `PATH` environment variable, you can issue the following command from a command prompt:

```
mysql -u root -p
```

You will be prompted to enter the root password specified during the MySQL server installation:

Enter password: `****`

After you have entered the password, the `mysql>` prompt appears, allowing you to issue commands against the server.

▓**Caution** The following discussion explains how to create the `mydb` database and `usr` user account in your MySQL server. The problem, though, is that you should already have them set if you followed the instructions provided in Chapter 1. To prevent an error from occurring, you start by issuing the DROP DATABASE and DROP USER statements in the following listings. However, if you haven't set the `mydb` database and `usr` user account yet, you can disregard the DROP statements in the following listings.

Now you are ready to create a new database. When issued, the statement shown in Listing A-1 creates a database named `mydb`.

Listing A-1. *Creating a New Database on the MySQL Server*

```
DROP DATABASE IF EXISTS mydb
CREATE DATABASE mydb;
```

Alternatively, you could issue the following statement:

```
DROP SCHEMA IF EXISTS mydb
CREATE SCHEMA mydb;
```

To make sure the database has been created, you can issue the following command:

```
SHOW DATABASES
```

This should output the databases that already exist:

```
Database
--------------------
information_schema
mysql
mydb
test
```

Note that the result includes several databases, most of which are predefined, installed during the server installation. The newly created mydb database is highlighted in bold.

Now that you have created the database, you need to create a user account that will be used to interact with that database. Assuming you are still connected to the server as the root user (alternatively you might be connected as another user granted the GRANT OPTION privilege), you can issue the query shown in Listing A-2.

Listing A-2. *Creating a New User Account and Granting It the Required Privileges*

```
DROP USER 'usr';
DROP USER 'usr'@'localhost';
GRANT CREATE, ALTER, DROP, SELECT, UPDATE, INSERT, DELETE
ON mydb.*
TO 'usr'@'localhost'
IDENTIFIED BY 'pswd';
```

The GRANT query shown in the listing accomplishes the following two tasks: creates the user account usr and grants to it the privileges required to work with the mydb database when connecting from the localhost. This assumes your application server and MySQL server reside on the same computer. In that case, limiting users to connect only from localhost is often a good security practice.

After you have created a user account, you can grant or revoke privileges to/from it at a later time. It is important to note that you are not limited to granting privileges to a user only on the resources created within a single database. You may grant to a user privileges on the resources located in different databases. For example, you might let the usr user select from the db predefined table located in the mysql database:

```
GRANT SELECT
ON mysql.db
TO 'usr'@'localhost'
```

Now you can connect as usr from a new terminal:

```
mysql -u usr -p
Enter password: ****
```

and instruct MySQL to use the mydb database:

```
use mydb
```

Then you can issue the following query:

```
SELECT host, db, user FROM mysql.db
```

This should produce the following output:

```
host    | db   | user
-------------------------------------------
localhost  | mydb  | usr
```

The previous example illustrates that a single user account can be granted the privileges allowing it to access database server resources stored in various databases. Figure A-2 gives a graphical depiction of this architecture.

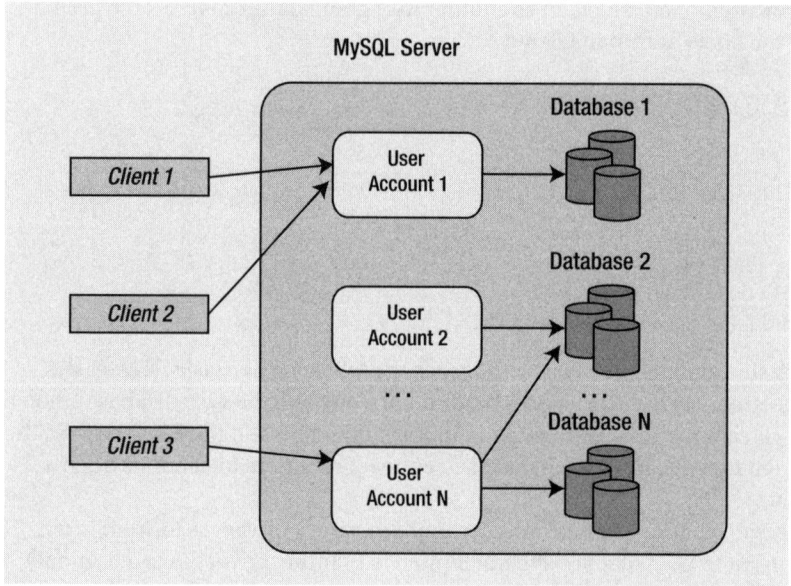

Figure A-2. *Client applications connect to the MySQL server using a user account defined on the server.*

As you can see in the figure, a client application connects to the server using one of the user accounts available. Accounts are different in the set of privileges they are granted. There may be accounts that allow the users connected through them to access only the resources belonging to a certain database. On the other hand, there may be accounts that are granted permissions to access the resources stored in more than one database. Also, this figure doesn't show the root user account that is used by the administrator to perform administrative tasks and that is allowed to perform any operations on the resources stored in any database on the server.

Note For more information on granting privileges to MySQL users, you can refer to the MySQL documentation's "SQL Statement Syntax" chapter, specifically, the section "GRANT Syntax." In this section, you will also find the entire list of privileges you can grant to a user account in MySQL.

You should now have a general idea of how data is logically organized in MySQL and how you can access that data. By now, you should know what the term *database* means in the context of MySQL and how to create one to be then utilized within your application.

How User Database Objects Are Organized in Oracle

Now, let's look at how things work in Oracle. To understand this, you first need to get at least a cursory knowledge of the Oracle architecture. In particular, you need to learn what the terms *instance* and *database* mean in Oracle. As you will learn in this section, the term *database* in the context of Oracle means a different thing than it means in the context of MySQL.

In simple terms, an Oracle database is simply a collection of database files that hold the database data and metadata. But what good is a set of files simply stored on disk if you have no mechanism to manage them? An instance comes to the rescue here. An Oracle database *instance* represents a set of operating system processes running on your machine and a shared memory pool used by those processes, making it possible for users to access the database mounted by the instance. An instance can mount a single database, as shown in Figure A-3.

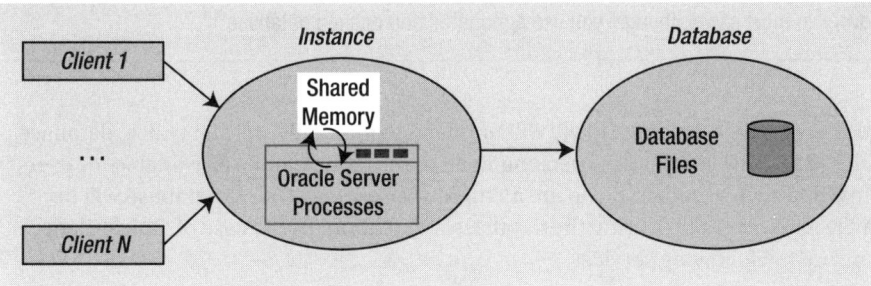

Figure A-3. *An Oracle database instance can be used to mount and open a single database.*

As you can see, the figure shows the one-to-one relationship between an instance and database, which is the most common type of relationship here.

> **■Note** It is interesting to note, though, that in some cases a database may be mounted and opened by more than one instance. The Oracle Real Application Clusters (RAC) technology assumes that a database can be manipulated by several instances simultaneously. For further information, you can refer to Oracle Database documentation. To find the documentation release corresponding to your Oracle Database release, you can visit the Oracle Documentation page at `http://www.oracle.com/technology/documentation/index.html`. You can find the Oracle Database documentation library corresponding to the most recent release of Oracle Database at `http://www.oracle.com/technology/documentation/database.html`. On this page, you can also find a link to the Oracle Database Express Edition (XE) Documentation page.

So, to make an Oracle database available for use, the following general steps must be performed:

1. Start an instance.

2. Mount the database.

3. Open the database.

It is important to note that Oracle can automatically perform the last two tasks when you start an instance. That means all three tasks can be performed in one step. One way to do this is to issue the STARTUP command from SQL*Plus, which is the Oracle SQL command-line tool bundled with all editions of Oracle Database. When executed, STARTUP starts an instance and reads a default initialization parameter file that contains the information required to find the database files and then mount and open the database specified in that file.

> **■Note** Actually, you can start an instance without mounting a database or start an instance and mount a database without opening it. For example, you might want to choose the latter when you need to perform full database recovery. In most cases, though, you use a mounted and opened database.

The good news is that you most likely will not need to manually start an Oracle database instance with the STARTUP command when you need to make the database available for users to connect to it and then access it. If you are a Windows user, your Oracle database will be started with the services set up during the database installation. In the case of Oracle Database XE, these are the following services:

- OracleServiceXE representing your Oracle database instance

- OracleXETNSListener representing the Oracle listener that enables clients to connect to the database

By default, the Startup Type property of these services is set to Automatic, which means they will automatically start upon starting the operating system, without you doing a thing.

In Linux, during the Oracle database software installation, you are asked whether you want the database to start automatically upon starting the computer. If your answer is Yes, you will have the database server up and ready for use every time the computer starts.

Now that you have a rough idea of how Oracle makes a database available for use, how can you create one? When installing an Oracle database server, a starter database is installed by default (you can turn off this option, though, for most editions of Oracle database). After the installing Oracle database server software, if needed, you can create a new database with the CREATE DATABASE command. However, this probably will not be the first thing you might want to do, if ever. In Oracle, the CREATE DATABASE command should be used with care, since it may erase existing data files, preparing them for initial use. The Oracle's CREATE DATABASE has a lot of ramifications, which you should know about before you use the command. Once you have created a new database, you will need to mount and open it with an instance to make it available for use.

Unlike in MySQL, when you need to create a working area for a new user in Oracle, you create a new user schema within an existing database with the CREATE USER statement. Listing A-3 shows how it could be done.

Listing A-3. *Creating a New User Schema and Granting It the Required Privileges*

```
CONNECT /AS SYSDBA
DROP USER usr;
CREATE USER usr IDENTIFIED BY pswd;
GRANT connect, resource TO usr;
```

In this example, you first connect to your Oracle Database instance as a privileged default user with AS SYSDBA, actually connecting to the default schema SYS. Then, you drop the user schema usr in the case you have it created. Next, you create a new user schema usr with password pswd. Finally, you grant the privileges to the newly created user so that it can connect to the database and create resources in the schema being created. Now you might want to select the information from the predefined DBA_USERS view to make sure the usr user schema has been successfully created:

```
SELECT username, created FROM dba_users;
```

■**Note** In MySQL, you would most likely issue both the SELECT user FROM mysql.user and SHOW DATABASES statements in this situation in order to obtain information about users and databases that can be used by those users. In Oracle, you obtain the information only about users because each user account is given a working area by default. When you grant a user to the RESOURCE role, you actually enable it to create and manipulate database objects in its working area.

The output might look like this:

```
USERNAME    CREATED
---------------------------------------
USR         12-DEC-07
```

```
SYS          25-NOV-07
SYSTEM       25-NOV-07
ANONYMOUS    25-NOV-07
HR           25-NOV-07
MDSYS        25-NOV-07
OUTLN        25-NOV-07
DIP          25-NOV-07
TSMSYS       25-NOV-07
FLOWS_FILES  25-NOV-07
CTXSYS       25-NOV-07
DBSNMP       25-NOV-07
XDB          25-NOV-07
```

This output shows all the schemas presented in the database. The newly created `usr` schema is highlighted in bold. All the other schemas are predefined Oracle schemas created during installation. Note that all these schemas are located within a single database, which is the one that is mounted and opened by the instance you're using now.

It is important to realize that even if you create a new database, you will have to create a new user schema within it anyway, unless you want to use a predefined one, which is not recommended, of course. The fact is that Oracle doesn't allow you to create tables and other database objects directly in a database. Instead, you create them in a certain user schema created within your database. So, in Oracle it's OK if you have a single database with a number of user schemas defined within it. Client applications use an appropriate schema to connect to the database and access its resources. Graphically, this might look like Figure A-4.

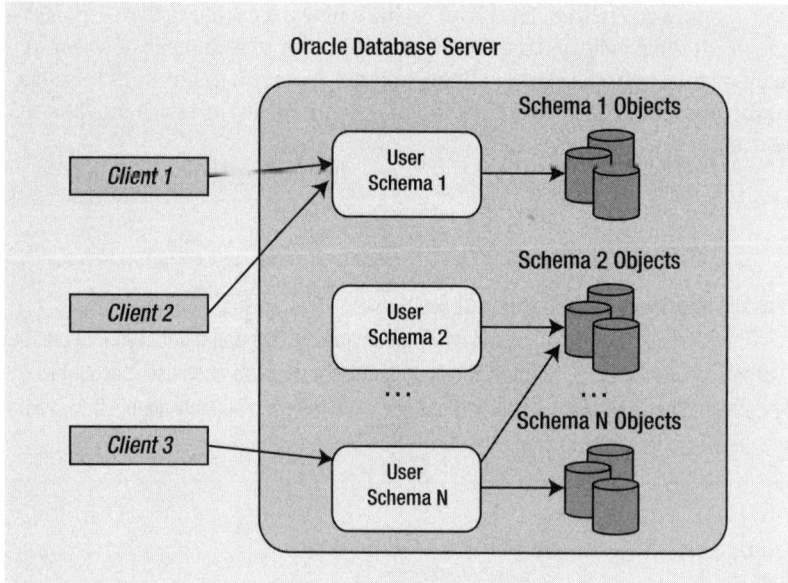

Figure A-4. *Database clients connect to the database using a user schema defined within that database.*

As noted earlier, you grant privileges to a user schema so that the clients using this schema can perform the tasks they need to accomplish. It is interesting to note that a user schema may be granted the rights to access database objects defined within another user schema. For example, you could grant the SELECT privilege on the departments default table located in the hr demonstration schema to a custom schema, say, usr:

```
CONN /AS SYDBA
GRANT SELECT ON hr.departments TO usr;
```

After that, you could connect as usr and issue the following statement against the hr.departments table:

```
CONN usr/pswd
SELECT * FROM hr.departments;
```

In this example, hr is followed by departments, explicitly telling Oracle that the departments table can be found in the hr schema.

■**Note** For more information on granting privileges and roles, you can refer to the "Authorization: Privileges, Roles, Profiles, and Resource Limitations" chapter in the Oracle Database Security Guide.

That concludes this concise discussion on how user database objects are logically organized in the MySQL and Oracle databases. By now, you should have a clear understanding that the term *database* means different things, depending on the database platform you're using. To create a new working area for a user account in MySQL, you create a new database with the CREATE DATABASE statement. To achieve this same goal in Oracle, you create a new user schema within an existing database with the help of the CREATE USER statement.

Knowing Your Database Features

As you learned in the preceding sections, databases may differ in the way they organize custom data, and even fundamental terms, such as *database*, may have different meanings in different database platforms. However, this is not the only part of what distinguishes databases from one another. Although all databases are designed to store and retrieve information, a set of the features provided may vary a lot from database to database.

The best way to learn what features are available is to look at the vendor documentation. For example, to find out what features are available in MySQL, you might visit the MySQL Reference Manual page at http://www.mysql.com/doc/en/index.html and look through the TOC of the MySQL Reference Manual.

This way, you will discover that MySQL lets you create stored programs and triggers, thus making it possible for you to implement key business logic of your application inside database. You can find some examples of MySQL stored routines in Chapter 6 of this book.

Scrolling down the MySQL Reference Manual TOC, you will learn that MySQL supports several storage engines, allowing you to handle both the transaction-safe and non-transaction-safe tables. Then, you will notice that MySQL supports enterprise-level features such as Replication and MySQL clusters.

To learn what features are available in Oracle, you might look at the book titles included in the Oracle Database Documentation Library. To start with, you might visit the Oracle Database Documentation page at `http://www.oracle.com/technology/documentation/database.html`. On this page, you should follow the View Library link to move on to the Oracle Database Documentation Library page, which in turn should contain the Master Book List link that brings you to the page containing the Oracle Database Documentation book titles.

Looking at the list of book titles, you may notice that Oracle Database is unparalleled in terms of the features provided. Aside from enterprise-level features such as Replication and Oracle Real Application Clusters (RAC), you may spot some features that you might want to use even when you are building a simple Oracle-backed application, such as PL/SQL, an Oracle database programming language that you might want to use when developing stored procedures and triggers. You can see PL/SQL in action in Chapter 6 of this book.

Another interesting Oracle feature you may know about when examining the documentation is Oracle XML DB, which actually represents a wide set of Oracle XML features that allow you to store, retrieve, update, and transform XML data and generate it from relational data. The purpose of Oracle XML DB is to simplify working with XML data, which, in the case of an XML-enabled application, lets you move a large amount of XML processing into the database.

It is interesting to note that, unlike Oracle, MySQL doesn't provide native XML support. So, if you choose MySQL as the underlying database for the application that operates on XML data, then you will have to implement logic performing XML processing in Java rather than employing the predefined solutions provided by the database. In that case, you will need to worry about shredding XML into relational data each time you have to persist it, as well as performing an inverse operation each time you have to extract XML from relational data stored in the database.

Although developing XML-enabled applications is beyond the scope of this book, the previous example perfectly illustrates that databases differ in the features they provide, so it is always a good idea to take some time to examine the documentation of several database vendors when deciding what database to choose as the back end for your application.

Using the SQL Database Language

As noted earlier, SQL provides a standard way to interact with a relational database. The following sections provide you with a brief introduction to SQL and its syntax, giving examples of the most commonly used SQL statements when interacting with MySQL and Oracle.

What Is SQL?

SQL stands for Structured Query Language. Being a nonprocedural language, SQL lets you define an instruction usually called a *SQL statement* to be issued against the database, describing the operation you want to be done. The SQL compiler then translates the statement into the code necessary to perform the desired task and execute it against the database.

■**Note** Despite that SQL is the standard language in all the major RDBMS systems today, many database tools allow you to interact with the database without explicitly building SQL statements. One of those tools is the TopLink Essentials used in GlassFish as the JPA implementation. As explained in Chapter 3, JPA doesn't require you to manually design SQL queries, leaving the details to the framework (TopLink Essentials in this case). It is important to realize, though, that tools like TopLink Essentials implicitly generate SQL statements and issue them against the database to fulfill the application's requests.

Although SQL is a standard language accepted by both ANSI and ISO, many database vendors add vendor-specific proprietary extensions to their implementations of SQL to increase the functionality provided. What this means is that each vendor uses its own SQL dialect to enhance the standard language. The easiest way to understand that SQL dialects used in different databases have some differences is by example. Just connect to your MySQL server as any user via the MySQL command-line client tool, and then issue the following command:

```
use
```

In response, MySQL should generate the following error message:

```
ERROR:
USE must be followed by a database name
```

This tells you that the USE statement exists in MySQL SQL dialect and must be followed by a database name.

Now if you connect to an Oracle database server with Oracle SQL*Plus and then issue the same command, you will see the following error message:

```
SP2-0042: unknown command "use" - rest of line ignored.
```

As you can see, Oracle SQL doesn't understand the USE statement. And this is not the only difference, of course. Some SQL statements are used in both databases but have a different syntax in each database when it comes to the clauses you can use with those statements. You already saw an example of using the CREATE DATABASE statement in MySQL. Unsurprisingly, this statement offers another set of branches in Oracle. As you might recall from the earlier section "Understanding the Architecture of Your Database," in Oracle the term *database* is treated differently than in MySQL. That is why in Oracle the CREATE DATABASE statement serves another purpose than it does in MySQL.

Categories of SQL Statements

Depending on the tasks they perform, SQL statements can be divided into several groups. Here are the most important categories of SQL statements:

- Data Definition Language (DDL) statements

- Data Manipulation Language (DML) statements

- Transaction management statements

- Database administration statements

Note, however, that vendor documentation will most likely give you a more detailed list specific to a particular database. For example, the Oracle documentation introduces the session control statements and embedded SQL statements categories in the list.

The following sections discuss the categories specified in the previous list, providing examples in both MySQL and Oracle as appropriate.

Performing DDL Operations

It is fairly obvious that before you can manipulate database data, you first need to create the database structures required to store that data. To address these needs, SQL provides DDL statements. Table A-1 lists the most commonly used DDL statements.

Table A-1. *Most Commonly Used DDL Operations*

DDL Operation	Description
ALTER	There is a set of statements beginning with ALTER, including ALTER DATABASE, ALTER TABLE, and ALTER VIEW. You use an appropriate ALTER statement when you need to change the structure of an existing database object.
CREATE	There is a set of statements beginning with CREATE, including CREATE DATABASE, CREATE TABLE, and CREATE VIEW. You use an appropriate CREATE statement when you need to create a new database object.
DROP	There is a set of statements beginning with DROP, including DROP DATABASE, DROP TABLE, and DROP VIEW. As opposed to CREATE, you use an appropriate DROP statement when you need to remove an existing database object.
GRANT	Enables you to grant privileges to user accounts. In MySQL, it also lets you create new user accounts.
REVOKE	As opposed to GRANT, you use a REVOKE statement to revoke privileges granted to a user account.

In the earlier section "Understanding the Architecture of Your Database," you saw examples of the CREATE DATABASE and GRANT statements in action. In the following sections, you will look at an example of how to create a single database table and then alter its structure, in both MySQL and Oracle.

Examples of DDL Operations in MySQL

Assuming you have created the mydb database in MySQL as described in Listing A-1, you can now create a table in that database. To do this, you first need to connect to your MySQL server as the usr user, as described in Listing A-2, by issuing the following command from a terminal:

```
mysql -u usr -p
Enter password: ****
```

As a result, the mysql prompt should appear. In the mysql prompt, you should issue the following command to instruct MySQL to use the mydb database:

```
use mydb
```

Now, you can create a table with the CREATE TABLE statement, as shown in Listing A-4.

Listing A-4. *Creating an* employees *Table in MySQL*

```
CREATE TABLE employees(
 empno INTEGER AUTO_INCREMENT PRIMARY KEY,
 firstname VARCHAR(24) NOT NULL,
 lastname VARCHAR(24) NOT NULL,
 salary NUMERIC(10, 2) NOT NULL,
 hiredate DATE NOT NULL
)
ENGINE = InnoDB;
```

If everything is OK, you should see the following message:

```
Query OK, 0 rows affected (0.11 sec)
```

Note the use of the AUTO_INCREMENT attribute in the previous statement. When specifying this attribute, you instruct MySQL to automatically generate a unique identity for each new row. In this particular example, specifying AUTO_INCREMENT with the empno column instructs MySQL to generate a subsequent integer value for this column each time you insert a new row. In other words, you don't need to worry about the value to insert for this column, since MySQL will do it for you, inserting a subsequent integer.

Another thing to note in the previous statement is that you explicitly instruct MySQL to use the InnoDB storage engine for the employees table being created, making it possible to use this table for storing the data used in transaction processing applications.

After you have created a table, you can populate it with data, as will be discussed in the "Performing DML Operations" section later in this chapter. Sometimes, however, you may need to modify the structure of an existing table. If so, you can use the ALTER TABLE statement. This statement has a great deal of branches, allowing you to perform a full set of alterations to an existing table structure. To look at the entire list of options available, you can refer to the MySQL documentation, specifically, the section "ALTER TABLE Syntax" in the chapter "SQL Statement Syntax." The following example illustrates how you could drop the primary key of the employees table created earlier in this section, with the help of the ALTER TABLE statement. First, you need to drop the AUTO_INCREMENT attribute. This could be done as follows:

```
ALTER TABLE employees MODIFY empno INTEGER;
```

Then, you can drop the primary key with another ALTER TABLE statement:

```
ALTER TABLE employees DROP PRIMARY KEY;
```

If the employees table has been successfully altered, each of the previous statements should generate the following message:

```
Query OK, 0 rows affected (0.14 sec)
Records: 0 Duplicates: 0 Warnings: 0
```

Now if you issue the DESCRIBE statement to obtain information about the columns in the employees table, you should see the following output:

```
Field     Type       Null   Key   Default   Extra
----------------------------------------------------------------------
empno     int(11)       No  0
firstname varchar(24) No
lastname  varchar(24) No
salary    decimal(10,2) No
hiredate  date        No
```

As you can see, the empno column is not the primary key column anymore, and the AUTO_INCREMENT attribute originally specified on this column is gone too.

Turning the primary key and AUTO_INCREMENT attribute back is surprisingly easy. To do this, you can issue the following ALTER TABLE statement:

```
ALTER TABLE employees MODIFY empno INTEGER AUTO_INCREMENT PRIMARY KEY
```

To make sure the primary key and AUTO_INCREMENT attribute have been set on the empno column again, you can issue the DESCRIBE statement:

```
Field     Type       Null   Key   Default   Extra
-----------------------------------------------------------------
empno     int(11)      NO   PRI   NULL      auto_increment
firstname varchar(24) NO
lastname  varchar(24) NO
salary    decimal(10,2) NO
hiredate  date      NO
```

This example illustrates how you might define a primary key on an existing table with the help of the ALTER TABLE statement.

Examples of DDL Operations in Oracle

Now that you have seen a few examples of DDL operations in MySQL, let's look at how these things work in Oracle. For that, you first need to connect to the Oracle server with SQL*Plus as the usr user created in Listing A-3 earlier in this appendix. To do this, you can issue the sqlplus command from a terminal window:

```
sqlplus
```

and then enter the username and password:

```
Enter user-name: usr
Enter password:
```

After you have connected, you can create an employees table in the usr schema by issuing the statement shown in Listing A-5.

Listing A-5. *Creating an* employees *Table in MySQL*

```
CREATE TABLE employees(
 empno NUMBER(6) PRIMARY KEY,
 firstname VARCHAR2(24) NOT NULL,
 lastname VARCHAR2(24) NOT NULL,
 salary NUMBER(10, 2) NOT NULL,
 hiredate DATE NOT NULL
);
```

If everything is OK, you should see the following message:

```
Table created
```

Looking through this statement, you may notice that the data types used here are different from those specified in the MySQL variation of the employees table created as shown in Listing A-4 in the previous section. In particular, you may note that Oracle uses the NUMBER datatype when it comes to defining numeric table fields, regardless of whether you are defining an integer or floating-point number column. When defining an integer number column, you use the NUMBER(p) syntax, where p is the maximum allowed number of decimal digits. In the case of a floating-point number column, you use the NUMBER(p, s) syntax, where s is the number of digits from the decimal point.

Also you may note that the Oracle variation of the employees table uses the VARCHAR2 datatype rather than VARCHAR. The fact is that the Oracle documentation encourages you to do so. For further details, you can refer to the Oracle Database SQL Reference Manual, specifically, the "Oracle Built-in Datatypes" chapter.

Taking the course of the MySQL example discussed earlier in this section, you might want to look at how the ALTER TABLE statement can be used in Oracle. To drop the primary key, for example, you might issue the following statement:

```
ALTER TABLE employees DROP PRIMARY KEY;
```

If the table has been successfully altered, you should see the following message:

```
Table altered
```

Note that, unlike the MySQL example discussed previously, you drop the primary key in one step. This is because you don't need to worry about removing the AUTO_INCREMENT attribute. The fact is that there is no such attribute in Oracle, and therefore, you cannot set it on or remove it from a column. Instead, in Oracle you can use a *sequence*, which is a database object allowing you to generate unique integers. To start with, you create a sequence as follows:

```
CREATE SEQUENCE empno_seq;
```

Once a sequence is created, you can use it when inserting a new row into the table. You will see this technique in action in the next section.

Returning to the employees table, you can restore the primary key as follows:

```
ALTER TABLE employees MODIFY empno NUMBER(6) PRIMARY KEY;
```

This ALTER TABLE statement modifies the empno column, setting it to NUMBER(6) and defining a primary key on it.

Performing DML Operations

Data Manipulation Language (DML) operations allow you to access and manipulate database data. Table A-2 lists the most commonly used DML statements.

Table A-2. *Most Commonly Used DML Operations*

DML Operation	Description
SELECT	Retrieves data from one or more database tables and/or views. SELECT may include subqueries. Also, you may write a UNION query combining the results from multiple SELECT statements.
INSERT	Inserts new rows into a database table. You can use INSERT with SELECT to insert new rows into a table from the dataset selected from another table or tables.
DELETE	Deletes rows from a database table.
UPDATE	Can be thought of as a delete followed by an insert operation. In the SET clause of this operation, you define how the rows should be updated in the target table or tables.

As you no doubt have realized, DML operations are used much more often in real life than DDL operations. Really, you use a DDL only when you need to define a new database object, say, a table, or when you need to modify the structure of an existing object. In other words, DDLs are used to define or modify metadata, whereas DMLs are used every time you need to retrieve from or save to the database a portion of the data your application is dealing with.

Examples of DML Operations in MySQL

Continuing with the example discussed in the previous sections, you might want to populate the employees table with data. To do this, you might use the INSERT statement as shown in Listing A-6.

Listing A-6. *Inserting Rows into the* employees *Table in MySQL*

```
INSERT INTO employees(firstname, lastname, salary, hiredate) VALUES ('Maya', ➥
'Silver', 3000, '2007-12-15'),('Bob', 'Browe', 3500, '2007-12-15');
```

This is an example of a multirow INSERT. If the rows have been successfully inserted, the following message should be generated:

```
Query OK, 2 rows affected (0.04 sec)
Records: 2 Duplicates: 0 Warnings: 0
```

Now you can issue the SELECT statement against the employees table:

```
SELECT * FROM employees;
```

You should see the following results:

```
empno firstname lastname  salary  hiredate
----------------------------------------------------------------------
1    Maya    Silver    3000.00 2007-12-15
2    Bob     Browe    3500.00 2007-12-15
2 rows in set (0.03 sec)
```

Although this SELECT statement retrieves all the rows in the employees table and shows all the fields in each row, the following query selects only the employee whose empno is 1, displaying just the first three fields:

```
SELECT empno, firstname, lastname FROM employees WHERE empno=1;
```

The output should look like this:

```
empno firstname lastname
----------------------------------------------------------
1    Maya    Silver
1 row in set (0.00 sec)
```

In a real-world situation, however, you often need to issue a SELECT statement querying more than one table. Typically, you have foreign key constrains established on such tables. You can find some examples of how to set foreign keys and then issue multitable queries in Chapter 5.

Examples of DML Operations in Oracle

Now let's look at how the examples discussed in the preceding section might look in Oracle. To start with, let's populate the employees table with data. For this, you might issue the two INSERT statements shown in Listing A-7.

Listing A-7. *Inserting Rows into the* employees *Table in Oracle*

```
INSERT INTO employees VALUES (empno_seq.NEXTVAL, 'Maya', 'Silver', 3000, ➥
 '15-dec-2007'
INSERT INTO employees VALUES (empno_seq. NEXTVAL, 'Bob', 'Browe', 3500, ➥
 '15-dec-2007');
```

If the rows have been successfully inserted, each of these statements should output the following message:

```
1 row created.
```

As you can see, this example uses two INSERT statements to insert two rows into the employees table. Unlike MySQL, Oracle doesn't support multirow INSERT statements. But what Oracle supports is multitable INSERTs that allow you to insert rows into one or more tables. The structure of a multitable INSERT may be complicated, though, and is beyond the scope of this section. If you want to learn more about the Oracle INSERT statement, you can refer to the Oracle Database SQL Reference, specifically the "SQL Statements" chapter's "INSERT" section.

Now that you have populated the employees table with data, you can issue the SELECT statement against it:

```
SELECT * FROM employees;
```

This statement should generate the following result:

```
EMPNOFIRSTNAME LASTNAME  SALARY HIREDATE
------------------------------------------------------------------------
1    Maya        Silver 3000.00 15-DEC-2007
2    Bob         Browe 3500.00 15-DEC-2007

2 rows selected
```

Like in the MySQL example discussed in the preceding section, you can also issue the SELECT statement that selects only the rows that satisfy the condition specified in the WHERE clause of the statement, as well as display only the columns specified in the select list. For example, to obtain information about the employee whose empno is 1 and display just the first three fields of the record, you might issue the following SELECT statement:

```
SELECT empno, firstname, lastname FROM employees WHERE empno=1;
```

The output should look like this:

```
empno firstname lastname
------------------------------------------------------------
1     Maya     Silver
```

Running ahead a little, it is interesting to note that Oracle automatically starts a transaction when you perform your first executable SQL statement and ends it when you explicitly commit or roll it back. What this means in this particular case is that the transaction automatically opened by the first INSERT statement shown in Listing A-7 earlier in this section is not committed yet. If, for example, you now connect to Oracle with another terminal as the usr user and issue a SELECT statement against the employees table discussed here, you will find out that the changes resulting from the INSERT statements performed in another session are not visible within this new session. To make the changes made to the employees table permanent and therefore visible to any other user's statements, you need to explicitly commit the transaction by issuing the COMMIT statement from within the same terminal window and in the same session (that is, you didn't reconnect to the server) in which you issued INSERT statements:

```
COMMIT
```

After that, the changes made to the employees table by the INSERT statements become permanent.

Performing Transaction Management Statements

As their name implies, the transaction control statements are used to manage transactions. The fact is that the list of transaction management statements used in MySQL is slightly different from that used in Oracle. This is mostly because these databases use different models when it comes to transaction management. To make a long story short, MySQL uses the autocommit mode by default, automatically committing the changes made by each successful DML operation. In contrast, Oracle expects you to explicitly commit a transaction.

Table A-3 lists the transaction management statements used in MySQL.

Table A-3. *The Transaction Control Statemements Used in MySQL*

Transaction Operation	Description
SET AUTOCOMMIT	Lets you to disable the autocommit mode, which is used in MySQL by default. To do this, you issue SET AUTOCOMMIT = 0.
START TRANSACTION	Disables autocommit until you explicitly end the transaction with COMMIT or ROLLBACK.
SAVEPOINT	Enables you to set a point in a transaction to which you will be able to roll back later.
COMMIT	Commits the current transaction, making the changes made in that transaction permanent.
ROLLBACK	Rolls back the current transaction, disregarding the changes made in it. You can use the ROLLBACK TO SAVEPOINT statement to roll back a transaction to the named savepoint set earlier with the SAVEPOINT statement.

Table A-4 lists the transaction management statements used in Oracle.

Table A-4. *The Transaction Control Statements Used in Oracle*

Transaction Operation	Description
SET AUTOCOMMIT	Enables you to specify how pending changes will be committed to the database. Actually, this is not an Oracle Database command. Rather, this is an Oracle SQL*Plus command.
SET TRANSACTION	Enables you to explicitly begin a transaction, establishing characteristics of it as needed. For example, you might instruct Oracle to begin a read-only transaction.
SAVEPOINT	Enables you to set a point in a transaction to which you will be able to roll back later.
COMMIT	Commits the current transaction, making the changes made within that transaction permanent.
ROLLBACK	Rolls back the current transaction, disregarding the changes made in it. You can use ROLLBACK TO SAVEPOINT statement to roll back a transaction to the named savepoint set earlier with the SAVEPOINT statement.

As you can see, Oracle, unlike MySQL, doesn't use the START TRANSACTION statement. As stated earlier, Oracle implicitly begins a transaction with the first executable SQL statement and ends it when you explicitly commit or roll it back.

Note Also Oracle implicitly commits the current transaction before and after executing a DDL statement. For example, if you insert a new row into a table with an INSERT and then issue an ALTER statement (not necessarily on this same table), then the changes made by the INSERT will be automatically committed. It is interesting to note that SQL*Plus also commits any uncommitted data when it exits.

The following sections provide some examples of how transactions work in MySQL and Oracle. Chapter 13 discusses building transactional Java EE applications in more detail.

Examples of Transaction Management Statements in MySQL

Let's look at an example to understand the concept of a transaction. Say you want to update the rows inserted into the employees table created and populated with the data as discussed in the preceding sections. You want to perform two update operations, making sure these updates become permanent only if each update has been successful.

To follow this example, you need to connect to your MySQL server as usr and then change database to mydb. Listing A-8 shows the statements you issue as well as the messages these statements generate. The statements are highlighted in bold.

Listing A-8. *Performing a Set of DML Operations in a Single Transaction in MySQL*

```
START TRANSACTION;
Query OK, 0 rows affected (0.00 sec)

UPDATE employees SET salary = 3500 WHERE empno=1;
Query OK, 1 row affected (0.06 sec)
Row matched: 1 Changed: 1 Warnnings: 0

UPDATE employees SET salary = 1000000000 WHERE empno=2;
ERROR 1264 (22003): Out of range value for column 'salary' at row 1

ROLLBACK;
Query OK, 0 rows affected (0.02 sec)
```

In this example, you explicitly start a transaction with START TRANSACTION, disabling the autocommit mode for the following two UPDATE statements. After executing these statements, you roll back the changes made by them, since the last UPDATE failed.

Now if you issue the following SELECT statement against the employees table:

```
SELECT empno, salary FROM employees WHERE empno=1 OR empno=2;
```

you should see that the values of the salary fields haven't changed for the employees whose empno are 1 and 2:

```
empno salary
------------------
1     3000
2     3500
```

As you might guess, the example discussed in this section assumes that you yourself decide whether to apply ROLLBACK or COMMIT, depending on whether both UPDATE statements have been successful. In reality, though, the process of issuing a set of required statements, as well as making the decision about whether to commit or roll back, is automated; that is, the entire process is implemented within a single program unit, say, a stored procedure. In that case, the program, not you, decides whether to apply ROLLBACK or COMMIT.

Examples of Transaction Management Statements in Oracle

Now let's look at how you might implement the example discussed in the preceding section in Oracle.

To start with, make sure to connect to Oracle as usr, and then you can issue the statements shown in Listing A-9. The listing shows the statements along with the messages generated. The statements are highlighted in bold.

Listing A-9. *Performing a Set of DML Operations in a Single Transaction in Oracle*

```
COMMIT;
Commit complete.
UPDATE employees SET salary = 3500 WHERE empno=1;
1 row updated.

UPDATE employees SET salary = 1000000000 WHERE empno=2;
ERROR at line 1:
ORA-01438 : value larger than specified precision allowed for this column

ROLLBACK;
Rollback complete.
```

You start this listing with COMMIT to make sure the following UPDATE is the first statement in the transaction. You execute two UPDATE statements in this transaction. Since the last UPDATE failed, you roll back the entire transaction, disregarding the changes made by both UPDATE statements.

To make sure this has been done, you might issue the following SELECT statement against the employees table:

```
SELECT empno, salary FROM employees WHERE empno=1 OR empno=2;
```

As the following output shows, the values of the salary fields haven't changed for the employees whose empno are 1 and 2:

```
EMPNOSALARY
-----------------------
1     3000
2     3500
```

Performing Administrative Tasks

To perform administrative tasks, you use statements that might be grouped into a category named, say, *database administrative statements*. According to vendor documentation, though, MySQL introduces the database administration statements, while Oracle offers the session control statements and system control statements instead.

Examples of Database Administration Statements in MySQL

It is interesting to note that MySQL documentation numbers account management statements such as CREATE USER, GRANT, and REVOKE with the database administration statements. If you recall, these statements were discussed in the "Performing DDL Operations" section earlier.

Perhaps the most interesting statement from the database administration statements category in MySQL is SHOW, which is used at the beginning of about thirty SHOW statements. You have already seen the SHOW DATABASES statement in action, and now you will look at some other uses of SHOW.

Suppose you want to look at how you might re-create the employees table you created as described in Listing A-4 earlier in this appendix. To find this out, you might connect to the MySQL server as root and then issue the following statement:

```
SHOW CREATE TABLE mydb.employees;
```

This should output the CREATE TABLE command that you might use for re-creating the employees table:

```
CREATE TABLE 'employees'(
  'empno' int(11) NOT NULL AUTO_INCREMENT,
  'firstname' varchar(24) NOT NULL,
  'lastname' varchar(24) NOT NULL,
  'salary' decimal(10, 2) NOT NULL,
  'hiredate' date NOT NULL,
PRIMARY KEY('empno')
) ENGINE = InnoDB DEFAULT CHARSET=latin1;
```

Before you could use the previous statement, though, you would need to remove the quotes before and after the table and column names.

Another interesting SHOW statement is SHOW PROCESSLIST, which shows information about the threads representing connections to the MySQL server. Being connected as root, you might use the following syntax to look at all current connections:

```
SHOW PROCESSLIST;
```

If you have two connections to the server, the output might look like this:

```
Id User Host           db Command Time State Info
------------------------------------------------------------------------
1  usr  localhost:1041 NULL Sleep 67NULL
2  root localhost:1042 NULL Query 0 NULL show processlist
```

Once you have obtained this information, you can terminate a connection with another administrative statement: KILL. For example, to terminate the thread whose ID is 1, you can issue the following statement:

```
KILL 2;
```

Now, if you try to issue any statement with the MySQL client that used the terminated connection, then the client will first reconnect to the server and then execute the statement issue.

Examples of Database Administration Statements in Oracle

Oracle doesn't use the SHOW syntax. Instead, you can query an appropriate v$ system view. For example, being connected via SQL*Plus as /as sysdba, you might obtain the list of the current sessions with the following statement:

```
SELECT sid, serial#, username FROM v$session;
```

Suppose you have opened two sessions, connecting as /as sysdba and usr, respectively. In that case, the output of the previous statement might look like this:

```
SID  SERIAL# USERNAME
--------------------------------------------------
26   26    USR
29   1
31   1
33   1
38   99    SYS
39   1
...
```

With that information in hand, you can terminate a session using the ALTER SYSTEM KILL SESSION statement and specifying the SID and serial number values of the session you want to terminate:

```
ALTER SYSTEM KILL SESSION '26, 26';
```

Now, if you try to issue a statement from within SQL*Plus whose session has been terminated, you will see the following error message:

```
ERROR at line 1
ORA-00028: your session has been killed
```

So, you first need to reconnect to the server.

Using Management Tools Shipped with Your Database

By now, you should have a good understanding of how to access and manage database data and metadata with command-line tools: the MySQL command-line tool and Oracle SQL*Plus, which are installed by default with MySQL and Oracle Database, respectively. However, since these tools will be used throughout the rest of this book when it comes to directly creating and manipulating database data and metadata, they are worth further investigation.

MySQL Command-Line Tool

Now that you've gotten your feet wet with the MySQL command-line tool, you might want to improve your experience of using this tool. In particular, this section discusses how you might execute SQL statements stored in a text file on your disk. You may find this technique useful when you need to execute statements that you have already saved in a file. If so, you don't need to type all those statements again. All you need to do is to specify the filename as an input parameter of the MySQL program or specify it as the parameter of the mysql's `source` command if you are already running MySQL.

Suppose you create the SQL script file `queryemp.sql` in the `c:\queries` folder. This file contains the following lines:

```
use mydb;
select * from employees;
```

Now you can run MySQL command-line tool as follows:

```
mysql -u usr -p < c:\queries\queryemp.sql
```

First, you will be prompted to enter the password. Then the following output should appear:

```
empno firstname lastname  salary hiredate
-------------------------------------------------------------------------
1 Maya Silver 3000.00 2007-12-15
2 Bob Browe 3500.00 2007-12-15
```

After this, the MySQL session ends, and you return to the operating system prompt. The most significant downside to this approach is that you can execute your SQL script file only once, upon starting the MySQL session. To execute it again, you need to start the MySQL again. Moreover, you cannot see the information messages generated by the server. For example, the previous output should be followed by the following message:

```
2 rows in set (0.03 sec)
```

However, it is not displayed.

Often, though, you need to execute a script file from within a `mysql` prompt and stay there after the execution is complete. In MySQL command-line tool this can be done with the `source` command, which you can issue from within the `mysql` prompt. Just connect to the server:

```
mysql -u usr -p
```

Then, enter the following command:

```
source c:\ queries\queryemp.sql
```

Now you should see the following output:

```
Database changed
empno firstname lastname  salary hiredate
-------------------------------------------------------------------
1 Maya Silver 3000.00 2007-12-15
2 Bob Browe 3500.00 2007-12-15
2 rows in set (0.00 sec)
```

After performing the `source` command, you stay at the `mysql` prompt, and all the information messages generated during the execution of the SQL script specified are displayed as if you had entered the statements manually.

For more complete information on MySQL command-line tool, you can refer MySQL documentation's "Client and Utility Programs" chapter, specifically, the section "The MySQL Command-Line Tool."

Oracle SQL*Plus

Now that you have seen a number of examples of how to access and manage database data and metadata with Oracle SQL*Plus tool, you might want to learn how to simplify entering SQL statements being executed with this tool.

You may find it exhausting to repeatedly type the same statement or sequence of statements at the SQL*Plus prompt. To make your life easier, Oracle SQL*Plus lets you create and execute scripts that can be stored to disk and edited with an operating system editor.

Run SQL*Plus, and connect as `usr`. Then, enter the `edit` command at the SQL*Plus prompt, specifying the name you want to be used for the script file being created:

```
EDIT scriptemp
```

As a result, your default operating system editor will open, and you will be asked to save the `scriptemp.sql` file to disk. Once you click Yes in the Save Changes dialog box, you can edit the newly create `scriptemp.sql` file, typing the SQL statements as if you were at the SQL*Plus prompt. To keep things simple, you might type just the following statement:

```
select * from employees;
```

Then, save the changes made to the file, and close the editor. Now, you can run the script from within SQL*Plus by entering the following command:

```
START scriptemp
```

This should execute the statements contained in the `scriptemp.sql` script file. As a result, you should see the following output:

```
EMPNOFIRSTNAMELASTNAME SALARYHIREDATE
-------------------------------------------------------------------------
1 Maya Silver 3000.00 15-DEC-2007
2Bob Browe 3500.00 15-DEC-2007
```

Now, if you want to edit the statement contained in the `scriptemp.sql` script or add another statement or statements, you can enter `EDIT scriptemp` command again and then edit the script in the editor as needed.

For complete information about Oracle SQL*Plus, you can refer to the SQL*Plus User's Guide and Reference.

Index

You Need the Companion eBook

Your purchase of this book entitles you to buy the companion PDF-version eBook for only $10. Take the weightless companion with you anywhere.

We believe this Apress title will prove so indispensable that you'll want to carry it with you everywhere, which is why we are offering the companion eBook (in PDF format) for $10 to customers who purchase this book now. Convenient and fully searchable, the PDF version of any content-rich, page-heavy Apress book makes a valuable addition to your programming library. You can easily find and copy code—or perform examples by quickly toggling between instructions and the application. Even simultaneously tackling a donut, diet soda, and complex code becomes simplified with hands-free eBooks!

Once you purchase your book, getting the $10 companion eBook is simple:

❶ Visit **www.apress.com/promo/tendollars/**.

❷ Complete a basic registration form to receive a randomly generated question about this title.

❸ Answer the question correctly in 60 seconds, and you will receive a promotional code to redeem for the $10.00 eBook. ·

THE EXPERT'S VOICE™

2855 TELEGRAPH AVENUE │ SUITE 600 │ BERKELEY, CA 94705

Offer valid through 3/1/09.